D1598196

University of California Press
Berkeley and Los Angeles, California

University of California Press, Ltd.
London, England

Library of Congress Cataloging-in-Publication Data

Lewis & Clark : legacies, memories, and new perspectives / edited by
Kris Fresonke and Mark Spence.
    p.   cm.
Includes bibliographical references and index.
    ISBN 0–520–22839–1 (cloth: alk. paper).—
    ISBN 0–520–23822–2 (pbk. : alk. paper)
    1. Lewis and Clark Expedition (1804–1806).   2. Lewis and
Clark Expedition (1804–1806)—Influence.   I. Title: Lewis and
Clark.   II. Fresonke, Kris, 1966–.   III. Spence, Mark David.
F592.7.L6945   2004
917.804′2—dc21
                                                    2003005228

Manufactured in the United States of America

13   12   11   10   09   08   07   06   05   04
10   9   8   7   6   5   4   3   2   1

The paper used in this publication is both acid-free and totally
chlorine-free (TCF). It meets the minimum requirements of
ANSI/NISO Z39.48–1992 (R 1997). ⊗

Lewis & Clark

Legacies, Memories, and New Perspectives

EDITED BY

Kris Fresonke and Mark Spence

UNIVERSITY OF CALIFORNIA PRESS

Berkeley   Los Angeles   London

CONTENTS

ILLUSTRATIONS

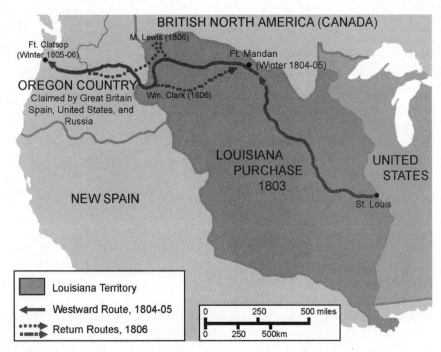

Map 1. Lewis and Clark expedition route and the imperial geopolitics of early nineteenth-century North America. (Map © Mark Spence)

Introduction

Kris Fresonke

*And Joshua . . . sent out of Shittim two men to spy secretly, saying, Go view the land,
even Jericho. And they went, and came into an harlot's house, named Rahab, and
lodged there.*

*. . . And [Rahab] said unto the men, I know that the Lord hath given you the land,
and that your terror is fallen upon us, and that all the inhabitants of the land faint
because of you.*

Joshua 2:1, 2:9

Despite the drab Sacagawea dollar, despite commemorative tourism, despite sentimental histories, despite Lewis and Clark souvenirs made from
authentic Dakota prairie grasses, despite the enforced invisibility of Native
Americans, despite national park gift shops, despite half-baked bicentennial hagiography, despite product placement, and despite the national
mood of hero worship, Lewis and Clark's achievement in the early nineteenth century is still absorbing, momentous, and of seemingly inex-
haustible interest. The purpose of this collection is to offer a selection of the
latest scholarship on the expedition, and to assess, on the occasion of the
bicentennial, its importance in American history and literature.

That importance is a given, but the exact line to take, or bead to draw,
has always been a source of debate. In literary studies, Lewis and Clark's redoubtable *Journals* have shown up only recently in the nineteenth-century
canon, signaled by the publication of Nebraska's scholarly edition; for many
years, exploration writing was simply a subliterary "artifact." In history,
scholars are still contending with the view that must be called Ambrosian,
after its only true begetter Stephen Ambrose: "Lewis and Clark are the real
thing. They're authentic heroes. They bind the continent together, they
bind together the American people in a way that nobody else can, or ever
will."[1] The New Western History has had its say, too: to the sentimental concept of Lewis and Clark's troupe as a "family," the dry-eyed Patricia Nelson
Limerick replied simply: *dysfunctional.* In the other social sciences, claims of
Lewis and Clark's sympathetic anthropology versus their aggressive manip-
ulation of tribes are hotly exchanged. Feminist scholarship has seen to it

that the woman whose name we misspell as Sacagawea, a Rahab to King Joshua's pair of spies, has finally been promoted from noble savage. The meanings of Lewis and Clark are more disputed, some would say, than the tribal lands they assessed for later seizure by the United States. All of these disputes and more are part of a story that scholarship at the bicentennial must acknowledge and try to retell.

The *Journals* and the ways they have been published and read seem a good place to start. We can see in their changing material fortunes, and the different meanings they've held for different readers, a glimpse of the reflected standing of Lewis and Clark. Every age has had its own edition of the *Journals,* and in something as minor as our changing editorial tastes we declare our intentions toward the historical meaning of the expedition.

Every Lewis and Clark fan has probably seen a page or two of Meriwether Lewis's elegant handwriting and perhaps a few of Clark's sketches of animals and plants. (See Figure 3, for an example.) For field records, subject to accident and abuse, the journals are extremely handsome: Lewis and Clark used brown ink that has aged beautifully and wrote in two kinds of book—one elkskin-bound, and the other red morocco with marbled endpapers. When you are permitted to examine these notebooks at the American Philosophical Society in Philadelphia, the sponsor of the expedition and its archive, you must put on a pair of white gloves.

Thomas Jefferson declared before anyone else that the *Journals* were "literary," a term that in 1803 conveyed the several fields of inquiry that would benefit from Lewis and Clark's findings. Jefferson meant, in his fine Augustan word choice, something we would clumsily have to call "interdisciplinary writerliness." The different genres that share a single text of exploration, such as journal, travelogue, scientific observation, military record, political theory, and so on, are all unified by their single goal of describing the new land, their use of written language to capture and commemorate those descriptions, and thus their single "literary" bearing.

It is odd, then, that this literary document passed quickly into subliterary status. Part of the problem was, of course, that the *Journals* didn't exist in print at all until 1814. The nineteenth century, in general, handled the editorial problems of the *Journals,* not to mention the elegance of the notebooks, inside and out, with less than the white glove treatment. Meriwether Lewis's last years were not happy ones; a variety of distracting miseries left him unwilling to satisfy Thomas Jefferson's requests to publish. Accounts written by the expedition members John Ordway, Patrick Gass, and others were published over Lewis's protests. Clark, dispirited by Lewis's death in 1808 but still eager to go to print, hired Nicholas Biddle to make over their laconic field notes into readable, narrative prose. Biddle was not a great writer, but he caught the purple spirit of his age and solved the problem of the dual authorship of the *Journals* by erasing it: he merged the two distinctive voices of Lewis and Clark into a third voice, unrecognizable as anyone's except, indelibly, Nicholas Biddle's. Here is a well-known passage from the *Journals* written by Clark on 7 November 1805:

> Great joy in camp we are in View of the Ocian, this great Pacific Octean which we been So long anxious to See. and the roreing or noise made by the waves brakeing on the rockey Shores (as I Suppose) may be heard distictly.[2]

Here is that passage made over by Biddle:

> We had not gone far from this village when the fog cleared off, and we enjoyed the delightful prospect of the ocean; that ocean, the object of all our labours, the reward of all our anxieties. This cheering view exhilarated the spirits of all the party, who were still more delighted on hearing the distant roar of the breakers.[3]

Here is another example, this time Lewis describing the Great Falls of the Missouri River on 13 June 1805:

> I hurryed down the hill which was about 200 feet high and difficult of access, to gaze on this sublimely grand specticle.[4]

And Biddle writes it this way:

> the hills as he approached were difficult of access and seating himself on some rocks under the center of the falls, enjoyed the sublime spectacle of this stupendous object which since creation had been lavishing its magnificence upon the desert unknown to civilization.[5]

Finding flaws in Biddle's prose is a turkey shoot; but even so, his rewrite does strike modern ears as a bit perverse. Lewis's sentence did not need revision. Biddle's version loses entirely the directness of Lewis's "hurryed down the hill" in order to ballast it with unwriterly, latinate excess about "stupendous magnificence." He also leaves out Lewis's endearing specificity, despite his joy and haste, of "200 feet high." Biddle, who sounds a bit like Charles Lamb on a bad day, seems altogether to have found the existing text insufficiently "literary." He brings to his project a windblown, or perhaps overblown, Romantic prerogative for passionate intensity. The Biddle edition was of no help to tastes like Jefferson's, nor probably to ours either. It was the only version of the expedition available throughout the nineteenth century, with one exception, and relegated the adventure undeservedly to the status of a sentimental journey.

Meanwhile, that one exception—the bestselling, unofficial account of Sergeant Patrick Gass—found its place among more complicated questions of literary sensibility. Gass's account irritated Lewis, who complained of "unauthorized and spurious publications"; the expedition merited the words of the commanders, he insisted, not of the supporting actors.[6] And

Figure 1. "A Canoe striking on a Tree." Courtesy of the Bancroft Library, University of California, Berkeley.

the Gass edition contained delightful woodcuts that do not so much illustrate events as concoct and color them.

The first plate in Gass, entitled "A Canoe striking on a Tree," was selected as the frontispiece to his journal, although it represents a pair of explorers at, perhaps, a fairly low moment: their canoe sinking, and their hands raised in alarm (Figure 1). Kenneth Haltman, an art historian who has written the only study of these illustrations to date, points out that the woodcut borrows its iconography from a popular eighteenth-century print of *Pilgrim's Progress,* namely *Christian and Pliable in the Slough of Despond* (1781).[7] Christian and Pliable, like Lewis and Clark, sink into a pond with raised hands, because, as John Bunyan tells it, "they, being heedless, did both fall suddenly into the bog." The caption of *Christian and Pliable* is a short colloquy from Bunyan on moral disorientation: "Then said Pliable ah! neighbour Christian, where are you now? Truly said Christian I do not know." Gass's pictures and diary found a simple but lasting moral in westering, in which the national quest narrative automatically served the righteous aims of moral geography.

Gass's publisher, David McKeehan, publicly answered Lewis's complaints about the infringement on his original *Journals.* First, Lewis, he argues, will bore his readers with "too long and learned dissertations," while Gass, "who does not speak scientifically," is at least "homespun." McKeehan unwittingly presents Lewis as a philosophe, or perhaps simply a quantitative drudge; in any case it is hard to miss the encyclopedic bent of Lewis's mind, even glimpsed through McKeehan's hostile account. Lewis, McKeehan hints and the *Journals* confirm, has a mind that finds truth in the sheer accumulation of knowledge, and that cannot take seriously any lesser effort to describe the natural world. The authoritative account of the expedition published in his own way provides for Lewis a certainty of knowledge with an audience who consent to that certainty. It is hard to imagine the Enlightenment mind more vividly.

On the other hand, flailing at Lewis for calling only his own account authoritative—the pirate pointing out piracy—McKeehan also illuminates a different side of Lewis's mind, one that may strike us now as Romantic. McKeehan contends that no one has the right to claim unique interest in the recent expedition, because the facts about Louisiana were probably plagiarized from Alexander Mackenzie.[8] Mackenzie had trekked across the Canadian Rockies to the Pacific for Great Britain in 1793. It is true that Lewis and Clark carried Mackenzie's account with them during the expedition; indeed, many explorers after Lewis and Clark carried the Biddle edition of Lewis and Clark with them. Lewis's obstinacy about "his" journal displays not only the Enlightenment impulse toward encyclopedic, "literary" presentations of knowledge, but also a Romantic's attachment to authentic, individual experience, rendered not as a corporate mission statement but as a direct chronicle of experience from the subject himself.

McKeehan's objections about Mackenzie, though—presented crossly, amid charges that Lewis walked to the Pacific and back only for the money—seem to me to get to the heart of the matter. *Of course* the Lewis and Clark journey was plagiarized; *of course* the route had essentially been traveled before; *of course* there was little novelty left in the Far West in 1806. Everyone knows the plot, McKeehan seems to be saying: you have no monopoly on it. What matters, McKeehan claims, is "spin," or what we would probably also call genre. Lewis, preoccupied in St. Louis with the governorship of Missouri, did not comment on McKeehan's accusation, nor did he return to work on his own manuscript. The Gass edition, in its confusing mix of moral signals and literary genres, and its unmixed emotions of nationalism, had won.

The sensibility of the Gass journal, which attacks both eighteenth- and nineteenth-century ideas of the "literary," and that of the Biddle journal, which pursues belles lettres like a bear treeing an explorer, were effectively the same thing in different wrappings, like the elkskin and the red morocco books kept by Lewis and Clark. Biddle created a single voice for the corporate Lewis-and-Clark, unrecognizable as either man's. Gass offered another. It is the privilege and inevitability of each age to ventriloquize Lewis and Clark, and the nineteenth century had two versions: Gass, the field soldier writing with the homespun morals of didactic Protestant literature, *Pilgrim's Progress;* and Biddle, with a rose-colored gaze and the prose to match.

In 1893 Elliott Coues prepared a version of Lewis and Clark that took even greater liberties and cannot rightly be designated an edition of the *Journals*.[9] Coues published chiefly for scientists, perhaps correcting the aestheticism of Biddle. The patchiness and randomness of the composition had only increased. It took the historian Reuben Gold Thwaites, under the aegis of the American Philosophical Society, to prepare a word-for-word, eight-volume edition in 1904–05, just in time for the centennial. (This history is reviewed in this collection's essay by Edward C. Carter II.) If the nineteenth century fumed over which voice the *Journals* should use, the twentieth century determined that all of them must be heard. Thwaites's verbatim approach is entirely to modern scholarly tastes, with its partiality to artifacts, its antisentimentality, its multiculturalism, and its skepticism about the limited notions of genre. As the literary critic Annette Kolodny cautions, in measured Jeffersonian terms, "the challenge is not to decide *beforehand* what constitutes literariness."[10]

It is the Thwaites edition that inspired both Bernard DeVoto, in his one-volume *Journals* digest from 1953, and Gary Moulton, in a multivolume work co-sponsored by the University of Nebraska Press and the American Philosophical Society, who corrected Thwaites even further for his definitive, scholarly, bicentennial edition.[11]

The scholars whose work is assembled here share the assumption that Lewis and Clark offer a classic case of Jeffersonian "literariness," or of interdisciplinary intrigue. The bicentennial of the Lewis and Clark expedition is thus a fitting occasion to see what mood we are in toward this pair of explorers, and why.

Literary criticism of the *Journals* has appeared in greater measure in the last few years, and its growing proportions surely prompted the Cambridge *History of American Literature* to include Myra Jehlen's long essay on Lewis and Clark.[12] (Frank Bergon's essay, in this collection, reviews this literature-anthology question in detail.) In general, the fortunes of exploration writings have risen among literary critics: the mood appears sympathetic. The field has acknowledged that writings declared "nonliterary" had been unjustly banished, and the canon has enlarged to take them in. Also, methodologies have changed: reverence for the well-wrought urn gave way, thankfully, to new-historicist approaches that could value the portmanteau, pastiche quality of the Lewis and Clark *Journals*.

And finally, a subterranean shift in attitudes toward American nature writing has renewed critical interest in texts like Lewis and Clark's. D. H. Lawrence once sneered that "absolutely the safest thing to get your emotional reactions over is NATURE";[13] but after the American pastoral was reread by Leo Marx, *Walden* by Stanley Cavell, the virgin land by Henry Nash

Smith, the nonvirgin land by Annette Kolodny, and the environmental imagination by Lawrence Buell, it was evident that sentimental naturalism had decamped for good, and we would have no more Biddling. Thus Smith's *Virgin Land* permitted scholars to examine the American West as a "drama . . . [and] the enactment of a myth."[14] Marx's *Machine in the Garden* elevated American arcadia to the most significant motif of New World discovery and conquest.[15] (Marx himself set the endpoint of the pastoral in 1963, when Robert Frost died; a new edition of *Machine* might have to stretch at least to Richard Brautigan's *Trout Fishing in America,* or to Meriwether Lewis's restored descriptions of the Missouri River plains.) Cavell and Buell found in Henry David Thoreau's *Walden* the evidence of a mind for whom writing about nature was not what came naturally, but what you did only after acquiring a generous knowledge of classical and contemporary languages, natural history, moral philosophy, Eastern religion, and basic gardening. Nature was not inert, exterior, and value-free; it was one's intellectual gymnasium.

Even after these studies appeared, Jefferson's *Notes on the State of Virginia* attracted far more critical attention than the epic journals of his protégé, Lewis, especially for three important works on landscape and literature: Wayne Franklin's *Discoverers, Explorers, Settlers: The Diligent Writers of Early America,* Richard Slotkin's *Regeneration Through Violence: The Mythology of the American Frontier, 1600–1860,* and Annette Kolodny's *The Lay of the Land: Metaphor as Experience and History in American Life and Letters.* And then, around 1992 (another significant anniversary of New World discovery), the literary draw was in the Southwest, among Spanish writers of conquest, coincident with Tzvetan Todorov's *The Conquest of America* and Stephen Greenblatt's *Marvelous Possessions: The Wonder of the New World.* Three works that finally addressed Lewis and Clark in aesthetic terms were Bruce Greenfield's *Narrating Discovery: The Romantic Explorer and American Literature, 1790–1855,* Robert Lawson-Peebles's *Landscape and Written Expression in Revolutionary America,* and Albert Furtwangler's *Acts of Discovery: Visions of America in the Lewis and Clark Journals.*[16]

Historians have also, in the twentieth century, offered a number of important studies of Lewis and Clark, and their mood has shifted over time. The centennial of the expedition that inspired Thwaites to bring forth a complete new edition of the *Journals* was also joined by Olin Wheeler's *The Trail of Lewis and Clark, 1804–1904,* which drew on the work of Thwaites and the author's own travels on the expedition route to present a century of historical change.[17]

Thwaites, Wheeler, and others were motivated by a certain postfrontier anxiety, that America had moved beyond its wilderness origins and would now lose the exceptional qualities that shaped its rise to global eminence. Progressive-era historians thus sought to resurrect and preserve the American West and its imagined values, such as its heartiness and masculine vigor—all for the edification of effete, cosmopolitan, urban readers. Frederick Jackson Turner's closed-frontier thesis, in effect, had opened the gates to the mythic claims of a backward-looking, redemptive West. In this respect, Lewis and Clark provided the nostalgic evidence of American virtue, which was even more appreciable from the perspective of an arid, amoral modernity.

While this approach to the expedition shaped a number of popular and scholarly treatments of the expedition, the anxious fears of the early twentieth century were tempered by that era's abiding belief in the future. Lewis and Clark were most commonly portrayed optimistically, as prophets of a new faith in material progress and overseas empire. No study of Lewis and Clark in the first decades of the century failed to reflect on the abundance of the western landscape, for instance, from the forests of the Pacific Northwest to the mines of the Rocky Mountains and new agricultural developments on the Northern Plains, and the comparable "abundance" promised in the enormous trade possibilities with East Asia. In this respect, Lewis and Clark not only connected the past with the present, and nature with nation, but merged all of these into a prophecy about the future.

Following the Great Depression, Lewis and Clark acquired new temperaments. Western historians like Walter Prescott Webb and Herbert Bolton rejected the emphasis on the frontier as a significant aspect of American history. In its stead, they focused on the ecologies and cultures that Americans encountered as they pushed westward. Webb defined the West as a land of hardship and scarcity, one that contained little of the promise it had for the earlier generation of historians. His central idea was westerners overcoming adversity: only through such ordeals did Americans convert the region into the mightiest of the United States. In a direct parallel of Webb's arguments, scholarship on Lewis and Clark at this time largely took place in the context of New Deal efforts to develop a series of national monuments and memorials that would inspire Americans to triumph over contemporary adversity (the crash of 1929), just as their forebears had done. Centered on what would become the Jefferson National Expansion Memorial in St. Louis, these studies did not so much connect Lewis and Clark with prophesies about the future as emphasize the American character, one with a special ability to overcome difficulties, whether they be mountains, waterfalls, Indians, or unemployment.[18]

By the 1950s Lewis and Clark took on the qualities of Cold Warriors in a world of clashing global empires. In Bernard DeVoto's magisterial *Course of Empire,* Lewis and Clark were the agents of Thomas Jefferson's geopolitical visions. The major threats to the expedition did not come from Native peoples or grizzly bears so much as the imperial designs of France, Spain, and England. It would be too much to state that DeVoto simply placed Lewis and

Clark in a Cold War context, but in *Course of Empire* and his single-volume edition of the journals, he did bring new emphasis to discipline and duty on the part of the captains. More significantly, DeVoto argued unequivocally that the expedition was one of the most pivotal episodes in all of American history.[19]

Service to a greater cause remains a central component of most popular approaches to Lewis and Clark, but these have been tempered by newer concerns for environmental and cultural issues. Both are at the heart of outstanding scholarly works like Paul Russell Cutright's *Lewis and Clark: Pioneering Naturalists* and James Ronda's *Lewis and Clark Among the Indians*.[20]

But the tendency to celebrate Lewis and Clark as triumphant nationalists has remained a constant aspect of most works on Lewis and Clark throughout the twentieth century. This celebration is clearly on display in the work of Stephen Ambrose, where his Lewis and Clark are a conglomeration of past descriptions: dutiful soldiers, virile frontiersmen, culturally sensitive diplomats, protoecologists, and visionaries of the future. Ambrose's work has not gone unchallenged by the so-called New Western History, though, which has sought to wean us from the guilty pleasures of nationalism. Patricia Nelson Limerick has made a point of critiquing the work of Ambrose with ready revisions of the more popular narratives of national glory. Led by Limerick's *Legacy of Conquest* and James Ronda's *Lewis and Clark Among the Indians,* the New Western History offered a skeptical corrective, only to have to confront its own analytical limits: as this collection, essay by essay, seeks to demonstrate, even revisionism is limited—by its devotion to a kind of unified Skeptical Field Theory.

The contributors to this volume variously tackle the expedition that opened the West for American expansion in the nineteenth century, and the ways it can be read, misread, and made over in tourist displays, paperback romances, natural history, suffrage propaganda, archives, legal codes, medical artifacts, and multivolume scholarly editions.

If major histories of the expedition have often operated in the field, doggedly retracing the expedition's steps, then it is fitting first to offer the judgment of Edward C. Carter II, who from 1980 until his death in 2002 was librarian of the American Philosophical Society (APS), where the expedition deposited its copious specimens and records, and where editors of the *Journals* have always worked. His essay narrates the crucial role of the APS in sponsoring the expedition, and the even more difficult task of organizing and publishing the troupe's geographic, ethnographic, and other scientific findings. Carter also details the trials of an institution that continues to serve as an intellectual headquarters for students and scholars of the expedition, especially during the busy bicentennial.

Frank Bergon evaluates the Nebraska scholarly edition of the *Journals.* We gladly reprint it from *American Literature* because it is undoubtedly the most thorough and thoughtful assessment of Lewis and Clark as writers and the vexing status of the *Journals* as literature. Dubbed by Donald Jackson "the writingest explorers," Lewis and Clark occupy a fascinating position in literary history and in the cross-currents of genres present in their epic text. Bergon describes the difficulties of publishing this text, as well as the rewards.

Charles Boewe reminds readers that among the less famous members of the expedition, George Shannon is worth our attention for his connections to the linguist and scientist C. S. Rafinesque. Rafinesque, who met Shannon and interviewed him about his experiences out west, was a keen reader of Biddle's edition of the Lewis and Clark journals and used it to assign scientific names to five animals that he had never seen. He also undertook significant linguistic researches among Native Americans and published widely on the topic. Thus the effects of the expedition were felt strongly among the scientists of the early nineteenth century.

Ronald Loge's medical expertise focuses our attention on the fascinating question of field medicine techniques during the Lewis and Clark expedition. Equipped with the most up-to-date medical information and, for all that, provided chiefly with laxatives, mercury, and opium, Lewis and Clark managed admirably during the various medical crises faced by the troupe.

Raymond Cross and Peter Appel approach the expedition from the perspective of legal history. Cross assesses Lewis and Clark from the perspective of the Native Americans (Mandan, Hidatsa, and Arikara) whom the expedition encountered and then infected with the twin plagues of disease and treaties. Not only does Cross decenter the "historic" significance of Lewis and Clark by viewing their efforts from a tribal perspective, he also offers this deflationary suggestion: that Lewis and Clark, far from being the heroes of their own expedition, more closely resemble Rosencrantz and Guildenstern, those minor flunkies of tragedy.

Appel queries the classic formulation by Alexis de Tocqueville, that political questions in America inevitably wind up in the courts. If that's the case, then where is the legal precedent set by Lewis and Clark? Appel answers: in the Louisiana Purchase. Jefferson's assumption of broad powers to purchase this million-mile landmass was, even to Jefferson himself, a breach of explicit constitutional limits. But Jefferson went ahead with the purchase, despite his Republican views on strict constructionism. This decision changed American federalism entirely, from the bare minimum sanctioned by the Republican Party to an excess still evident in land-use policies and in policies regarding Native Americans.

John Spencer's essay takes on the Lewis and Clark centennial and shows that the anniversary hype of 1904 came from turn-of-the-century railroad pamphlets, boosterism, and Teddy Roosevelt's expansionist wars—just as later hype about the glories of the expedition also came from current events, such as ecological consciousness raising and the Vietnam War's lessons in racial conquest. Spencer interrogates the revisionism of our own age and candidly reviews the ongoing divide between the perspectives of buffs and scholars.

Joanna Brooks examines the enduring, exasperating romance of Sacajawea, thinly masked as the title character Cogewea in Mourning Dove's 1927 novel. We know relatively little about Sacagawea (historians don't even agree whether she died in 1814 or 1884) and yet her heroics have been taken over and retold by figures ranging from Susan B. Anthony to Charles Eastman to the Unites States Department of the Treasury, which recently put her image on the gold dollar. Lewis and Clark's famous appearance on the Pacific coast in *Cogewea* is not the tragic melodrama of Indian conquest, stirring the "patience" and "endurance" for which Sacagawea was canonized by the women's suffrage movement. Instead, Mourning Dove makes over Indian awe at the western heroes—into the bafflement of the nonplussed. Cogewea even quarrels with her white lover to defend her grandmother's eyewitness observation that Lewis and Clark simply were *not* the first white explorers in Oregon. As Brooks points out, Red Progressives at the turn of the century (Native political activists grappling with the question of assimilation) were similarly nonplussed by the tragic role that Indianness offered them.

Wallace Lewis's essay offers a review and a critique of the commemoration of Lewis and Clark, from roadside plaques and monuments to ersatz Fort Clatsops on display at the St. Louis World's Fair. The greatest commemoration, Lewis points out, has been the trail itself, a tourist destination 3,700 miles in length, and of mixed authenticity and purity—especially after the massive construction effort of hydraulic dams in the twentieth century, which obliterated many camp and fort sites.

Through a juxtaposition of the expedition's original purposes with present understandings of Lewis and Clark, Mark Spence demonstrates that the bicentennial is celebrated as an opportunity for national redemption. With millennial zeal, Lewis and Clark fans see the bicentennial as an opportunity to reenact the virtues of a mythic past, bury the mistakes of two centuries, and press ahead with a newly restored environmental and cultural sensitivity. Because the experiences and goals of the expedition do not support this interpretation, the bicentennial cannot address historical problems or start the process of actively addressing their difficult legacies. Indeed, Spence argues that these issues are actively avoided. Current plans for the bicentennial place great emphasis on outdoor recreation where individuals can "relive a spirit of adventure" and "discover the past." This tendency to conflate the distant past with the tourist's immediate present makes the historical roots of ecological and social problems disappear—the very issues that shape current ideas of Lewis and Clark. As Spence concludes, therein lies the real appeal of these newly constituted heroes for the new millennium, and there also can be found reason for deep concern about the challenges of the next century.

Andrew Gulliford offers an upbeat and thoughtful account of many aspects of the bicentennial of the Lewis and Clark expedition, assessing not only the actual physical problems associated with walking in the footsteps of the explorers (especially when the terrain is fragile and the archaeological record has vanished) but also the subtle, less tangible difficulties that come to every tourist who faces changes in stereotypes and conventional historical wisdom along the route of the trail.

Roberta Conner's chapter offers her call for meaningful attention to the Indian perspective on the bicentennial and also presents the views of Wishlow-too-la-tin, Raymond Burke, of the Umatilla nation. Both documents not only expand the Native American standpoints on the expedition collected in this volume but offer a sharp corrective to the univocal and patriotic commemorations originating in Washington, D.C. and in the federal agencies overseeing the festivities of 2003–06.

Finally, Dayton Duncan, in the epilogue to this volume, offers the perspective of a documentary filmmaker who has traveled the Lewis and Clark trail twice and has found particular inspiration in the unofficial motto of the expedition, "We proceeded on." The phrase appears frequently in the *Journals* and tells us of the persistent values of the expedition—the perseverance of their scientific inquiry and their progress in covering huge distances, along with the beauty and wonder of western landscapes. Duncan takes Lewis and Clark on an imaginary tour of the trail and offers reflections on its contemporary state.

Why study Lewis and Clark? Because we have to. It is already studying us. Two important and related facts arise from it. The first is that Lewis and Clark, from the evidence of the last hundred years, are very much with us, from uncirculating golden dollars to the prospering enterprise of national myth. The material proof of their popularity should not necessarily cheer us up. Like all legacies, these bequests from the expedition—in the form of the Sacagawea coin or the Genuine Dakota Prairie Grass Tote Bag or the sorry state of Native American rights—are a burden. Efforts to ignore these burdens or consider them "in the past" are a basic misunderstanding of the laws of inheritance.

The corollary of this burden is the second fact: the West and its effect on national history. Of course, to call the importance of the West in American history an "effect" is to crop half of its glory and half of its doom, for the

West is also a first cause, a prime mover. Recovering from the European delusion that we discovered the New World, we find that all along it discovered us: the West has, at least since 1803, set the agenda, wagged the dog, and written the plot. This collection acknowledges that we might better perceive Lewis and Clark themselves as the undiscovered country and instead now write the biography of the territory that apprehended them. And how it was willed to us.

A fistful of dollars—now there's a Western theme. The Sacagawea dollar will be spent in, approximately, fistfuls during the bicentennial by the many tourists who visit the Lewis and Clark trail. Having Sacagawea on that coin is good luck for the bicentennial, a series of events hungry for publicity and commemoration, not to mention product endorsements. And her image there is either a joke on white people, or it is not: so far no one is quite sure. Either the Native has had the last laugh, circulating cool and golden in white hands and offering herself as the medium of exchange for souvenirs and Diet Cokes and gasoline for the drive down the trail to the Pacific; or whites have won again, shriveling Indian brass into its most abject form: a dollar coin available only from Wal-Mart, just big enough to be rejected by parking meters and vending machines, and with a gold finish that bank tellers in my town lament "turns dirty after a few weeks."

It is probably the latter. Commemoration always works this way: tackily, with tarnish, fitting ill. A friend who is a Cherokee recently wrote to me about the Sacagawea dollar with this hilarious story of memorial tarnish in her own family:

> For years family mythology had it that Sacagawea was my great great great great great great grandmother. . . . In 1976 I was asked to represent her in a pageant so I began a lengthy research into Shoshone beadwork to be used to decorate a four-hundred-dollar buckskin dress I had made for the occasion. . . . To cut to the chase, my research revealed that we were not related to Sacagawea but to her no-account husband, Toussaint Charbonneau, and to him illegitimately. Now several relatives no longer speak to me, others flatly deny the validity of my work and go on with the myth, and I have a four-hundred-dollar dress minus beadwork that I never wore.[21]

Four hundred Sacagawea dollars worth of buckskin later, this friend still harbors great admiration for her nonancestor. Many people share this view or offer its corollary, admitting that political correctness must have had a hand in the choice of Sacagawea but shrugging that, like a family myth, such a pleasant frailty can be indulged.

I myself am less certain. I write about Lewis and Clark and the dynamo of manifest destiny in the nineteenth century. My sympathy is not with the empire. But rather than declare the dollar a good or bad thing by looking at it on its own, I follow it into circulation. What is it trying to buy?

If the Sacagawea dollar were a success, it would mean, for one thing, an uncontroversial entry into our wallets, when it has been anything but. We should be spending it; but at the moment no one is, preferring to collect it like the fifty-states quarters or the doomed old Susan B. Anthony dollar. In a survey of friends I have found their responses to the new dollar to range from glee ("all money is beautiful") to resignation ("at least it is better looking than the nickel") to isolationist hauteur ("I live in Paris"), to classic Manhattanite confusion: "Whassat? Like the Euro, but for the West Coast?" But nobody has yet exchanged it for food, drink, or half a gallon of gasoline. This unspent dollar is not so much a reminder of Sacagawea's heroism as an incoherent bit of national *omertá*, a bribe to ourselves, to doctor the slightest amount of historical inquiry into dusty monuments to heritage. Hoarding the dollar, we're keeping its meaning out of circulation.

I see this fact in the ancient prototype for the mythic Sacagawea who appears in the book of Joshua. The tale of Rahab gives me an inclination to dislike and distrust the Sacagawea dollar, and not merely for its effortless condescension to Native Americans. A pair of spies from Israel, so the story goes, traveled west into Canaan to reconnoiter for Joshua's invasion. A Canaanite woman named Rahab, grasping "that the Lord hath given [the spies] the land," and that Zion was coming and hell followed with it, helps them; she has her life spared during the massacre that follows. The spies spilled neither ink nor blood to thank her or make her famous, and she's no Canaanite heroine today. Rahab, therefore, is a key player in Israel's exaltation, but she is so predefeated in the terms of the story that her survival is to Israel's credit, not her own. Like Sacagawea with Jefferson's pair of spies, the enterprise she might have once been leading changed directions, so that she had to follow.

The Navajo Mary Brown, who was the model for Sacagawea on the new coin, has been touring the country, signing autographs. The coeditor of this collection wants to know, quite sensibly: what name is she signing? Sakakawea? Sacajawea? Sacagawea? Mary Brown? or perhaps Rahab?

It's a cheap shot to say that any commemoration is unhistorical, that Jefferson wasn't as noble as he looks on Mount Rushmore (or in the book of Joshua), that Kennedy never had a day in his life when he looked as unraffish as he did on a previous dollar coin. Those would be boring little beefs to make. What matters is that American history is once again wriggling out of the grip of commemoration. It simply won't go into the neat coin-shape of legend, with a happy ending, or at least an ending, and some sort of moral. Only stories do this. But history, in the hard-edged definition of Gibbon, thinking of antiquity and of the old Old World, is "little more than the story of the Crimes and Follies of Mankind." We like to think the New World is Zion, that it reveals a plan or at least a plot, that it unrolls destinies that are manifest. But the theme of New World history is just conquest: the conquest by displaced Europeans over the huge land, its inhabitants, and

finally over the world. Conquest is the dominant theme from the days of
Columbus on Hispaniola to the days of globalization.

To be an adult means shouldering historical original sin and holding on,
with dry eyes, to a counterfeit ornamented buckskin hanging in your closet.
When it comes to buying peace of mind, I am against symbols of contrition
and would rather traffic in contrition itself. We cannot, if we want to think
clearly, entirely regret the triumphant American conquest, since it makes
our world, and we are all to some degree beneficiaries of it. But nor can we,
in good conscience, merely celebrate the pageant of the lush American centuries. We are all players, most with comfortable bit parts, in that tragic
avalanche of human resettlement along the Lewis and Clark trail: Sacagawea the kind collaborator with the process of her nation's obliteration,
Mary Brown the elegant poster girl, and I myself the coeditor of a book published amidst the commotion of the bicentennial.

NOTES

1. Stephen Ambrose's remarks appear online at a PBS web site entitled "Lewis
and Clark" (http://www.pbs.org/lewisandclark/archive/idx_int.html).

2. Gary E. Moulton, ed., *The Journals of the Lewis & Clark Expedition* (Lincoln: University of Nebraska Press, 1983–99), 6:33.

3. Nicholas Biddle, *History of the Expedition Under the Command of Captains Lewis
and Clarke to the Sources of the Missouri, Thence Across The Rocky Mountains And Down
The River Columbia To The Pacific Ocean. Performed During The Years 1804–5–6. By Order of the Government of The United States* (1814; reprint, New York: Allerton Book,
1922), 2:328.

4. Moulton, *Journals*, 4:283.

5. Biddle, *History*, 1:159.

6. The facts of this little-known story, and the quotations from Lewis's and Mc-
Keehan's letters, appeared first in Donald Jackson, "The Race to Publish Lewis and
Clark," *Pennsylvania Magazine of History and Biography* 85 no. 2 (1985); and are retold by Gary E. Moulton, introduction to *The Journal of Patrick Gass, May 14,
1804–September 23, 1806* (vol. 10 of *Journals*).

7. Kenneth Haltman, "Figures in a Western Landscape: Reading the Art of Ti-
tian Ramsay Peale from the Long Expedition to the Rocky Mountains, 1819–1820"
(doctoral diss., Yale University, 1992). "Christian and Pliable in the Slough of Despond" (1791), anonymous line etching, 14 × 25.7 cm, Print Collection, Win-
terthur Library, Delaware. See also my *West of Emerson: The Design of Manifest Destiny*
(Berkeley: University of California Press, 2002), ch. 1, where I present this argument
about Gass and Bunyan in terms of the Lewis and Clark *Journals*.

8. In "Race to Publish" Jackson reprints McKeehan's diatribe (first published in
the *Pittsburgh Gazette*, 14 April 1807) and adds, "It occupied the whole of page 2 . . .
and seems to have been overlooked by the biographers of Lewis and Clark and
the subsequent editors of their journals." It appears, of course, in Moulton, *Journals*,
vol. 10.

9. Elliott Coues, *History of the Expedition Under the Command of Lewis and Clark,* 3 vols. (New York: F. P. Harper, 1893).

10. Annette Kolodny, "Letting Go Our Grand Obsessions: Notes Toward a New Literary History of the American Frontiers," *American Literature* 64 (March 1992): 14.

11. Bernard DeVoto, ed., *The Journals of Lewis and Clark* (New York: Houghton Mifflin, 1953).

12. Myra Jehlen, "The Final Voyage," in *The Cambridge History of American Literature* (Cambridge: Cambridge University Press, 1994), 1:149–168.

13. D. H. Lawrence, *Studies in Classic American Literature* (Garden City: Doubleday, 1951), 33.

14. Henry Nash Smith, *Virgin Land: The American West as Symbol and Myth* (New York: Vintage Books, 1959), 18.

15. Stanley Cavell, *The Senses of Walden* (New York: Viking, 1972); Leo Marx, *The Machine in the Garden: Technology and the Pastoral Ideal in America* (New York: Oxford University Press, 1964); Annette Kolodny, *The Lay of the Land: Metaphor as Experience and History in American Life and Letters* (Chapel Hill: University of North Carolina Press, 1975); Lawrence Buell, *The Environmental Imagination: Thoreau, Nature Writing, and the Formation of American Culture* (Cambridge, Mass.: Harvard University Press, Belknap Press, 1995).

16. Wayne Franklin, *Discoverers, Explorers, Settlers: The Diligent Writers of Early America* (Chicago: University of Chicago Press, 1979); Richard Slotkin, *Regeneration Through Violence: The Mythology of the American Frontier, 1600–1860* (Hanover, N.H.: Wesleyan University Press, 1973); Kolodny, *Lay of the Land;* Tzvetan Todorov, *The Conquest of America* (New York: Harper and Row, 1984); Stephen Greenblatt, *Marvelous Possessions: The Wonder of the New World* (Chicago: University of Chicago Press, 1991); Bruce Greenfield, *Narrating Discovery: The Romantic Explorer and American Literature, 1790–1855* (New York: Columbia University Press, 1992); Robert Lawson-Peebles, *Landscape and Written Expression in Revolutionary America* (New York: Cambridge University Press, 1988); Albert Furtwangler, *Acts of Discovery: Visions of America in the Lewis and Clark Journals* (Urbana: University of Illinois Press, 1993). See also Paul Russell Cutright's *A History of the Lewis and Clark Journals* (Norman: University of Oklahoma Press, 1976).

17. Olin D. Wheeler, *The Trail of Lewis and Clark, 1804–1904: A Story of the Great Exploration across the Continent in 1804–06, with a Description of the Old Trail, Based upon Actual Travel over It, and of the Changes Found a Century Later* (New York: Putnam, 1904; reprint, New York: AMS Press, 1976).

18. Walter Prescott Webb, *Divided We Stand: The Crisis of a Frontierless Democracy* (New York: Farrar and Rinehart, 1937); Herbert E. Bolton, *Wider Horizons of American History* (New York: Appleton-Century, 1939).

19. Bernard DeVoto, *The Course of Empire* (Boston: Houghton Mifflin, 1952).

20. Paul Russell Cutright, *Lewis and Clark, Pioneering Naturalists* (Urbana: University of Illinois Press, 1969); and James P. Ronda, *Lewis and Clark among the Indians* (Lincoln: University of Nebraska Press, 1984).

21. Thanks to my friend Dr. Betty Donohue of Bacone College, Muskogee, Oklahoma, for this missive.

PART I

Contexts

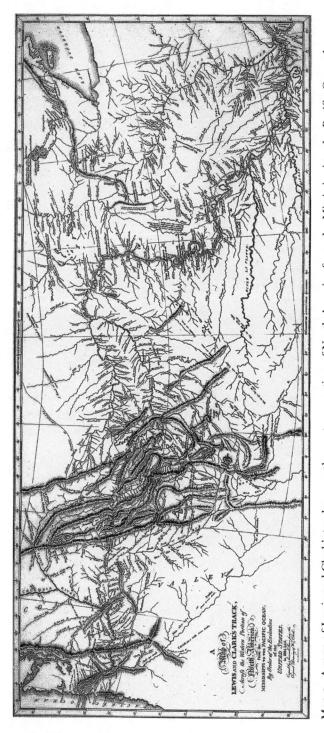

Map 2. A map of Lewis and Clark's track across the western portion of North America from the Mississippi to the Pacific Ocean by order of the executive of the United States in 1804, 5, & 6. By Samuel Lewis, 1814, from the original drawing of Wm. Clark, 1810. (American Philosophical Society)

Based on William Clark's careful observations, and augmented with information from the 1805–7 expedition of Zebulon Pike, this full-scale map of the entire Lewis and Clark trail is crowded with references to rivers, mountain ranges, and Native groups. Clark added new details to an original version of this map throughout a thirty-year career that combined his private interests in the fur trade with his official obligations as an Indian agent and superintendent of Indian affairs for the Upper Louisiana Territory. The updated map that he kept in his offices in St. Louis served as a guide to fur trading enterprises, policy makers, and military planners for nearly half a century.

Though largely neglected by scholars and the general public for most of the nineteenth century, the Lewis and Clark expedition has attracted a great deal of attention since the centennial celebrations of 1904 and 1905. It would seem that the past one hundred years might be enough to exhaust the subject. After all, the expedition has a clear beginning and end, the route across the continent is well known and documented, various issues of the journals are widely available, and hundreds of authors have already written about the subject. Yet the increasing flood of books, articles, and films on the expedition suggests there may be no end to the appeal of Lewis and Clark and the ways it can be described or interpreted.

The most remarkable feature of writings on Lewis and Clark is not the sheer volume of material, but its narrow scope. Indeed, the Lewis and Clark expedition might be likened to a favorite national children's bedtime story—which like young children, Americans insist on hearing over and over. The physicality of the expedition generally receives the most attention, with Lewis and Clark and wild nature set up as antagonists in a classic tale of adversity and triumph. There is more to the appeal of the expedition than this, and it is unfair to suggest that recent scholarship on Lewis and Clark fits into this narrow story line. Nevertheless, there remains a great deal of work to be done on the broader contexts and meaning of the expedition. This section presents new views on the expedition, with particular emphasis on the conditions and concerns that shaped its purposes and ensured its lasting significance. The first three essays assess the support of organizations like the American Philosophical Society, the manner in which the journals fulfilled Jefferson's description of the expedition as a "literary pursuit," and the social aspects of disease and injury and their medical treatments.

Chapter 1

Living with Lewis & Clark

The American Philosophical Society's Continuing
Relationship with the Corps of Discovery from the
Michaux Expedition to the Present

Edward C. Carter II

Both Benjamin Franklin's 1743 proposal for the creation of the American Philosophical Society and its 1780 charter charged the organization with fostering discovery and exploration through surveys, charting, and mapping of the unknown expanses of North America and its "Sea-coasts, or Inland Countries; Course and Junctions of Rivers and Great Roads, Situations of Lakes and Mountains," and describing "the variety of its climate, the fertility of its soil," all of which offered to "these United States . . . the richest subjects of cultivation, ever presented to any people upon the earth." Over the years, the society has taken its responsibility seriously, occasionally mounting its own expeditions, subsidizing others, actively promoting exploration of the American West and the polar regions with federal agencies and the general public, regularly publishing the reports of expeditions and individual explorers, and amassing a vast array of rare manuscripts, printed works, and graphic collections of North American and oceanic exploration in its library. Admirable and valuable as these activities may be, in the eyes of the general public and the scholarly community, they are no match for the American Philosophical Society's role in helping plan and execute the Lewis and Clark expedition, preserving its records and fostering publication of those accounts for more than 185 years.

Thomas Jefferson was president of the American Philosophical Society from 1797 to 1814. During the first four years of his presidency, he was a "hands-on" leader and attended and chaired many meetings of the society, setting policy and initiating programs. After his removal from Philadelphia to Washington upon becoming the third president of the United States, he carried out his leadership through correspondence and surrogates. For the next decade Jefferson (APS 1780) was mostly concerned with the organization, training, and execution of the Lewis and Clark expedition between

1803 and 1806, the allocation of the Corps of Discovery's booty, the flawed effort at publication of the journals, and the final donation of those invaluable documents to the society. Until his death on 4 July 1826, Jefferson gave books and manuscripts to the American Philosophical Society and successfully urged others to do likewise. Thomas Jefferson's principles, interests, generosity, and example have helped shape the American Philosophical Society's history and mission right up to the present time.[1]

Knowing that the American Philosophical Society constituted the single greatest concentration of scientific talent and resources in the United States, he promoted its cause not only at home but also during his residence in Europe. Thus while the American Philosophical Society and its Philadelphia members provided Jefferson with intellectual stimulation and all-important friendship, it primarily served him as a source of inspiration by defining the level of scientific and technological competence Americans might achieve. The society also served as an instrument for advancing and diffusing American science and technology and, when constitutionally appropriate, assisting in or even executing federal projects. For his part, Jefferson not only materially enriched the society through donations of books, manuscripts, apparatus, and natural history items; provided active, interested leadership; but also added his great prestige to the society's name for nearly half a century.

Specifically, Jefferson's agenda for the society can be discovered in his great *Notes on the State of Virginia* (1787), probably the most important scientific book written by an American before 1790. First, Jefferson was eager to push western exploration and American claims beyond the Mississippi to the southwest and seek a water passage to the northwestern coast at the mouth of the Columbia. Second, he wanted to learn as much as possible about the Native inhabitants of all of North America—their languages, social and political organization, their means of livelihood, and ultimately their actual origins. Third, in response to the comte de Buffon's negative judgments on the degeneracy of American species, Jefferson was determined to identify American animal and plant species, measure them accurately, and compare them to supposedly superior European ones. He was also confident that the American environment that fostered such superior examples as larger and more numerous quadrupeds would extend its beneficent influence to his countrymen's physical, intellectual, and social well-being, as well as their political character and behavior.[2]

The American Philosophical Society proved to be a valuable asset in Jefferson's "Westerning" efforts. In 1792–93, he drafted instructions on behalf of the society for a fact-finding mission up the Missouri River, and thence to the Pacific to be led by the French botanist André Michaux. The instructions from Jefferson to Michaux were a précis of those he drafted for Meriwether Lewis (APS 1803) a decade later. Interestingly, the eighteen-year-old Lewis, farming near Charlottesville, evidently volunteered to accompany the Frenchman, but Jefferson refused his request.[3] In any case, the expedition was diplomatically and politically aborted. The Michaux expedition, however, was not a total loss for either Jefferson or the American Philosophical Society. The process of reviewing "instructions" by qualified members of the society was begun and an intellectual and organizational framework was created for future exploration. André Michaux bore no ill will toward the society, which today holds the nine-volume manuscript of his North American botanical journal, 1787–96. His famous son and assistant, François-André Michaux (APS 1809), had close contacts with the society and bequeathed it 92,000 francs at his death in 1855 to contribute to the progress of agriculture and silviculture in the United States. Today the Michaux Fund's value is approximately $850,000.[4]

Jefferson and the American Philosophical Society did not allow the failure of the Michaux expedition to deter them from pressing forward with what would become a major component of the Lewis and Clark expedition—an investigation of trans-Mississippi Native American social and political organization, trade patterns, and demographic distribution. In 1797 Jefferson joined the recently created History Committee charged with gathering a wide range of documents relating to the creation of the United States and also with searching for general information about and artifactual examples of Indian cultures, the meaning of the trans-Appalachian mounds, and evidence of the American mastodon. Many valuable manuscripts and printed documents were gathered in, but as time went by the committee's focus intensified on "the Customs, Manners, Languages and Character of the Indian nations, ancient and modern, and their migrations."[5] By this time, Jefferson had become president of the United States and the American Philosophical Society was the nation's first and most prominent center of Indian linguistics and ethnohistory. Its members proved to be important resources for Lewis and Clark in how best to deal with and study the Indians of the Missouri. The History Committee then became dormant but began to revive in 1811 and was formally reestablished in 1815 as the Historical and Literary Committee devoted to the study of general (European and Asian) linguistics and Native American languages and linguistics.

The driving forces on the committee were the society's librarian, John Vaughan (APS 1784) and the famed international lawyer and the committee's corresponding secretary, Peter S. Du Ponceau (APS 1791). Together these two men built up a world-famous printed and manuscript collection of linguistics and anthropology. Jefferson himself was involved and most helpful in scouting out key documents of early American history like the 1728 survey between Virginia and North Carolina. The committee held regular meetings and published its own *Transactions*. By 1817, it was an ongoing, vigorous quasi-independent body within the American Philosophical Society devoted to linguistics, anthropology, and history—the latter topic pleasing Jefferson who always thought "we were too much confined in the practice to the Natural and Mathematical Departments."[6] The significance of this somewhat lengthy discussion is to demonstrate that when the time came for Thomas Jefferson to decide where the Lewis and Clark expedition journals and associated documents should be finally deposited after Nicholas Biddle (APS 1813) and William Clark had concluded their editorial and publication work, the Historical and Literary Committee was a ready and appropriate home for these great documents.[7]

The record of the transfer negotiations of the Lewis and Clark journals and other materials can be found in Donald Jackson's second volume of the *Letters of the Lewis and Clark Expedition and Related Documents 1783–1854*.[8] Vaughan responded to Jefferson's initial letter of 28 June 1817, offering to gather the Lewis and Clark materials together for deposit with the committee, and informed Jefferson "that the Society had [already] received the manuscript journals of Zebulon Pike's expedition up the Mississippi and of William Dunbar's travels on the Ouichita, these having been presented to the Society by Daniel Parker, adjutant and inspector of the army."[9] If Jefferson needed any further precedent for making his deposit of the Lewis and Clark journals, this probably sealed the deal. And so they came to the American Philosophical Society in 1817–18, where they have resided and been cared for with great affection and professional proficiency ever since.

We now return to 1801 and the immediate years thereafter that witnessed the dramatic voyage of the Corps of Discovery. In March 1801 Thomas Jefferson assumed the presidency of the United States and Meriwether Lewis, an Albemarle County neighbor, became his private secretary, residing either in the White House or at Monticello. Most likely Lewis was selected not with an eye to his leading an expedition, but for his knowledge of the political opinions and convictions of the U.S. Army Officer Corps. But once Jefferson decided to go forward with a federal transcontinental exploratory enterprise, Lewis was ready, as was the American Philosophical Society. The Lewis and Clark expedition, a joint effort of President Jefferson, the U.S. Army, and the society, was the first major exploratory mission sponsored by the federal government. Clearly it was the greatest use of the society made by Jefferson, who submitted his draft instructions to the society for review and then enlisted society members to tutor Captain Meriwether Lewis in surveying, astronomy, medicine, natural history, and Indian ethnology. Members of the society were also assigned roles in the unsuccessful attempts at publishing the scientific findings recorded in the journals. Today the society is fulfilling its obligation by cosponsoring, with the University of Nebraska, Gary Moulton's definitive, award-winning, modern edition of *The Journals of the Lewis & Clark Expedition*.

A list of the society members who instructed and advised Meriwether Lewis in 1803 constitutes a contemporary pantheon of American science and medicine: in Philadelphia, Benjamin Smith Barton (APS 1789), natural history and the preservation of specimens; Caspar Wistar (APS 1787), anatomy and paleontology; Benjamin Rush (APS 1769), medicine and medical supplies; Robert Patterson (APS 1783), mathematics to support Lewis's astronomical skills; in Lancaster, Andrew Ellicott (APS 1785), astronomy and training in use of its instruments; and in Washington, D.C., Albert Gallatin (APS 1791), secretary of the treasury, Missouri River geography and cartography.[10] Jefferson wrote letters of introduction to his society colleagues asking their assistance in training Lewis in the purchase of the correct supplies and instruments required, and in helping to assemble a working reference library for the expedition. The president swore his correspondents to secrecy because the Louisiana Purchase was not yet a reality and the expedition's Corps of Discovery's proposed path lay through foreign territory, and no one, as yet, envisioned the sudden purchase of Louisiana from Napoleon.

At the same time, April 1803, Jefferson wrote Lewis to inform him that "your destination is known to Mr. Patterson, Doctrs. Wistar, Rush & Barton" and instructed Lewis to submit the enclosed "copy of the rough draufht of the instructions I have prepared for you . . . for their perusal so that they may suggest any additions that they think useful. . . . A considerable portion of [the instructions] being within the field of the Philosophical society, which once undertook the same mission, I think it my duty to consult some of its members, limiting the communication by the necessity of secrecy in a good degree."[11] Jefferson's friends took their duties seriously and probably reviewed and amended the draft "Instructions" for the expedition several times. Patterson and Ellicott rejected a number of the astronomical and surveying instruments proposed by Jefferson as not practical for such a rough voyage and, by implication, because they were too sophisticated for a novice like Lewis. All (especially Benjamin Rush) were helpful in outfitting of the expedition in Philadelphia and the safe packaging of Lewis's fragile and perishable purchase of medical instruments and drugs.

This collaboration between members of the society continued during and after the voyage of discovery but with diminishing success. As Lewis and Clark pushed off upriver from the Mandan villages in April 1805, a major shipment of natural history specimens and Indian artifacts were sent back east to Jefferson. Many of these were then sent to the American Philosophical Society for study, classification, and, in the case of seeds, planting in the city's botanical gardens. The same process continued when Lewis and Clark returned in 1806, but with uneven results. Naturalists failed to prepare the materials for publication; much of the Lewis and Clark booty was dispersed and some eventually lost; and the publication plan announced to the public by Meriwether Lewis in 1807 floundered after his death two years later.[12] However, as we have seen, the partnership took on new life with the 1814 publication of Biddle's two-volume narrative history of the expedition and William Clark's great printed map of its routes, and with the journals' final deposit at the society several years later.

While the Lewis and Clark expedition was itself a triumph, the publication of its vital geographic, ethnographic, and other scientific findings was less satisfactory. Lewis, who was charged with arranging for the publication of the expedition's various reports, did little after selecting a Philadelphia publisher and apparently consulting with naturalists to work up those materials. Then Lewis died tragically in 1809, probably by his own hand, leaving the unfinished business for Jefferson and Clark to salvage as best they could with the planned publication. In fact, although the historical literature on Lewis and Clark is immense, it was not until the late twentieth century that the Corps of Discovery's definitive record would be made available in the multivolume modern edition.

Meriwether Lewis had announced in 1807 publication plans for a three-volume expedition report together with a separately issued large map documenting the Corps of Discovery's outbound and inbound routes and its principal geographic and ethnographic findings. The first volume was to be a chronological narrative of the expedition; the second was to deal with the geographic and other physical aspects of the territory traversed; and the third and final volume would be confined "exclusively to scientific research"—natural history and physical science. In the end, the first publication of the Lewis and Clark journals would be limited to Biddle's two-volume chronological narrative containing the engraved map. By the time of Lewis's death, Jefferson had retired to Monticello and Clark was deeply involved in his official duties in St. Louis, where he served as the Louisiana Territory's superintendent of Indian affairs. With his friend and comrade's death, William Clark took possession of all the records of the expedition. He traveled east in 1809–10 determined to discover a way to publish at least the narratives of the expedition—a task Clark felt was far beyond his own capabilities.

The ultimate solution lay in the recruitment of young Nicholas Biddle of Philadelphia to undertake the work. Biddle was a lawyer, man of culture, and an important literary figure and editor. After the war of 1812, he would become the president of the Second Bank of the United States and in the 1830s President Andrew Jackson's archenemy in the realm of national fiscal policy. Biddle at first refused Clark's invitation but eventually spent about three weeks in the spring of 1810 with Clark at the family home of the captain's wife in Fincastle, Virginia. Together they studied the journals and discussed the expedition in great detail. It was agreed that Biddle would write a narrative account of the great enterprise, leaving scientific matters

to experts. Clark turned over to Biddle the journals and other papers related to further publication. Upon Clark's return to St. Louis the two men
corresponded about unanswered questions and publication problems. Biddle's synthesis was brilliant but unfortunately excluded the greater portion
of Lewis's insightful natural history observations and descriptions.[13]

When William Clark returned to his duties in St. Louis, he threw himself
into the task of pulling all the cartographic records of the Corps of Discovery together, analyzing them, and producing the great "large Connected
[manuscript] Map" of the Northwest based upon earlier composite maps,
the expedition's highly accurate route maps, and Native American maps.
Clark's masterpiece of American cartography also attempted to show some
of the results of the exploratory efforts into the upper Arkansas and Rio
Grande river basins by Captain Zebulon M. Pike (1805–7) and the individual travels of two former members of the corps: John Colter (1807–8),
through the northeastern quarter of present-day Wyoming; and George
Drouillard (1808), through some of the territory covered by Colter and
through the Bighorn River's drainage area. Clark's manuscript map, now in
the collections of Yale University, was sent in December 1810 to Biddle, who
had it copied by the Philadelphia cartographer Samuel Lewis. This version
was then engraved for inclusion in the 1814 publication (the engraved copper plate today resides in the society's collections).

William Clark's final cartographic achievement stands as one of the great
maps of all times and perhaps the single most influential one of the American West, for it was upon this visual essay that our modern understanding
of the topography of that vast area would evolve.

By this point, readers have noticed that the date of APS election follows
the names of all the major figures in this essay—all, that is, but one—that
of William Clark. It seems both incredible and immensely unjust that Clark,
who shared the leadership of the expedition so brilliantly and tried to tidy
up its loose ends after Lewis's death, was never elected to the American
Philosophical Society. How might this have happened? The society retained
records of the elections' results, never of the preceding deliberations. Occasionally, members kept brief personal notes (against the laws of the society) and these have been found in personal papers. Nothing in Jefferson's
correspondence or any known clandestine notes refer to Clark on such a
matter.

Lewis himself was elected at the meeting of 21 October 1803 when he
was in Clarksville, Indiana Territory, across the Ohio River from Louisville,
Kentucky, recruiting the Corps of Discovery's first enlisted men with Clark.[14]
Up to this point, Meriwether Lewis had really not accomplished anything
of major consequence. Why was he elected at this time? The easy answer
might be that he was the protégé, confidant, and friend of the society's president, who had urged his election. Perhaps a more likely reason is Lewis's

"tutorial" visit to Philadelphia, during which he worked closely with the leading lights of the society. A number of them commented very favorably on Lewis, his character, and qualifications when responding to Jefferson's letters of introduction. I suspect that the Philadelphians thought Lewis a likely candidate for fame and put his name forward at the onset of his voyage of discovery.

But what about William Clark? Lewis himself had an opportunity to push for his best friend's election in the spring of 1807, a year after the Corps of Discovery's return from the West. By that time, William Clark was one of the most famous "scientists" in the United States and was well known to the society's Philadelphia members. Lewis attended three meetings of the society (17 April, 17 June, and 17 July 1807),[15] which gave him an opportunity to propose and engineer Clark's election under the society's rules of the time. (Ironically, at the 17 April meeting, the society elected Ferdinand R. Hassler, professor of mathematics at West Point, who later attempted unsuccessfully to make sense out of Lewis's and Clark's astronomical computations and readings aimed at establishing the expeditions longitude and latitude at key locations.) We probably never will know if Lewis ever attempted to have his friend elected.

Jefferson always seemed to favor Lewis over Clark, primarily because of his close association with, and high regard for, his young Virginia neighbor. Their relationship cooled in the years before Lewis's death mainly because of the younger man's failure to push forward with the expedition's publications or to inform Jefferson about his personal or professional life. After 1806, Lewis did make clear to Jefferson the immense role Clark played in the expedition's achievements. Later, Jefferson worked closely with Clark and Biddle to publish the history and major findings of the expedition. Biddle was elected in 1813 to the society presumably because of this work, but Clark (a non-Philadelphian) was not.

In 1815, Jefferson gave up the society's presidency without seeing that William Clark received his proper reward from an organization that had benefited and would continue to benefit from the captain's co-leadership of the greatest act of exploration in the history of the United States.

When Thomas Jefferson died on 4 July 1826, the Lewis and Clark expedition was fading from the collective American memory—diminished by the stories of others who followed the Corps of Discovery's track and the ensuing national tensions like the 1820 Missouri Compromise that, in part, were engendered by western migration and settlement. But at the American Philosophical Society, their great president's western dreams and accomplishments were remembered and celebrated (if only momentarily) on 11 April 1827 when the *Eulogium* on Thomas Jefferson was delivered by Nicholas Biddle.[16] In a fair, balanced manner, he described Jefferson's long-term interest in western exploration, highlighting the achievements of the

Corps of Discovery while placing them in context with other federal expeditions instituted by Jefferson like those of Pike, Freeman, and Hunter Dunbar. Biddle, the author of the 1814 *History,* made no mention of his own work. Perhaps he passed over the subject out of respect for Jefferson's thwarted hopes for full-scale, European-standard exploratory reports, including transcriptions of the journals themselves, the full cartographic record, and scientific assessments of the natural history and ethnographic discoveries.

There was little Lewis and Clark interest or activity at the American Philosophical Society until the end of the nineteenth century. The journals were not lost or buried at the society, as Elliott Coues (APS 1878) later claimed. They were listed in the society's two printed catalogs of the library's collections and occasionally the historically curious asked to see and even study them.[17] In 1896, a monumental discovery was made when Thomas Meehan, a botanist at Philadelphia's Academy of Natural Sciences, acting on a tip from a colleague, searched the society and located 179 of Lewis's plants "stored away, probably untouched for three-quarters of a century and somewhat decimated by beetles."[18] These were placed on permanent loan at the academy, where today they constitute the majority of the 227 specimens of the Lewis and Clark Herbarium (eleven other items are at Kew Gardens and one is at the Charleston Museum). The society's botanical holdings proved to be an important element in the renewed scholarly and public interest in Lewis and Clark that developed at the opening of the twentieth century.

The subject of the Lewis and Clark expedition also benefited from two contemporary developments of the late nineteenth century: the propensity to mark important national anniversaries and the professionalism of social science. The celebration of the centennial of American independence in Philadelphia during the summer of 1876 set off an anniversary frenzy that stimulated the nation's patriotic, historical, and promotional appetites. There were famous extravaganzas like the Columbian World Exposition held at Chicago in 1893 and lesser known ones like that of August 1887 when "the Village of Lititz, in Lancaster County, Pennsylvania celebrated its one-hundredth birthday."[19] At the same time, the founding of the American Historical Association in 1884 marked the rise of professionalism in the field of history—a development that also took hold at the American Philosophical Society, which began electing leading university-trained historians. When the American Historical Association appointed its Historical Manuscript Commission to promote the collection, editing, and publication of American historical documents in 1895, the society responded two years later by creating its own Committee on Historical Manuscripts to examine the library's historical documents and its early American imprints and consider ways to make them more available for study. These two movements—

popular celebrations and historical professionalism—coalesced at the American Philosophical Society when under the auspices of its committee, the publishers Dodd, Mead issued Reuben Gold Thwaites's eight-volume edition (1904–05) of the journals of the Lewis and Clark expedition, consisting mainly of materials Jefferson had sent to Philadelphia. The committee's sponsorship of the edition was strongly motivated by two forthcoming centennials: the 1904 Louisiana Purchase celebration in St. Louis and the 1905 Lewis and Clark Centennial and American Exposition and Oriental Fair held in Portland, Oregon.[20]

Elliott Coues had already published in 1893 his enlarged three-volume edition of Biddle's *History*, but Coues's work was not an edition of the journals![21] After their 1817–18 deposit, the journals and associated materials were only occasionally consulted throughout the balance of the century until Coues, a former army surgeon, a leading American ornithologist, and an APS member, "rediscovered" the journals in the society's collections. Coues proposed to undertake a new edition of Biddle's *History*, consulting all the previously excluded natural history commentary and data. With the society's permission, he removed the journals to his home in Washington, D.C. in 1892, and set to work on the project. While his 1893 edition of Biddle's *History* would prove to be "in many ways a masterly work," his treatment of the journals by current standards—and even those of the times—was scandalous.[22]

To make the journals easier to work with, Coues defaced them in a shameless manner. He organized the materials chronologically, placed labels on each notebook, providing each with an alphabetic codex (an identification system that continues today), and paginated the lot. He removed brass holding clasps and presented them to friends, added interlinear notes in the manuscript text, and trimmed ragged pages. Nevertheless the doctor-scientist-editor wrote excellent natural history annotations and brought a degree of order to Biddle's 1814 effort.

Coues's publication, for all its virtues, was not an exact transcription of the captains' words but an expansion of Biddle's paraphrased narrative of 1814. The first true edition of the materials would be Thwaites's *Original Journals of the Lewis and Clark Expedition*. Thwaites, the director of the State Historical Society of Wisconsin and an experienced editor of western historical materials, discovered new Lewis and Clark "documents that greatly enhanced his edition."[23]

Following the publication of Thwaites's edition there was an upsurge of Lewis and Clark interest, discovery of more critical documentation, and an expansion of the literature by scholars like Milo M. Quaife, Bernard De-Voto, Donald Jackson, and Paul Russell Cutright. A number of abridged editions of the journals were produced as well, but no one undertook a complete, modern, definitive edition until the 1970s. Gary E. Moulton, with the co-sponsorship of the University of Nebraska Press and the American Philosophical Society, undertook that task. Opening with a brilliant atlas volume containing the entire cartographic work, the distinguished edition advanced with remarkable speed through ten volumes of journals (including those of Sergeants Charles Floyd, Patrick Gass, and John Ordway, and Private Joseph Whitehouse), concluding in 1999 with a natural history volume on the expedition's herbarium. One hundred and ninety-three years after the Corps of Discovery's return to St. Louis, Moulton's *Journals of the Lewis & Clark Expedition* not only fulfilled but also far exceeded the dreams of Thomas Jefferson, Meriwether Lewis, and William Clark for the publication of the records and achievements of the great enterprise.

The American Philosophical Society took its sponsorship of the project seriously and over the years provided valuable technical and financial support for Moulton's work. The society not only allowed him free and unlimited access to the journals but also provided microcopies of all the journals, photographs of individual pages when necessary, photographed all the Lewis botanical specimens from the Philadelphia Academy of Natural Sciences for the final volume, and made significant annual grants to the project (matched by the National Endowment for the Humanities). For more than a decade the editor spent several two-week visits in the library reading all the project's transcriptions against the original text. Our staff came to regard Moulton as not only a friend but also an honorary member of the library. Professor Moulton generously claims that the sponsorship and financial support of the American Philosophical Society opened doors at foundations and the pocketbooks of private donors.

Of course, the Lewis and Clark journals represent only a very small part of the society's large and distinguished research collections on western, polar, and oceanic scientific research and their accompanying holdings in anthropology and Native American linguistics and ethnohistory. Over the years thousands of researchers have visited the society to use these resources—visits that have resulted in hundreds of notable scholarly articles and books.

The early 1990s seemed an appropriate time to think of undertaking a conference on the progress and current state of North American exploration studies. A resurgence of western history was under way, heightening scholarly and popular interest in scientific expeditions and surveys. Readership in the society's manuscript and printed exploration and anthropological collections, always vigorous, was on the rise, perhaps helped along by the library's 1991 publication of William Stanton's *American Scientific Exploration 1803–1865: Manuscripts in Four Philadelphia Libraries,* which highlighted our extensive and varied holdings. On 14–16 March 1997, the Library of the American Philosophical Society held a three-day conference on North American scientific exploration attended by some one hundred and fifty scholars and interested members of the general public, who heard twenty-seven presentations organized into nine plenary sessions.

The meeting was intended to examine and, we hoped, illuminate new historical approaches to scientific expeditions and surveys, and to stimulate discussion and intellectual interchange between the new generation of scholars and their more established colleagues. To accomplish these goals the Program Advisory Committee invited participation of historians, art historians, historical geographers, anthropologists, archaeologists, historical botanists, and others. We proposed to investigate broad topics that represented both new directions of inquiry and those more traditional ones that should be revisited. By employing "Surveying the Record" as the conference title, we hoped that participants would look at the actual history of specific expeditions through a variety of disciplinary lenses and also reevaluate earlier scholars' accounts of the explorative enterprise.

The conference was a resounding success and certainly demonstrated that exploration studies were alive and well, imaginative and diverse. Two years later the society published *Surveying the Record: North American Scientific Exploration to 1930* containing sixteen of the conference papers (including two on Lewis and Clark topics).[24]

In 1979 the society had taken a modest step in making original Lewis and Clark documents available to the public. It reused the engraved plate of the 1814 map to print 10 extremely clear and sharp unnumbered copies and 150 numbered ones, selling the latter for the benefit of the Friends of the Library before retiring the plate from service because of its fragile state. Then in 1998 the librarian called upon one of the nation's most distinguished fine printing and facsimile presses, the Stinehour Press of Lunenburg, Vermont, using offset lithography, to produce another "run" of 2,500 copies of the unnumbered map, together with an explanatory booklet. In essence, the 1814 printed map is a précis of the Lewis and Clark expedition itself—a concluding page of the great enterprise's tale. It can be "read" with pleasure and enlightenment in tandem with either a modern historical account or an edition of the journals.

A more recent dramatic example of the society's Lewis and Clark public outreach was made possible by a generous 1998 grant from the Pew Charitable Trusts of Philadelphia supporting the production and complimentary distribution of a facsimile edition: *Three Journals of the Lewis & Clark Expedition* in 2000. A total of 1,200 complimentary sets was presented to federal repositories, state libraries and historical societies, major independent research libraries and historical societies, state and federal historical interpretive sites along the Lewis and Clark trail, some two hundred tribal centers, high schools, colleges and universities in the Delaware Valley, and selected colleges and research universities throughout the United States.

With the assistance of Professor Moulton, we selected three journals to comprise the facsimile publication. As all thirty codices are filled with interesting and exciting descriptions and events, the selection was a difficult one. We picked journals from different stages of the expedition reflecting a variety of geographic landscapes, climates, seasons, and activities. We felt it was important for the reader to have the benefit of both Meriwether Lewis's and William Clark's reporting, insights, and literary styles.[25]

From a viewpoint of enlightened self-interest, the response to these facsimile editions was highly favorable. Tens of thousands of individuals who had never heard of the American Philosophical Society will now learn something about the society and its mission. The greater significance of these facsimile publications is that numerous students, scholars, and members of the general public can study at firsthand these key documents of America's creation.

What of the present and future relations of the American Philosophical Society with Lewis and Clark? The tidal wave of the Lewis and Clark bicentennial is already upon us, pulled along by the amazing national response to Stephen Ambrose's record-breaking best-seller of 1996, *Undaunted Courage: Meriwether Lewis, Thomas Jefferson, and the Opening of the American West,* and the widely viewed PBS documentary by Ken Burns and Dayton Duncan, *Lewis & Clark: The Journey of the Corps of Discovery.* The society's librarian has served as a director of the National Lewis and Clark Bicentennial Council since its founding in 1994. This national body is officially charged with the tasks of raising public awareness of the celebration; working with federal, state, tribal, and local organizations to produce meaningful events and lasting results; and offering its good offices as a general coordinating body. The American Philosophical Society already is feeling the increased pressure of coping with numerous Lewis and Clark queries and requests for TV and newspaper interviews about the Corps of Discovery, the society's role, and related library holdings. There is also a rising tide of e-mail questions from members of the general public (of all ages), scholars, and publishers; and numerous requests for permission to film Lewis and Clark materials for documentaries. The society is working closely with the Missouri Historical Society on planning and mounting the major national traveling exhibit that will include items from our collections. In 2003 we will welcome the annual convention of the Lewis and Clark Trail Heritage Foundation to Philadelphia, and the society is planning to hold a symposium with Monticello on "Thomas Jefferson, the American Philosophical Society, and the Lewis and Clark Expedition."

Although at present we are handling all these requests efficiently and generally with good spirits, it is clear we must become more selective in carrying out our Lewis and Clark mission over the next few years. Even the best public projects have a way of getting out of hand. A good example is our *Three Journals,* a facsimile edition that will reach thousands of students, scholars, and members of the general public throughout the United States. What seemed like a fairly straightforward project required the full-time attention of a senior staff member and his assistant for half a year after the design and photography were completed.

Regardless of such diversions, the American Philosophical Society is ready to meet the new, and perhaps most challenging, Lewis and Clark adventure of modern times under way since January 2003. To echo the sentiments of Meriwether Lewis on his departure from the Mandan villages en route to the Rocky Mountains and the Pacific Ocean beyond—the society will succeed in a voyage which has formed a darling project of ours for more than two hundred years.

NOTES

1. Not much has been written on Jefferson's leadership of the APS other than Gilbert Chuinard, "Thomas Jefferson and the American Philosophical Society," *Proceedings of the American Philosophical Society* 87 (September 1943): 163–276. A portion of the following text is taken from Edward C. Carter II, "Jefferson's American Philosophical Society Leadership and Heritage," in *"The Most Flattering Incident of My Life": Essays Celebrating the Bicentennial of Thomas Jefferson's American Philosophical Society Presidency, 1797–1814* (Philadelphia: Published for the Friends of the APS Library, 1997), 9–15.

2. For Jefferson's thoughts on these specific topics see William Peden, ed., *Notes on the State of Virginia by Thomas Jefferson* (New York: W. W. Norton, 1972), 7–10, 15–16, 92–107, 43–63.

3. The possible early involvement of Lewis in the Michaux expedition is based on a statement in Jefferson's "Life of Captain Lewis," which served as an introduction to Nicholas Biddle's 1814 two-volume *History of the Expedition Under the Command of Captains Lewis and Clarke to the Sources of the Missouri, Thence Across The Rocky Mountains And Down The River Columbia To The Pacific Ocean. Performed during the Years 1804–5–6. By Order of the Government of The United States* (1814; reprint, New York: Allerton Book, 1922), wherein Jefferson states that when Lewis was on recruiting duty in Charlottesville in 1792 he applied for the job but was turned down. Most historians have merely repeated Jefferson's statement although Lewis did not volunteer for the militia until 1794 when he was twenty. Anthony F. C. Wallace recently pointed these facts out and sets the date of Lewis's raising the issue as 1799, when he was in Charlottesville on recruiting duty (*Jefferson and the Indians: The Tragic Fate of the First Americans* [Cambridge, Mass.: Harvard University Press, Belknap Press, 1999], 342). Lewis himself seems to place the date earlier; upon departing from Fort Mandan on 7 April 1805, he joyfully wrote in his journal about his "most confident hope of succeading in a voyage which had formed a da[r]ling project of mine for the last ten years [of my life]" (Gary E. Moulton, ed., *The Journals of the Lewis & Clark Expedition* [Lincoln: University of Nebraska Press, 1983–99], 4:10).

4. For excellent biographical sketches of the dramatic, productive lives of the two Michaux see their entries in John A. Garraty and Mark C. Carnes, eds., *American*

National Biography (New York: Oxford University Press, 1999), 15:414–417. For a more modern and intriguing "Michaux story," see the amazing and even amusing account of how a 1979 high school summer intern discovered one of the society's most famous and valuable documents, the manuscript of the Michaux expedition instructions and subscription list, in a small 1770 package of the old Silk Society (Whitfield J. Bell, Jr.'s "Report of the Committee on Library," *APS Year Book* [1979]: 159–160). On the document are all the signatures of the contributors—who joined the APS in 1780—and the amounts they gave: George Washington, $100; John Adams, $20; Thomas Jefferson and Andrew Hamilton, each $50. No historian or biographer for 175 years had seen this breathtaking document until it was found by young Robert E. Mooney. "There cannot be many documents which bear the signatures of the first four Presidents of the United States" (Bell, "Report," 159). Through the generosity of the Pew Charitable Trusts it was conserved in 1999 and recently exhibited in the APS library's lobby (November 1999 to August 2000).

5. Quoted in Wallace, *Jefferson and the Indians,* 158.

6. Quoted in ibid., 320.

7. For a more detailed discussion of the committee see ibid., 139, 156–157, 319–321.

8. Jefferson to Vaughan, Monticello, 28 June 1817; Jefferson to Peter S. Du Ponceau, Monticello, 7 November 1817; Du Ponceau to Jefferson, Philadelphia, 5 December 1817; Clark to Biddle, Washington, D.C., 27 January 1818; Biddle to William Tilghman (APS 1805), chairman of committee, Philadelphia, 6 April 1818, Vaughan to Biddle, 8 April 1818; all in Donald Jackson, ed., *Letters of the Lewis and Clark Expedition with Related Documents 1783–1854,* 2d ed. (Urbana: University of Illinois Press, 1978), 2:630–637. For a summary of the negotiations through which the journals were acquired see also the minutes of the APS Historical and Literary Committee, especially entries of 19 November 1817 and 8 April 1818.

9. Jackson, *Letters,* 2:74.

10. The Philadelphians were also distinguished faculty members of the University of Pennsylvania.

11. These quotations are from Jefferson to Lewis, Washington, D.C., 27 April 1803 in Jackson, *Letters,* 1:44.

12. For an excellent review of postexpedition history of the numerous plant and animal specimens, Indian artifacts, and other objects collected see Paul Russell Cutright, *Lewis and Clark, Pioneering Naturalists* (Urbana: University of Illinois Press, 1969), 349–402. Moulton ably brought the botanical aspect of this story up to date in his edition's twelfth volume, *Herbarium of the Lewis & Clark Expedition* (Lincoln: University of Nebraska Press, 1999), 1–10.

13. Biddle, *History.*

14. Entry for 21 October 1803, in *Early Proceedings of the American Philosophical Society . . . Compiled . . . from the Manuscript Minutes of Its Meetings from 1744 to 1838* (Philadelphia: McCalla and Stovely, 1884), 343.

15. Entries for those dates in ibid., 396–398.

16. Biddle, *Eulogium on Thomas Jefferson Delivered before the American Philosophical Society on the Eleventh Day of April 1827* (Philadelphia: Robert H. Small, 1827), 33–35.

17. *Catalogue of the Library of the American Philosophical Society* (Philadelphia: Joseph R. A. Skernett, 1824) [the society's first printed catalog]; and *Catalogue of the American Philosophical Society Library*, 4 parts (Philadelphia: C. Sherman, Son., 1863–84).

18. Moulton, *Herbarium*, 6.

19. Michael Kammen, *Mystic Chords of Memory: The Transformation of Tradition in American Culture* (New York: Alfred A. Knopf, 1991), 141.

20. Edward C. Carter II, *"One Grand Pursuit": A Brief History of the American Philosophical Society's First 250 Years, 1743–1993* (Philadelphia: APS, 1993), 44–45, 49, and 54.

21. The following discussion of Coues's publication and three modern editions is taken from Edward C. Carter II, ed., introductory booklet to *Three Journals of the Lewis & Clark Expedition 1804–1806*, from the Collections of the American Philosophical Society: a facsimile edition (Philadelphia: APS, 2000), 17–21.

22. Moulton, *Journals*, 2:39.

23. Ibid., 40. Reuben Gold Thwaites, ed., *Original Journals of the Lewis and Clark Expedition, 1804–1806*, 8 vols. (New York: Dodd, Mead, 1904–05).

24. See Gunther Barth, "Strategies for Finding the Northwest Passage: The Roles of Alexander Mackenzie and Meriwether Lewis," and Albert Furtwangler, "Do or Die, But Then Report and Ponder: Palpable and Mental Adventures in the Lewis and Clark Journals," both in *Surveying the Record: North American Scientific Exploration to 1930*, ed. Edward C. Carter II (Philadelphia: APS, 1999), 253–266, 267–278. As the APS librarian, Carter also organized and directed the conference.

25. The final selections were William Clark Codex A journal 13 May–14 August 1804 (getting the expedition under way up the Missouri); Meriwether Lewis Codex E journal 24 May–16 July 1805 (going westward from the Mandan villages up the Missouri to the Great Falls and around them); and Meriwether Lewis Codex J journal 1 January–20 March 1806 (damp and rainy winter at Fort Clatsop with splendid summary of flora and fauna, descriptions of northwestern coastal tribes, and preparations for the homeward journey). See Carter, introductory booklet, *Three Journals*, 19–21.

Chapter 2

Wilderness Aesthetics

Frank Bergon

The Lewis and Clark expedition, like the adventures in the *Epic of Gilgamesh* and the *Odyssey,* was a trek into an unfamiliar and often frightening wilderness—the first, longest, and largest of nineteenth-century United States government expeditions into terra incognita. Launched from St. Louis in 1804 in a 55-foot masted keelboat and two pirogues carrying more than 8,000 pounds of food and equipment, the Voyage of Discovery, as it was called, lasted two years, four months, and ten days. Round-trip, it covered 7,689 miles between the mouth of the Missouri River and the Pacific outlet of the Columbia River. To a young nation—the United States was barely seventeen years old at the time—Lewis and Clark brought back maps of previously uncharted rivers and mountains, specimens of previously unknown plants and animals, amazing artifacts, and even representatives of previously unseen peoples of the West. But the explorers' most valuable contribution came in an elkskin-bound field book and red morocco-bound journals, stored in tin boxes. Written in an odd, fragmented style that vacillated between the languages of art and science in accordance with the aesthetic expectations of the day, these remarkable journals offered a new natural history of the West. More significant—and surprising—is that the strange, vacillating style of the journals came to characterize the entire genre of American nature writing in the nineteenth century.

Beginning in 1983, *The Journals of the Lewis & Clark Expedition* have been appearing piecemeal from the University of Nebraska Press in a standard edition of thirteen volumes, including an oversize atlas, a volume of natural history materials, the diaries of four enlisted men, and the complete journals of the expedition leaders, Meriwether Lewis and William Clark, once dubbed "the writingest explorers of their time."[1] More than a million words of journal entries in over five thousand pages of text and annotation culminated this twenty-year project. Edited by Gary E. Moulton, professor of history at the University of Nebraska-Lincoln, this joint venture of several institutions and numerous scholars, the product of both private and government funding, came to completion just shy of the bicentennial of the 1804–06 expedition. According to a reviewer's puff quoted on a publisher's brochure, "These journals of exploits and courage in a pristine West have a simplicity and timelessness about them—never failing to capture the imagination of the ordinary reader or to interest the historian, scientist, or geographer."

But what about students and teachers of American literature? Do these expeditionary materials stimulate their interest with the same intensity as that of historians, scientists, and geographers? If for an answer we turn to current canon-forming literary histories and college anthologies, the response would be no. The journals are absent from major commercial anthologies of American literature published by Norton (1994), Heath (1994), HarperCollins (1994), Macmillan (1993), and Prentice Hall (1991), while the recent *Columbia Literary History of the United States* (1988) advises readers to forego the complete journals and explore a modern abridgment because "[t]edious detail so clutters their narrative."[2] Perhaps a change is imminent. The more recent *Cambridge History of American Literature* (1994) discusses the journals at length, and the new scholarly Nebraska edition now provides an opportunity to see that these writings—with their logs of temperature and weather, astronomical observations, tabulations of longitude and latitude, descriptions of flora and fauna, anthropological data, misspellings, and neologisms—do indeed constitute a classic "literary pursuit"—a natural history of the lands, animals, and native peoples of the West that rises to the level of an American epic.

"Epic" is a word frequently and loosely applied to the expedition itself—the historic act of exploration—with respect to its magnitude, but the term might also characterize the journals as literary texts.[3] In 1989, when asked to produce a popular abridgment of the journals not unlike those recommended by the *Columbia Literary History of the United States,* I found myself arguing in the introduction that "no abridgment can fully convey the dazzling epic quality of the complete journals or their splendid achievement in the literature of natural history, for their effect is monumental and cumulative." I organized the abridgment into the paradigmatic twelve-book epic scheme, and with the freewheeling hyperbole welcome to such editions, I argued that from the hindsight of almost two centuries, these uneven, fragmented, and unpolished journals offer the equivalent of a national poem. In a multistyled language as distinctive as those that characteristically identify ancient epics, they tell a heroic story of a people's struggles through a wilderness and the return home. Better than more artful poems or novels or plays, they embody with the directness and plainness of an oral tale the mythic history of a nation. They tell the story of the tribe, moving west. Not the conventional mythic story of the lone frontiersman facing the wilderness, this tale depicts a cooperative enterprise: a fluctuating community of some thirty-five to forty-five people, including soldiers, woodsmen, blacksmiths, carpenters, cooks, French engagés, a black slave, a Lemhi Shoshone woman, and a newborn baby of mixed race, all heading west. In retrospect, the journals also dramatize the disturbing design of a nation committed to the arrogant belief that—as William Gilpin expressed it seventy years after the expedition ended—the *"untransacted* destiny of the American people is to subdue the continent."[4] In portending the destruction of one civilization and the rise of another, the journals reveal the dark imperialistic underside of the epical adventure.

To Lewis and Clark themselves, however, and the expectant readers of their time, the account of this particular epic followed the format of a work in natural history that conformed to a well-established New World genre. In 1526, when the Spanish naturalist and friend of Columbus, Gonzalo Fernández de Oviedo y Valdés, published his *Natural History of the West Indies,* he initiated a freshet of works in this genre from New Spain, New France, New England, and other New Founde Lands that left Lewis and Clark the inheritors of an American literary tradition more than 250 years old. As with many of their predecessors, Lewis and Clark's conception of "natural history" was rooted in the double meaning of *history* as it had evolved from Aristotle and Pliny. History, or 'ιστορια, to the Greeks meant "an inquiry" or "an account of one's inquires," so that natural history came to mean an inquiry into the natural world and a systematic account (without relation to time) of its observable forms. But *history* in the Aristotelian sense also meant "a narrative or tale or story" in time. Since many naturalists combined their "inquiry into nature" with a narrative of their journeys and adventures, it came to be accepted that natural history was an eyewitness account of nature encountered on one's travels. For the natural historians of the Americas, observable phenomena included landforms, water bodies, minerals, plants, mammals, birds, reptiles, fishes, amphibians, invertebrates—all the expected and unexpected flora and fauna—as well as the commodities and manners of the people in these areas, especially those native inhabitants of the Americas known as Indians.

Lewis and Clark were heirs to this genre that, in the eighteenth century, despite increasing specialization in the sciences, remained for the most part a branch of literature. When Benjamin Smith Barton, scientific adviser to Lewis and author of the first American textbook of botany—a book the explorers carried on their journey—wrote to the naturalist William Bartram in 1788 thanking him for botanical information, he said, "I know not how to repay your goodness, and attention to my literary pursuits." He urged Bartram to publish his manuscript of natural history because it would be of "essential benefit to the cause of Science [and] would be considered a very valuable presente to the literary world."[5] He was right. William Bartram's *Travels through North and South Carolina, Georgia, East & West Florida,* published in 1791, quickly passed into no fewer than nine European editions. It seems only appropriate that this remarkable work, given the importance of its genre to the New World, was arguably the first book published in the United States to become internationally recognized as a literary classic. Coleridge copied passage after passage into his own notebooks and acclaimed it "a work of high merit [in] every way." Images from Bartram's *Travels* made their way into Goldsmith's "Deserted Village," Coleridge's "Kubla Khan," Wordsworth's "Ruth," and Chateaubriand's "Atala." Carlyle asked Emerson, "Do you know *Bartram's Travels?* . . . treats of *Florida* chiefly, has a wonderful kind of floundering eloquence in it. . . . All American libraries ought to provide themselves with that kind of book; and keep them as a kind of future *biblical* article."[6]

That type of comprehensive book, with its particular fusion of scientific and literary concerns, was what Jefferson had in mind for Lewis and Clark. A fine naturalist himself, with a particular interest in phenology (the study of relationships between climate and periodic biological phenomena), Jefferson gave the explorers careful written instructions for observing and recording in detail the natural world. As a result, Jefferson's influence informs the journals like that of a muse. The Voyage of Discovery was his dream, and the journals his inspiration. For twenty years he had sought to have someone do what Lewis and Clark were finally accomplishing. As a congressman in 1783, Jefferson had unsuccessfully tried to enlist General George Rogers Clark, the Revolutionary War hero and William's older brother, to explore the lands west of the Mississippi. As minister to France in 1786, Jefferson supported the Connecticut adventurer John Ledyard in his daring but frustrated attempt to cross the continent by traveling eastward over Siberia and the Bering Sea and then walking from the Pacific Coast, over the Rockies, to the Missouri River. In 1793, as secretary of state and vice president of the American Philosophical Society, Jefferson backed another aborted exploration when he instructed André Michaux, France's most accomplished botanist, to "find the shortest & most convenient route of communication between the U.S. & the Pacific ocean."[7] A current misconception found in several recent books is that when Jefferson, as president in 1803, finally received congressional approval and funds to launch his expedition across the continent, he invited Bartram to serve as the expedition's naturalist.[8] An admirer of Bartram's work and one of the first public officials, along with President George Washington and Vice President John Adams, to order Bartram's *Travels,* Jefferson did later try to enlist Bartram on an expedition up the Red River, which the sixty-five-year-old naturalist politely declined.

For the more demanding trek across the continent, Jefferson had had his
eye on young Meriwether Lewis ever since the nineteen-year-old boy requested Jefferson's permission to accompany Michaux to the Pacific. For two
years before the expedition, Lewis had virtually lived with Jefferson, serving
ostensibly as the president's private secretary while training to lead the
Corps of Discovery. In 1803, when Jefferson sent Lewis to scientists and physicians in Philadelphia for brief but intensive instruction in botany, zoology,
celestial navigation, and medicine, he confided to Barton that he needed
not just a trained specialist but someone with "firmness of constitution &
character, prudence, habits adapted to the woods, & a familiarity with the
Indian manners & character, requisite for the undertaking. All the latter
qualifications Capt. Lewis has."[9] As an ensign in the army, Lewis had earlier
served briefly in a rifle company under the command of Captain William
Clark, who became his immediate choice as a cocommander of the expedition. In both Lewis and Clark, Jefferson found men capable of "a remarkable mass of accurate observation." In their ability to keep "a sharp lookout"—as the naturalist John Burroughs describes it[10]—Lewis and Clark
shared with other naturalists, like John James Audubon, Thoreau, John
Muir, and Burroughs, a trait that surpassed their formal scientific training.
They were not scientific specialists; the word *scientist* in its modern sense had
not yet been invented. They were natural historians whose range encom-
passed all of nature. The strange landforms and new watercourses the explorers encountered were the primary concerns of Clark, who served as the
main cartographer and geographer, while Lewis was the botanist and zoologist. Both compiled a valuable ethnographic record of Indian people, especially of the Lemhi Shoshone, whose meeting with Lewis and Clark
marked their first encounter with whites.

In 1803 the writing of this natural history faced political obstacles. The
vast stretch of lands that Jefferson wanted documented was still a foreign
territory subject to murky claims by Great Britain, Spain, France, and Rus-
sia. Jefferson tried to assure these nations that his encroachment into their
possessions was a "literary" endeavor, undertaken in the disinterested spirit
of expanding scientific and geographic knowledge. He also couched his secret congressional request for exploratory funds in careful terms. In addition to increasing the literary store of natural history, he was interested in
looking for possible trade routes, he told Congress, for external commerce.
Everyone knew otherwise, especially the European powers who were anxious to keep the original colonies of the United States tidily contained along
the continental eastern seaboard. Jefferson's grand design, they knew, was
imperial, to make way for American expansion from sea to shining sea.

As with earlier accounts of American explorers, the enterprises of natural
history writing and colonization became intertwined. "Westward the Course
of Empire Takes Its Way" was the eighteenth-century sentiment that seemed

to become reality when Napoleon, short of cash after failing to overcome the slave revolt in Haiti, abandoned his own imperial ambitions in North America and tried to frustrate Britain's by selling the vast Louisiana Territory to the United States for three cents an acre. The United States suddenly doubled its holdings, and expansion to the Pacific became a virtual certainty. "The consequences of the cession of Louisiana," President Jefferson predicted, "will extend to the most distant posterity." Scarcely six months after congressional ratification of the sale in October 1803, Lewis and Clark were on their way across the continent, writing their journals, and the United States was on its way to becoming a world power. After hearing of the Louisiana Purchase, the Federalist Fisher Ames fearfully warned, "We rush like a comet into infinite space!" [11]

Although the political and commercial ramifications of Lewis and Clark's trek are well known, they should not overshadow what Jefferson told Congress were the "literary purposes" of the venture. In fact, it might be argued that the expedition succeeded more spectacularly as Jefferson's "literary pursuit" than in some of its other aims. Lewis and Clark failed in their primary commercial purpose of finding a practical water route across the continent to link the United States in trade with China. There was no Northwest Passage. They also failed to establish workable routes up the northern tributaries of the Missouri to capture the Canadian fur trade for the United States. And they failed to establish a lasting peace with the native peoples, especially those who controlled passage on the Missouri, and the killing of two Blackfeet warriors actually aggravated relations with tribes of the Northern Plains. It is also questionable how firmly the expedition reinforced the nation's claim to the Oregon territory. But as a "literary pursuit"—a report on the lands, animals, and native peoples of the American West—the expedition succeeded in ways that only now, after nearly two hundred years, are fully appreciable.

In 1806 Jefferson greeted the return of Lewis and Clark to the United States with "unspeakable joy," noting that even the "humblest of it's citizens" looked forward with impatience to publication of the explorers' journals. The president envisioned a revised, polished version of the raw journals, similar to the literate accounts of Bartram's travels and Captain Cook's voyages. Within weeks Lewis released a prospectus announcing the 1807 publication of a three-volume history of the expedition, including all the "scientific results . . . which may properly be distributed under the heads of Botany, Mineralogy, and Zoology," "a view of the Indian nations," and "Lewis & Clark's Map of North America." [12] This project was delayed and then ended with Lewis's death, an apparent suicide, in 1809. Responsibility for the edition shifted to Clark, then serving as Indian agent for the Louisiana Territory, who engaged the Philadelphia lawyer and self-styled litterateur Nicholas Biddle to deal with the journals. Meanwhile, a number of apocryphal patchwork accounts, composed of older explorers' journals and Jefferson's message to Congress, had appeared in popular editions, as did the bowdlerized diary of the expedition sergeant and carpenter, Patrick Gass, whose *Journal of the Voyages and Travels of a Corps of Discovery*, published in 1807, quickly went through seven editions. Finally in 1814, Biddle's authorized *History of the Expedition under the Command of Captains Lewis and Clarke* appeared, much to Jefferson's disappointment, because all the scientific material given to Barton for preparation had not been completed and was therefore excluded from what Jefferson called the "mere journal."[13] Biddle's version was a paraphrase of the original journals written in the first person plural that compressed the two captains into a composite "we," with accounts of Indian sexual activity translated into Latin. This edition stood as the only representation of the explorers' writings for nearly a century. In 1893 the redoubtable ornithologist and military surgeon Elliott Coues edited Biddle's history with massive annotations that brought attention to the previously neglected scientific material. In the process, however, Coues took liberty in emending the original journals, and his numerous interlineations on the manuscript earned him the derision of later scholars despite his valuable editorial achievement. Coues, however, wasn't the only person who had left his smudges on the pages. At the turn of the century, on the eve of the Lewis and Clark centennial, when the American Philosophical Society authorized a verbatim edition of the original journals, the manuscripts were a palimpsest of interlineations and emendations in different shades of ink by Coues, Biddle, Clark, and at least one other unknown person. Biddle's notes in red reflected his own words as well as those of George Shannon, a member of the expedition who, along with Captain Clark, had helped Biddle in his interpretation of the journals. The American Philosophical Society considered asking the Western writer Owen Wister to edit the manuscripts, but it finally selected the historian Reuben Gold Thwaites, who had just edited the 73 volumes of the *Jesuit Relations* (1896–1901). Thwaites chose to reproduce the journals in their current marked-up state, using a variety of typographic pyrotechnics to indicate authorship of most emendations and interlineations except extensive ones by Coues. With a surprising paucity of annotation about the scientific and geographic achievement, Thwaites's edition focused on transcription and compilation of extant materials, so that in 1904–05, one hundred years after the expedition, there at last appeared a *verbatim et literatim et punctuatim* edition of the *Original Journals of Lewis and Clark,* and the captains' actual words were published for the first time.

I have hovered over this history of the manuscripts because the new *Journals of the Lewis and Clark Expedition,* edited by Moulton, expands and updates the 1904–05 Thwaites edition. Moulton adapts Thwaites's format of printing Lewis's and Clark's entries in tandem with appropriate sections introduced by the writer's bracketed name. As in Thwaites's edition, chapter divisions follow the chronological and geographic demarcations inherited from Biddle's edition, and the journals of enlisted men are consigned to separate volumes. Like Thwaites, Moulton has identified emendations and interlineations in the text; only he adds the emender's italicized initials. Moulton relies on reproductions of the Thwaites text as scanned by the optical character recognition (OCR) process but checked, for the first time in a century, against the original journals to ensure accurate transcription. In the last ninety years, misplaced or lost expeditionary documents, unavailable to Thwaites, have been found and published, most notably Lewis and Clark's 1803 eastern journal and Sergeant Ordway's three-volume journal, edited by Milo Milton Quaife. Quaife's 1916 publication of the eastern journal, which recounts the preliminary trip from Pittsburgh on 30 August 1803 to the Mississippi River, presented the captains' earliest writings and extended the documented length of the expedition to three years and one month. Clark's field notes, discovered in 1953 and dubbed the "Dubois Journal" and the "River Journal," were edited by Ernest Staples Osgood and published in 1964. Other valuable materials became available in 1962 with the publication of Donald Jackson's *Letters of the Lewis and Clark Expedition with Related Documents, 1783–1854*. These and other important books in the last fifty years have rendered Thwaites's scanty notations antiquated, and previously neglected achievements of the expedition in the realms of botany, zoology, medicine, ethnography, linguistics, and geography/cartography have become documented.

Moulton's stated purpose is to gather these scattered materials into the first comprehensive, collated edition with a reliable, definitive text and a thorough, uniform annotation. No newly discovered, previously unpublished materials appear in this edition. Accurate transcription is the primary task. "I'm very concerned," Moulton has written, "to get every jot and tittle correct. . . . We're supposed to do the final edition that will stand for all time."[14]

A comparison of sample passages from the Thwaites and Moulton editions exhibits the measure of care taken in rendering an accurate text. Here is Thwaites's 1904 transcription of Lewis's well-known departure from the Mandan villages for the great unknown after sending the keelboat with 18 men and important expeditionary materials back to St. Louis on 7 April 1805:

> Our vessels consisted of six small canoes, and two large perogues. This little fleet altho' not quite so rispectable as those of Columbus or Capt. Cook, were still viewed by us with as much pleasure as those deservedly famed adventurers ever beheld theirs; and I dare say with quite as much anxiety for their safety and preservation.   we were now about to penetrate a country at least two thousand miles in width, on which the foot of civilized man had

never trodden; the good or evil it had in store for us was for experiment yet
to determine, and these little vessells contained every article by which we were
to expect or subsist or defend themselves.   however, as the state of mind in
which we are, generally gives the colouring to events, when the immagination
is suffered to wander into futurity, the picture which now presented itself to
me was a most pleasing one.   enterta[in]ing as I do, the most confident hope
of succeeding in a voyage which had formed a da[r]ling project of mine for
the last ten years, I could but esteem this moment of my departure as among
the most happy of my life.[15]

And here is Moulton's corrected version:

Our vessels consisted of six small canoes, and two large perogues. This little
fleet altho' not quite so rispectable as those of Columbus or Capt. Cook were
still viewed by us with as much pleasure as those deservedly famed adventurers ever beheld theirs; and I dare say with quite as much anxiety for their safety
and preservation.   we were now about to penetrate a country at least two
thousand miles in width, on which the foot of civillized man had never trodden; the good or evil it had in store for us was for experiment yet to determine, and these little vessells contained every article by which we were to expect to subsist or defend ourselves.   however as this the state of mind in
which we are, generally gives the colouring to events, when the immagination
is suffered to wander into futurity, the picture which now presented itself to
me was a most pleasing one.   entertaing <now> as I do, the most confident
hope of succeeding in a voyage which had formed a da[r]ling project of mine
for the last ten years <of my life>, I could but esteem this moment of my <our>
departure as among the most happy of my life. (4:9–10)[16]

Moulton has made nine alterations in vocabulary, spelling, and punctu-
ation. The slight difference between the two renditions, hardly noticeable
to the normal reader, demonstrates that Thwaites did a good job in his original transcriptions, but Moulton's are even better. No one can anticipate
when a minuscule alteration might significantly affect interpretation, and
care in transcription now gives scholars a text to rely on. The same care is
extended to the correction of Thwaites's notations. For example, Thwaites's
binomial identification of a Lewis zoological discovery misnames the bushy-
tailed woodrat as *Neotama cinera* (2:205), which Moulton silently corrects to
Neotoma cinerea (4:354). The few typographic errors that appear in the new
edition pop out of the editorial scaffolding rather than the texts themselves,
where, I assume, editors properly applied more scrupulous proofreading.
For example, Prickly Pear Creek is misspelled as "Prickley" in footnotes
(4:406n. 5, 406n. 9, 410n. 2) though correctly spelled in the index, and
Lewis's entry for 29 May 1805, is mislabeled without notation "1905"
(4:215). The typographic slip of spelling "allitudes" for "altitudes" in the
editorial front matter of volume 3 was apparently caught and corrected
in subsequent volumes. After such evidence of careful editing, it may seem

unfair to suggest that the reading of a passage in Moulton is affected less by transcriptive changes than by the awkward three-to-four pound volumes in which they appear. Better suited to the scholar's desk than the reader's lap, these boxy books are less friendly to the general reader than is the Thwaites's edition with its compressed, old-fashioned print. Thwaites's notes, skimpy as they may be, do appear conveniently at the bottom of the page, a good place for many brief items that simply identify geographic location or the scientific denominations of plants and animals. Moulton's blocks of notes at the conclusion of daily entries, rather than in footnotes or chapter endnotes, are not always easy to locate, and their varied appearance within the text at the top, middle, or bottom of a page creates much shuffling back and forth between text and annotation.

In his arrangement of texts, however, Moulton has done a significant service by moving materials that were chronologically out of place in the Thwaites edition. For example, the extensive summations about rivers, Indian tribes, and botanical and mineralogical collections prepared during the winter at Fort Mandan, which Thwaites tucked into an appendix in volume 6 of his edition, now properly appear with the other writings of that winter to give a better sense of the captains' enterprise among the Mandan. In other instances, however, interspersion of new materials, particularly from Clark's field notes, is not clearly noted. In the Moulton edition a passage about the Mandan by William Clark for 30 March 1805, in part, reads: "All the party in high Spirits, but fiew nights pass without a Dance they are helth. except the—vn. [venereal]—which is common with the Indians and have been communicated to many of our party at this place—those favores bieng easy acquired. all Tranquille" (3:322). This passage is absent from Thwaites, but whether the earlier editor neglected to transcribe it or whether the passage has been inserted into the journal from Clark's rediscovered field notes is not made clear. In other instances, one wishes controversial interpretations of transcriptions were noted. For instance, a longstanding problem in geographic nomenclature has concerned the captains' naming of the Milk River (in present-day Montana). Lewis refers to the Milk River as the "scolding river" (3:367), the one called by Hidatsa *the river that scolds at all others*"(4:248). The scholars Donald Jackson and Paul Russell Cutright both claim that "scolding river" makes no sense; they assume that Thwaites, in transcribing Lewis, mistook "scalds" for "scolds." They argue that "scalds" or "scalding" could be a reference to the color and temperature of scalded milk, an interpretation supported by an entry in a paraphrased version of Private Joseph Whitehouse's journal, discovered in 1966: "Our officers gave this River the name, Scalding Milk River."[17] To my surprise, the Moulton edition shows that Jackson and Cutright are wrong. Thwaites did indeed correctly decipher Lewis's handwriting and properly transcribed "scolds" and "scolding." The Indian terms do make sense when referring to the only stream of any magnitude above the mouth of the Yellowstone to discharge with enough force into the Missouri to churn, or "scold," it. But Moulton offers no commentary on nomenclature that has puzzled historians since the appearance of the *Original Journals of Lewis and Clark* ninety years ago.

In 1980, at the start of the project, Moulton wrote, "The most difficult and time-consuming work on the journals will be in the area of annotation. In hundreds of footnotes, the staff will clarify and expand upon the manuscript diaries. If we were to edit the journals only in terms of placing the original material into print we could complete the project in short order, even considering the extreme care we will give to this dimension. But a great deal of effort will be required to search out the writers' numerous obscure references to people, places, and events."[18]

The editorial staff relied not only upon published scholarship for its annotations but also upon direct consultation with experts in various fields around the country. The result is a fund of information gleaned from anthropologists, archaeologists, astronomers, botanists, geologists, geographers, ornithologists, cartographers, historians, linguists, and zoologists. Identifications of plants, animals, people, places, and events along the route are excellent, but notes occasionally reflect incomplete assimilation of such varied sources. For example, in the sections on the Lemhi Shoshone the staff relied on the noted linguist and anthropologist Sven Liljeblad for clarification of Shoshone words and phrases. Information about the Lemhi Shoshone as a group, however, is spotty despite the extensive account Lewis and Clark provided. In volume 4, when Lewis's first use of the word Shoshone ("Sosonees or snake Indians" [4:398]) appears, a note tells us that "[i]t was not the Shoshone name for themselves" (4:401n. 3) but does not say what that name was or what "snake" signified. Later, in volume 5, we learn that the Shoshone "call themselves *n i m i* (singular), 'person' or *n i m i n ii* (plural), 'the people,'" and the Lemhi Shoshone were a "division of the Northern Shoshones of the Rocky Mountains, known to the Great Plains tribes as 'Snakes'" (5:85n. 7), but the staff offers no cultural or linguistic identification of the various Northern Shoshone "divisions" (some of whom, including Bannocks, were also called "Snakes") or the related "divisions" of Eastern Shoshone or Western Shoshone, information that Sven Liljeblad or recent studies by Brigham Madsen, Wick Miller, Robert Murphy, and Yolanda Murphy could easily have provided. In a subsequent footnote, the "Tukudikas" *[sic]* are described as a "Shoshonean group . . . later referred to by whites as 'Sheepeaters' because they ate the bighorn sheep" (5:94n. 8), but it would be helpful to know that they are also called Agaideka (eaters of salmon) and they are a group of Northern Shoshone with an important relationship to the Lemhi Shoshone. Both the Tukudeka and Lemhi Shoshone had a common cultural origin and were virtually indistinguishable until they diverged after the arrival of the horse. Today, however, both groups are still compositely referred to in the Shoshone language as Agaideka. In the annotations the generic term "Shoshone" causes confusion because it is repeatedly applied to the Lemhi Shoshone, despite the term's correct reference to a large language group of culturally distinct peoples ranging from northern Idaho to southeastern California. The staff's use of the term "Shoshonean" obscures matters even more because this linguistic category properly includes peoples as different as the Paiute, Ute, Comanche, and Hopi. Tossing around terms like "Shoshonean" and "Tukudikas" might produce the illusion of precision, but the uninformed reader remains so. In contrast, the staff provides full, clear annotations about other Native American peoples like the Mandan and the seven divisions of Teton, "those Sioux who spoke the western or *Lak'ota* dialect" (3:109n. 4). The excellent note about the Hidatsa amounts to a concise interpretive essay (3:206–207n. 8).

Although the Moulton edition includes no previously unpublished writings or stylistic changes to transform or subvert our general impression of the explorers' journals, it does radically improve the Thwaites edition in its weakest dimension—maps. As one wrestled with the boxed set of maps in the Thwaites edition, it was difficult to make heads or tails out of the sometimes mislabeled, accordion-pleated reproductions of poor quality. In contrast, the first volume of the Moulton edition is a folio-size *Atlas of the Lewis and Clark Expedition* reproducing in facsimile on thick, creamy pages the maps Clark sketched on the expedition, those the captains consulted beforehand, and those executed after the trip, all clearly organized, labeled, and described. It is a beautiful set. Many were unavailable or unknown to Thwaites. Of the 129 maps in the atlas, 118 are at original size, and 42 have never been previously published. Many of Clark's lost maps have been reproduced from accurate copies of his originals prepared for the 1833 expedition of the naturalist Prince Maximilian of Wied Neuwied and the great Swiss artist Karl Bodmer. The only disappointment is the omission of the 1802 Aaron Arrowsmith Map of North America. Moulton explains in a note that it is not printed because the Nicholas King 1803 map, which is printed, largely duplicates it. The reason doesn't hold up when one considers the overlap of other maps as well as Moulton's admission that King made significant modifications from Arrowsmith's map. As James Logan Allen notes, the Arrowsmith map was "the single most important item of cartographic data" available to the explorers; more detailed than the King map in representing the upper Missouri basin, it served as a template for the explorers' cartographic corrections of the area.[19] Jefferson had ordered a copy in the summer of 1803, and it is virtually certain that Lewis and Clark carried the map with them on the transcontinental trek. When gathering information about the upper Missouri from the Mandan during the winter of 1803–04, Lewis refers to the errors "I see that Arrasmith in his late map of N. America has laid down" (4:266). Its absence from the atlas is unfortunate.

Nevertheless, thirty-four of the maps in the atlas show about 900 previously undetailed miles of the trip, and all reinforce the achievement of Clark as a geographer who sketched the course of the journey with impressive care. He records the longitude and latitude, though not always accurately, of all important geographic features as well as compass readings of each twist and turn in the streams and rivers he explored (Figure 2). As he sailed up the Missouri, Clark estimated distances by eyesight, recording, for instance, that the expedition had traveled between the mouth of the Missouri and the Platte River a distance of 600 miles. A surveying team several years later concluded from their instruments that the distance was actually 611 miles.

What does all of this material add up to in relation to those teachers and students of literature I referred to at the beginning of this survey? The maps suggest an answer. They are not just illustrative enhancements of the Moulton edition; they heighten our understanding of the explorers' writings, for they offer a detailed portfolio of the exploratory process itself, which is dramatized to a greater extent than in most expedition accounts in the journals' day-by-day record of route finding and decision making in the field. The 129 maps of the atlas also reflect a concern for measurement and demarcation informing much of the language of the journals. Almost any page offers the explorers' counts and measurements or estimates of size, weight, and time. On 21 July 1804 Clark observes the Platte River with typical detail:

> the Rapidity of the Current of this river which is greater than that of the Missourie, its width at the Mouth across the bars is about ¾ of a mile, higher up I am told by one of the bowmen that he was 2 winters on this river above and that it does not rise <four> 7 feet, but Spreds over 3 miles at Some places, Capt Lewis & my Self went up Some Distance & Crossed found it Shallow. This river does not rise over 6 or 7 feet.

> The Otteaus a Small nation reside on the South Side 10 Leagues up, the Panies on the Same Side 5 Leagues higher up—about 10 Leagus up this river on the S. Side a Small river Comes into the Platt Called Salt River. (2:401, 403)

After killing a rodent that the explorers eventually name the prairie dog, Clark notes: "The toe nails of his fore feet is one Inch & ¾ long, & feet large; the nails of his hind feet ¾ of an Inch long, the hind feet Small and toes Crooked, his legs are Short and when he Moves Just Suffcent to raise his

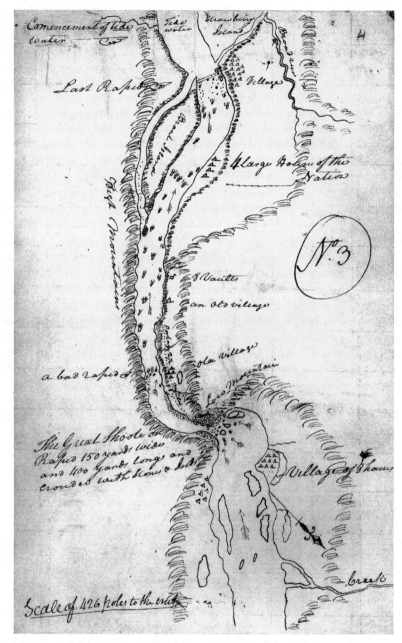

Figure 2. Great Rapids of the Columbia River, sketch-map by Clark.
(American Philosophical Society)

body above the Ground" (2:430). On 5 May 1805, Lewis similarly considers the corpse of a terrifying grizzly:

> it was a most tremendious looking anamal, and extreemly hard to kill notwithstanding he had five balls through his lungs and five others in various parts he swam more than half the distance across the river to a sandbar & it was at least twenty minutes before he died; he did not attempt to attact, but fled and made the most tremendous roaring from the moment he was shot. We had no means of weighing this monster; Capt Clark thought he would weigh 500 lbs. for my own part I think the estimate too small by 100 lbs.   he measured 8 Feet 7½ Inches from the nose to the extremety of the hind feet, 5 F. 10½ Inch arround the breast, 1 F. 11 I. arround the middle of the arm, & 3 F. 11 I arround the neck; his tallons which were five in number on each foot were 4⅜ Inches in length. (4:113)

The explorers are here engaged in their work as scientific collectors of objective data about the natural world. These details, when added to astronomical symbols and tabulations of longitude and latitude, produce those texts that the *Columbia Literary History of the United States* finds so cluttered with tedious detail. But the cumulative effect of this detail is monumental. Clark's hunters shoot 1,0001 deer. In one day Lewis with ten men catch 800 fish. Gifts for Indians include 2,800 fishhooks, 4,600 assorted needles, and 130 twisted rolls of tobacco. Among medicines are 3,500 pills to counter sweats, 1,100 doses of emetics to induce vomiting, and over 600 pills, appropriately named "Rush's Thunderbolts" after their inventor, to counteract constipation. On the Missouri a floating mass of white feathers 70 yards wide and 3 miles long lead to an island covered with thousands of pelicans. The petrified backbone of an ancient fish is 45 feet long. The carcass of a beached whale measures 110 feet. July hail 7 inches in circumference hits the ground and bounces 12 feet into the air. Under the unbearably difficult circumstances of their composition, the writing of such detailed accounts was the most heroic of acts. Bristling with factual matter characteristic of scientific enterprises in the New World, the texts also reflect early American literary fascination with registering the density of the physical world and ways of encountering it. The extensive language of measurement and demarcation elevates the journals into an epic of the quotidian.

In contrast to the language of contemporary science, the journals also offer the explorers' subjective responses in language borrowed from the prevailing lexicon of art, including literature, painting, sculpture, music, and architecture, to produce a vacillating style. The language of eighteenth-century science with its penchant for objective observation and quantification vies with that of art in its figurative modes of classifying the natural world. Both forms of expression, however, are ordered by the prevailing aesthetic expectations of the day. "Nature does nothing in vain" was the scientific position of the seventeenth-century physician William Harvey, and the eighteenth-century naturalist Thomas Jefferson concurs in *Notes on the State of Virginia*, "Such is the oeconomy of nature, that no instance can be produced of her having permitted any one race of her animals to become extinct; of her having formed any link in her great work so weak as to be broken." The stable relationships and processes of nature's economy, the concept that the great naturalist Baron Karl von Linné (or Carolus Linnaeus, as the master Latinist dubbed himself) coined in *Oeconomia naturae* (1749), were apparent to both eighteenth-century naturalists and poets. Everything is in balance in the vast chain of being, according to general laws, to produce "the amazing whole," as Alexander Pope writes, "Where, one step broken, the great scale's destroyed." The key to such beliefs comes with Popian succinctness: "ORDER is Heaven's first law," and "The general ORDER, since the whole began, / Is kept in nature, and is kept in Man."[20]

In the 1780s such aesthetic assumptions intertwined with political ideology to shape Jefferson's argument with the French naturalist, the comte Georges-Louis Leclerc de Buffon, about the character of the natural world in the Americas. Jefferson offered measurements of everything, from the height of American mules to the size of strawberries from his own garden, to counter Buffon's theory that flora and fauna had degenerated in the inferior environment of the New World so that "animals of America are tractable and timid, very few ferocious and none formidable. . . . All animals are smaller in North America than Europe. Everything shrinks under a 'niggardly sky and unprolific land.'" About America's wild animals, Jefferson exclaimed, "It does not appear that Messrs. de Buffon and D'Aubenton have measured, weighed, or seen those of America." In the aftermath of this debate, Lewis and Clark's descriptions of large bison and fierce grizzlies became both scientific and patriotic weapons. Jefferson's view that the bones of what he called the Megalonyx in Virginia provided triumphant evidence against the purported degeneracy of American animals, along with his belief that the economy of nature disallows the annihilation of any species, led him to order Lewis and Clark to look out for signs of animals deemed rare or extinct, like the mammoth. According to the "traditionary testimony of the Indians," as Jefferson reports in *Notes on the State of Virginia*, "this animal still exists in the northern and western parts of America."[21]

As for the native peoples of the New World, Jefferson is happy "for the honor of human nature" to dismiss Buffon's claim that Indians are feeble, insensitive, timid, cowardly, and listless—lower than animals—lacking passion, intelligence, honor, body hair, and developed sexual organs. Lewis and Clark's detailed accounts of native habits and physical characteristics support Jefferson's defense, including his riposte that the "Indian is neither more defective in ardor nor more impotent with his female than the white man."[22] The explorers even comment on the bare breasts of women and other "parts" of both men and women "usually covered from formiliar view." When a Chinookan woman wearing a short cedar-bark skirt "stoops or places herself in many other attitudes, this battery of Venus is not altogether impervious to the inquisitive and penetrating eye of the amorite" (6:435). Many tall, well-proportioned Indians, like the Flatheads, who "are a very light coloured people of large stature and comely form" (5:197) and the Nez Perces—"Stout likely men, handsom women, and verry dressey in their way" (5:258)—counter French claims of physical degeneracy. As evidence against moral degeneracy, numerous accounts of kindness and honor include the story of a man who walked all day to catch up with the expedition to return a hatchet left behind in camp.

No ideologues of Noble Savagery, Lewis and Clark also report what they perceive as brutality, thievery, and squalor. Their mixed accounts of unsavory and noble behavior create a complex ethnographic record of culturally diverse native peoples in their historical situation. "I think the most disgusting sight I have ever beheld," Lewis notes about some northwestern coastal women, "is these dirty naked wenches" (6:436), and Clark finds a coastal Cathlamet village "the dirtiest and Stinkingest place I ever Saw" (7:10). The cultural biases of certain reports are clear, as when Lewis watches some starving Lemhi Shoshone eating raw venison innards—kidney, spleen, liver—"blood running from the corners of their mouths"; one man "with about nine feet of small guts one end of which he was chewing on while with his hands he was squezzing the contents out at the other. I really did not untill now think that human nature ever presented itself in a shape so nearly allyed to the brute creation. I viewed these poor starved divils with pity and compassion" (5:103). Just three months earlier Lewis had delightedly praised his own cook's preparation of *boudin blanc*—composed of buffalo innards, intestine, and a "moderate portion" of what normally "*is not good to eat*"—as "one of the greatest delacies of the forrest" (4:131). Those Indians the explorers find least aesthetically pleasing and most corrupt are tribes on the northwestern coast who have had extensive commerce with whites. Deteriorating and demoralizing conditions even extend to the speech of coastal Indians who "inform us that they speak the same language with ourselves, and gave us proofs of their veracity by repeating many words of English, as musquit, powder, shot, nife, damned rascal, sun of bitch &c." (6:187).

In pursuing Jefferson's directions to gather linguistic information, Lewis and Clark engage in the search for the possible origin of Native Americans and their interconnections within the human family. The explorers collect extensive vocabulary lists, make comparative observations, and note inflectional distinctions in Indian speech. The Flatheads, they notice, appear to have a brogue as they speak a "gugling kind of languaje Spoken much thro the Throught" (5:188). Reluctant to harden their data into a premature theory, the captains do not write down what Joseph Whitehouse reports in his journal: "we take these Savages to be the Welch Indians if their be any Such from the Language. So Capt. Lewis took down the names of everry thing in their Language, in order that it may be found out whether they are or whether they Sprang or origenated first from the welch or not."[23] The legend that certain light-skinned Indians were offshoots of a Welsh prince named Madoc and his companions who had traveled to America in the remote past was a popular theory of origin based on speculation that Native Americans were descendants of Old World peoples like the Phoenicians, Egyptians, Chinese, Greeks, or even one of the Lost Tribes of Israel. Jefferson had lamented the destruction of so many tribes before their languages had been recorded, for he firmly believed that comparative linguistics would eventually "construct the best evidence of the derivation of this part of the human race."[24]

Apparent in Jefferson's views of native peoples and the natural world are the aesthetic underpinnings of value and meaning provided by the Linnaean concept of *oeconomia naturae*—the governing plan that sustains the processes of nature and the existence of individual species so that all natural things are interconnected, chained together, in a common, ordered function. The antecedents of such an aesthetic view extend at least as far back as Plato, but Linnaeus approached the question of nature's balance, or nature's economy, as a scientific problem, albeit one with a mythological basis as old as Plato's *Protagoras* and a theological basis in its manifestations of the creator's benevolent disposition. What Linnaeus found in nature was an economy that worked for the good of the whole and the preservation of individual species. What Lewis and Clark found in the wilderness did not consistently support such an amiable view. A shadow world of disorder, underlying every aesthetic scheme, thus provides dynamic tension to the language of the journals.

Still, an aesthetics of order, moderation, regularity, and stability shaped Jefferson's and the explorers' preconceptions of western rivers and mountains. Long navigable rivers flowing eastward suggested their counterparts in the West. One supposedly could anticipate the western course of the Missouri from the eastern course of the Ohio. The same apparent symmetry affected the order of mountains. "Our mountains," Jefferson writes, "are not solitary and scattered confusedly over the face of the country; but that they commence at about 150 miles from the sea-coast, are disposed in ridges one behind another, running nearly parallel with the sea-coast." Jefferson adds that "as the tract of country between the sea-coast and the Mississippi becomes narrower, the mountains converge into a single ridge."[25] A country seemingly ruled by such balance and economy had given rise to the myth of the Northwest Passage, a fantasy bolstered by the dreams of earlier explorers and substantiated by the illusory documentation of maps, including those Lewis and Clark consulted in preparation for their journey. A single "pyramidal height of land" (5:1), as the Arrowsmith map showed, would offer an easy portage between the eastward-flowing Missouri River and the westward-flowing Columbia River.

Lewis and Clark's subjective responses to the western wilderness also drew from artistic tropes ruled by Enlightenment assumptions of harmony and order. Lewis finds a pleasing neoclassic balance between wildness and sweetness in the songs of birds, described as those "feathered tribes who salute the ear of the passing traveler with their wild and simple, yet s[w]eet and cheerfull melody" (4:266); and he likens a stretch of the Great Plains to a "beatifull bowlinggreen in fine order" (3:80). Expectations of encountering fertile, well-watered lands across the country trigger frequent, hopeful notations on areas suitable for agrarian settlement. Adjacent to "lofty and open forrests," Lewis finds "one of the most beatifully picteresque countries that I ever beheld . . . it's borders garnished with one continued garden of roses" (4:266). Even late in the journey when the country does not quite measure up to its promise, Clark can speculate that it would be fine when cultivated. The explorers do seem at times like new men in a new Eden, walking peacefully among hundreds of animals that will not scare: "the whol face of the country was covered with herds of Buffaloe, Elk & Antelopes; deer are also abundant, but keep themselves more concealed in the woodland. the buffaloe Elk and Antelope are so gentle that we pass near them while feeding, without apearing to excite any alarm among them, and when we attract their attention, they frequently approach us more nearly to discover what we are" (4:67).

Horror shatters this Edenic world in the form of enraged grizzlies, rampaging buffalo, violent storms, flash floods, smashed boats, horses rolling down hillsides, feet torn and bleeding from cactus needles, incessant rain, fleas, and mosquitoes. The thick, multiridged labyrinth of lines "scattered confusedly"[26] on Lewis and Clark's Map of the West denotes the actual Rocky Mountains the explorers enter, where, as Lewis writes, "every object here wears a dark and gloomy aspect. the tow[er]ing and projecting rocks in many places seem ready to tumble on us" (4:402). Rather than the easy two-day portage the explorers anticipated, the trek spanned some 45 days of hardship from the headwaters of the Missouri to those of the Columbia. A reverential distance from wilderness might allow one to see reflected there a benevolent order and a peaceable millennium, but in the space of one day, Lewis is chased into a river by a bear, attacked by a "tyger cat," and charged by three buffalo bulls. "It now seemed to me," he writes, "that all the beasts of the neighbourhood had made a league to distroy me" (4:294). The wilderness becomes animate in a way that is as primal as it is gothic. Measurable topography and objective events melt into romantic "seens of visionary inchantment" (4:226) and "curious adventures" that "might be a dream" (4:294). In the woods we return to reason and faith, Emerson was to say, but not in the West of Lewis and Clark where "evil gennii" (4:225) lurk. The journals often become an epic story of confrontations with dark monsters and inexplicable powers. But the real snake in the garden hideously follows the explorers themselves. In the wanton smashing of a wolf's skull with a spontoon, the slaughtering of animals, and the proprietary attitudes toward the land, the explorers reveal sad glimpses of the dark side of American imperialism. Their first council with Native American likewise becomes both a threat and an omen. Characterized as the president's "red children," the Otos and Missouris are warned not to displease "your great father, the great chief of the Seventeen great nations of America, who could consume you as the fire consumes the grass of the plains."[27] As a military expedition, the Corps of Discovery made way for others, seemingly bent on transforming what Clark calls "a land of Plenty" (3:66) into a land of waste.

When the conventions of the age fail to encompass the western wilderness, Lewis opts for the conventional trope of noting such failures. While trying to describe the Great Falls of the Missouri, Lewis "truly regretted" that he had not brought along a camera obscura, sometimes called a Claude glass, the popular device carried by tourists that projected an image though a lens onto the back wall of the box. The reflected photographic image could then be traced onto a sheet of paper, rendering the scene into the ordered perspective of picturesque art. But as commentators like Robert Edson Lee and Robert Lawson-Peebles have noted, the Great Falls of the Missouri would only elude the tranquil principles of Claude Lorrain's aesthetics. To apprehend these extravagant waterfalls, Lewis also "wished for the pencil of Salvator Rosa . . . or the pen of Thompson," but the aesthetic framework informing the wild, desolate scenes of the seventeenth-century Italian painter and the eighteenth-century Scottish poet would be "fruitless and vain" for Lewis to achieve (4:285). Only the concept of the Burkean sublime, which, as Ernst Cassirer notes, had shattered the "conceptual framework of previous aesthetic systems," could suggest the grandeur that "fills [Lewis] with such pleasure and astonishment" (4:285).[28] Enlightenment order collapses into sublime asymmetry, and the aesthetic of measurement shifts to the aesthetic of the measureless to accommodate natural disorders like floods and earthquakes. Still, Lewis feels he can offer only an "imperfect description" of these "truly magnificent and sublimely grand" torrents of falling water (4:285). Unlike Jefferson, who confidently described the Natural Bridge on his own Virginia property as the "most sublime of Nature's works,"[29] Lewis wrestles for two days to covey a "faint idea" (4:285) of the beauty and sublimity that distinguish the twin falls, only to come up with his own uneasy, qualified categorization of them: "nor could I for some time determine on which of those two great cataracts to bestoe the palm, on this or that which I had discovered yesterday; at length I determined between these two great rivals for glory that this was *pleasingly beautifull*, while the other was *sublimely grand"* (4:290).

It is now a commonplace of Lewis and Clark criticism to characterize the stylistic extremes of the two explorers as reflections of their sensibilities. Laconic, measured, and scientifically objective accounts of the environment are identified with Clark. Effusive, romantic, and subjective literary responses are identified with Lewis. The styles supposedly mirror the personalities of the two men as polar opposites: Lewis as a brooding introvert given to melancholy speculation, Clark an even-tempered, sociable extrovert inclined toward good-natured self-effacement. Charles Willson Peale's famous portraits, now hanging in the Independence National Historical Park in Philadelphia, seem to emphasize these contrasting images. Clark, a husky man with a high forehead and shock of red hair, looks boldly from the canvas directly at the viewer, while Meriwether Lewis, tall and slender with sensitive bow lips and an aquiline nose, gazes dreamily toward the side of the canvas. The contrasting careers of the two men after their renowned expedition have also reinforced the image of Clark as a gregarious public official and Lewis as a moody loner. Clark pursued a long and distinguished career as superintendent of Indian affairs at St. Louis, while Lewis experienced a brief and troubled governorship of the Louisiana Territory—ridden with alcoholism and abruptly terminated by a murky death.

The stylistic differences of the two men cannot be ignored, nor can their differences of temperament—Lewis is more subjective, circumlocutory, and polished, Clark more terse, objective, and direct—but the journals do not bear out the rigid categorizations of either style or personality imposed from the hindsight of their subsequent careers. Lewis employs the descriptive discourse of science as scrupulously as Clark, even more so in many cases, particularly in regard to flora and fauna, where his command of technical terminology is greater. Lewis's rhetorical nod to the "truly magnificent and sublimely grand" (4:285) Great Falls of the Missouri occupies only a brief moment in pages of careful observation and measurement. At times Clark's quantitative topographic recordings also might break into brief rhetorical flourishes about "butifull fertile picteresque Country" (7:223), or a place he called "bad humered Island as we were in a bad humer" (3:114). The distinction between verbose Lewis and laconic Clark also needs qualification, for Clark contributed to the journals many more of the 862,500 total words than did Lewis. Unless some journals were lost, Lewis made entries for only 441 of the 863 days, while Clark provided entries for all but 10 days, which he later summarized.

Moments even occur where the two men seemingly reverse personalities, and Clark becomes the melancholy loner depressed by bad weather and bugs, while Lewis retains his joie de vivre amid misfortune and longs for the

companionship of friends and civil society. "O! how horriable is the day,"
Clark writes in November 1805, during winter encampment on the Pacific
Coast (6:79). "!O how Tremedious is the day. This dredfull wind and
rain. . . . O! how disagreeable is our Situation dureing this dreadfull
weather" (6:92); "Small bugs, worms, Spiders, flyes & insects of different
kinds are to be . . . Seen in abundance" (6:94); "Since we arrived in Sight
of the Great Western; (for I cannot Say Pacific) Ocian as I have not Seen one
pacific day Since my arrival in its vicinity . . . tempestous and horiable"
(6:104); "The winds violent Trees falling in every direction, whorl winds,
with gusts of rain Hail & Thunder, this kind of weather lasted all day, Certainly one of the worst days that ever was!" (6:126); "The fleas are So trou-
blesom that I have Slept but little for 2 nights past and we have regularly to
kill them out of our blankets every day for Several past" (6:138). On Christmas Day 1805 Clark complains, "we would have Spent this day the nativity
of Christ in feasting, had we any thing either to raise our Sperits or even
gratify our appetites, our Diner concisted of pore Elk, So much Spoiled that
we eate it thro' mear necessity, Some Spoiled pounded fish and a fiew roots"
(6:138). On New Year's Day 1806, as the weather improves, Clark flatly
notes, "This morning proved cloudy with moderate rain, after a pleasent
worm night during which there fell but little rain" (6:153). In contrast,
Lewis is able to keep his spirits elevated as he faces the new year: "our repast
of this day tho' better than that of Christmass, consisted principally in the
anticipation of the 1st day of January 1807, when in the bosom of our
friends we hope to participate in the mirth and hilarity of the day, and when
with the zest given by the recollection of the present, we shall completely,
both mentally and corporally, enjoy the repast which the hand of civilization
has prepared for us" (6:151–152).

The expeditionary record shows that Lewis and Clark form an alliance
that transcends their differences of personality and style. They seem to command, effortlessly and without conflict, as one; over the course of the journey, both demonstrate cunning, intelligence, and dignity in their leadership of others. In chronicling their trials and achievements, the heroes of
this epic adventure sing of themselves, becoming—in a modern literary
twist—their own bards. Where modesty commends one to silence about his
own achievement, history compels the other to document the worthiness of
the event, producing an absence of boastfulness that Theodore Roosevelt
found so impressive. The effectiveness of this strange alliance, a sharing of
command that defies military hierarchy, is unique to military history. While
Lewis enjoys eating dog meat and Clark hates it, Lewis craves salt and Clark
dismisses it as a luxury, and Lewis likes eating black currants and Clark favors yellow ones, the two leaders otherwise form a perfectly harmonious relationship. A moving aspect of the journals is how much they care for each
other. They remain friends to the end.

It is the composite character of these leaders—their pervasive outpour-ing of intellectual and moral energy—that sustains the expedition and guarantees its success. This composite character manifests itself in the thou-sands of right decisions the leaders jointly make to avert disaster. Only when Lewis and Clark are apart on the return journey does tragedy strike, when two Blackfeet Indians are killed. Clark's declamations against the harsh win-ter weather also peak when the men are separated. While they are still apart, Lewis is almost killed when accidentally shot by one of his own hunters. It is as if the division of the classical hero into two men allows Lewis and Clark to embody heroic impulses in believable ways. They become heroes cut down to credible size, eighteenth-century men who merge into a compos-ite character acceptable to the skepticism of the modern age. Of all the heroic moments recorded in the journals, however, none surpasses the writ-ing of the journals themselves. In a touching moment, Lewis notes "the ink feizes in my pen" (5:133), and yet he continues to write. When the explor-ers copy from each other's field notes or journals, original authorship some-times becomes blurred or lost. The "I" of some entries becomes that com-posite hero and author whom Clark seemed to honor, after his cocaptain's death, when he named his son Meriwether Lewis Clark. The journals ap-propriately end with William Clark's last brief entry on 25 September 1806: "a fine morning we commenced wrighting &c" (8:372).

The vacillating style of this composite authorship is less the product of differing sensibilities than of the era's competing languages of art and sci-ence. That two men happened to write the journals conveniently symbolizes the split in discourse that had characterized American nature writing since the eighteenth century. In the 1787 edition of his *Notes on the State of Vir-ginia,* Jefferson typically jumps from the language of science to that of art when his quantitative description of Virginia's topographic features breaks into paeans to the sublimity of the Natural Bridge or the Potomac River. Even more extreme are the wild swings in style in William Bartram's 1791 *Travels.* Bartram's sudden flip-flops between neoclassic poetic tropes and scientific Latinate descriptions now cause student wonderment that such a schizophrenic text was actually written by one person. A similar tension continued into the nineteenth century, evident in the split between Thoreau's transcendental flights and those journalistic observations once dismissed as dry, meaningless factual details about grasses, snowfalls, tree rings, lichens, and seeds. After the Civil War, the prose of trained geologists like John Wesley Powell, Clarence King, and Clarence Dutton vacillates between technical description and metaphors drawn from mythology and architecture to shape a visionary, aesthetic response to an apparently inanimate landscape. Static buttes, mesas, and canyon lands become ani-mate dramas of shifting forms under the violently changing pressures of wind, water, fire, and light. In *My First Summer in the Sierra* (1911), John

Muir's prose undergoes extravagant stylistic shifts not seen since Bartram's *Travels* 120 years earlier. Technical descriptions of lateral moraines, *Quercus Douglasii*, residual glaciers, albicaulus pines, and bituminous beds erupt into ecstatic renderings of the "spiritual affinities" binding the personalities of trees, ants, people, and "noble rock . . . full of thought, clothed with living light." The birds of John Burroughs, reduced at one moment to conventional poetic epithets of "widowed mothers" or "happy bridegrooms," are rendered vivid in subsequent sentences of astonishing transparency yet scientific accuracy.[30]

Part of the reason for the vacillating style of American nature writing lies in the increasing professionalization of scientific pursuits and scientific language in the eighteenth century. Earlier writers of American natural history drew from a common language, free of specialized terminology, to record both natural phenomena and personal experience, so that Thoreau could refer to the "strong and hearty but reckless hit-or-miss style" in the early works of John Josselyn and William Wood, "as if they spoke with a relish, smacking their lips like a coach-whip, caring more to speak heartily than scientifically true."[31] By William Bartram's time, "natural philosophy," a term once loosely encompassing all scientific pursuits, had become sharply differentiated from "natural history," which in turn was splintering into the specifically termed studies of botany, zoology, geology, and mineralogy. Specialization of scientific tasks was making way for the nineteenth-century invention of the word *scientist*, and the specialized language of naturalists like Bartram pointed toward James Fenimore Cooper's caricature of Dr. Battius in *The Prairie* (1827), floundering through the wilderness, a danger to himself and others, oblivious to everything except new species, while gibbering in the Latin derivatives of the Linnaean system.

Why Lewis and Clark avoided the Linnaean system of taxonomy and nomenclature has puzzled many commentators. Recent studies have shown Lewis to be better trained and more scientifically competent than is often assumed. His careful descriptions of plants include no fewer than two hundred technical botanical terms. He had studied Latin as a young man and had worked for two years with Jefferson who, as Cutright observes, "took to binomials like a poet to iambic pentameter." At Fort Clatsop in 1806 Lewis exhibited familiarity with Linnaean principles in the organization of his ethnobotanical and ethnozoological data. Because they provided the first detailed, formal descriptions of new flora and fauna, the explorers are now credited with the discovery of 178 plants and 122 birds, animals, fish, and reptiles, including the cutthroat trout, mountain quail, pack rat, western hog-nose snake, western meadowlark, kit fox, Lewis's woodpecker, and Clark's nutcracker (see Figure 3). But in their journals Lewis and Clark employ Latinate classifications only three times and an actual binomial only

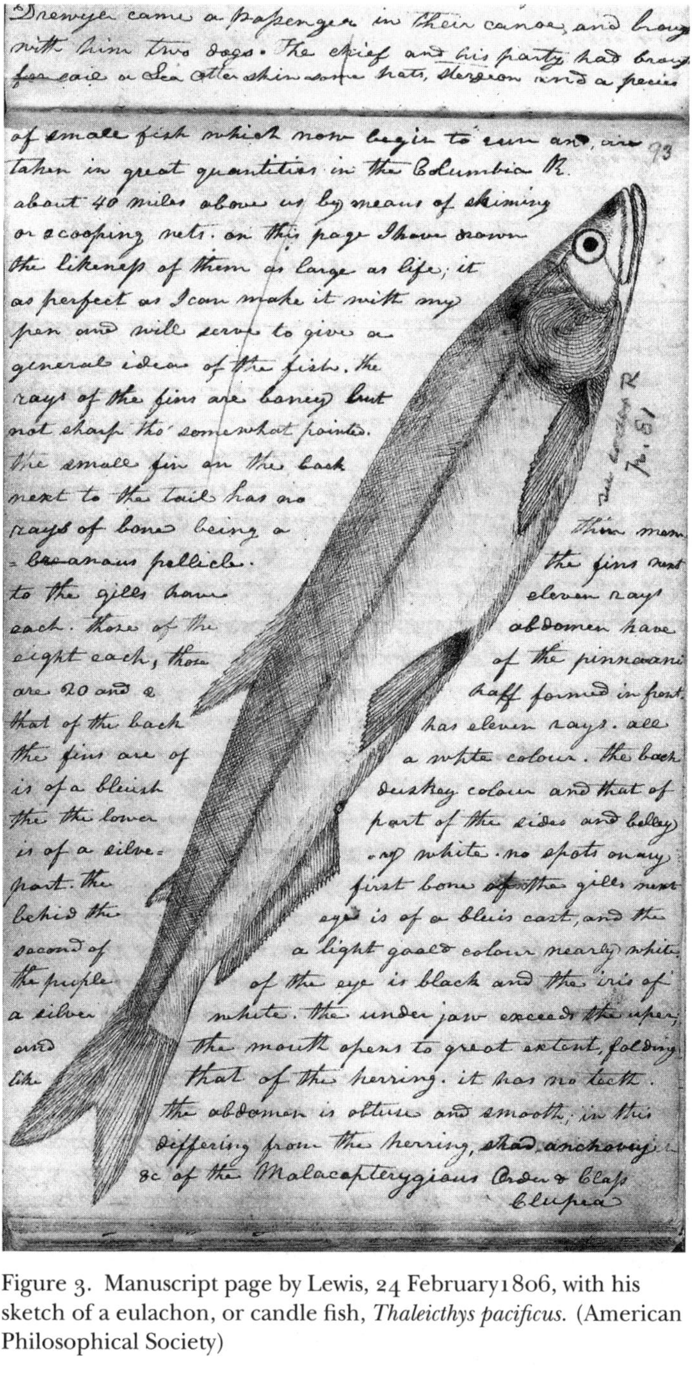

Figure 3. Manuscript page by Lewis, 24 February 1806, with his sketch of a eulachon, or candle fish, *Thaleicthys pacificus*. (American Philosophical Society)

once. As a result, their prose does not reach the extreme vacillations of diction marking other works of natural history such as Bartram's.[32]

The explorers' scrupulous adherence to Jefferson's instructions during the trip west suggests that their use of the vernacular met with the president's charge and approval. "Your observations are to be taken," Jefferson wrote, "with great pains & accuracy, to be entered distinctly, & intelligibly for others as well as yourself." Although Jefferson himself used scientific names as often as the vernacular in his own writings, and although he believed in the aesthetic and theoretical order of nature's economy, he maintained the first task of good science to be the accurate collection and precise description of data. "A patient pursuit of facts, and cautious combination and comparison of them is the drudgery to which man is subjected by his Maker, if he wishes to attain sure knowledge." A faulty scientific investigator like Buffon too precipitously selects "facts, and adopts all the falsehoods which favor his theory, and very gravely retails such absurdities as zeal for a theory alone could swallow." As a Lockean empiricist, Jefferson notes that "he who attempts to reduce [the natural world] into departments, is left to do it by the lines of his own fancy."[33] Here, Jefferson joins hands with his old intellectual avatar, Buffon, who had attacked the Linnaean system from its inception, arguing that its categories of classes, orders, genera, and species imposed an enormous abstraction on the natural world.

Jefferson's views dramatize what Linnaeus himself had come to realize: the *systema naturae* is actually a *systema Linnaei*. The system is artificial, Linnaeus grudgingly acknowledged, although he maintained that it was a step toward the discovery of the natural system he felt sure existed. In searching for the structure of nature and—his favorite slogan—the "object itself," he sought to rid science of figurative language and allusion. But while rejecting the falsity of rhetoric, in Hobbesian and Lockean terms, as powerful instruments of error and deceit, Linnaeus found himself replacing one rhetorical trope for another. His "kingdoms" of plants and animals in the "empire" of nature, composed of "phalanxes," regiments," and "recruits" underscore the imperialist thrust of his scientific enterprise to dominate both the study of nature and nature itself. In his last edition of *Systema naturae*, however, Linnaeus no longer insisted on the immutability of species, the concept that had sustained the aesthetic order and metaphor of nature's economy. The Linnaean system, prior to the moment of its widest acceptance, was already crumbling.

By the time Lewis and Clark trekked into the West, rejection of Linnaeus's system and method was widespread. The breakdown was anticipated in Bartram's *Travels*, where an Ovidian world of metamorphosis shattered the Linnaean economy of nature. Likewise, in *Elements of Botany* (1803), appropriately illustrated with Bartram's pre-Darwinian drawings, Benjamin

Barton Smith provided a running criticism of Linnaeus's ideas. Newly proposed systems had begun to dominate the sciences. Antoine Laurent de
Jussieu's new botanical system was superseding that of Linnaeus. In zoology,
Baron Georges Cuvier completely revised Linnaeus's classifications of animals, and Jean-Baptiste de Monet de Lamarck subverted the economy of
nature with a theory of organic evolution. In the age of Romanticism, old
metaphoric notions of teleology and animism that Linnaeus had tried so
hard to kick out the door of science would reenter through the window
newly guised in the acceptable concept of "life." But to Jefferson, such scientific revolutions merely added more arbitrary systems to the old. He criticized Lavoisier's standardized nomenclature in chemistry for prematurely
closing the door to discovery and retarding the "progress of science by a jargon." One new discovery, he said, could send the whole system crumbling.
"We can no longer say there is nothing new under the sun," Jefferson wrote.
"The great extent of our republic is new. Its sparse habitation is new."[34]

Lewis and Clark's disregard of Latinate terminology coincides with a
need to forge language appropriately descriptive of a new country and its
inhabitants. While the explorers never completely abandon the literary and
scientific conventions of their age, a qualitative change does occur over the
course of the journals as those conventions diminish. Most of Clark's topographic descriptions in quantitative scientific language appear early in the
journals. Conventional rhetoric and cultural assumptions break down as
the country, animals, and native peoples of the West effect new forms of
perception. Less often as they move west do the explorers encounter landscapes that "exhibit a most romantic appearance" (4:225). On the return
home, the Rocky Mountains become to Lewis "that icy barier which seper-
ates me from my friends and Country, from all which makes life esteemable"
(7:267). Conceptual frameworks and aesthetic orderings, like instruments
of measurement hauled from the East, crack, as did the expedition's three
thermometers. Two streams the explorers tried to name in honor of the Enlightenment virtues of Wisdom and Philanthropy are now called Big Hole
and Stinking Water. At the Great Falls of the Missouri, where Lewis finds his
aesthetic descriptions shaky, he watches helplessly as his collapsible iron
boat, designed and built in the East, sinks into a western river. In the Rockies, the explorers abandon their canoes and depend on Indian horses to
cross the Bitterroot Range to where they can chop and carve native cotton-
woods into dugouts for the final run down the Snake and Columbia Rivers
to the sea. Attempts to render their experience, the country, and its wildlife
through conventional expression give way to new terms. Language itself has
to be altered in the process; words coined and twisted to fit the occasion
produce in the journals, according to the lexicon compiled by Elijah
Criswell, the first usage of 1,004 new words or extended meanings in the
American language, some adapted from Native American languages and

frontier French, others jammed into new linguistic hybrids. Instead of being honored for using scientific terms like *Odocoileus hemionus,* Lewis and Clark are remembered for adding the names "mule deer," "prairie dog," and "whistling swan" to the American language.

The best linguistic study of the journals, Elijah H. Criswell's *Lewis and Clark: Linguistic Pioneers,* appeared as a quarterly issue of University of Missouri Studies in 1940. Although photocopies are currently available from the Lewis and Clark Trail Heritage Foundation, this fine 313-page monograph has never been republished. This is a shame, for Criswell's investigations of Lewis and Clark's Americanisms—ripe for correction and expansion—offer fruitful entry into the explorers' achievement as writers. The Nebraska edition, for example, might have noted how Lewis and Clark, as masters of the vernacular, use American words that in some cases had recently entered the language, like *cut-off, tote, overalls, barefoot, cloud up, overnight, shut of, lick* (as a verb), *jerk* (in reference to cured meat) and *balance* (in the sense of "remainder" or "leftover"). Criswell presents 301 examples of new words or new meanings of old words that antedate their earliest usage cited in the *Oxford English Dictionary.* The *OED* does note that some Americanisms like *noon it* (as in "we nooned it just above the entrance of a large river" [4:124]) mark their first recorded appearance in the journals, but it leaves out others like the specific definition of *cheek,* as Clark uses the word, when he observes after Lewis is shot that the bullet "cut the cheek of the right buttock for 3 inches in length" (8:290).

The new Nebraska edition of the journals does not gloss words or extended meanings that Lewis and Clark contributed to the language, nor does it note when they use recently coined Americanisms, but it does draw on Criswell's lexicon to define some nonce words, like *happerst* as "some form of knapsack, perhaps from 'hoppas,' an Indian knapsack" (4:253n. 10). Other apparent nonce words or individualisms like *dismorallity* remain unglossed. We learn from Criswell that *dismorallity* is Lewis's humorous combination of *disease* and *morality* to describe flatulence as "a dismorallity of order in the abdomen" from smoking intoxicating Indian tobacco (6:179). As these examples show, not all neologisms in the journals have entered the language. Neither did the maxim, "accidents will happen in the best families," nor the adage, "to push a tolerable good pole" (4:423), but such coinages do invest the journals with lively, inventive prose responsive to fresh experience. Given the excellent annotations of the Moulton edition in other fields, one can only wish that it might have more fully built on these preliminary linguistic investigations and filled their gaps. For example, the term *hair pipe* baffled Criswell. "I do not know," he writes, "the identity of this article apparently taken along for Indian trade."[35] Moulton offers no help. The term *hair pipe* receives no gloss. But as one can readily see in Karl Bodmer's and George Catlin's paintings of Great Plains Indians, hair pipes are tubular lips of conch shells, about the size of normal pipe stems, drilled through the center from end to end so that they can be strung in the hair. They were as popular among Plains Indians as the famous blue beads that the explorers also brought with them.

Besides freshly minted words that would eventually make their way into dictionaries, the explorers' diction and syntax reveal the survival of obsolete words and the frequent use of archaisms in American speech. Many words, though departing from today's standard English, extend back to older forms, even to Middle English. When Lewis refers to a woman's breast as a "bubby," his use of this obsolete word lacks the vulgar connotations of later slang and employs its former acceptable usage in prose and poetry by writers like John Dryden. When Clark writes "for to" (as in "I prepare Some presents for to give the Indians of the *Mahars* nation" [2:474]) and Lewis writes "same of" for "same as," the result is not bad grammar but use of once standard forms that have survived in American dialect into the twentieth century.

Irregularities of grammar and spelling in the journals have given commentators much to chuckle over. A favorite observation is that the explorers spell the word *Sioux* at least twenty-seven different ways. In an age when orthographic variants were common, even Jefferson consistently began sentences without capital letters and spelled words inconsistently. But the absence of standardized spelling before the publication of Noah Webster's dictionary in 1828 cannot account for the extremes of the journals. Who but Clark, one scholar asks, could create such a "classic howler" as "feeMail" for *female*?[36] Yet in spelling *accent* "axcent" and *sagacity* "segassity," the explorers are clearly striving to spell words phonetically. Rather than howlers and malapropisms the explorers often accurately present the vernacular as it was heard at the time in the speech of Virginia and Kentucky backwoodsmen. Sharp ears, rather than ignorance or subliteracy, account for much of the inventive orthography in the journals.

While Criswell's study is primarily one of vocabulary, not of grammar or orthography, his work offers a valuable starting point for investigation of the journals as a compendium of colloquial pronunciation. Some spellings produce dialect reminiscent of Mark Twain's best efforts to put colloquial speech on the page, as when we read "fur" for *far*, "git" for *get*, "jest" for *just*, "tegious" for *tedious*, "furin" for *foreign*, "pint" for *point*, and—sounding much like Natty Bumppo—"sarvis-berry" for *serviceberry*. In certain words, consonants intrude or disappear, as can still be heard in some regional dialects today, as in "idear" for *idea*, "onced" for *once*, "musquetor" for *mosquito*. The same is true for the formation of doubly inflected participles like "drownded."

Variations in spelling, along with departures from current standard usage in the forms of nouns and the tenses of verbs, sometimes reflect not only regional pronunciation but also the survival of once acceptable forms, as in "catched" for *caught*. In fact, the word *fitten*, whose usage in England is last noted in the *OED* in a quotation for 1642, continued to survive in America to become a favorite colloquialism of Twain. To study the journals in this way, as reflecting speech in the time of Lewis and Clark, opens a resource for understanding the development of American English. Perhaps an analogy with the interpretation of Mayan transcriptions is not inappropriate. For years, Mayan glyphs had eluded decipherment until scholars overcame the mistake earlier decoders had made in thinking that glyphic writing did not reflect spoken language. Reading the journals as largely oral transcriptions reveals Lewis and Clark's mastery of the vernacular in their achievement as effective, vigorous writers.

We might argue that the vernacular adds a competing strain to the literary and scientific languages of the journals. In a way it does, producing a linguistically tense, multistyled text common to epics, like Dante's, that employ the vernacular. In such tensions, symbolically reinforced through dual authorship, the journals characterize the vacillation in much American nature writing between, on the one hand, scientific precision and poetic extravagance, or on the other, scientific reductiveness and poetic vision. The vernacular occasionally offers a way out of this split by fusing literary and scientific concerns in untechnical language. When Lewis describes how antelopes are like birds on the plains, figurative language anticipates the metamorphosis of post-Darwinian science. Anthropocentrism diminishes. One aspect of nature is defined in terms of another. When Clark documents the rise and fall of a river in the animistic speech of a backwoodsman, his writing fuses the relicts of an older language with that of future geologists like Powell or King whose visions of landscapes are more alive than conventional science would allow. The literary result of such composition, unlike a scientific experiment, is as unrepeatable as a Twain novel.

The new Nebraska edition of *The Journals of the Lewis & Clark Expedition* in its inclusiveness takes an important step in fostering appreciation of the journals as an important contribution to American literature. On display are those monumental accumulations of data and varied systems of notation—a massive achievement in the genre of natural history—that take on epic characteristics. Ragged and unpolished, the journals now bear comparison to oral tales that are often even more expansive, digressive, and tediously detailed, unlike the doctored versions that survive in popularly printed editions. The unpolished journals appropriately become an unfinished epic for a nation still discovering its ties to the natural world. Like other great nature writers, Lewis and Clark often move against contemporary conventions toward an apprehension of the unknown and the uncategorized in imaginative ways that abandon technical terms and stock conceits for fresh, flexible uses of the vernacular. Such writing anticipates future moments in Thoreau's *Maine Woods* (1864), Burroughs's *Signs and Seasons* (1886), and Muir's *Mountains of California* (1894), where fusions of documentary and visionary expression through a vernacular style will continue to invigorate the genre of American nature writing at its best.

NOTES

1. Donald Jackson, ed., *Letters of the Lewis and Clark Expedition with Related Documents, 1783–1854* (Urbana: University of Illinois Press, 1962), v.

2. William L. Hedges, "Toward a National Literature." *Columbia Literary History of the United States,* ed. Emory Elliott et al. (New York: Columbia University Press, 1988), 202.

3. In 1893 Elliott Coues comments on his edition of the journals, "This is our national epic of exploration" (introduction to *History of the Expedition Under the Command of Lewis and Clark,* ed. Elliott Coues [1893; reprint, New York: Dover, 1965], 1:v). In 1988 the editor Gary Moulton agrees, "It is our national epic of exploration" ("Lewis and Clark: Our 'National Epic of Exploration' Worthy of Monumental Editing," *Nebraska Alumnus,* 1 March–1 April 1988, 8). John L. Allen notes that the expedition "has long been recognized as the American exploratory epic" (review of *The Journals of the Lewis & Clark Expedition,* vols. 2–4, ed. Gary E. Moulton, *William and Mary Quarterly* 46 [1989]: 630). Marius Bewley observes that the "community that existed between Lewis and Clark" and the members of the expedition "was very much of that character we find described in heroic poetry" ("The Heroic and the Romantic West," *New York Review of Books,* 8 April 1965; reprinted in *Masks and Mirrors: Essays in Criticism* [New York: Atheneum, 1970], 214).

4. Frank Bergon, introduction to *The Journals of Lewis and Clark,* ed. Frank Bergon (New York: Viking, 1989), xvii; William Gilpin, *Mission of the North American People, Geographical, Social, and Political,* rev. 2d ed. (Philadelphia: J. B. Lippincott, 1874), 130.

5. Benjamin Smith Barton, letters to William Bartram, 19 February and 13 December 1788, in Bartram Papers, Historical Society of Pennsylvania, Philadelphia, 5, 4.

6. Samuel Taylor Coleridge, quoted in Francis Harper, introduction to *The Travels of William Bartram: Naturalist's Edition,* ed. Francis Harper (New Haven: Yale University Press, 1958), xxvii; Thomas Carlyle, letter to Emerson, 8 July 1851, in *The Correspondence of Emerson and Carlyle,* ed. Joseph Slater (New York: Columbia University Press, 1964), 468.

7. Jackson, *Letters,* 669.

8. The erroneous claim seems to have originated with N. Bryllion Fagin's *William Bartram: Interpreter of the American Landscape* (Baltimore: Johns Hopkins University Press, 1933), but it reappears in Josephine Herbst's *New Green World* (1954); Joseph Ewan's introduction to *William Bartram, Botanical and Zoological Drawings, 1756–1788* (1968); and Joseph Kastner, *A Species of Eternity* (New York: Alfred A. Knopf, 1977), among others.

9. Jackson, *Letters,* 17.

10. John Burroughs, *A Sharp Lookout: Selected Nature Essays of John Burroughs*, ed. Frank Bergon (Washington, D.C.: Smithsonian Institution Press, 1987), 333.

11. Jefferson is quoted in Dayton Duncan, *Out West: A Journey Through Lewis & Clark's America* (New York: Viking, 1987), 10; Fisher Ames, *Works of Fisher Ames*, ed. Seth Ames (Boston, 1854), 1:324.

12. Jackson, *Letters*, 350, 591, 394–396.

13. Thomas Jefferson, *Writings: Autobiography, Notes on the State of Virginia, Public and Private Papers, Addresses, Letters*, ed. Merrill D. Peterson (New York: Library of America, 1984), 1313.

14. Howard Goodman, "Lewis and Clark Redux," *We Proceeded On* 19, no. 4 (1993): 25–26.

15. Reuben Gold Thwaites, ed., *Original Journals of the Lewis and Clark Expedition, 1804–1806* (New York: Dodd, Mead, 1904–05), 1:284–285.

16. Gary E. Moulton, ed., *The Journals of the Lewis & Clark Expedition*, 13 vols. (Lincoln: University of Nebraska Press, 1983–99). Any parenthetical page citations in chapter 2 text and notes are to this edition. The phrases in angle brackets are partly illegible words that Moulton has had to decipher.

17. Paul Russell Cutright, *A History of the Lewis and Clark Journals* (Norman: University of Oklahoma Press, 1976), 258.

18. Gary E. Moulton, "The Journals of the Lewis and Clark Expedition: Beginning Again," *We Proceeded On* 6, no. 4 (1980): 15.

19. John L. Allen, *Passage through the Garden: Lewis and Clark and the Image of the American Northwest* (Urbana: University of Illinois Press, 1975), 79.

20. Jefferson, *Writings*, 176; Alexander Pope, "An Essay on Man," in *Alexander Pope*, ed. Pat Rogers (New York: Oxford University Press, 1993), 279, 300, 276.

21. Kastner, *Species of Eternity*, 123; Jefferson, *Writings*, 177, 176.

22. Jefferson, *Writings*, 183, 184.

23. Thwaites, *Original Journals*, 7:150–151.

24. Jefferson, *Writings*, 227.

25. Ibid., 142.

26. Ibid.

27. Jackson, *Letters*, 206.

28. Ernst Cassirer, *The Philosophy of the Enlightenment*, trans. Fritz C. A. Koelln and James P. Pettegrove (Princeton: Princeton University Press, 1951), 329; Jefferson, *Writings*, 148.

29. John Muir, *My First Summer in the Sierra* (Boston: Houghton, 1911), 129; Burroughs, *A Sharp Lookout*, 36. It is interesting to note that Stephen Fender discerns in the journals, letters, and diaries of 1849 transcontinental travelers a similar "double style," varying between formal and factual description, picturesque and scientific rhetoric, or literal and figurative language. Fender extends his examination of the "forty-niners' 'double style'" to include "their better known contemporaries, Hawthorne, Thoreau, and Melville, whose prose also exhibits (though more designedly and much more famously) the strategic fracture between fantasy and documentary fact" (*Plotting the Golden West: American Literature and the Rhetoric of the California Trail* [Cambridge: Cambridge University Press, 1981], 14). Although Fender has been criticized for a vague shifting of dualistic categories, his stylistic observations about

midcentury travel accounts, particularly those of John Charles Frémont, are valuably pertinent to this study of nature writing.

30. Henry David Thoreau, *The Journal of Henry D. Thoreau,* ed. Torrey Bradford and Francis H. Allen (Boston: Houghton, 1908), 7:108.

31. Cutright, *History,* 8.

32. Paul Russell Cutright, *Lewis and Clark, Pioneering Naturalists* (Urbana: University of Illinois Press, 1969), 8. Field collectors like Lewis and Clark would normally not presume to name new species but would turn over their descriptions and samples to taxonomic specialists (usually noncollectors), like the German botanist Frederick Pursh, who received Lewis's herbarium and credited the explorers with providing 122 specimens of the new plants scientifically named and classified in his two-volume *Flora Americae Septentrionalis* (1814), including ones tagged with newly coined genera and species honoring their discoverers as *Lewisia* and *Clarkia.* Field collectors, however, would commonly use Latinate binomials for the identification of known species and Linnaean terms for the classification of new species, as Lewis does when comparing the eulachon or candle fish to "the herring, shad anchovy &c of the Malacopterygious Order & Class Cupea" (6:344) or when describing the magpie as a "bird of the *Corvus genus"* and "order of the pica" (3:83).

33. Jefferson, *Writings,* 1127; Jefferson, quoted in Charles A. Miller, *Jefferson and Nature: An Interpretation* (Baltimore: Johns Hopkins University Press, 1998), 44; Jefferson, *Writings,* 1261, 1330.

34. Jefferson, quoted in John C. Greene, *American Science in the Age of Jefferson* (Ames: Iowa State University Press, 1984), 33; Jefferson, *Writings,* 1086. Resistance to the Linnaean system coincided with widespread American suspicion of specialized terminology. The earlier objection of some poets like Joel Barlow to foreign terms in the American language, especially a Latinity equated with monarchy, also shaped the views of those in the sciences, like Charles Willson Peale. Although Peale's museum in Philadelphia provided an orderly exposition of natural history according to Linnaean principles, Peale himself rejected Linnaean terminology and complained to Jefferson that "men pretending to a knowledge must be humored with the high sounding names made from the dead Languages" (Jackson, *Letters,* 308–309).

35. Elijah Harry Criswell, *Lewis and Clark: Linguistic Pioneers,* University of Missouri Studies, no. 15 (Columbia: University of Missouri Press, 1940), 45.

36. Robert B. Betts, "'we commenced wrighting &c.' A Salute to the Ingenious Spelling and Grammar of William Clark," *We Proceeded On* 6, no. 4 (1980): 11.

Chapter 3

"Two dozes of barks and opium"

Lewis & Clark as Physicians

Ronald V. Loge, M.D.

After the purchase of the Louisiana Territory in 1803, President Thomas Jefferson entrusted the fate of the expedition to explore the Missouri River headwaters to his capable friend and personal secretary, twenty-eight-year-old Meriwether Lewis. Having planned the expedition for ten years, Jefferson outlined detailed and precise goals. He was interested in opening up the west in order to establish trade routes, particularly for the fur trade, and he wanted to lay claim to the Pacific Northwest. In addition, Jefferson wished to learn more about the indigenous peoples, their cultures, and their health. He provided Meriwether Lewis with the necessary instruction to prepare for this journey. Lewis invited a former fellow army officer and experienced frontiersman, thirty-two-year-old William Clark, to serve as co-captain of this expedition of discovery.[1]

This remarkable journey of 8,000 miles up the Missouri River, over the Rocky Mountains, down the Columbia River, and back again was successfully completed because of rigorous preparation, frequent good luck, and exceptional tenacity. Although the voyagers on this journey faced extreme weather, many types of injury and disease, and encounters with hostile Indian tribes and grizzly bears, only one of the expedition members died. The skillful leadership and care provided by Lewis and Clark were central to this successful outcome.

Possessing a low opinion of most physicians and their treatments, Thomas Jefferson considered a physician to be an unnecessary encumbrance on the expedition and assumed that all illnesses and injuries would be handled effectively by Captains Lewis and Clark.[2] Some background about the state of medicine of the early 1800s helps explain how the capable army captains were able to function as physicians.

Medicine in 1804 had evolved very little in the two thousand years from the time of Galen and Hippocrates. Thus, the theories and treatments used in medical practice persisted into the nineteenth century. Newer scientific discoveries, however, had changed the names of some of these descriptors from good and ill humors of the Greeks to inflammation, morbid conditions, and nervous irritability. Purging and bloodletting endured as the standards of therapy.[3]

The first medical school in the colonies was founded in 1765, and by 1800 the five medical schools in the new republic had graduated a cumulative total of 250 physicians. Many practitioners had little or no training. One doctor in ten held a medical degree. Though many nondegree physicians had legitimate apprenticeship training, impostors were widespread. A New York City newspaper from the late 1700s described the city as having forty doctors, "the greatest part of whom were mere pretenders to a profession of which they were entirely ignorant."[4]

Frontier areas had few, if any, trained physicians, and most of medicine was practiced with only a basic understanding of first aid. Midwives and "yarb" (herb) doctors were common. One of the better known yarb doctors in Albemarle County, Virginia, was Lucy Marks, the mother of Meriwether Lewis. She was undoubtedly a source of his knowledge of herbal remedies.[5]

With an abiding interest in medicine, Thomas Jefferson had an extensive medical library and corresponded with leading physicians of the day. Jefferson understood very well the limitations of both insight and abilities possessed by his contemporaries. Succinctly summarizing the state of early-nineteenth-century medicine, he wrote: "Thus, fulness of the stomach we can relieve with emetics; disease of the bowels, by purgatives; inflammatory cases, by bleeding; intermittents, by the Peruvian bark; syphilis, by mercury; watchfulness, by opium; etc. So far I bow to the utility of medicine."[6] These principles of medical practice outlined by Jefferson were the basis of treatments used by Lewis and Clark.

Therapeutic bleeding goes back to the time of the Greeks and was probably practiced even before written history. In Jefferson's time few maladies escaped treatment with the phlebotomy lancet. "Intermittents" described intermittent fever, usually malaria, but the term was also applied to any sort of fever. Peruvian bark, or cinchona, contains quinine and other alkaloids that reduce fever. "Bark," the aspirin of its day, was used frequently by Lewis and Clark.

Syphilis was treated with mercurial salts. Mercury had been used for nearly three centuries to treat syphilis, both the primary and secondary forms, and was standard therapy through the end of the nineteenth century.[7] Watchfulness, a diagnosis that included insomnia, anxiety, and probably even depression, was treated with opium.

To prepare Meriwether Lewis better for his formidable journey, President Jefferson sent him to Philadelphia to receive scientific instruction

from some of Jefferson's fellow members of the American Philosophical Society. He expected Lewis to enhance his skills in natural history, zoology,
botany, and astronomical navigation, and also to become proficient in field
medicine.[8] The principal teacher in Lewis's brief medical study was Benjamin Rush, whom Jefferson knew from the days of the Declaration of Independence, which they both signed.[9] Dr. Rush was considered to be the
most influential physician of his time. A zealous advocate of bleeding and
purging techniques, probably to the extreme, Rush was said to have shed
more blood than any general in history.[10]

Although there is no record of any detailed medical training that Dr.
Rush provided Meriwether Lewis, he did give Lewis a list of instructions for
the health and hygiene of the men under his command and probably
helped Lewis assemble medical supplies. Assessing Lewis's abilities for the
mission, Rush wrote to President Jefferson, "Mr. Lewis appears admirably
qualified for it," thereby confirming to Jefferson that Lewis could be captain, naturalist, and physician.[11]

Congress initially allocated $2,500 for the entire expedition, expected to
field only a dozen men and take up to two years. Meriwether Lewis bud-
geted $55.00 for medicine and $696.00 for Indian presents, a ratio that
reflected the relative needs he anticipated.[12] As the journey unfolded, however, medicine, rather than the presents, secured the beneficial relationships with the northwestern natives.

A list of the medical items originally packed for this journey reflects the
medical treatments of that era (see Table 1). George Gillaspy and Joseph
Strong were Philadelphia physicians who owned the apothecary that supplied the medications. The total cost was $90.69, appreciably over budget.
One-third of the expenditures, $30.00, was for Peruvian bark.

Other items included several laxatives (rhubarb, magnesia, and jalap, a
powerful laxative derived from the Mexican morning glory) and substances
to induce vomiting (ipecac and cream of tartar). Most frequently employed
of the medical supplies were the bilious pills (fifty dozen) of Benjamin
Rush, a potent laxative combination of jalap and calomel. Although inexpensive, Rush's bilious pills produced powerful results. Approximately
1,300 doses of laxatives were prepared for this journey. A medicine that
would prove of great worth was vitriol, a topical solution of zinc sulfate and
lead acetate, used for eye diseases.

Lewis, aware of reports from the upper Missouri River that syphilis was
endemic amongst the Mandan Indians, anticipated that the sexual behavior of his men would require a store of mercurials.[13] Calomel (mercurous
chloride) was given orally as a laxative and also to treat syphilis. Lewis
bought clyster syringes (enema and penis syringes). Although the penis sy-
ringe was designed to treat gonorrhea by urethral irrigation, it may have

TABLE 1. Medical Items Purchased for the Lewis and Clark Expedition

Bought of Gillaspy & Strong the following article for use of M. Lewis Esquire on his tour up the Mississipi [sic] River, & supplied by his Order (Phila., May 26, 1803). —Viz.

15 lb. Pulv. Cort. Peru	$30.00	4 oz. Laudanum	.50
½ " " Jalap	.67	2 lb. Ung. Basilic Flav. 50	1.00
½ " " Rhei [rhubarb]	1.00	1 " " [. . .] Calimin 50	.50
4 oz. " Ipecacuan.	1.25	1 " " Epispastric.	1.00
2 lb. " Crem. Tart.	.67	1 " " Mercuriale	1.25
2 oz. Gum Camphor	.40	1. Emplast. Diach. S.	.50
1 lb. " Assafoetid.	1.00	1. Set Pocket Insts. Small	9.50
½ lb. " Opii Turk.opt.	2.50	1 " Teeth	2.25
¼ lb. " Tragacanth	.37	1. Clyster Syringe	2.75
6 lb. Sal Glauber 10	.60	4. Penis do.	1.00
2 " " Nitri 33½	.67	3. Best Lancets .80	2.40
2 " Copperas	.10	1. Tourniquet	3.50
6 oz. Sacchar. Saturn. opt.	.37	2 oz. Patient Lint	.25
4 " Calomel	.75	50. doz. Bilious Pills to	
1 "Tartar Emetic	.10	Order of B. Rush .10	5.00
4 " Vitriol Alb.	.12	6. Tin Canisters 25	1.50
½ lb. Rad. Columbo	1.00	3. 8 oz. Gd. Stopd. Bottles 40	1.20
¼ " Elix. Vitriol	.25	5 4 " 0 Tintures do	1.85
¼ " Ess. Menth. Pip.	.50	6 4 " Salt Mo.	2.22
¼ " Bals. Copaiboe	.37	1. Walnut Chest	4.50
¼ " " Traumat.	.50	1. Pine do.	1.20
2 oz. Magnesia	.20	Porterage	.30
¼ lb. Indian Ink	1.50		————
2 oz. Gum Elastic	.37		$90.69
2 " Nutmegs	.75		
2 " Cloves	.31		
2 " Cinnamon	20		
	$46.52		

SOURCE: Donald Jackson, ed., Letters of the Lewis and Clark Expedition, with Related Documents, 1783–1854 (Urbana: University of Illinois Press, 1962), 1:80–87.

been more effective as a deterrent. Three of the best lancets were included in the inventory.

After securing the plans, training, and materials needed for the expedition, Captain Lewis traveled down the Ohio River and met his friend, William Clark, at Clarksville, Indiana Territory. They proceeded on to Camp DuBois, near St. Louis, where, during the winter of 1803–04, they assembled and prepared a crew of hearty woodsmen and army volunteers, now numbering forty-five.

In May 1804 the Corps of Discovery set off upriver on the mighty Missouri River at high water in a heavy iron keelboat and two smaller boats, called pirogues. The strenuous voyage had begun. These boats had to be rowed, sailed, poled, and pulled up the 2,300 miles of the Missouri River.

The voyagers had not traveled far before some men complained of sore eyes, probably from blowing sand and ultraviolet keratitis from the bright sun on the water. But the first real medical problem occurred on 4 July 1804, when one of the men suffered snakebite on his foot, which immediately began to swell. Captain Lewis applied a poultice of gunpowder and Peruvian bark to the wound.[14] Lewis did not ignite the poultice, as was the practice in some quarters to treat snakebite.

No one was severely ill until mid-August when the group arrived at what is now the area of Sioux City, Iowa, where the only fatality on the entire journey occurred. Sergeant Charles Floyd died of an acute illness that was described as "bilious colic." Floyd had complained of being ill for several days in late July but had soon improved. On 19 August, however, Floyd developed crampy abdominal pain, vomiting, and diarrhea and died the next day.[15] Although no treatment is described in the journals, the customary use of purgatives and bleeding for such illnesses may have been employed, with catastrophic consequences. A ruptured appendix with peritonitis has been the traditional historical diagnosis used to explain Floyd's death. Floyd was about twenty years old, and certainly appendicitis is common in this age group. Arsenic poisoning and cholera-like illnesses have also been suggested as etiologies.[16] Chronic peptic ulcer disease with perforation and peritonitis has not been previously considered and should be added to the list of possible causes of Floyd's illness and death. Undoubtedly, apprehension arose thereafter whenever anyone developed the frequently occurring symptoms of colic or abdominal pains.

Medical events were infrequent until the explorers reached Fort Mandan, where the corps spent its first winter on the banks of the Missouri River, adjacent to Mandan and Hidatsa Indian villages. These friendly Indians provided food for the visitors in exchange for trinkets and important blacksmith goods. But of greater significance, the captains acquired knowledge of the upper Missouri, the uncharted waters ahead of them.

Also traded were sexually transmitted diseases! Clark wrote: "they are helth. except the—vn. [venereal]—which is common with the Indians and have been communicated to many of our party at this place—those favores bieng easy acquired" (3:322). The natives believed that powers or "medicine" could be transferred through sexual relations. Thus, it was a common practice for esteemed visitors to have the honor of sexual intercourse with the Indian women.[17] Since syphilis was endemic in the tribes, Lewis and Clark administered mercurials throughout that winter.

Clark learned that smallpox had previously decimated some of the Mandan villages. Although helpless against smallpox epidemics, the Indians might have been aided by Lewis and Clark if President Jefferson's plans could have reached fruition. Jefferson and Rush, both ardent advocates of Jenner's new cowpox (kine-pox) vaccination methods, believed that the scourge of smallpox could be prevented. In his final instructions to Meriwether Lewis in June 1803, Jefferson wrote, "Carry with you some matter of the kine-pox," and he encouraged Lewis to teach its use to and vaccinate especially those with whom they would spend their winter encampment.[18] The potentially historic opportunity to vaccinate the Mandan and Hidatsa tribes never came about because, as Lewis reported in a letter to Jefferson in October 1803, "the Vaxcine matter," supplied by the president, "has lost it's virtue."[19]

During that cold Dakota winter when the group experienced forty days of temperatures below zero, frostbite was common. In January they found a young Indian boy who had spent a 40-degrees-below-zero night out on the prairie wrapped only in a buffalo robe. He had badly frostbitten toes, which turned gangrenous. Three weeks later, the captains sawed off the boy's affected toes (3:281). His recovery likely left a favorable impression on the Indians.

The most significant event of the winter at Fort Mandan was the captains' introduction to Sacagawea, a Shoshone woman who had been captured by the Hidatsa Indians four or five years earlier. Lewis and Clark immediately perceived that she would be a key link to the western Indians. She was about sixteen years old, married to a French fur trapper named Charbonneau, and pregnant. In February 1805 Sacagawea began a long and difficult labor. Captain Lewis was approached by Ren Jessome, another French fur trapper, who said that in situations like this "he had frequently administered a small portion of the rattle of the rattle-snake" (5:291). Lewis had a rattle that Jessome broke into small pieces, mixed with water, and gave to Sacagawea. Lewis, in his only foray into obstetrics, observed that within ten minutes the patient delivered a healthy baby boy.

With the breakup of the Missouri River in the spring of 1805, the Corps of Discovery resumed its upstream travel. Lewis, a gifted naturalist and botanist, described plant and animal life extensively, including fruits and wild vegetables that grew along the way. Sacagawea—now part of the corps—would occasionally dig roots to supplement their meat diet (4:15). And with buffalo and elk abundant on the prairie, there was never a shortage of food.

When the group neared the Great Falls of the Missouri, Lewis became afflicted with abdominal pain and fever. Would he, while experiencing "violent pain in the intestens" (4:278), have remembered Sergeant Floyd's fatal illness and recognized the perilous balance that such new intervening diseases created? He did recall what was presumably one of his mother's herbal remedies made from chokecherry twigs boiled in water. After drinking this black decoction, Lewis described feeling remarkably better. By the next day he was able to march twenty-seven miles (7:279).

At about the same time Sacagawea became gravely ill, the infirmity lasting nine days. William Clark wrote in his journal on 10 June 1805: "Sah cah gah, we a, our Indian woman verry Sick I blead her" (7:277). Like a sagacious and attentive physician, Meriwether Lewis noted the following in his journal on 16 June 1805:

> about 2 P.M. I reached the camp found the Indian woman extreemly ill and much reduced by her indisposition. this gave me some concern as well for the poor object herself, then with a young child in her arms, as from the consideration of her being our only dependence for a friendly negotiation with the Snake Indians on whom we depend for horses to assist us in our portage from the Missouri to the columbia River. . . . I found that two dozes of barks and opium which I had given her since my arrival had produced an alteration in her pulse for the better; they were now much fuller and more regular. I caused her to drink the mineral water altogether. When I first came down I found that her pulse were scarcely perceptiable, very quick frequently irregular and attended with strong nervous symptoms, that of the twitching of the fingers and leaders of the arm; now the pulse had become regular much fuller and a gentle perspiration had taken place; the nervous symptoms have also in a great measure abated, and she feels herself much freer from pain. she complains principally of the lower region of the abdomen, I therefore continued the cataplasms of barks and laudnuum which had been previously used by my friend Capt Clark. I beleive her disorder originated principally from an obstruction of the mensis in consequence of taking could. I determined to . . . restore the sick woman. (4:299–301)

Sacagawea did recover with, or in spite of, the treatment. Lewis's observations suggested a pelvic disorder. The syndrome of lower abdominal pain, fever, and occasional delirium may have been pelvic inflammatory disease (PID), a likely possibility considering the presence of gonorrhea among the Hidatsa Indians of that era. History suggests that she did have another child in about 1812.[20] In that so many infertile years passed before this presumably sexually active young woman had a second child, PID may be a credible retrospective diagnosis.

The exhausting portage around the Great Falls of the Missouri was made worse by a trio of pests: mosquitoes, gnats, and prickly pears. All three made the next leg of the journey to the three forks of the Missouri River unpleasant. The hard, sharp thorns of prickly pears penetrated their moccasins, broke off in the flesh, and caused abscesses. The three forks of the Missouri, the convergence of the Gallatin River, the Madison River, and the Jefferson River, had been the site of Sacagawea's abduction by the Hidatsa tribe five years before. Near this key geographic point, Lewis and Clark anticipated finding the Shoshone Indians. The expedition, however, was unexpectedly forced to halt here. Captain Clark had become alarmingly ill. Several days earlier he had complained of blisters and prickly pear thorn wounds on his feet. On 26 July 1805 he felt "verry unwell & took up Camp" (4:432). On the 27th, as described by Lewis: "at 3 P.M. Capt Clark arrived very sick with a high fever on him and much fatiegued and exhausted. he informed me that he was very sick all last night had a high fever and frequent chills & constant aking pains in all his mustles." Lewis noted that Clark was "somewhat bilious and had not had a passage for several days." He persuaded Clark to take a dose of Rush's pills, which Lewis had "always found sovereign in such cases" (4:436).

Captain Clark did take five of Rush's pills, a very large dose, and though sick throughout the night, began to feel somewhat better, particularly after the medicine had "operated." The following day Clark had improved, although he was still very languid and complained of a general soreness in all his limbs. He took Peruvian barks, which probably assuaged his symptoms. The following day, 30 July, he was well enough to travel (5:14).

What was the cause of Clark's febrile illness at Three Forks? Although this illness caused Captain Lewis to suspend their voyage at this critical juncture, scores of previous analyses have simply dismissed this infirmity as constipation, exhaustion, malaria, or infection from prickly pear punctures. Current knowledge of infectious diseases and epidemiology suggests that a person presenting now with these symptoms during the summer season in southwestern Montana would usually be suffering from Colorado tick fever. This viral infection, transmitted by wood ticks, is endemic today in the Three Forks area. The 1805 journal account of Clark's illness may be the first clinical description of Colorado tick fever, written by two good clinical observers.

The captains must have been elated when, on 8 August, Sacagawea recognized the Beaverhead Rock and stated that beyond it they would find her people. Indeed, reunion with her Shoshone tribe took place a few days later just south of present-day Dillon, Montana. Cameahwait, a Shoshone chief and Sacagawea's brother, agreed to provide horses and a guide for the corps to make the overland journey.

A heavy September snowstorm made the seven-day crossing of the rugged Bitterroot Range a severe struggle. With no wild game, the captains staved off starvation with horse meat and "portable soup," a canned soup concentrate purchased by Lewis in Philadelphia. Some scholars have suggested that, by this time, the party had developed scurvy, because Captain Clark made frequent mention of skin infections and boils.[21] The journals, however, provide no clues to any illness with the clinical manifestations of scurvy in the men. Furthermore, they had adequate sources of vitamin C from rosehips, plums, chokecherries, serviceberries, and currants.

Descending to the Clearwater River valley, in what is now Idaho, the group reached a Nez Perce Indian village. The Corps of Discovery troops were famished. The natives provided a feast of dried salmon, berries, and roots. Apparently because of the food, all of the men became extremely ill for several days with what may have been some type of bacterial enteritis to which the Indians were immune. Lewis was, in fact, so weakened by vomiting, abdominal pain, and diarrhea that he could not ride his horse. And what treatment did Captain Clark administer to all of these men with dysentery? None other than the "sovereign" bilious pills of Dr. Rush!

After this two-week delay, the expedition proceeded down to the Columbia River in hand-hewn canoes, establishing contact with Indian tribes as they went. On this part of the journey Lewis and Clark began their medical practice with the Indians by treating their very common eye complaints with vitriol eye drops. The Indians suffered from sore eyes and blindness, perhaps caused by trachoma, still the leading cause of blindness in the world today.

On 7 November 1805 Clark wrote, "Great joy in camp we are in View of the Ocian" (6:33). The winter camp, Fort Clatsop, was fairly quiet, except for some interaction with the local Indian tribes. These natives had the same sexual mores as the Mandan Indians. In spite of admonitions of chastity, the captains had again to treat many of the men with mercurials for "the venerial" (6:416).

Three men were dispatched from Fort Clatsop to the ocean to make salt by boiling seawater. In February 1806 one of them, Bratton, became ill with a cough and low back pain. The back pain persisted for four months and caused him to be totally disabled. On the return journey, while camped along the Clearwater River in May, Bratton asked that he be sweated in an attempt to restore his health. After a set of vigorous sweats in a sweat hole, followed by immersion in cold water, his back finally began to improve, and he was soon able to resume his duties (7:283).

Captain Lewis had purchased nearly $700 worth of gifts and trinkets for the Indians to be used to barter for food, horses, canoes, and goodwill. Returning up the Columbia, they lacked resources to complete the return trip, and their supply of trade items was depleted. Although they resorted to cutting buttons off their clothes to trade for food and horses, it was the medical practice of Captain Clark that saved the day. Word of the red-haired doctor and his "Big Medicine" had gotten out to the Columbia River tribes, and on the return voyage, natives were waiting for him with their medical problems. And Captain Clark had many important successes.

Lewis wrote that Clark gave an Indian man some liniment to rub on his knee and "the fellow soon after recovered and has never ceased to extol the virtues of our medicines and the skill of my friend Capt. C. as a phisician" (7:209). Word of the medical skills of Lewis and Clark traveled fast and far.

Indians came from as distant as two days' ride on horseback just to seek medical attention. Captain Clark would see as many as fifty people a day at his clinics, while Captain Lewis carried on diplomatic negotiations with tribal leaders.

The expedition lacked sufficient numbers of horses to cross back over the mountains. Captain Clark's medical practice produced the needed horses. One of the many horses came from an Indian man whose wife had an abscess in the small of her back. He promised a horse for the treatment of the abscess. Captain Clark received a second horse in exchange for medicine for a little girl with rheumatism. Lewis noted, "[M]any of the natives apply to us for medical aid which we gave them cheerfully so far as our skill and store of medicine would enable us. schrofela, ulcers, rheumatism, soar eyes, and the loss of the uce of their limbs are the most common cases among them" (7:243).

One of the most interesting patients among the Nez Perce was a paralyzed chief. Lewis wrote,

> a Cheif of considerable note at this place has been afflicted with it for three years, he is incapable of moving a single limb but lies like a corps in whatever position he is placed, yet he eats heartily, digests his food perfectly, injoys his understanding, his pulse are good, and has retained his flesh almost perfectly, in short were it not that he appears a little pale from having lain so long in the shade he might be taken for a man in good health. (7:243)

Lewis perceptively observed that the chief's muscles were not atrophied and he looked well. The usual remedies of sulfur, purgatives, and dietary changes did not help. Relatives of this chief had seen Bratton's sweat therapy and subsequent recovery. They persuaded Lewis and Clark to sweat the chief even though the Indians could have done this themselves. Before the first sweat, the captain-physicians sedated the chief with a dose of laudanum. After the sweat the chief began to use his arms, and after several more treatments, he regained the use of his limbs. After a month in the camp "hospital," he had nearly recovered.

Like Clark's fever at Three Forks, this illness has undergone little analysis by medical historians. The chief was possibly disabled by a conversion reaction resulting from past psychological trauma that remained unresolved in the male Indian tradition and culture of the time.

Why were these Army captains effective healers among the Indians? Lewis noted that "everything which is incomprehensible to the Indians they call big medicine, and is the opperation of the presnts and power of the great sperit" (4:101). Since Lewis and Clark presented a novel appearance, spoke a strange language, dressed differently, had unusual-colored skin or hair (Clark had red hair and Clark's servant, York, was black), and employed unique remedies, they were perhaps considered to be personifications of the Great Spirit. Their treatments seemed to produce powerful results for the Indians.

Lewis gave credit to his partner, Captain Clark, as the Indians' "favorite phisician." Lewis and Clark acknowledged they were not actual physicians, but in their circumstance they felt that it was "pardonable to continue this deseption for they will not give us any provision without compensation in merchandize and our stock is now reduced to a mere handfull" (7:209, 210). This "pardonable deseption" enabled the Corps of Discovery to secure the critical provisions and packhorses needed to return over the mountains.

Similarly to Hippocrates, Lewis stated: "we take care to give them no article which can possibly injure them" (7:210). Their journals give evidence that as good physicians, the captains truly cared for these native people and desired as good an outcome as possible.

In June 1806 they re-traversed the rugged Bitterroot Range and proceeded on their homeward voyage. In August of that year an accident of grave potential occurred at the junction of the Yellowstone and Missouri Rivers, when Meriwether Lewis was accidentally shot in the leg by one of his own men. Fortunately, it was only a superficial wound. He recovered quickly, and shortly thereafter the Corps of Discovery "proceeded on." Arriving in St. Louis on 23 September 1806, the troops "received a harty welcome." Writing from St. Louis to President Jefferson, Meriwether Lewis summarized the importance of their health: "The whole of the party who accompanyed me from the Mandans have returned in good health, which is not, I assure you, to me one of the least pleasing considerations of the Voyage."[22]

The role of Captain Lewis and Captain Clark as expedition physicians was vital to the overall success of this mission. Included among the physician-captains' patients were their troops, Sacagawea, her baby, the Native Americans, and each other. Their aid to the Indians assured the success of travel and prevented starvation. With the exception of one tragic encounter with a Blackfeet hunting party on Lewis's return, their interaction with the native people was friendly. By using diplomacy, honesty, and their medical skills, Lewis and Clark achieved more than any conquering army might have for their president and for their country.

NOTES

Acknowledgment: the author would like to thank Edward W. Hook, M.D., for his encouragement to publish this Medical Center Hour presentation and for his assistance with manuscript editing. Thanks are extended also to Joyce S. Garver for manuscript preparation, and especially to my wife, Charlene, for editing and encouraging me in this endeavor.

1. Donald Jackson, ed., *Letters of the Lewis and Clark Expedition, with Related Documents, 1783–1854* (Urbana: University of Illinois Press, 1962), 1:57–60.

2. E. G. Chuinard, *Only One Man Died: The Medical Aspects of the Lewis and Clark Expedition* (Glendale, Calif.: Arthur H. Clark, 1979), 415.

3. Ibid., 67–80.

4. J. T. Flexner, *Doctors on Horseback: Pioneers of American Medicine* (New York: Fordham University Press, 1992), 9.

5. Chuinard, *Only One Man Died,* 108.

6. Ibid., 415.

7. J. G. O'Shea, "Two Minutes with Venus, Two years with Mercury: Mercury as an Antisyphilitic Hemotherapeutic Agent," *Journal of the Royal Society of Medicine* 83 (June 1990): 392–395.

8. Jackson, *Letters,* 1:16–19.

9. D. F. Hawke, *Benjamin Rush: Revolutionary Gadfly* (Indianapolis: Bobbs-Merrill, 1971), 392.

10. Flexner, *Doctors on Horseback,* 113.

11. The quotation is from Jackson, *Letters,* 1:54.

12. Ibid., 1:8–9.

13. James P. Ronda, *Lewis and Clark among the Indians* (Lincoln: University of Nebraska Press, 1984), 106.

14. Paul Russell Cutright, *Lewis and Clark, Pioneering Naturalists* (Urbana: University of Illinois Press, 1969), 63.

15. Gary E. Moulton, ed., *The Journals of the Lewis & Clark Expedition* (Lincoln: University of Nebraska Press, 1983–99), 2:495. Any parenthetical page citations in chapter 3 text and notes are to this edition.

16. Chuinard, *Only One Man Died,* 230–238.

17. Ronda, *Among the Indians,* 107.

18. Jackson, *Letters,* 1:64.

19. Ibid., 1:130.

20. Ibid., 2:639.

21. Chuinard, *Only One Man Died,* 320.

22. Jackson, *Letters,* 1:324.

PART II

Legacies

Map 3. A new map of Texas, Oregon, and California: with the regions adjoining. Compiled from the Most Recent Authorities. Philadelphia: S. Augustus Mitchell, 1846. (Library of Congress, Geography and Map Division)

In terms of acquisition, incorporation, and the administration of peoples and territories, this odd mix of imaginary geography, jingoism, and geopolitical reality amply illustrates the unsettled legacies of the Lewis and Clark expedition. Here, the American West is made up of six huge geographic entities: Texas, Iowa Territory, Missouri Territory, Indian Territory, Upper or New California, and Oregon—which extends to latitude 54′40″. References to Indian tribes have completely disappeared, except for the carefully delineated lines of new reservations in Indian Territory that have been set aside for tribes removed from the East. This conglomerate of newly conquered lands and loosely administered territories is visually stitched together by the tracings of various routes across the map, namely the explorations of Lewis and Clark and John C. Frémont, as well as the overland commercial routes to Santa Fe and the California coast.

The Lewis and Clark expedition is almost universally described as the greatest and most successful exercise in overland exploration ever attempted. Even today, it is hard to conceive how one might organize thirty-five to forty-five individuals to cross the continent by foot, horseback, and small watercraft, then return by similar routes and modes of travel. Trying to accomplish the same feat in the early nineteenth century, and lose only one person to an inoperable case of appendicitis, truly boggles the imagination. Of course, the completion of this transcontinental journey depended on the assistance of Native peoples—who themselves were quite capable of covering vast distances in a relatively short time. The success of the expedition was not a simple matter of miles traveled, mountains crossed, or mosquitoes tolerated, nor should its significance be assessed in terms of persistence or assistance. Rather, the successes of Lewis and Clark, as with any enterprise of similar magnitude, are best measured in terms of their historical consequences.

The first two essays in this section, both by legal scholars, examine the immediate and ongoing legacies of Thomas Jefferson's Corps of Discovery. The consequences of the Louisiana Purchase and the subsequent expedition of Lewis and Clark had far-reaching constitutional implications that raised fundamental questions about slavery, the legality of territorial expansion, and the nature of the federal public domain. The explicit objectives of the expedition also left a series of disturbing legacies in its wake. For the Mandan, Hidatsa, and Arikara peoples of the upper Missouri River, who occupied a central place in the commercial, diplomatic, and geographic designs of Jefferson and the two captains, the past two centuries have been an epic struggle to regain the strength and autonomy they possessed at the time of their encounter with Lewis and Clark. Together, these two essays force us to broaden the contexts in which we understand the expedition and remind us of its direct and lasting significance on subsequent generations. The third essay extends our understanding of the significance of the expedition in terms that are too easily forgotten. To the degree that Lewis and Clark set out on a "literary enterprise," scholars have largely regarded their efforts as a failure—yet the expedition had an immediate and lasting effect within learned circles.

Chapter 4

The Louisiana Purchase and the Lewis & Clark Expedition

A Constitutional Moment?

Peter A. Appel

"Scarcely any political question arises in the United States," noted Alexis de Tocqueville, "that is not resolved, sooner or later, into a judicial question."[1] If Tocqueville is correct, then the Lewis and Clark expedition—in some ways, the culmination of the Louisiana Purchase—ought to be a constant reference in the case law of American courts. Instead, the legal researcher combing through Westlaw or Lexis unearths such mundane and irrelevant matters as cases involving Lewis and Clark College in Portland, Oregon, Lewis and Clark County, Montana, a recent decision of the Supreme Court entitled *Lewis v. Lewis and Clark Marine, Inc.*, and a series of cases involving a boat captain named Lewis N. Clark.[2] Even the important cases, involving Indian tribes that had their first contact with the government of the fledgling United States through the expedition, treat the expedition more in passing reference.[3] The case most directly involving the expedition itself concerns a dispute over the fate of Clark's diary.[4] These cases surely are not the resolution of great political matters by the judiciary.

This lack of attention in the reported decisions is unusual, given the sweeping claims made for the impact of the Louisiana Purchase on the legal system. For Henry Adams, the Louisiana Purchase was the absolute beginning of nineteenth-century politics; it was "in historical importance next to the Declaration of Independence and the adoption of the Constitution—events of which it was the logical outcome."[5] Everett Sommerville Brown concluded in 1917 that the purchase "serves as the corner stone for all interpretations of the constitutional right of the United States to acquire and govern foreign territory; and such acquisitions have been one of the most significant features in the history of the United States."[6] Frederick Jackson Turner agreed with Adams and argued that "[w]hen the whole sweep of American history and the present tendencies of our life are taken

87

into view, it would be possible to argue that the doctrines of the Louisiana Purchase were farther-reaching in their effect upon the Constitution than even the measures of Alexander Hamilton or the decisions of John Marshall."[7] The great constitutional thinker and judge Thomas Cooley argued that, after the Louisiana Purchase, congressional debate over whether the federal government had limited powers or not died down.[8] More recently, Merrill Peterson wrote that the ratification of the treaty with France worked "a revolution in the Constitution. A momentous act of Jeffersonian statesmanship unhinged the Jeffersonian dogmas and opened, so far a precedent might control, the boundless field of power so much feared."[9] (Not all writers are quite so gushing in describing the constitutional effects of the Louisiana Purchase. For example, one modern critic allows that the Louisiana Purchase "is a good example of early constitutional change," but only as "constitutional change on a relatively small scale.")[10]

But scholarly and historical claims about the constitutional importance of Jefferson's purchase are lacking in three important areas. First, for the most part they do not identify exactly how the Constitution changed as a result of the Louisiana Purchase. To be sure, the reach of the federal government expanded after the Louisiana Purchase, but to what did that reach extend? Did the federal government now possess power over local (sometimes called municipal) issues, or did its expanded power still have well-defined limits? Second, to the extent that writers like Brown do identify how the federal government's power expanded as a result of the Louisiana Purchase, few of these historians attempt to spell out the precise effect that the Louisiana Purchase had on the inner workings of the federal government. Was the expanded power equally divided among the three branches? Or was it largely vested in one or two? Third, and finally, the past argument concerning the Louisiana Purchase ignores the signal event that made the purchase truly part of the United States, namely the Lewis and Clark expedition. The instructions that the explorers received on setting out and the public adulation that they received on their return complete the story of the constitutional effects of the Louisiana Purchase. The instructions directed the explorers not only to go beyond the physical boundaries of the United States but also to investigate matters beyond the powers of the federal government.

One solution to these inquiries, and one that allows us to sidestep the purely judicial question, may reside in the work of the constitutional scholar Bruce Ackerman. Ackerman theorizes that the Constitution can change fundamentally through two means. The first way is obvious to anyone who has had high school civics, namely the formal means of amendment contained in article 5 of the Constitution, where two-thirds of each house of Congress proposes an amendment and three-fourths of the states ratify that change. The other means of achieving change in the fundamental law is through what Ackerman has named a "constitutional moment."[11] Ackerman's concept of the "constitutional moment" looks for a pattern of interchange between the People and their government, and among the different branches of government, to arrive at an altered understanding of the constitutional structure that courts eventually invest with the force of law.[12] These states of interchange include signaling, where the People make their representatives aware of the need for constitutional change; proposing, in which the desired change takes concrete form; mobilized deliberating, where the citizenry debates proposals that embody transformative change; and finally codifying by the courts, in reformed legal doctrine.[13]

Some scholars have criticized Ackerman's theory about the development of constitutional law, arguing that its flexibility makes it verge on the tautological. Any historical event that has the qualities Ackerman defines is a constitutional moment; a historical event that appears to have these qualities but does not result in change—or does not result in change that Ackerman would approve of—is a failed constitutional moment.[14] Others urge that, as a normative matter, courts should not take it upon themselves to figure out when they are in the midst of a constitutional moment and can start reshaping and codifying new constitutional principles. Rather, argues this school, courts should rely on more traditional sources of legal authority such as text, original intent, constitutional structure, and precedent.[15]

Regardless of the merits of Ackerman's general theory, his concept of a constitutional moment, at least in a looser form than Ackerman might allow, aptly conjures up a phenomenon in constitutional law, namely the establishment of precedent through means other than a change in the text of the constitution, or even a decision of a court embracing a particular interpretation of the preexisting text. The Supreme Court has recognized that a consistent pattern of accommodation between the legislative and executive branches can eventually develop into constitutional doctrine that the courts will apply in future cases.[16] This essay uses this expanded notion of a constitutional moment to explain how the Louisiana Purchase and the subsequent Lewis and Clark expedition affected American governance under the Constitution. These two intertwined events altered received understandings about the powers of the federal government generally and the power of the executive branch within that government, especially over the acquisition and management of public lands. One can then trace the effects of these changes through decisions of the courts concerning public lands. Although these decisions might not make up the great political cases of all time, they nevertheless shaped the governance and physical appearance of the nation.

To approach this subject, I first address a basic question: why did Jefferson and his allies in Congress believe that the Louisiana Purchase was constitutionally suspect? An answer to this question requires a background in the history of the United States government's acquiring and governing land in the West. I then turn to the debates over the Louisiana Purchase and the outcome of that debate from a constitutional perspective, meaning the immediate effects of the purchase as a precedent. Then, after looking at how the Lewis and Clark expedition cemented that understanding, I identify traces of these two intertwined events in modern jurisprudence concerning federally owned lands. The basic constitutional principles arising out of the Louisiana Purchase and the Lewis and Clark expedition still exist, if one looks for them carefully.

The general question of expansion of the United States beyond the Mississippi River did not occupy much of the attention of the founders at the constitutional convention. This oversight did not necessarily come from a lack of interest in the West or of expansionist intent. Indeed, the topic of actually acquiring lands beyond the Mississippi occupied the thoughts of some of the founders. But the new nation faced larger hurdles to overcome before tackling westward expansion beyond the Mississippi. For example, the free navigation of the Mississippi greatly interested the South and the West, and the efforts by John Jay to negotiate with the Spanish to limit free navigation of the river by Americans greatly distressed these interests. The controversy over free navigation of the Mississippi—which, in turn, led to the Louisiana Purchase—almost led to a split in the fragile union.[17] Disputes over land claims make up a surprising number of the debates over the Constitution in the late eighteenth and early nineteenth century.

Perhaps the constitutional convention did not bother itself with the lands west of the Mississippi because the convention had to grapple with the far more immediate question about the western land claims. Seven of the states (Connecticut, Georgia, Massachusetts, New York, Virginia, and the Carolinas) claimed grants of land that extended far beyond their present boundaries, with some states pointing to crown charters granting them lands as far as the South Sea. The states without such claims (Delaware, Maryland, New Hampshire, New Jersey, Pennsylvania, and Rhode Island and Providence Plantations) were understandably envious of their better-endowed neighbors. The controversy over the western lands formed one of the most fractious issues facing the country during the Revolutionary War through the period of the Articles of Confederation. The dispute loomed so large that for two years Maryland refused to adopt the Articles of Confederation.

The nonlanded states objected to the landed states' claims for a number of reasons, ranging from principles to politics to greed. As a matter of principle, the nonlanded states argued that all of the states had fought to liberate these lands from the British, and all should therefore benefit from their disposition by the nation as a whole. States without western land claims saw the western lands as their just, shared reward for services rendered in the revolution. After all, observed New Jersey in its consideration of the proposed articles of confederation, "It was ever the confident expectation of this State, that the benefits derived from a successful contest, were to be general and proportionate; and that the property of the common enemy, falling in consequence of a prosperous issue of the war, would belong to the United States, and be appropriated to their use."[18] Although New Jersey believed that the state ceding the territory should retain political jurisdiction over it, all of the states "have fought and bled for" the western territory "in proportion to their respective abilities, and therefore the reward ought not to be predilectionally distributed."[19] Rhode Island similarly proposed that the United States should receive ownership of the western lands with the landed states retaining political jurisdiction over them.[20]

Maryland's objections to the Articles of Confederation went beyond those of New Jersey and Rhode Island, because Maryland urged that the states with western land claims should cede both the ownership of and political jurisdiction over these lands. In Maryland's view, the western lands, "if wrested from the common enemy by the blood and treasure of the thirteen states, should be considered as a common property, subject to be parcelled out by Congress into free, convenient and independent governments, in such manner and at such times as the wisdom of that assembly shall hereafter direct."[21] Maryland predicted that if states like Virginia retained their western lands, they could easily pay off their share of the collective war debt through land sales, and, because landless states like Maryland would have only the option of raising ruinous taxes to satisfy their war debts, overtaxed Marylanders would emigrate to Virginia, thus depopulating Maryland. In addition to its stand based on principle and politics, Maryland had another motive in demanding that Virginia and the other states cede their western lands: prominent Marylanders had invested in land speculation companies that had made claims in Virginia's western territory, and resolution of the conflicting claims in Congress held out the best hope for these speculators to succeed in their investments. Virginia and New York eventually ceded their lands to the United States, and Maryland signed on to the Articles of Confederation (although pressure from the French government may have forced Maryland's hand).[22]

As adopted, the Articles of Confederation did not expressly grant the United States power to acquire or manage any land, or to admit any new colonies to the confederation without the concurrence of nine states (although Canada could join if it agreed to the Articles of Confederation). The articles were therefore poorly adapted for the national government to do the work cut out for it. Virginia and New York had already ceded their land claims and the other states were expected to by the time that Maryland acceded to them. The general view held by Maryland that United States should own the ceded lands as a common fund and exercise political jurisdiction over them won the day. Despite the lack of express authority in the articles, Congress enacted three important statutes to govern the western lands before the constitutional convention, one of which was the Northwest Ordinance of 1787. That ordinance framed a system for the establishment of territorial governments and, among other provisions, banned slavery in the Northwest Territory. In urging subsequent adoption of the Constitution, Madison would later point to these acts as a sign of the weakness of the Articles of Confederation. Congress enacted all of this legislation, Madison complained, "without the least color of constitutional authority."[23]

The constitutional convention of 1787 met to address the general lack of power in the federal government, including an express lack of power over the western lands. At each turn in the proceedings, the constitutional convention broadened federal authority over these lands and did not foreclose the possibility that the United States might acquire territory beyond the Mississippi. For example, the initial drafts concerning the authority of the federal government over the territories and other property of the United States vested in the federal government only the power to "dispose of the unappropriated lands of the United States."[24] But the Constitution, as adopted, vests in Congress the significantly greater power "to dispose of *and make needful Rules and Regulations respecting* the Territory and other Property belonging to the United States."[25] Similarly, the original drafts concerning the authority of Congress to admit new states concerned only those "lawfully arising within the limits of the United States" and expected that Congress would form these new states either by joining two existing states or carving a new state out of an existing state.[26] The convention considered a motion that would vest Congress with the power "to erect new States within as well as without the territory claimed by the several States,"[27] but it passed over this proposal to adopt language much like the present language concerning the admission of new states, which is silent as to whether these new states must be within the boundaries that the United States then claimed.[28]

Thus, the constitutional convention worded the grants of authority to Congress over the territories and new states broadly when it confronted the issues of territorial governance, regulation of federal property, and the admission of new states. In addition to these direct grants of authority to Congress, the Constitution also granted power to the federal government to acquire territory, at least by implication. In article I, the Constitution vested in Congress the power to declare war.[29] Second, article II of the Constitution vested in the president the power to make treaties with the advice and consent of two-thirds of the senate, and article VI made the Constitution and treaties made under its authority "the supreme Law of the Land."[30] The common understanding at the time of the ratification of the Constitution was that the United States, as a corporate whole, constituted the nation-state for purposes of international law, and that the individual states (such as New York and Georgia) ceded their role as potential nation-states to the United States. Settled principles of international law at the time recognized that nation-states could transfer territories in several ways, including conquest (war) and voluntary cession (treaty).

Stopping the story here could give support to the argument that a constitutional moment had occurred. The Constitution, unlike the Articles, granted Congress express authority to manage the territories and other property of the United States. This authority, wrote Madison, was of paramount importance because Congress needed it, and, if it did not have it, it would grab it, just as Congress did when it enacted the Northwest Ordinance "without the least color of constitutional authority." Not that Madison disagreed with the content of the Northwest Ordinance, but he objected to the process. Forcing the legislature to act when it lacked express authority to do so—vesting in the United States the western land claims but not granting it the power to legislate for them—led inevitably to "dissolution or usurpation."[31] Ackerman has argued that the adoption of the Constitution in 1787 was the first of three important constitutional moments.[32] If he is correct, then this first constitutional moment also happened to involve the ownership and management of the territories and other property of the United States. The Constitution established Maryland's objection to the articles as the principle that would continue to govern the territories and federal lands: these lands were to serve as a common fund to be used by the United States for the good of all the states. This reading, while plausible, would be simplistic because one of the first large constitutional questions that faced the new nation was the acquisition and governance of more territory.

With the determination that the United States would dispose of the western lands and govern it while these new lands developed into political units worthy of statehood, thoughts could turn to the possibility of American dominion over more of the continent. In the earliest discussions of the powers of the federal government, the question of its authority to acquire lands outside of the boundaries of the original states arose in somewhat strange circumstances, namely the creation of the first Bank of the United States. When George Washington considered the first bill to incorporate the Bank of the United States in 1791, he solicited opinions from many members of his cabinet, notably Alexander Hamilton and Thomas Jefferson. Hamilton—Washington's secretary of the treasury and a staunch supporter of a strong national government—submitted his opinion that the federal government had the authority to charter a corporation to further national ends. There, Hamilton expressly considered the possibility that the United States would acquire territory through war and concluded that "if the United States should make a conquest of any of the territories of its neighbors, they would possess sovereign jurisdiction over the conquered territory. This would rather be a result from the whole mass of the powers of the Government, and from the nature of political society, than a consequence of either of the powers specially enumerated."[33]

Before Hamilton wrote his opinion, Jefferson—Washington's secretary of state and an advocate of limited government—weighed in on the bank and objected to the expansion of federal powers that such an institution would represent. He did not, as Hamilton did, raise the question of acquiring new territory outside United States boundaries as a test of his doctrine; he simply urged that the proposed bank exceeded the powers granted to Congress in the Constitution. "To take a single step beyond the boundaries thus specially drawn around the powers of Congress," warned Jefferson, "is to take possession of a boundless field of power, no longer susceptible of any definition."[34] How this view would play out when Jefferson confronted the actual possibility of acquiring more territory for the United States as president lay several years in the future.

Unlike the plan to acquire the western lands from the states as a common fund, any plans that the United States had toward westward expansion obviously and necessarily involved the claims of other countries, particularly France and Spain. The Louisiana Territory had belonged to the French at the time of the French and Indian War, and France had ceded its interest in it to Spain in the 1762 Treaty of Paris. After the end of the Revolutionary War and the ratification of the Constitution, France reacquired its interest in the Louisiana Territory through the October 1800 Treaty of Ildefonso. This switch in ownership complicated matters for American politics both externally and internally. Externally, the renewed presence of France in Louisiana made things difficult for the expansion of the United States. Although Spain was an easy foe, Bonaparte's France was a major world power. In a war against France, the United States might very well lose. This provided a reason for the United States to acquire territory at the mouth of the Mississippi.

The internal dispute involving free navigation of the Mississippi reached a head as Spain closed the duty-free cargo deposit that American ships used in New Orleans, a move that arguably violated an earlier treaty that the United States had negotiated with Spain. Whether Spain took this step as a deliberate move to combat American smuggling or whether, as the Jefferson administration portrayed it, the closure of the cargo deposit was simply the unauthorized action of a Spanish local official is immaterial.[35] Whatever its origin—and modern historians believe that Madrid took this action deliberately—the loss of this important transshipment point raised hackles in the South and West and thus created a potential crisis for the administration. Robert Livingston, the representative of the United States in France at the time, did not inspire much confidence in the Jefferson administration. Livingston had been in France for almost a year before Spain closed New Orleans to American goods and had made no progress on acquiring two essential areas, namely New Orleans and a portion of the Floridas. Members of Congress from the West and South were up in arms about losing their transshipment point in 1802, and members of the Federalist Party used the disruption to try to persuade citizens of these states to form a new allegiance with the Federalists. These forces also called for the United States to take steps toward war if negotiations with France did not succeed. Senator James Ross of Pennsylvania was particularly hawkish toward France and Spain. "Why not expel the wrongdoers?" he asked. "Plant yourselves on the river, fortify the banks, invite those who have an interest at stake to defend it; do justice to yourselves when your adversaries deny it; and leave the event to Him who controls the fate of nations."[36] To placate the southerners and westerners, Jefferson appointed James Monroe—a Virginian with investments in the West—as minister extraordinary and plenipotentiary to France to negotiate acquisition of New Orleans and the Floridas. By the time he arrived in Paris, Napoleon had already decided to sell Louisiana to the United States. Napoleon concluded that France could not defend Louisiana from invasion, based in part upon a failed attempt to repress a slave revolt at Saint-Domingue in the Caribbean. The saber-rattling of some members of Congress may well have solidified his impression of an American threat.[37]

At the time that Monroe and Livingston concluded the treaty with France that sold France's interest in Louisiana to the United States for $12 million, the constitutional law on this subject was not entirely clear to some advocates at the time. Hamilton had advocated territorial expansion, but in a different setting. In other words, the purchase of Louisiana might be unconstitutional. National politics also confused the constitutional issue. The Federalists, seeking to embarrass Jefferson in the West and South, had called for the United States to acquire a small part of Louisiana by force. Now the United States had acquired all of Louisiana through treaty. Would Jefferson's opponents reverse their usual doctrinal position and become strict constructionists to oppose this acquisition? In the meantime, Jefferson's envoys had acquired much more from Bonaparte than Jefferson had sent them for, and Jefferson had argued against such broad increases in federal power such as the bank (although his opinion on the bank might not have been widely known at the time).[38] If creating the bank was too broad a use of federal power, surely buying Louisiana was too. Would Jefferson's desire to acquire this territory and to send an expedition through it overcome his strict constructionist principles? Was a constitutional moment about to occur?

Jefferson received news of the Louisiana Purchase on 3 July 1803, and the newspapers for the most part loudly proclaimed it as a victory. Some Federalist newspapers raised questions about the extent of the purchase, but for the most part, even they were supportive (although they argued that the Jefferson administration deserved no credit for the purchase). The Republican newspapers were unstinting in their praise, hailing the coincidental date of the news as the greatest news since the Declaration of Independence itself.[39]

The treaty called for ratification by 30 October 1803. Thus, Jefferson had to reconvene Congress to ratify the treaty and to appropriate the money necessary to implement it. Over the course of that summer and fall, then, Jefferson had ample time to think about the constitutionality of the purchase. The contemporary written record in Jefferson's letters suggests that Jefferson believed the Louisiana Purchase dubious at the very least and quite possibly unconstitutional. Two issues arose from the purchase, the question of acquisition (buying the land) and the question of incorporation (making it part of the United States). Jefferson apparently believed that acquisition of territory might pass strict constitutional muster, but incorporation of that territory into the United States presented a different problem. As he wrote to his secretary of the treasury, Albert Gallatin, in January 1803, "there is no constitutional difficulty as to the acquisition of territory, and whether, when acquired, it may be taken into the Union by the Constitution as it now stands, will become a question of expediency." But Jefferson thought that relying on principles of expediency could prove dangerous, and thus he thought it would be "safer not to permit the enlargement of the Union but by amendment of the Constitution."[40] After receiving news of the treaty, Jefferson set to work in the summer of 1803 drafting two different possible constitutional amendments that would empower the United States to acquire and incorporate Louisiana. Both recognized the acquisition of Louisiana after the fact and limited the ability of the United States to admit new states from a zone north of the 31st parallel. The second laid out more explicitly the rights and duties of the citizens to be admitted to the United States.[41]

Jefferson's letters after he learned of the treaty also reveal his constitutional qualms about acquiring and incorporating Louisiana. In a letter to John Dickinson, Jefferson wrote, "The general government has no powers but such as the constitution has given it; and it has not given it a power of holding foreign territory, & still less of incorporating it into the Union."[42] An exchange of letters between Jefferson and Virginia Senator Wilson Cary Nicholas also shows Jefferson's belief that strict construction of the Constitution should prevail over expediency. Nicholas urged Jefferson not to make any opinion of his on the unconstitutionality of the treaty known, for it would either scuttle the treaty or scuttle the party. "I shou'd think it very probable," wrote Nicholas, "if the treaty shou'd be by you declared to exceed the constitutional authority of the treaty making power, that it would be rejected by the Senate, and if that should not happen, that great use wou'd be made with the people, of a wilful breach of the constitution."[43] In response to Nicholas, Jefferson wrote a classic defense of strict construction of the Constitution.

> When an instrument admits two constructions, the one safe, the other dangerous, the one precise, the other indefinite, I prefer that which is safe and precise. I had rather ask an enlargement of power from the nation, when it is found necessary, than to assume by a construction which would make our powers boundless. Our peculiar security is in the possession of a written Constitution. Let us not make it a blank paper by construction.[44]

These words, read alone, would make any strict constructionist proud.

In the end, however, the depth of Jefferson's constitutional objections to the Louisiana Purchase remains uncertain. Some of Jefferson's letters show his wavering. In his letter to John Dickinson, Jefferson stated his belief that a constitutional amendment was necessary. "In the meantime," Jefferson conceded, "we must ratify & pay our money, as we have treated, for a thing beyond the constitution, and rely on the nation to sanction an act done for its great good, without its previous authority."[45] In his letter to Nicholas urging that the Constitution should not be made "blank paper by construction," Jefferson yielded to expediency. "If, however, our friends shall think differently, certainly I shall acquiesce with satisfaction; confiding, that the good sense of our country will correct the evil of construction when it shall produce ill effects."[46] Jefferson also believed that Congress should do whatever it judged best, "with as little debate as possible, and particularly so far as respects the constitutional difficulty."[47] Similarly, Jefferson had earlier written to Senator John Breckenridge of Kentucky that although the "Constitution has made no provision for our holding foreign territory, still less for incorporating foreign nations into our Union," nevertheless the overall good of the country justified the purchase.

> It is the case of a guardian, investing the money of his ward in purchasing an adjacent territory; and saying to him when of age, I did this for your good; I pretend to no right to bind you: you may disavow me, and I must get out of the scrape as I can: I thought it my duty to risk myself for you. But we shall not be disavowed by the nation, and their act of indemnity will confirm and not weaken the Constitution, by more strongly marking out its lines.[48]

Ackerman's theory of constitutional change echoes this notion: Jefferson advocated that the representatives of the People take a stand that incorporates what lies beyond the accepted bounds of the Constitution, and present it to the People for their ratification.

Furthermore, many of Jefferson's actions stand in stark contrast to his written statements expressing concern and doubt over the constitutionality of the purchase. After all, Jefferson instructed Livingston to gain some French territory to bolster American shipping interests on the Mississippi, and he sent Monroe to France to help in this task. What must have surprised Jefferson about Bonaparte's eventual offer was not the thought of the United States annexing land so much as the amount of land that the French ceded to the United States. Although he set about drafting possible constitutional amendments to add Louisiana to the United States, Jefferson never submitted them to Congress. In fact, Jefferson called Congress to convene and deliberate over ratifying the treaty with France on 17 October 1803, when ratification had to occur by 30 October 1803, leaving just less than two weeks for the Senate to ratify the treaty and for both houses to enact a constitutional amendment (should they determine one was necessary). Of course, in the days before fax machines and New York to Washington shuttles, communication and travel time between the far-flung states and the capital limited the amount of time that Jefferson could convene Congress. Nevertheless, Jefferson used the time before Congress convened not to prepare an amendment so much as to shore up support for the purchase among his political allies and to quell interest in the constitutional questions it raised.

Moreover, and in some ways more significantly, Jefferson organized the Lewis and Clark expedition before the United States had even acquired the Louisiana Territory from France, and the reasons he gave to justify the expedition changed for each audience. To the Spanish authorities who still claimed the territory, Jefferson said that the planned expedition was scientific and literary in nature. These reasons may have placated those authorities, but strictly read the Constitution does not vest any authority to promote science or literature in the federal government with the narrow exception of the clause that empowers Congress to create copyrights and patents.[49] In his secret message to Congress of 18 January 1803—still months before the United States had actually acquired the land that Lewis and Clark would explore—Jefferson stressed that the expedition would serve to further commerce through navigation of rivers and promotion of the fur trade. "The interests of commerce place the principal object within the Constitutional powers and care of Congress," argued Jefferson, "and that it should incidentally advance the geographic knowledge of our continent, cannot but be an additional gratification."[50] Again, even with this happy coincidence, strictly read, the Constitution does not empower Congress to promote interstate and foreign commerce but only to "regulate" it. Even so, Dumas Malone recognized that Jefferson may have made this shift in emphasis because "he doubted the constitutional authority of that body [Congress] to make an appropriation for a 'literary expedition.'"[51]

Finally, in his instructions to Lewis, issued after the United States had actually acquired some of the territory to be explored, Jefferson emphasized three missions. The first two—exploring the Missouri to discover whether it provided a transcontinental route for commerce and exploring the potential for commerce with the Indian tribes Lewis and Clark met along the way—arguably were linked to powers granted to the federal government in the Constitution, namely the power to regulate commerce with foreign nations and with Indian tribes. The third purpose of the expedition—collecting data on the soil, vegetation, and animals discovered "especially those not of the U.S."[52]—had no direct connection with any express power of the federal government. Arguably, exploring the land that the United States bought from France would be an exercise of the government's power to manage its property. But Jefferson's mission expressly directed the Corps of Discovery to exceed even the bounds of the United States with the Louisiana Purchase. Exploring the territory of another country for its soil, vegetation, and animals has no obvious connection to an express power of the federal government. Indeed, this instruction is mystifying until one recalls Jefferson's wide-ranging interests in science and nature. Jefferson wanted to know about latitudes and longitudes of rivers, the nature of soil, vegetation, and animals, the types of Indians found in the territory, and all of this information unrelated to the regulation of commerce because he wanted to *know* the country. Jefferson was, after all, the author of the *Notes on the State of Virginia,* in which he cataloged the different flora and fauna of his state. That analysis of Virginia can be seen as a template for the later survey he envisioned of the western lands. If there was a mastodon living in the West, Jefferson wanted to know everything about it, and not just how it could be used in the regulation of commerce.[53]

In sum, although Jefferson advocated strict construction and although the politics of the day may have driven Jefferson to stake out an even stricter constitutional view than he might otherwise—after all, Hamilton could not have been right about the bank—Jefferson's keen scientific and literary interests pulled him in the opposite direction. If actions speak louder than words, Jefferson's actions shout down his protests about the constitutionality of the Louisiana Purchase.[54]

In the context of modern constitutional law, Jefferson's quandary is hard to understand. Jefferson and the advocates of the Louisiana Purchase had all of the tools at their disposal that a modern constitutional lawyer would find necessary to justify the Louisiana Purchase, namely the text of the Constitution and the record of the debates at the constitutional convention. First, the Constitution vested in the national government the power to declare war and the power to conclude treaties. Jefferson himself recognized this power. Although one could argue that the disposal of new territory is domestic and would therefore fall within the power of individual states under this theory, the acquisition of territory from another nation is clearly something that common practice would place in the realm of the nation. Indeed, Jefferson's attorney general, Levi Lincoln, suggested to Jefferson a plan along those lines to obviate any constitutional concern, namely that the land obtained through the Louisiana Purchase would be attached to existing states, thereby preventing the need of a constitutional amendment to incorporate the territory into the United States. But Albert Gallatin, Jefferson's secretary of the treasury, argued that such a tortured process was unnecessary. Thus, even at the time, many recognized the constitutionality of the purchase based on the text of the Constitution and the structure of government.

Second, the record of the debates at the constitutional convention showed that the founders expected the United States to have extensive power over its property, and that it had to have the authority to acquire more. After all, Georgia and North Carolina did not cede their western lands until after the ratification of the Constitution. Because the participants to the constitutional convention all expected these cessions eventually, the federal government must have had the authority to acquire and incorporate new territory. To be fair to the strict constructionists of Jefferson's day, though, this expectation may not have uniformly extended to territory outside the agreed boundaries of the United States. Moreover, Gouveneur Morris, who drafted the language in the Constitution granting Congress the power over the territories, later wrote that he believed it did not allow Congress to admit new territory as potential states but only as provinces with "no voice in our councils."[55] Placed in context, it is clear that Morris did not believe that his views represented those of the convention as a whole.

Nevertheless, the constitutional lawyer of today would likely dismiss Morris's sentiments because they were not contemporaneous with the drafting of the Constitution. But these are the arguments of today's constitutional lawyer. Even if they were persuasive to the party of broad construction, times had changed, and now the Republicans, who had won their ascendancy in part on the principle of strict construction, controlled Congress. The historian dismisses Morris's argument because it so clearly had its basis in the politics of the moment. When Morris lodged his objection to the incorporation of Louisiana into the United States, Congress debated the steps of the Louisiana Purchase, a debate marked by how times had changed. The expansionist party advocated express constitutional authority and against Jefferson's treaty with France, and the party associated with strict construction advocated, of all things, expedience.

The debate in the Senate over ratification of the treaty itself went quickly, and with few hitches. When the act to carry the treaty into effect and to appropriate the money to pay France hit the House, the Federalists immediately brought up the constitutional question, asking where in the Constitution the president and Senate obtained the authority to expand the boundaries of the United States through the treaty-making power. As Jefferson's allies pointed out, however, this argument came from the same people who had advocated going to war to seize territory from the French. Similar issues came up at each step, led by the Federalists. In the end, most of the measures required to acquire Louisiana, incorporate it into the United States, and establish a provisional government for it, passed by party-line votes.[56]

Lewis and Clark set out on their journey and returned to a great reception. "Never did a similar event excite more joy through the United States," Jefferson later wrote. "The humblest of its citizens had taken a lively interest in the issue of this journey, and looked forward with impatience for the information it would furnish."[57] Congress ratified the expedition by awarding the soldiers double pay and homestead allowances from public lands.

If one looked for the close of a constitutional moment, this ratification of the expedition after loud acclaim by the people might serve as the final step of Ackerman's process. For most recitations of the constitutional history and impact of the Louisiana Purchase, the story ends there, or even a little sooner. Jefferson and his Republican allies swallowed their principles, accepted the expansion of the United States through the vast Louisiana Purchase for the sake of expediency, and thereby established precedent for future expansion. To the eyes of a constitutional scholar, however, this telling of the story is incomplete. The Louisiana Purchase and the subsequent Lewis and Clark expedition were certainly momentous. That does not mean, however, that they necessarily completed a "constitutional moment." The subsequent treatment of the Louisiana Purchase and the Lewis and Clark expedition by the People and the courts—the signaling and codifying steps of events that become a constitutional moment—lay in the future. Moreover, the steps would take two different directions, one for the extent of federal powers over the territories, and one for the way the government would exercise that power and through what agency.

The first question raised by the Louisiana Purchase was the extent of congressional authority over the territory that the United States acquired from France. It would seem at first that this power was vast and unlimited, for the Constitution vests in Congress the "Power to dispose of and make all needful Rules and Regulations respecting the Territory or other Property belonging to the United States." A crude use of Ackerman's theory might describe the Louisiana Purchase as a constitutional moment in this sense: before the Louisiana Purchase, the Constitution was seen by many in Congress as depriving the federal government of needed authority to acquire and manage new territory outside of the bounds of the original states and their chartered limits. With the restrictions that Spain placed on the Mississippi at New Orleans, Ackerman's People rose up and demanded action from their government. Their government responded and went beyond the strict needs of the People, rewarding them not only with new lands, but with a scientific and heroic exploration. The Supreme Court subsequently codified this new expansive view of the power of the federal government through decisions that found the power of the federal government over the territories to be almost without limit. Thus, within a generation after the Louisiana Purchase, the Supreme Court codified the principles behind the Louisiana Purchase in several cases that stand for the rule that the federal government has broad power over the territories.[58]

This telling of the story would be only half right. The key dispute of the country before the Civil War was slavery, and at the federal level the fight over slavery often took the form of disputes over how Congress would or could legislate for the territories. Here, the story returns to the Lewis and Clark expedition and specifically to the actions of William Clark. After the expedition, Lewis was appointed governor of the Louisiana Territory, but his tenure ended with his early (and mysterious) death. Clark lived much longer. He was appointed to deal with the Indians in the area and was eventually appointed to be the territorial governor of what would become the state of Missouri. And, unlike any other member of the expedition, Clark brought along with him a slave, a man named York. York had been a slave of Clark's family, and the evidence suggests that York was roughly Clark's age and was a companion from Clark's youth. The only thing that may have separated Clark and York was York's race and thus legal status.[59] Despite his legal status within the United States, York contributed to the expedition in many ways. The *Journals* report many surprising stories about York, which indicate that he was considered a full member of the expedition. For example, York is reported shooting animals, even though slaves could not legally carry firearms. He voted in the deliberations of the expedition, thus becoming perhaps the first African American to have a legal voice in government. The most noteworthy aspect of York's race, it appeared, was the fascination he held for the Native Americans that the expedition encountered. These tribes had never seen a black person before, and York apparently played it to the hilt.[60] One could even argue that York's racial difference made the difference between success and failure for the expedition, because the Shoshone Indians from whom the expedition needed horses were willing to keep stalling Lewis until Clark showed up with York.[61]

Yet, unlike any other member of the expedition, York did not receive double pay—indeed, he did not and could not receive any pay, because he was a slave. Instead, York asked for his freedom from Clark. Clark was, to say the least, not forthcoming with the request. Instead, he hired York out as a wage-earning slave. We think of slavery as the most objectionable position a person could be in, yet being a wage-earning slave was one of the lowest positions that a slave could find himself or herself—in some ways, the lowest of the low. York toiled for a few years in this capacity and died in Tennessee, unable to enjoy the freedom that Clark bestowed upon him eventually.[62]

The federal government should have granted York land in the West. Instead, York's reward for his toil lay in Clark. Unfortunately, Clark's refusal to grant York his freedom and the sad story it tells embodies the larger price that the United States would pay for the Louisiana Purchase. In the Northwest Ordinance, the first effort that the federal government made for managing territory wholesale—and one, incidentally, drafted by Jefferson, himself a slave owner—the United States banned slavery. By contrast, the United States dithered over the status of slavery in the newly acquired Louisiana Purchase. The most noteworthy act that Congress took about slavery in the period following acquisition was the Missouri Compromise, in which Congress admitted Missouri to the union as a state that had slaves but banned slavery in the rest of the Louisiana Purchase. Slavery flourished in Missouri, and apparently St. Louis, where Clark had taken York, was a particularly inhospitable place for slaves. "Though slavery is thought, by some, to be mild in Missouri, when compared with the cotton, sugar and rice growing states," wrote William Wells Brown in a slave narrative, "yet no part of our slaveholding country is more noted for the barbarity of its inhabitants than St. Louis."[63]

Over the course of the 1840s and 1850s the question of Congress's power over the territories festered. It took several forms. For example, in 1846, Congress debated and ultimately rejected the Wilmot Proviso, which would have banned slavery in any territory acquired from Mexico in the Mexican-American War. Although the proviso failed, the fight spilled out into other arenas, such as the organization of the territorial governments for Kansas and Nebraska, which led in turn to civil war breaking out in Kansas.

During this period, opinion about congressional power over the territories divided into roughly four schools of thought. Some, like John Calhoun of South Carolina, argued that Congress could not constitutionally ban slavery in the territories, but instead that Congress was obligated to protect slave owners in their property. Others, like Stephen Douglas of Illinois, argued for popular sovereignty in the territories, namely that Congress could not ban slavery but territorial governments could. A third school argued for the practical determination that Congress should simply extend the line of the Missouri Compromise across the country or make individual decisions for individual territories. Obviously, this school appealed to practical compromise, not constitutional principle. Finally, some argued that Congress could ban slavery in the territories if it wished, and that it should. The Republican Party platform for 1856 embodied this view and declared, "the Constitution confers upon Congress sovereign power over the Territories of the United States for their government; and that in the exercise of this power, it is both the right and the imperative duty of Congress to prohibit in the Territories those twin relics of barbarism—Polygamy, and Slavery."[64] The first and last schools based their claims most expressly on the Constitution, the second and third on compromise.

This political question became, as Tocqueville would have predicted, a judicial one. And, just as inevitably, a question about territory became a question about slavery. The Supreme Court answered the question in its deservedly infamous *Dred Scott* decision. The facts of the case fit a common fact pattern then but seem bizarre and arcane now. The basic question was what events would render a slave free. Courts had struggled with this question against a variety of fact patterns, such as where the slave escaped into free territory, where the master had taken the slave voluntarily into free territory for a short period but returned to slave territory, or where the master had lent the slave to another who took the slave into free territory. In Dred Scott's case, Scott claimed to be free because John Emerson, one of Scott's previous masters and an officer in the United States Army, had taken Scott from Missouri (a slave state) to what was the territory of the United States and is now Minnesota (free soil by virtue of the Missouri Compromise), and also to Illinois (a free state). Scott argued that his presence on free soil freed him. Scott originally sued the wife of his master in the Missouri courts, where the court decided against him. The Missouri Supreme Court had case law that supported Scott's claim, but it could have distinguished that body of precedent on the ground that Emerson never established residency in free territory since the army had ordered him to move each time. Instead the Missouri Supreme Court overruled its own prior authority and held that Scott was still a slave.[65]

Undaunted by this loss, Scott sued John Sanford (whose name is misspelled in the official reports as "Sandford"), who was Mrs. Emerson's brother, and either had acquired the Scotts or acted as the executor of Dr. Emerson's estate.[66] Sanford was a citizen of New York, so Scott sued in federal court asserting that the court had jurisdiction because of the diverse citizenship of the parties. Thus to determine whether it had jurisdiction, the federal court had to decide whether Scott, a putative slave, was a "citizen" of Missouri in the way that Sanford was a citizen of New York. Scott lost in the trial court, and the case wound its way to the Supreme Court.

The opinions of the Supreme Court run over two hundred pages, and, because each justice wrote separately, it is difficult to determine whether the Court held anything. But it is generally accepted that Chief Justice Taney's opinion for the Court probably gives a sense of the majority, and in his opinion, Taney reaches two basic conclusions. First, Taney held that Scott was not a citizen of Missouri because of his race. The practice of the founders was not to treat blacks as citizens since before the founding of the United States, in Taney's words, they were "regarded as beings of an inferior order,

and altogether unfit to associate with the white race, either in social or political relations; and so far inferior, that they had no rights which the white
man was bound to respect; and that the negro might justly and lawfully be
reduced to slavery for his benefit."[67] If Scott was not a citizen of Missouri,
then he could not sue Sanford in federal court claiming that the parties
were "citizens" of different states.

Despite the lack of jurisdiction, Taney went on to a second conclusion.
Did Scott's presence on free soil make him free? To answer that question,
Taney decided to rule on whether Congress could mandate that the territory of the United States be free. Taney held that it could not, and that the
Missouri Compromise was unconstitutional. Taney's reasoning on this point
is hopeless. Turning to the text of the Constitution, Taney found that the
clause of the Constitution that grants Congress power over the "Territory
and other Property belonging to the United States" applied only to the territory that Virginia and the other states had ceded to the United States before the ratification of the Constitution. The term "territory" must have had
a definite and fixed meaning, not an expansive one, and it must have been
fixed at the time of the founding. Of course, the problem with Taney's interpretation of the territorial power was that Congress had made legislation
for the territories, and lots of it, and the Supreme Court itself had approved
of these arrangements. Even justices who agreed with Taney had trouble
with his reasoning. Justice Catron disagreed for personal reasons. "It is due
to myself to say," he wrote, "that it is asking much of a judge, who has for
nearly twenty years has been exercising jurisdiction, from the western Missouri line to the Rocky Mountains, and, on this understanding of the Constitution, inflicting the extreme penalty of death for crimes committed
where the direct legislation of Congress was the only rule, to agree that he
had been all the while acting in mistake, and as a usurper."[68] But Catron, a
southerner, did not dissent from the overall decision.

To drag himself out of the logical quagmire he created, Taney argued the
federal government could pass laws for the territories under the inherent
power that a sovereign has over its territory. This power did not, however,
include the power to act in excess of constitutional authority. Therefore
Congress could not ban slavery in the territories, Taney argued, because it
amounted to a deprivation of private property without due process of law—
an act in excess of constitutional authority. Because slaves were property,
banning slavery in the territories was like telling a person that he could not
take his clothing or other personal property with him when moving to the
territories.

Earlier, I stated that Taney decided to rule on the constitutionality of the
Missouri Compromise. Taney's decision had to be deliberate and result-
driven, because it was unnecessary. There was no reason that Taney had to
discuss the Missouri Compromise, given how he decided the rest of the case.

Recall that Scott had traveled with his then master Emerson not only to a territory made free by the Missouri Compromise but also to the free state of Illinois. Did the voluntary action of a master taking a slave to a free state and establishing permanent residency there make the slave free? The Court had earlier suggested this possibility in a case involving slaves living in Kentucky who, with their master's permission, went occasionally into Ohio. On one trip, the slaves kept going from Kentucky to Ohio and then to Canada, and the owner of the slaves sued the master of the boat that had enabled the slaves to go to Ohio claiming the value of the escaped slaves. In that case, *Strader v. Graham,* the Court held, "Every state has an undoubted right to determine the *status,* or domestic and social condition, of the persons domiciled within its territory."[69] Since the escaped slaves were domiciled— permanently residing—in Kentucky, their escape to the free state of Ohio did not affect their status because Kentucky law determined their status. But in Dred Scott's case, he had moved and permanently resided in Illinois be- cause his master took him there on purpose. Would not his permanent res- idence, his domicile, in Illinois change his status from slave to free man since Illinois had the "undoubted to determine the *status* . . . of the persons domiciled within its territory"? Taney answered no, because Scott's status was not to be determined by the law of Illinois, but by the law of Missouri, where Scott was most recently domiciled. And Missouri law held that Scott's presence in Illinois did not affect his status in Missouri—indeed, the Mis- souri Supreme Court created that rule especially for Scott, overturning ear- lier Missouri case law. Assuming that Missouri law governed Scott's status, then the Court did not need to decide whether Congress could ban slavery in the territories under the Missouri Compromise, for, even if it could, Scott's return to Missouri rendered him slave regardless. The only reason that Taney needed to decide whether the Missouri Compromise was consti- tutional, then, was to settle once and for all the question of congressional power over slavery in the territories.

Although it is frequently overlooked in much of the modern discussion of *Dred Scott,* the part of the decision invalidating the Missouri Compromise provoked the most heated debate at the time of the decision. At least two reasons explain this focus. First, although the Supreme Court held that Scott was not and could not be a citizen of Missouri—the aspect of the de- cision considered most odious today, especially because of its language— relatively few people at the time of the decision in *Dred Scott* argued that African-Americans were citizens. There was no state (except, perhaps, Maine) in which they could freely vote, serve on juries, hold public office, serve in the militia, or undertake other tasks that citizens performed. In- deed, an editorial in *Harper's Weekly* at the time stated that the uproar over the case was overblown. After all, the editors coolly reasoned, the decision had no practical effect on daily life in the United States. Since whites did not treat blacks as fellow citizens, what harm could come from the Supreme Court declaring that blacks could not be citizens for purposes of invoking the special jurisdiction of the federal courts?[70] (Similarly, continued the editors, the holding that Congress could not ban slavery in the territories would have had importance earlier during the debate over the Kansas-Nebraska bill, but it was of no practical effect in 1857 since the Democrats— "certain to be in power in two branches of the Government at least for the next four years—have announced it as their fixed and unalterable determination to leave the question of slavery to the Territories themselves. When then, or how is the case to arise, which shall give this branch of the decision any practical force?")[71] Pro-slavery southerners would also use this line of reasoning to quiet criticism of the *Dred Scott* opinion on this ground, as antislavery northerners were not necessarily for racial equality—in fact, they generally opposed it.[72]

The second reason that the territorial aspect of Court's decision caused great consternation was how it fundamentally changed the terms of debate over slavery in the territories. Democrats like Stephen Douglas could argue before *Dred Scott* for popular sovereignty in the territories—let the territories decide whether they would be free or slave. With the decision in *Dred Scott*, however, the possibility of popular sovereignty was undermined at the very least and probably shattered entirely. If territorial governments were creatures of Congress, how could they ban slavery when Congress itself lacked the power to do so? Douglas attempted to explain this problem away in an lengthy article in *Harper's Monthly*, for which he was rewarded with nasty rejoinders in pamphlet form written by leaders of his own party.[73] Southerners, meanwhile, latched onto Taney's reasoning that a ban on slavery was an unlawful deprivation of property to argue that Congress had a positive duty to protect slavery in the territories. Given that many state constitutions had provisions similar to the due process clause in the United States Constitution, some pro-slavery advocates even argued that no state could ban slavery. The Democratic Party began to collapse in on itself as the internal struggle over slavery consumed its time and energy. Meanwhile, the Republicans—with their strident but clear platform and arguments by Abraham Lincoln to ignore the territorial aspect of the *Dred Scott* decision— won the presidential election of 1860.

Once the Civil War began, Congress acted in direct defiance of the Supreme Court. In 1862, Congress made good on the Republican Party platform and banned both slavery and polygamy in the territories.[74] The Court's response to these new laws reveals either its own weakness or the weakness of *Dred Scott* as a precedent. If the Court had adhered to its position in *Dred Scott*, it could have found many of these regulations unconstitutional. Obviously, the Thirteenth Amendment settled the constitutionality of the congressional ban on slavery in the territories. On the broader question of congressional power over the territories—such as whether Congress could ban polygamy—the Court caved in. It upheld the statute banning polygamy in the territories, holding even that the United States could dismantle institutions of the Mormon Church. It upheld the power of Congress to override decisions of a territorial legislature, acknowledging in amazing understatement that "[t]here have been some difference of opinion as to the particular clause of the Constitution from which the power is derived, but that it exists has always been conceded."[75] Through their representatives, the People had acted to deny what the Supreme Court had said in *Dred Scott,* and the Court codified their beliefs.

Thus, returning to Ackerman's concept of a constitutional moment, the story of the constitutional effects of the Louisiana Purchase does not end until after the Civil War. It is not until then that the principle of congressional authority over the territories is unquestionably settled. The pattern of signaling, proposing, mobilized deliberating, and codifying—the back and forth between the People, their representatives, and the judiciary—had all taken place. The People demanded unfettered access to the Mississippi River and trading in New Orleans. Jefferson and his political allies responded and gave the People what they wanted and more, even though the constitutional authority was, in their own view, slim at best. The representatives of the People then presented this action to them as a guardian would say to a ward "when he came of age, I did this for your good; you may disavow me, and I must get out of the scrape as I can." Along with the purchase, the government presented the People with a successful exploration of the territory, a wildly popular move. The discussion over congressional power to acquire territory may have ended there, but the debate over congressional power did not, for buried within the Louisiana Purchase were the seeds of its potential destruction. Slavery existed in the territory that the United States acquired from France, and Congress did not deal with the problem adequately or comprehensively. As the general fight over slavery took on growing importance in the 1840s and 1850s, the debate at the federal level took the form of regulating slavery in the territories. This culminated in the *Dred Scott* decision, which held that the federal government lacked such regulatory power. When the Civil War began, Congress enacted a law that contradicted this holding outright and continued to assert municipal authority over the territories. In response to this action and the lessons learned in the Civil War—and not in response to an express constitutional amendment, unlike the post-Civil War amendments freeing the slaves and establishing their rights—the Supreme Court accepted the repudiation of its holding and buried *Dred Scott.* Not until a generation later did the Supreme Court tangle with the legal decision in *Dred Scott* and declare it essentially irrelevant.

Thus, the development of congressional power over the territories and other property belonging to the United States forms the first "constitutional moment" that the Louisiana Purchase starts. The second constitutional change that occurs from the purchase and the subsequent Lewis and Clark expedition concerns how the federal government would manage these lands. Jefferson drafted the instructions to Lewis without assistance from Congress, and, as described above, one of Jefferson's primary missions for the explorers, exploring and cataloging the soil, flora, and fauna of foreign territory, had nothing to do with an express power of the federal government. The exploration was a success in every measure. Lewis and Clark lost only one man, and the reaction to the things they found was exciting to the general population. Had the exploration not succeeded—had, for example, the party died while navigating the upper reaches of the Missouri or at the hands of a hostile tribe of Native Americans—the reactions would undoubtedly have soured some Americans on the notion of a bold exploration of the West. Counterfactual history is always a questionable enterprise, but had the Lewis and Clark expedition failed, or had it not succeeded so well, the People may have questioned the wisdom of exploration of the West or have expected their representatives to place more checks on it. But the expedition succeeded, and with that success came increased power of the president.

The development of Indian law provides a useful trace of this increase in power in the executive branch. Originally, the United States dealt with Indian tribes as if they were foreign nations, and the logical and expected agreement between the two sovereigns would be a treaty. Nevertheless, the United States accepted that Indian tribes were domestic sovereigns and that the Indian tribes could not have, for example, their own foreign policy; perhaps this recognition led to placing responsibility for Indians within the Department of the *Interior*. Later, the United States abandoned the policy of treaties and dealt with tribes largely through executive agreement and general legislation. Congress apparently acquiesced in this transformation. To the extent that Indian policy represents public land policy, the shift in power may have been complete.

This is not to say that the Lewis and Clark expedition alone accounts for expanded presidential power over the territories and public lands. To be fair, expedience explains this growth of power as well. After all, at the time of the Lewis and Clark expedition, no other branch of the government could carry out such an expedition. Moreover, the United States Army, under the ultimate control of the president as commander-in-chief, presented itself as the logical unit of the United States to explore the West, especially foreign territory. Until the establishment of the Department of the Interior in 1849, the army had the primary responsibility for negotiating with Indian tribes because no other federal agency logically had that role. Even after that time, the army had the principal role in dealing with hostile Indian tribes. Moreover, Congress may not have had the resources effectively to address the myriad questions of Indian policy that the United States faced in its aggressive expansion.

Nevertheless, the success of the Lewis and Clark expedition marked the first step in a move toward recognizing presidential power over public lands that the Constitution itself does not confer. The Constitution grants to Congress the power to "dispose of and make all needful Rules and Regulations respecting the Territory and other Property belonging to the United States." It says nothing about presidential authority in this area. The president's power to explore the West became the president's power to protect these public lands. As early as 1868, the Supreme Court recognized that the president had the power to withhold public lands from disposition under otherwise applicable federal laws because the practice dates "from an early period in the history of the government."[76] By 1915, the principle was firmly established. Executive orders had reserved millions of acres of land for Indian tribes, military reservations, and bird sanctuaries, even though no statute authorized the president to reserve these lands.[77] Moreover, Congress has vested broad discretion in the president to reserve federal lands for certain purposes.

The power of the president to withdraw public lands from disposal from allocation under public land law sounds boring and inconsequential. It is not. Presidential orders spared thousands of acres of national forests from the ax.[78] For good or for ill, presidential orders placed Native Americans on reservations that survive to this day. More recently, the Supreme Court has recognized that Alaska cannot drill for oil in the tidelands of the National Petroleum Reserve in Alaska because President Warren Harding reserved these lands and prevented them from passing to Alaska upon its admission to the union.[79] Thus, the entire look of this country, especially the West, has its roots in presidential proclamation, some of which rests on pure assertion of executive authority. In addition, the Supreme Court has upheld broad congressional delegations of authority to the president. For example, the Court upheld grazing regulations that the Forest Service issued, even though the relevant legislation gave the Forest Service no express authority over grazing.[80] These Supreme Court decisions came at a time when the Court viewed presidential authority narrowly.

To return again to Ackerman's theory of the constitutional moment, one can see again the steps of signaling through codifying. After the Louisiana Purchase, Congress created a territorial government for Louisiana and vested much of the authority over that government in the president. Jefferson directed Lewis and Clark to undertake an exploration of the West, and, with their successful return, directed others to do the same. The Supreme Court gradually recognized a broad area for executive authority in this area, in part from expedience and in part from the accommodation that the political branches had reached. Thus, a greater scope of power for the president arose from the Louisiana Purchase and the Lewis and Clark expedition, one that the People apparently wanted and the courts eventually codified.

NOTES

1. Alexis de Tocqueville, *Democracy in America* ed. Phillips Bradley, trans. Henry Reeve, rev. Francis Bowen (New York: Alfred A. Knopf, 1948), 1:280.

2. For the cases involving Lewis N. Clark, see *Ullery v. The Mayflower*, 75 F. 842 (W.D. Pa. 1896), *Bovard v. The Mayflower*, 39 F. 41 (W.D. Pa. 1889), and *Poor v. The Geneva*, 26 F. 647 (W.D. Pa. 1886). There is also a *Lewis v. Clark*, 129 F. 570 (C.C.A. Idaho 1904).

3. On this point see chapter 5, Raymond Cross's excellent essay.

4. *United States v. First Trust Co.*, 251 F.2d 686 (8th Cir. 1958).

5. Henry Adams, *History of the United States of American During the Administrations of Thomas Jefferson* (New York: Library of America, 1986), 1:334–335.

6. Everett Somerville Brown, *The Constitutional History of the Louisiana Purchase 1803–1812* University of California Publications in History, no. 10 (Berkeley: University of California Press, 1920), 196; he cites Turner and Cooley on 2. I have uncovered no attempt to redo Brown's general constitutional history of the Louisiana Purchase, and I am indebted to his work for my own approach to constitutional arguments over the purchase.

7. Frederick J. Turner, "The Significance of the Louisiana Purchase," *The American Monthly Review of Reviews* 27 (1903): 584.

8. According to Cooley, the Louisiana Purchase "established a precedent which was certain to be followed whenever occasion should invite it, and it would be vain to contend that the Constitution did not sanction what had thus with public approval been so successfully accomplished" (Thomas M. Cooley, "The Acquisition of Louisiana," *Indiana Historical Society Publications* 2 [1887]: 87). Cooley nevertheless saw a dark side of the Louisiana Purchase, arguing that its inattention to constitutional principle "gives unbridled license" to "every reckless fanatic or anarchist," leaving to "every man to judge for himself of the times and occasions when he will elevate his own discretion above that great charter of national unity" (89).

9. Merrill D. Peterson, *Thomas Jefferson and the New Nation* (New York: Oxford University Press, 1970), 775.

10. Stephen M. Griffin, *American Constitutionalism: From Theory to Politics* (Princeton: Princeton University Press, 1996), 32.

11. Professor Ackerman appears to have used the term first in 1984 (Bruce A. Ackerman, "The Storrs Lectures: Discovering the Constitution," *Yale Law Journal* 93 [1984]: 1022), as he recalled in later correspondence with me. He has elaborated on his theory in several articles that culminated in *We the People*, vol. 1, *Foundations*, and vol. 2, *Transformations* (Cambridge, Mass.: Harvard University Press, 1991–98), and shared with me a manuscript version of the next volume in the series. Although this draft did not discuss the Lewis and Clark expedition, I am nevertheless indebted to Professor Ackerman for his generosity.

12. In this context, Ackerman capitalizes the word "People" not only as a reference to the preamble to the Constitution—"We the People"—but also to emphasize that during the course of a constitutional moment, the citizenry act not only out of self-interest but also as a mobilized force searching for fundamental change.

13. Ackerman, *We the People*, 1:272–290.

14. For an example of criticism along this line, see Michael W. McConnell, "The Forgotten Constitutional Moment," 11 *Constitutional Commentary* (1994): 115–144. Professor McConnell argues that the era of Jim Crow at the end of Reconstruction fits all of the criteria of Ackerman's theory yet is not incorporated into it because of the uncomfortable implications of including it. For Ackerman's initial response to McConnell, see Ackerman, *We the People*, 2:471–474.

15. For select criticisms of Ackerman, see Michael J. Klarman, "Constitutional Fact/Constitutional Fiction: A Critique of Bruce Ackerman's Theory of Constitutional Moments," *Stanford Law Review* 44 (1992): 759–797; Suzanna Sherry, "The Ghost of Liberalism Past," *Harvard Law Review* 105 (1992): 918–934; and Laurence H. Tribe, "Taking Text and Structure Seriously: Reflections on Free Form Method in Constitutional Interpretation," *Harvard Law Review* 108 (1995): 1221–1303.

16. For example, the Supreme Court has relied on a long series of acts in which Congress has authorized the president to take command in foreign affairs to support its conclusion that the president has broad powers in this area (*United States v. Curtiss-Wright Corporation*, 299 U.S. 304, 322–329 [1936]).

17. For a detailed account of the Mississippi River question and its influence on the constitutional convention, see Eli Merritt, "Sectional Conflict and Secret Compromise: The Mississippi River Question and the United States Constitution," *The American Journal of Legal History* 35 (1991): 117–171.

18. Worthington Chauncey Ford et al., eds. *Journals of the Constitutional Convention* (Washington, D.C.: Government Printing Office, 1906–37), 11:650.

19. Ford et al., 11:650.

20. Ford et al., 639.

21. Ford et al., 14:622.

22. For the argument that Maryland acted on principle and general political considerations, see Herbert B. Adams, *Maryland's Influence in Founding a National Commonwealth*, Maryland Historical Society Fund Publication, no. 11 (Baltimore: John Murphy, 1877). For the argument that Maryland acted primarily to support land speculators, see Merrill Jensen, "The Cession of the Old Northwest," *Mississippi Valley Historical Review* 23 (1936): 27–50; and Merrill Jensen, "The Creation of the National Domain," *Mississippi Valley Historical Review* 26 (1939): 323–342. For a rebuttal to Professor Jensen's articles, see Lemuel Molovinsky, "Maryland and the American West at Independence," *Maryland Historical Magazine* 72 (1977): 353–360. For the argument that the French ambassador influenced Maryland to adopt the articles by threatening to withhold military assistance, see Jensen, "Cession of the Old Northwest," 27; and Edmund S. Morgan, *The Birth of the Republic, 1763–89*, 3d ed. (Chicago: University of Chicago Press, 1992), 112. Good general histories of the disputes over the western land claims and related controversies include Thomas Perkins Abernathy, *Western Lands and the American Revolution* (New York: Russell and Russell, 1937); and Peter S. Onuf, *The Origins of the Federal Repub-*

lic: Jurisdictional Controversies in the United States, 1775–1787 (Philadelphia: University of Pennsylvania Press, 1983). My own treatment of this history can be found in Peter A. Appel, "The Power of Congress 'Without Limitation': The Property Clause and Federal Regulation of Private Property," *Minnesota Law Review* 86 (2001): 16–36.

23. Clinton Rossiter, ed., *The Federalist Papers* (New York: New American Library, 1961), 239–240.

24. Max Farrand, ed., *The Records of the Federal Convention of 1787* (New Haven: Yale University Press, 1937), 2:321.

25. United States Constitution, article IV, section 3, clause 2 (emphasis mine). Gouveneur Morris drafted the language that became this provision (Farrand, 2:466).

26. Farrand, 1:22. On the requirement that new states arise within the lawful limits of the United States (which presumably means within the Mississippi), see also Farrand 1:117, 1:231, 2:39, 2:133, 2:147, 2:173, 2:188.

27. Farrand, 2:457.

28. Farrand, 2:458.

29. United States Constitution, article I, sec. 8, clause 11.

30. United States Constitution, article VI, clause 2.

31. *The Federalist Papers*, 239–240.

32. Ackerman, *We the People*, 2:32–68. Under Ackerman's theory, the drafting and ratification itself was a constitutional moment because it represented an unauthorized amendment of the Articles of Confederation, and the founders exceeded their authority in drafting a constitution rather than simply amending the articles. This process fits his pattern of change coming from the People through their representatives overcoming the written constitution of government.

33. Opinion of Alexander Hamilton, on the constitutionality of a national bank, in *Legislative and Documentary History of the Bank of the United States including the Original Bank of North America*, comp. Matthew St. Clair Clarke and D. A. Hall (Washington, D.C.: Gales and Seaton, 1832; reprint, New York: Augustus M. Kelley, 1967), 96.

34. Opinion of Thomas Jefferson, in *Legislative and Documentary History*, 91.

35. On this controversy, see Dumas Malone, *Jefferson the President: First Term, 1801–1805*, vol. 4 of *Jefferson and His Times* (Boston: Little, Brown, 1970), 264–266.

36. *Annals of Congress*, 7th Congress, 2d sess. (Washington, D.C.: Gales and Seaton, 1851), 86.

37. The influence that actions in Congress may have had on the Napoleon's decision is discussed in David A. Carson, "The Role of Congress in the Acquisition of the Louisiana Territory," *Louisiana History* 26 (1985): 369–383.

38. Malone, 311, argues, "It seems unlikely that [Jefferson] was as closely identified with this doctrine [of strict construction] by his contemporaries at this time as he was afterwards by historians who had access to more sources of information. His opinion on the constitutionality of the Bank of the United States had not been published."

39. For accounts of the newspaper coverage of the purchase, see Malone, 284–285; and Peterson, 760.

40. Henry Adams, ed., *The Writings of Albert Gallatin* (Philadelphia: J. B. Lippincott, 1879), 1:115.

41. Paul Leicester Ford, ed., *The Works of Thomas Jefferson* (New York: G. P. Putnam's Sons, 1905), 10:3–12.

42. Ford, *Works,* 10:29.

43. Nicholas to Jefferson, quoted in Brown, 27.

44. Jefferson to Nicolas, reprinted in Andrew A. Lipscomb, ed., *The Writings of Thomas Jefferson* (Washington, D.C.: Thomas Jefferson Memorial Association, 1904), 10:418–419.

45. Ford, *Works,* 10:29.

46. Lipscomb, *Writings,* 10:420.

47. Lipscomb, *Writings,* 10:418.

48. Lipscomb, *Writings,* 10:411.

49. United States Constitution, article I, sec. 8, clause 8, vests in Congress the power "To promote the Progress of Science and useful Arts, by securing for limited Times to Authors and Inventors the exclusive Right to their respective Writings and Discoveries."

50. *Annals of Congress,* 26.

51. Malone, 276.

52. Jefferson's instructions to Lewis, in *The Journals of Lewis and Clark,* ed. Bernard DeVoto (Boston: Houghton Mifflin, 1953), 483.

53. On Jefferson's scientific interest, see Kathleen Tobin-Schlesinger, "Jefferson to Lewis: The Study of Nature in the West," *Journal of the West* 29, no. 6 (1990): 54–61.

54. One scholar has argued that Jefferson did not sell out his principles by agreeing to the Louisiana Purchase, but that the purchase furthered Jefferson's republican principles of individualism and agrarianism by affording Americans more room in which to spread out (Barry J. Balleck, "When the Ends Justify the Means: Thomas Jefferson and the Louisiana Purchase," *Presidential Studies Quarterly* 22 [1992]: 679–696). Nevertheless, Balleck's argument does not account for the Lewis and Clark expedition or in particular explain why Jefferson directed the explorers to make particular notes about the soil, vegetation, and animals outside of the United States. Perhaps Balleck would argue that these inquiries simply laid the groundwork for further expansion when necessary, but the better view is that they were motivated primarily by Jefferson's personal scientific interest.

55. Gouveneur Morris to Henry W. Livingston, in Farrand, 3:404. The full quotation is instructive, however, of Morris's views:

> I always though that, when we should acquire Canada and Louisiana it would be proper to govern them as provinces, and allow them no voice in our councils. In wording the third section of the fourth article, I went as far as circumstances would permit to establish the exclusion. Candor obliges me to add my belief, that, had it been more pointedly expressed, a strong opposition would have been made.

56. The congressional debates over the Louisiana Purchase are summarized nicely in David A. Carson, "Blank Paper of the Constitution: The Louisiana Purchase Debates," *The Historian* 54 (1992): 484–490.

57. Thomas Jefferson, "Memoir of Meriwether Lewis," in *History of the Expedition Under the Command of Lewis and Clark,* ed. Elliott Coues (New York: Francis P. Harper, 1893; reprint, New York: Dover, 1965), 1:xxxvi.

58. A typical listing of such cases would include *American Insurance Co. v. Canter,* 26 U.S. (1 Pet.) 511 (1828); *United States v. Gratiot,* 39 U.S. (14 Pet.) 526 (1840); and *Cross v. Harrison,* 57 U.S. (16 How.) 164 (1853), as well as certain statements in *Sère v. Pitot,* 10 U.S. (6 Cranch) 332 (1810), *McCulloch v. Maryland,* 17 U.S. (4 Wheat.) 316 (1819). *American Insurance Co. v. Canter* arose in Florida, and the Supreme Court held that Congress could establish territorial courts that did not resemble federal courts established under Article III of the Constitution. (The judges on the territorial courts involved did not have life tenure.) In *United States v. Gratiot,* the Supreme Court held that the United States could retain land within the states and was not required to dispose of it by sale. Finally, *Cross v. Harrison* upheld the constitutionality of the military government established for California.

59. The most detailed attempt at a biography of York is probably Robert B. Betts, *In Search of York: The Slave Who Went to the Pacific with Lewis and Clark* (Boulder: University Press of Colorado, 1985).

60. DeVoto, 48–49.

61. Ibid., 209.

62. The foregoing account is based largely on Betts. Betts speculated that York may not have died but instead returned to the West to live among Indians (Betts, 135–143).

63. William Wells Brown, *From Fugitive Slave to Free Man: The Autobiographies of William Wells Brown,* ed. William L. Andrews (New York: Penguin Books USA, 1993), 34.

64. "Republican Platform," appendix to "The Republican Party: 1854–1864," in *History of U.S. Political Parties,* by Hans L. Trefouse, vol. 2, *1860–1910: The Gilded Age of Politics,* ed. Arthur M. Schelsinger, Jr. (New York: Chelsea House Publishers, 1973), 1204. The other competing views are summarized in Don E. Fehrenbacher, *The Dred Scott Case: Its Significance in American Law and Politics* (New York: Oxford University Press, 1978), 135–147. My own earlier treatment of the Dred Scott case appears at Appel, 36–55.

65. *Scott v. Emerson,* 15 Mo. 576 (1852).

66. There is considerable debate over the exact legal relationship between the Scotts and Sanford. On this question, see Fehrenbacher, 270–271; and Vincent C. Hopkins, *Dred Scott's Case* (New York: Fordham University Press, 1951), 23–24.

67. Scott v. Sandford, 60 U.S. (19 How.) 393, 407 (1857).

68. Ibid., 522–523.

69. Strader v. Graham, 51 U.S. (10 How.) 82, 93 (1850).

70. "The Dred Scott Case," *Harper's Weekly Journal of Civilization* 1 (1857): 193, reprinted in *The Dred Scott Decision: Law or Politics,* ed. Stanley I. Kutler (Boston: Houghton Mifflin, 1967), 48–50. The editorial on this point is worth quoting at length, if only to convey the general sense of race relations at the time, even in a northern publication:

Nor does it appear that the question of the citizenship of our free black population is a question likely to take any practical shape capable of profoundly agitating the public mind. We are indeed a consistent and reasonable people! We have among us a small representation of a tropical race of human beings, marked off from us by the unmistakable line of color, if by nothing else, and over whom we daily arrogate to ourselves of the Caucasian stock a complete and absolute superiority. We will not marry with them, we will not eat with them, as a general rule we do not let them vote, we will let them hold no office. We do not allow them to kneel beside us to worship the Great Father of all; not even when we approach the end of our weary journey will we allow our miserable dust to repose side by side with theirs in the common receptacle of humanity. And yet, when half a dozen old lawyers at Washington, after racking their heads for two years over a question that has bothered the Robe for half a century, announces as their decision that *free blacks are not citizens of the United States,* and as such not permitted to sue in certain courts of limited and special jurisdiction, we fume, and fret, and bubble, and squeak, as if some dreadful injustice and oppression were committed. It really does not seem to us that this part of the Dred Scott decision is likely to produce any very serious practical results.

71. *Harper's,* 193.

72. Fehrenbacher, 429–430.

73. Douglas's article appears as Stephen A. Douglas, "The Dividing Line Between Federal and Local Authority," *Harper's New Monthly Magazine* 19 (1859): 519. The nasty responses include [Jeremiah Black,] *Observations on Senator Douglas's Views of Popular Sovereignty as Expressed in Harpers' Magazine, for September 1859* (Washington, D.C.: Thomas McGill, 1859), which was written by President Buchanan's attorney general; and [Reverdy Johnson,] *Remarks on Popular Sovereignty, as Maintained and Denied Respectively by Judge Douglas and Attorney-General Black* (Baltimore: Murphy, 1859), which was written by a prominent Democrat, who served as President Zachary Taylor's attorney general and Sanford's lawyer before the Supreme Court.

74. Act of 19 June 1862, ch. CXI, 12 Stat. 432; Act of 1 July 1862, ch. CXXVI, 12 Stat. 501.

75. *National Bank v. County of Yankton,* 101 U.S. 129, 132 (1879). The Court upheld the limitation on polygamy in *Reynolds v. United States,* 98 U.S. 145 (1878), and the repeal of the articles of incorporation for the Mormon Church in *Late Corporation of the Church of Jesus Christ of Latter-Day Saints v. United States,* 136 U.S. 1 (1890).

76. *Grisar v. McDowell,* 73 U.S. (6 Wall.) 363, 381 (1868).

77. *United States v. Midwest Oil Co.,* 236 U.S. 459, 469–473 (1915).

78. Most of these reservations were undertaken under congressional authorization (Charles F. Wilkinson, *Crossing the Next Meridian: Land, Water, and the Future of the West* [Washington, D.C.: Island Press, 1992], 120–124).

79. *Alaska v. United States,* 521 U.S. 1, 36–46 (1997).

80. *Light v. United States,* 220 U.S. 523 (1911); *United States v. Grimaud,* 220 U.S. 506 (1911).

Chapter 5

"Twice-born" from the Waters

The Two-Hundred-Year Journey of the Mandan, Hidatsa, and Arikara Indians

Raymond Cross

Christian salvatory lore requires that you be "twice-born" from the waters to merit everlasting life. Perhaps in a similar manner, the sacred and secular birth and rebirth of the Mandan, Hidatsa, and Arikara people from the waters may merit them everlasting life. Their first birth from beneath the waters of Spirit Lake conferred a sacred character on their endeavors to develop an economically and culturally vibrant life along the bottomlands of the upper Missouri River.[1] According to the Hidatsa creation story, they came from beneath the waters of Spirit Lake, that body of water non-Indians now call Devils Lake in present-day North Dakota. A vine grew downward into the underworld where the Indians lived beneath the waters. Some of the Hidatsa climbed that vine into the upper world of the sunlight. But a very fat Hidatsa woman pushed her way to the head of the line and when she tried to climb the vine, it broke. Many of the Hidatsa remain, to this day, marooned beneath the waters of Spirit Lake.[2]

These Indian people's second birth was from beneath the waters of Lake Sakakawea, the 118-mile-long federal flood control and hydropower reservoir created in 1953 by the world's fourth-largest earth-filled dam, the Garrison. The creation of Lake Sakakawea—named by the U.S. Army Corps of Engineers to commemorate the memory of the young Shoshone Indian who assisted the Lewis and Clark expedition in 1805–6—required the removal of over 90 percent of the Mandan, Hidatsa, and Arikara people from their historic settlements along the bottomlands of the Missouri River. Their rebirth from beneath the waters of that manmade lake occurred in 1992 when Congress awarded $149.5 million in just compensation for taking the Garrison.[3] The Three Affiliated Tribes must, by statute, use these funds to overcome the social and economic devastation wrought by Lake Sakakawea so as to rebuild their tribal world—which has been constantly undermined by the ongoing encounter with American power since the arrival of the Lewis and Clark expedition in 1804. In doing so, the tribes must address the interlacing of sacred and secular duties that confront their people. They will accomplish this by drawing from the strengths that have allowed them to survive the hardship and devastation that has characterized their two-hundred-year relationship with the United States and once again exercise the cultural and economic independence they possessed when they first encountered the American explorers.[4]

Water, disease, and words—these are the three basic human factors that have defined the long relationship between the United States and these Indian people from 1804 to the present. My essay evaluates how the interaction of these three human factors, and their different significance for Indians and non-Indians, have fundamentally altered the tribal life worlds of the Mandan, Hidatsa, and Arikara people over the course of two-hundred years. I divide this span of two centuries into four key historical periods, concluding with a fourth human factor—hope—to illustrate how these Indian people's enduring resilience and tenacity will enable them to survive and perhaps even triumph over their ongoing hardships. The ultimate "test case" of my hypothesis evaluates the likelihood that these Indian people will recover from the federally engineered destruction wreaked in 1953 by the flooding of the Fort Berthold Indian Reservation.

Disease, particularly smallpox, is the human factor that dominates the first historical period, from the arrival of Lewis and Clark in 1804 to the devastating epidemic of 1837 that forced the surviving members of the Mandan, Hidatsa, and Arikara tribes to consolidate within one village. Words, those contained in an 1886 federal agreement between these Indian people and the United States, open my second historical period. This agreement created the contemporary Fort Berthold Indian Reservation and obligated the Mandan, Hidatsa, and Arikara people to farm and ranch the bottomlands along the Missouri River. Through arduous effort these Indian people had clearly lived up to the words of the 1886 agreement by recreating a self-sufficient agricultural economy and a renewed tribal cultural life within the forbidding environment of the Fort Berthold reservation in northwestern North Dakota. But in 1949 the federal government chose to break its word by taking the Indians' last remaining river bottomlands as the site for the federal hydroelectric and flood control reservoir known as Lake Sakakawea. Water, embodied in those billions of gallons unleashed on the Fort Berthold reservation by the federally engineered flood of 1953, frames the tribal life world of these Indian people during my third historical period. Beginning with the mass removal and relocation in 1953 of over 90 percent of these Indian peoples from their reservation homes to accommodate the closure of the flood gates of the Garrison Dam, this third historical period ends in 1985 with Interior Secretary Donald P. Hodel's reluctant creation of the Joint Tribal Advisory Committee (JTAC) to hear these Indians' just compensation claim arising from the flooding of their historic tribal homelands. Hope is the factor that animates the tribal life world during my fourth historical period, which begins in 1986 with the release of the pivotal JTAC report to Congress and may close in 2004 with these Indian people's development of a social and economic recovery plan based on the 1992 congressional payment of $149.5 million in just compensation.

FRAMING THE LEWIS AND CLARK ENCOUNTER

The Mandan, Hidatsa, and Arikara people long ago made the "elongated oases" of the upper Missouri River valley their home. By their successful exploitation of the river valley's resources these Indian peoples—particularly the Mandan—had by 900 A.D. established a vibrant cultural and economic life along the bottomlands, terraces, and bluffs of the Missouri River in what are now the states of South Dakota and North Dakota.[5] By the time of their 1804 encounter with the so-called Corps of Discovery, these Indian people had long flourished through their use of the waters and riparian lands of the upper Missouri River. They had evolved varieties of quick-maturing corn that were well adapted to the short growing season of the upper Missouri River valley, thus becoming the northernmost outpost of the Mesoamerican corn culture. Their exploitation of the extensive flood plain of the river, when cleared of brush, allowed the tribal women to plant and cultivate their large gardens of squash, corn, beans, and sunflowers. Likewise, the surrounding terraces and bluffs created by the river provided suitable sites for their earth lodge villages that could be easily defended from potential attack by their enemies. The surrounding prairie was well stocked—not only with abundant deer, elk, and antelope—but with the big game animal the Mandan valued most as their source of food and material supply—the bison.[6]

Well before the arrival of Lewis and Clark in 1804, the Mandan had substantially expanded their horticulture and used their large food surplus in a flourishing intertribal trade, particularly with their nomadic neighbors to the west. Situated on the big bend of the Missouri, and downstream from the mouth of the Yellowstone River, they enjoyed an enviable geographic position that attracted trade goods from far-flung regions such as obsidian from present-day Yellowstone National Park, copper from the Great Lakes area and conch shells from the Gulf Coast. Later, with the coming of the horse and gun to the Great Plains, the Mandan and Hidatsa villages became the center of an even more complex web of trade that eventually incorporated trading representatives from the fabled Hudson Bay and Northwest Companies.[7] It was in this last context, as confident and adaptive peoples who were well situated in regional, continental, and imperial trade networks, that the Mandan, Hidatsa, and Arikara first encountered Lewis and Clark.

John Seelye has rightly described the Corps of Discovery as a pragmatic "nationalistic reconnaissance with a paramilitary, quasi-diplomatic scope and purpose."[8] One of its acknowledged, if publicly unstated, missions was to dislodge the well established British and French fur trading interests from the upper Missouri by securing the resident Indian tribes' acceptance of American sovereignty and their commitment to trade exclusively with those American companies that would come upriver from St. Louis. Native peoples were to be left in no doubt about the United States' intent and power to impose its control over the Indian trade within that region. Toward these ends, the Lewis and Clark expedition exerted a significant measure of "gunboat diplomacy" as its means of impressing on the Indian peoples the might of their new master—the United States government.[9]

Meriwether Lewis made sure that the first general council meeting in the late fall of 1804 with the assembled Mandan and Hidatsa chiefs would highlight the "gunboat diplomacy" aspects of his mission. In his journal, he described this meeting as held "under an awning of our sails, stretched so as to exclude the wind . . . [and so t]hat the impression might be the more forcible, the men were all paraded, and the council was opened by a discharge from the swivel [gun] of the boat. We then delivered a speech which, like those we already made, intermingled advice with the assurances of friendship and trade." At least one Hidatsa chief, Caltarcota, expressed his anger at being lectured but, Lewis blandly noted, "was instantly rebuked with great dignity by one of [his fellows] for this violation of decorum at such a moment."[10]

According to Roy Meyer, the Indians' real assessment of this first meeting was that Captain Lewis "had a wicked design on their country." They likewise judged Captain Lewis's flowery speech, and his professed his wish for undying peace and friendship with the Indians, as political farce.[11] But the Mandan and Hidatsa Indians' critical assessment of the expedition did not deter a thriving Indian trade with the American explorers. In exchange for Mandan corn and buffalo the expedition's blacksmiths mended the Indians' hoes, repaired firearms, and late produced implements of intertribal warfare such as Indian battle-axes. Although this trade seriously undermined the expedition's putative objective of promoting intertribal peace, Lewis defended his blacksmiths' practices as a "happy resource to us in our present situation as I believe it would have been difficult to have devised any other method to have procured corn from the natives."[12]

Viewed in isolation, the impact of the Lewis and Clark expedition on the Mandan, Hidatsa, and Arikara people was virtually nil—in both diplomatic and commercial terms. A Mandan chief complained about the lack of

American trade goods and concluded that "had these Whites come amongst us with charitable views they would have loaded their 'Great Boat' with necessaries. It is true they have ammunition, but they prefer throwing it away idly rather than sparing a shot of it to a poor Mandan."[13] As federal diplomats, Lewis and Clark sought to impose what James Ronda has called a "simplistic diplomatic model" that did not require their understanding of the deep complexity of tribal economic and governmental life. Their simple formulation of the Indians' revised political status as "dutiful Indian children" with a new and powerful "White Father" who resides in Washington, D.C. was certainly not welcomed by the Mandan, Hidatsa, and Arikara people.[14] Nevertheless, these misunderstandings formed the basis for the unequal relationships between these Indians and the increasingly powerful United States.

DISEASE AND DEPENDENCE, 1837 TO 1886

When President Thomas Jefferson was devising his instructions for the Lewis and Clark expedition, he apparently considered the vaccination of the Indians of the upper Missouri River against smallpox. After all, as Ronda put it, "[d]ead Indians could not participate in an American trade network and dying natives could only blame the explorers for spreading the disease." Jefferson ultimately decided against this precaution, since he believed it would overburden his Corps of Discovery by adding an unwieldy medical function that might detract from the performance of their other duties.[15] His views were reflected in the observations of expedition members, who commented on the consequences of past epidemics with clinical detachment. Fortunately, no one on the expedition carried a fatal infectious disease, a fact that no doubt helps account for Lewis and Clark's ability to garner much needed assistance from various Native communities during the successful return to St. Louis in 1806.

Disease followed in the wake of the expedition. Increased trade through St. Louis brought greater exposure to European diseases, which had a debilitating effect on all the Native peoples of the upper Missouri. It was not until the late 1830s, however, that the Mandan, Hidatsa, and Arikara Indians would face epidemiological catastrophe. At the waning height of the peltry trade, when American fur trade posts had long since dislodged these Indian communities from their central position in the Great Plains trading networks, the waters of the upper Missouri River and American commerce joined to bring to the Mandan, Hidatsa, and Arikara villages an unwelcome guest—smallpox—which arrived on the American Fur Company steamer, *St Peters*, at 3:00 P.M. on 19 June 1837. Although the presence of smallpox had been suspected aboard the steamer when a mulatto servant had come down with the disease, the captain refused to put the man ashore because he did not wish to lose the man's services. Apparently, some three Arikara women, who had been visiting their Pawnee relatives, came aboard the boat and soon contracted the disease. The disease spread rapidly, devastating the Hidatsa and Arikara people, and virtually wiping out the Mandan. From a historic high population of 8,000, the Mandan had been reduced to a pre-epidemic population of 3,200. By the time the disease had run its course, only 120–130 individuals survived.[16]

The journal of the Indian agent Francis A. Chardon, starting on 14 July, references just one or two Indian deaths a day from smallpox. But his reported number of Indian fatalities from that disease increases by the date of his August entries from four to seven a day. By 20 August, he estimated the rate of Indian fatality from smallpox to have reached eight to ten a day. By August's end he concluded that at least five hundred Mandan and Hidatsa Indians had been killed by smallpox and by 19 September he raised that number to eight hundred dead. Chardon later remarked that the "Mandan and Rees gave us two splendid dances, they say they dance on account of that they do not have long to live, as they expect to all die of the smallpox, and as long as they are alive they will take it out in dancing." Aside from their dancing, some of the village Indians responded more directly to the disease by committing suicide. A young widow killed her two children and then hanged herself. A young Arikara man asked his mother to dig his grave and then walked into it, saying that all his young friends were gone and he wished to follow them.[17]

Roy Meyer remarks that the Indians surprisingly sought no vengeance against those who had brought the disease to them.[18] Still, the Mandan chief Four Bears (ca. 1795–1837) sought vainly to rally his supporters to attack the whites. Reflecting on his own relationships with Americans since the time of Lewis and Clark, Four Bears noted that more than three decades of peaceful trade only resulted in the ultimate undoing of his people:

My friends one and all, listen to what I say—Ever since I can remember, I have loved the Whites, I have lived with them ever since I was a Boy, and to the best of my Knowledge, I have never Wronged a White Man, on the Contrary, I have always Protected them from the insults of Others, Which they cannot deny. The 4 Bears never saw a White Man hungry, but what he gave him to eat, Drink, and a Buffaloe skin to sleep on, in time of Need, I was always ready to die for them, Which they cannot deny. I have done everything that a red Skin could do for them, and how have they repaid it! With ingratitude! I have Never called a White Man a Dog, but to day, I do Pronounce them to be a set of Black harted Dogs, they have deceived Me, them that I always considered as brothers, has turned out to be My Worst enemies. . . . Listen well what I have to say, as it will be the last time you will hear Me. Think of your Wives, Children, Brothers, Sisters, Friends, and in fact all that you hold dear, are all Dead, or Dying, with their faces all rotten, caused by those dogs the whites, think of

all that My friends, and rise all together and Not leave one of them alive. The
4 Bears will act his part.[19]

Weakened both physically and spiritually, and displaced within their own
trading systems, the three tribes became increasingly dependent on American commercial and military interests in the decades following the 1837
epidemic. By 1845 several Mandan and most of the Hidatsa moved further
upriver to jointly establish a new town, Like-a-Fishhook Village—which
soon attracted the looming presence of a new American trading establishment, Fort Berthold. It is not altogether clear why the new village was established, but Hidatsa legend holds that all the timber was gone at the old
sites by 1845 and some new village location had to be found. In any event,
by 1862 the consolidation of all the remaining Mandan and Arikara in that
village became the focus of life for the upper Missouri tribes over the next
forty years.[20]

The political integration of these three distinct Indian groups into an
affiliated or amalgamated tribal people was clearly the result of the 1837
pandemic. Though Mandan, Hidatsa, and Arikara individuals and groups
maintained distinct ethnic identities, from this time forward village leaders
and federal policy makers operated as if the Like-a-Fishhook community
represented a single tribe. Such amalgamation presented difficult challenges for tribal leaders, but also gave the village a numerical strength that
approximated the size of their once numerous town sites along the river. If
the Mandan, Hidatsa, and Arikara continued to live separately, they would
have been overwhelmed by the much larger equestrian groups on the plains
or become lost in the world of day labor that defined life in American trading establishments. While amalgamation presented necessary benefits, so
too did isolation. As Meyer notes, the Three Tribes remained "largely free
of overt white pressures, [and] retained their languages, their traditions,
their values, most of their material culture, and a heartening amount of
their dignity and sense of identity."[21] Nevertheless, the Three Tribes had
lost much in the decades following the epidemic—a fact that is probably
best measured by the magnitude of land they were forced to relinquish to
the United States. By executive order in 1870 and 1880, their land base was
diminished by approximately 80 percent to make way for a new railroad and
again reduced a further 60 percent in 1886.In all, about 11,424,513 acres
of tribal lands were taken, reducing the Indians' land base to approximately
the present-day size of the Fort Berthold Indian Reservation.[22]

NEW WORLDS AND OLD WATERS, 1886 THROUGH THE 1940S

The contemporary Fort Berthold Indian Reservation was formally established by agreement in 1886 "for the sole use and benefit" of the Mandan,

Hidatsa, and Arikara people.[23] By that agreement those Indians ceded to the United States all their lands north of the 48th parallel and west of a north-south line drawn six miles west of the most westerly point in the big bend of the Missouri River. The stated purpose of this reservation was to enable the Mandan, Hidatsa, and Arikara Indians "to obtain the means necessary to enable them to become wholly self-supporting by the cultivation of the soil and other pursuits of husbandry."[24] Though it involved a significant reduction of their land base, the Three Tribes kept true to the words in the 1886 agreement. This was recognized by the House Subcommittee on Public Lands in 1949 when it remarked that the Indians' development of an agricultural livestock industry [on the Fort Berthold reservation had] rendered them "in sight of complete economic independence."[25] By making full use of their reservation's available natural resources—"the wild game, the fruits and berries, the timber that grew in the river bottoms and along the tributary ravines, [and] the lignite coal," they continued to draw on their long-developed abilities to make a living from the "forbidding" country and climate of the Dakotas.[26]

The road to independence was also built during a long struggle to receive fair compensation for the lands ceded to the United States by the executive orders of 1870 and 1880. After three decades of petitions from tribal leaders, the U.S. Court of Claims eventually heard the Indians' arguments and in 1930 awarded them $4,923,093.47. However, the United States requested an offset of $2,753,924.89, ostensibly representing the amount it had expended gratuitously for the "support and civilization" of these Indians. The court granted that federal offset request and reduced the Indians' final award to $2,169,168.58. The joint congressional resolution of 1931 that approved this final award also directed that the money be doled out in per capita installments of about $200 to each eligible Indian beneficiary, for a total of $1,191.50 per individual. Although the agency superintendent feared that these per capita payments would be misspent on illegal liquor, most of the money seems to have gone toward housing improvements, and the purchase of beef and dairy cattle, and farm equipment.[27]

This money did not shield the beneficiaries completely from the worst effects of drought and economic depression in the mid-1930s. In 1934, the worst drought year on the Fort Berthold reservation, neither the Indian farm and ranch operators, nor their non-Indian lessees, earned any income from the parched earth. The Indian livestock operators had to radically destock their herds, selling their starving or diseased animals for disposal to the federal government and selling their healthy animals for whatever price they could get on the depressed livestock markets. Federal Indian rations, something the Indians had long foregone out of pride and self-sufficiency, returned during the depression years to the Fort Berthold reservation.[28]

As in its dealings with other Native communities, the federal government was slow to extend its "New Deal" public employment and works projects to the Fort Berthold reservation. By the late 1930s, however, a small Indian Conservation Corps became fairly active on the reservation, rebuilding bridges, developing dams and springs, latrines, garbage pits, or cattle guards, and helping in land revegetation efforts. Much of this came in the wake of the Indian Reorganization Act (IRA), the brainchild of the ambitious new Commissioner of Indian Affairs, John Collier. At its core, the IRA was Collier's effort to extend a constitutionally based, representative democracy to Indian country. Indian tribes that did not affirmatively vote to reject the IRA were required to adopt tribal constitutions and establish democratically elected, representative tribal councils. Collier assumed that the Fort Berthold reservation would be receptive to the IRA idea and he was proven right. On 17 November 1934 the Mandan, Hidatsa, and Arikara people voted to become one of the first "IRA-tribes" by a margin of 477 to 139. The biggest selling point was the federal promise of economic development aid to IRA tribes. Section 17 of the IRA allowed the tribal government to become a federally chartered corporation empowered to exercise the usual corporate powers of a for-profit business entity. Although the new tribal council voted to reorganize itself, the federal government once again broke its word: nothing came of the promised federal economic aid or the expected business development on the Fort Berthold Indian Reservation.[29]

Strengthened by the challenges of drought, depression, and the IRA, and sustained by the age-old gifts of the Missouri River, the Three Tribes entered the 1940s on solid footing. Environmental and political change would soon undermine their relationship to the river, and the tribes would be forced to draw on all the lessons of the past to navigate their way through a daunting future. The upper Missouri River was a friend to these Indians, but non-Indian settlers and later downstream city dwellers viewed the river's changeable nature as a menace to their lives and property. A huge flood in 1943 wreaked havoc on downstream cities, industries, and farms, and led the downstream Missouri River states to demand a comprehensive congressional plan for flood control. Ironically, one of their greatest concerns involved protection of the channels and dikes that had taken several decades and millions of dollars to construct on the lower Missouri—but had also contributed to the disastrous magnitude of the flood.[30]

While the flood of 1943 inundated portions of the Fort Berthold reservation, its effects on the Three Tribes were relatively minor. However, its consequences would become permanent. When Congress passed the Flood Control Act of 1944, it called for a comprehensive approach to the development of the Missouri River basin for the purposes of flood control, irrigation, and navigation. Though a number of congressional representatives may have been ignorant of it at the time, the act also set the United States on a course to breach the central premise of its 1886 agreement with the Mandan, Hidatsa, and Arikara: namely, to reserve a stretch of the fertile bottomlands along the Missouri River to ensure the Three Tribes could "obtain the means necessary to enable them to become wholly self-supporting by cultivation of the soil and other pursuits of husbandry." The consequence of these broken words would be the greatest threat to the survival of these tribal people since the epidemic of 1837.

SURVIVING THE ENGINEERED FLOOD, 1953 TO THE 1980S

The Flood Control Act incorporated two competing proposals, one championed by Colonel Pick of the Army Corps of Engineers and one from W. Glenn Sloan of the Bureau of Reclamation. The Pick-Sloan Program was hailed as the answer to the region's prayers for an end to the twin devastations caused by recurring summer dust bowls and spring floods. The program called for a mammoth multipurpose water development program that entailed the construction of four major main-stem dams along the Missouri River: three in South Dakota, Gavins Point near Yankton, Big Bend at Fort Thompson, and Oahe at Pierre; and one in North Dakota, Garrison at Riverdale. The Pick-Sloan Program was carefully planned so that its reservoirs would not inundate any non-Indian towns along the Missouri River. But the Mandan, Hidatsa, and Arikara people were not so fortunate. The Garrison Dam was intended to serve as the "high dam"—the major regulating structure—in the Pick-Sloan Program, and its reservoir would inundate all of the riparian lands that had been reserved to the Three Tribes by the terms of the 1886 agreement with the United States.[31]

The Flood Control Act of 1944 had been adopted by Congress without any consultation with the Mandan, Hidatsa, and Arikara people. The first real experience of these Indians with the coming of the Garrison Dam occurred when the Corps of Engineers entered the reservation to begin construction in April 1946. The Mandan, Hidatsa, and Arikara people—led by their tribal chairman, Martin Cross—petitioned Congress to prohibit the construction of the Garrison Dam on their reservation as a direct violation of the terms of their 1886 agreement with the United States. Their efforts in this regard inspired the creation of a congressionally established group known as the Missouri River Basin Investigations (MRBI), which essentially affirmed the Indians' basic argument that constructing one of the world's largest earth-filled dams on the Fort Berthold reservation would irretrievably disrupt the economic and social life of an ancient tribal people.[32]

The MRBI reports highlighted the expected adverse impacts of the Garrison Dam. First, approximately 90 percent of the Indian people would have to be removed from their historic settlements along the bottomlands of the Missouri River. Second, the agricultural treaty purposes of the Fort

Berthold reservation would be frustrated due to the flooding of the Indians' arable land base. Third, the only agriculturally self-sufficient Indian tribes on the Great Plains would have their economic and social base destroyed by the proposed flooding and would likely be reduced to dependence on the federal government for their future subsistence and maintenance.[33]

Indian resistance to the dam eventually received a partial response from Congress, which statutorily forbade the corps's building of any of the dam's major structural features until the secretary of war located and offered an adequate replacement reservation to the affected Indians.[34] While tribal leaders were cool to the idea of a new reservation, dam proponents argued that this standard of compensation was too high and would set a dangerous precedent for the corps's negotiations with the downstream Indian tribes who likewise opposed the taking of their lands for the Pick-Sloan Program.[35] The secretary of war seemed to share the concerns of this latter group and suggested that it would be hard to convince local non-Indian communities to accept the creation of a large replacement reservation for the relocated Mandan, Hidatsa, and Arikara Indians. Nevertheless, he did locate and propose a few potential new reservation sites, but the tribal council and the secretary of interior alike rejected them on the grounds that they failed to meet the requirement that the replacement lands be of "like quality and quantity" as the taken Indian lands. Project proponents then contended that the Indians' refusal to accept these replacement lands demonstrated the impracticability of this congressional compensation scheme.[36] Mounting constituent pressure forced Congress to move speedily on the construction of the Garrison Dam, and it responded in kind. Once the Indians and the secretary of the interior rejected the war secretary's last offer of replacement lands, Congress rescinded the construction ban and ordered the removal of the Mandan, Hidatsa, and Arikara Indians from their soon-to-be-inundated lands.[37]

Once it became clear to tribal leaders that they could not stave off the construction of Garrison Dam, they focused their energies on obtaining just compensation. While the value of their lands was considerable, just compensation would also have to ensure that tribal members could effectively operate in a cash economy. As the Interior Department reported to Congress in 1949, "Most of the natural resources upon which the Indians depend for subsistence will be wiped out by the completion of the Garrison project. . . . Most of the surface coal deposits from which the Indians mine their coal will be flooded. . . . [F]amilies obtain almost all of their fuel, a large portion of their meat and fruit, a considerable amount of garden vegetables, and most of their building materials without the expenditure of any cash. After the inundation of these natural resources by the Garrison Reservoir Project, the amount of cash will be greatly increased."[38] The Corps of Engineers and Congress pressured the Indians to accept a quick settlement, and a certain degree of fatalism among the Mandan, Hidatsa, and Arikara made them susceptible to these outside demands. Nevertheless, tribal leaders insisted that any agreement must preserve their right to sue for just compensation at a future date. They eventually proved successful in this matter, forcing the inclusion of a provision that would allow them to bring a just compensation suit in the Court of Claims for any additional damages "of any treaty obligation of the Government or in any intangible cost of reestablishment or relocation for which the said tribes are not compensated."[39]

Just compensation and future legal rights were not easily secured, however. Senator Arthur V. Watkins, chair of the Senate Indian Affairs Committee, reasoned that Congress, not the courts, was the appropriate forum for determining the appropriate compensation for the Indians. Watkins rightly claimed there was a "substantial unanimity of opinion [in the Senate on this matter,] to the effect that Congress should provide a definitive settlement with the Three Affiliated Tribes." Watkins's views stemmed from his interpretation of Congress's plenary power over Indian lands, and he assured the Indians that any congressional settlement would be "both just and generous, . . . thereby removing any reason [or] necessity for further action in the Court of Claims." The Mandan, Hidatsa, and Arikara Indians remained unconvinced of Senator Watkins's sincerity and were forced to watch in horror as the Utah Republican's control of a key committee allowed him to override standard legislative processes for determining just compensation.[40]

The House Committee on Public Lands and the Senate Indian Affairs Committees did briefly debate the cost-versus-loss basis for just compensation.[41] For example, the House committee was clearly uneasy with the corps's cavalier assertion that payment of fair market value to individual Indian landowners would adequately compensate the Mandan, Hidatsa, and Arikara people for their losses from this taking: "The Committee . . . feels that [the corps's figure of $17 million] is small compensation for the disruption forced upon the 2,215 Indians. A conservative estimate of the basic value of the lands and their annual use value is approximately $21,981,000. Therefore, the United States . . . will obtain the reservoir right-of-way at about two-thirds of its basic value and its annual use value."[42] Individual congressmen, such as Mr. Lemke from North Dakota, colorfully expressed their dismay that the Indians were to be paid an amount of compensation substantially less than the real economic value of their treaty-reserved lands: "Here is a factory . . . that produced a net income last year of $774,000. That alone capitalized at 4 per cent equal about twenty million. Surely no one would voluntarily surrender an income of 4 per cent on twenty million for less than twenty million cash. . . . In taking these lands, we are . . . depriving these tribes of their land for less than its value."[43]

Despite the clarity of these arguments, which tended to favor an earlier MRBI report that had capitalized the value of the taken Indian lands at a conservative estimate of $21,981,000, the House and Senate jointly proposed a settlement of approximately $17 million. This smaller total was based on the following elements: $5.1 million for the fair market value of the inundated Indian trust lands and related relocation costs; $3 million for a land readjustment fund that would be used to consolidate fragmented land holdings of tribal members into viable economic units and to purchase private lands for needy tribal members; $6.5 million as additional compensation to the Three Affiliated Tribes for "values not compensated for under the contract;" and approximately $2.4 million for 20,000 kilowatts of electric power (when available from the Garrison Dam) "for sale and distribution by the . . . Tribes . . . delivered at such points or points on the reservation . . . as may be determined by the Secretary of the Interior;" and of "any irrigation works and related facilities which . . . the Secretary of the Interior determines to be feasible. . . . If constructed, the irrigation works must be operated on a basis not less favorable than to non-Indian lands, and the costs thereof must be repayable in accordance with the terms of other laws applicable to Indian lands."[44]

However unjust, the compensation for taking the Garrison Dam never followed hard economics. Instead, the amount was ultimately determined by the comparative power of the House Committee on Public Lands and the Senate Indian Affairs Committee. The minimum just compensation amount proposed in the joint resolution of the House and Senate was repeatedly reduced by Senator Watkins's committee.[45] When all the "horse trading" was completed, the House and Senate committees ultimately agreed on a compensation figure of $12.6 million, and on 15 March 1950, the Fort Berthold Indians reluctantly agreed to accept that final amount.[46] The dramatic downward spiral of the original compensation proposal did not escape the attention of tribal leaders' attention, who advised tribal members "that if we should reject the Act, the next offer of the government probably would not be even as good as the one we are considering."[47] However, they knew another day might come.

Their removal to make way for the Garrison Dam in 1953 was perhaps the most traumatic event that the Mandan, Hidatsa, and Arikara people faced since the 1837 smallpox epidemic. While this trauma often played out in destructive personal reactions—such as increased domestic violence and alcoholism—it took place in a broader context of internal divisions among tribal leaders, external political threats, and the geographic fragmentation of the reservation community. These were all graphically illustrated on the April 1953 cover of the *Fort Berthold Agency News Bulletin* in which Lake Sakakawea was portrayed as a sea serpent spreading its tentacles over a radically segmented and divided Fort Berthold reservation.[48]

How to spend the compensation for the Garrison taking fueled political in-fighting between two powerful tribal leaders—Martin Cross and Carl

Whitman, Jr. Cross favored a per capita distribution of virtually all of the monies to individual tribal members while Whitman favored the retention of most of these monies in tribal programs to address the long-term needs of the Indian people. Cross used his position on this key issue to defeat Whitman in the 1950 tribal council election, but the matter dominated tribal politics until the U.S. Congress agreed to a per capita payment in 1957. This internal debate within the tribe was shadowed by the new Indian policy of termination, which sought to "terminate" federal treaty obligations and end the unique government to government relationship between Indian tribes and the United States. In this context, the Bureau of Indian Affairs (BIA) attempted to exploit both sides of the per capita debate on the Fort Berthold reservation. If funds went to the tribe as a whole, reasoned Indian Commissioner Dillon S. Myer, and the tribal government had confidence that it could manage and spend millions of dollars, then it no longer needed a treaty relationship with the United States or the supervision of the BIA. Yet BIA officials also viewed per capita distribution of the Garrison taking as a sort of de facto detribalization: if individuals received all the money, then they apparently no longer thought in tribal terms and thus had no need to operate under the terms of past treaties. Cross and the tribal council responded in an artful manner to Commissioner Myers's desire to terminate the tribe on any grounds: "We are opposed to the withdrawal by the government of any *help* that they give us. . . . We only oppose their *interference* with our management of our own property and money."[49]

The Three Tribes effectively staved off termination, but the BIA-administered relocation of tribal members away from the areas flooded by Garrison Dam had severe consequences for the reservation community. The BIA sought to use relocation as an opportunity to recreate Fort Berthold as new, dispersed tribal communities on the residual high plains of the reservation. These new communities—Mandaree, Twin Buttes, and New Town—sought to fuse the three tribal groups into one new tribal identity. Indeed, the name Mandaree is a composite of the syllables *Man*(dan), (Hi)*da*(tsa) and (Arika)*ree*. But the reality of physical separation on the desolate high plains imposed severe limits on governmental and economic integration of the Fort Berthold reservation. The resulting geographic of the reservation community onto far-flung, unproductive parcels of land was reflected in the Indians' deteriorating social welfare status and the substantial decline in their incomes from farming and grazing leases. While 39 percent of their income came from such leases during the World War II years, only 10 percent of their income derived from these sources after the Garrison Dam. Welfare that had amounted to just 1 percent of reservation income for the years prior to the dam accounted for over 9 percent of reservation income after the dam.[50]

Besides fragmenting the reservation's social geography, the creation of

Lake Sakakawea eroded the tribal integrity of the Fort Berthold community by fostering the absorption of tribal members into surrounding non-Indian institutions and economy. When their distinctive Indian schools disappeared under the waters of the vast reservoir, most Indian children either attended public schools on the reservation or made the long trek to off-reservation BIA-run boarding schools. Young Indian men and women also began to see themselves primarily as wage laborers, hiring out as help on non-Indian-run farms and ranches or relocating to off-reservation establishments. This change was especially marked in the early 1960s, as wage income increased from 14 percent in the pre-dam era to 43 percent in the post-dam era. While the scope of psychological damage cannot be fully summarized in statistics, the Mandan, Hidatsa, and Arikara peoples clearly had to face substantial adjustment challenges in adapting to their new reservation setting.[51]

The new federal program of relocation only exacerbated these tendencies, as the BIA encouraged young men and women on reservations throughout the West to move to urban areas such as Denver, Oakland, or Chicago where their chances for employment might be better. Many young people from the Fort Berthold reservation went through the "relocation" process during the 1950s and 1960s, but most did not experience any substantial improvement in their material circumstances. The reservation community sorely missed their presence, however—notwithstanding the claims of Superintendent Ralph Shane, who in 1954 asserted that the Indians would one day thank the United States because all the changes on the reservation were "by no means the end of the trail for any people, any culture, any way of life, nor an ascending economy." He believed that the challenges of the post-dam era, just like the trials they had undergone in the past, would ultimately benefit the members of the Three Tribes if they could arise to meet them.[52]

MAKING WORDS MATTER, 1984 TO 1992

Rising to meet challenges was never a virtue in short supply among the Mandan, Hidatsa, and Arikara Indians. Yet the devastation wrought by the Army Corps of Engineers and the Bureau of Indian Affairs had terribly undermined the Three Tribes and transformed them from a self-sufficient people to a fragmented and weakened community that was increasingly dependent on outside political and economic developments. In a slowly disintegrating situation, the Three Tribes had only one real strategy for overcoming the consequences of Lake Sakakawea and reclaiming the independence they had once almost achieved, and it hinged on tribal efforts: convince the government to revisit the costs of the 1949 Taking Act. They finally succeeded in 1984, when Congress established the Garrison Diversion Unit Commission (GDUC). This eleven-member body—charged with reviewing a host of issues including problems involving land acquisition, environmental impacts, irrigation rights, and international treaties over shared water resources with Canada—quickly determined that the Three Tribes had borne a disproportionate share of the economic burden in having the Garrison Dam and reservoir located on their most productive tribal homelands. The GDUC based this finding on its review of the legislative record of the 1949 Taking Act and concluded that the Indians had suffered devastating economic, cultural, and social losses from the seizure of their most productive agricultural lands. In short, they paid the price for a project that benefited only downstream communities and industries. The GDUC, moreover, found that Congress may have failed to make the Mandan, Hidatsa, and Arikara people whole for these economic losses.[53]

According to its mandate, the GDUC directed Secretary of the Interior Donald P. Hodel to hold administrative hearings on the Indians' just compensation and related claims arising from the 1949 taking. Hodel subsequently established the Joint Tribal Advisory Committee (JTAC), which was charged with examining whether the federal government had failed to justly compensate the Three Tribes for their economic losses and, if so, to recommend appropriate implementing legislation to make appropriate amends.[54] On the urging of the Indian people, the JTAC construed its charter so as to allow relevant lay and expert testimony about the devastation of tribal culture and economy. And the hearings before the JTAC provided the organizational catalyst for the Mandan, Hidatsa and Arikara people to join together. They urged the JTAC to review the entire circumstances surrounding this federal taking, and to ensure a reliable and comprehensive inquiry into its fairness.[55]

Whether the federal government had made a good faith effort to justly compensate the Mandan, Hidatsa, and Arikara people was the most significant issue confronted by the JTAC. Focusing on the administrative and legislative record that ostensibly justified the 1949 Garrison taking, the committee paid particular attention to Indian claims that demonstrated the failure to fulfill the "make whole" standard of the Just Compensation Clause.[56] The Indians argued that Senator Watkins's Indian committee failed to justly compensate them for their taken lands, given that their lands should have been valued on the same basis as non-Indian lands that served comparable governmental and public welfare functions. They contended that this valuation standard would fulfill two important underlying goals of the Just Compensation Clause. First, such a valuation standard would ensure the continued viability of the affected Indian peoples as a recognized government consistent with the purpose of their 1886 agreement with the federal government. Second, such a valuation standard would discourage future "rent-seeking" initiatives by Indian congressional committees that sought to exploit their plenary power over Indian lands for their non-Indian constituents' benefits.[57]

The Indians' treaty-reserved lands formed the essential trust that supported their economic and governmental infrastructure. In particular, the destruction of 156,035 acres of easily irrigable bottomlands imposed economic losses that could be measured only by the capitalized value of the expected future incomes that those lands would have generated. The JTAC recognized that the federal government had a legal duty to make the Indians whole for their economic losses based on known and accepted 1949 valuation standards. Such a valuation approach replicated the 1946 congressional valuation standard that required the War Department to provide the Indians with the "in-kind" replacement value of their taken lands.[58] The JTAC's next task was to determine the amount of replacement or substitute value that would adequately compensate Indians for the loss of their lands. Such an alternative valuation standard had been endorsed by the Supreme Court in the federal taking of lands that served essential governmental or public welfare functions. That the Indians' taken lands provided the social welfare and governmental benefits described by the Court was evidenced by their use within the tribal farming and ranching activities as contemplated by the 1886 agreement. Only the continued existence of those lands, or the just compensation equivalent, would ensure that the Indians would be able to fulfill those treaty-defined goals embodied in that agreement.

The JTAC issued its final report in 1986 and recommended that the secretary of the interior propose federal legislation on behalf of the Mandan, Hidatsa, and Arikara people that would award just compensation to those Indians for the 1949 taking of the Fort Berthold Indian Reservation. As the JTAC chairman Major General C. Emerson Murry noted, the enactment of just compensation legislation would allow the tribes to reestablish a viable economic base "that was destroyed by the construction of the [Garrison dam and reservoir]." The amount that Congress should provide as just compensation was based on two valuation formulas, and the JTAC recommended a range of $178.4 million to $411.8 million as just compensation.[59]

Interior Secretary Hodel declined to accept the JTAC report or implement any of that commission's recommendations. Instead, the Senate Select Committee on Indian Affairs and the House Interior Subcommittee on Water and Power initiated joint oversight hearings on the JTAC's final report in 1986.[60] The JTAC's just compensation recommendation was referred by the Select Committee to the General Accounting Office (GAO) for its analysis and response. The GAO report, issued in 1990, concluded that the JTAC's findings provided a substantial basis for Congress to consider an equitable award of just compensation to the Indians in the amount of $149.5 million.[61] After lengthy discussions with the various interested groups, such as the National Rural Electric Cooperatives Association, tribal leaders crafted an agreement that authorized the deposit of a specified amount of Pick-Sloan hydropower receipts into a treasury account on behalf of the Three Affiliated Tribes.[62] In addition, the Indians were required to submit an economic and social recovery plan to the interior secretary that would govern the future expenditure of the accumulated interest on that account once the principal had reached $149.5 million. President George H. W. Bush threatened to veto the legislation but eventually signed the just compensation act into law in November 1992 as part of a larger water resources development bill.[63]

CLOSING THE CIRCLE

The Mandan, Hidatsa, and Arikara people have survived much, endured much, along their two-hundred-year journey from 1804 to 2004. They now confront a new "disjunctive" moment in their collective life as an Indian people: can they effectively use the $149.5 million in just compensation to reverse history and recover socially and economically as an Indian people? Unlike the "one-shot" decision in the 1957 tribal referendum to "per-cap" the government's compensation for the Garrison taking, the governing statute on the use of the $149.5 million precludes any such self-interested solution. Because only the accrued interest from this trust fund will be distributed on an annualized basis to the tribe as a whole, the members of the Three Affiliated Tribes will be forced again and again collectively to redecide the best use of the distributed interest income for their economic and social recovery as a tribal people.[64]

As "repeat players," the various advocates for competing social and economic recovery projects will be forced to build coalitions and alliances to convince the interior secretary, who holds the trust fund, that a majority of the Indian people support a particular approach to social and economic recovery on the Fort Berthold Indian Reservation. There is some evidence that such a process is already under way among the Mandan, Hidatsa, and Arikara people. Between 1992 and 1999, the accrued interest on this fund of $149.5 million had accumulated to $33 million. The current tribal business council has proposed a plan for investing $30 million of the monies in a tribal endowment fund that would be managed by a private investment firm. It promises that this investment will earn an expected annual interest rate of 10 percent, compared to a 6.5 percent annual rate of interest those funds would earn if they are administered by the federal Office of Trust Funds Management. Under the council's plan, about 50 percent of the endowment's annual income would be reinvested into the corpus of the fund. The remaining 50 percent of the annual income would be made available for tribal programs consistent with the council's proposed tribal social and economic recovery plan.[65]

Not surprisingly, the appropriate use of such a large sum of money has prompted much heated discussion among various tribal constituencies. Because the tribal business council's plan authorizes that body to invade the fund's corpus and use up to 25 percent of its principal as security for any borrowing authorized by the tribal council, many tribal members have greeted such plans with skepticism. They question whether stepping away from federal trust management of this major tribal resource is a good idea. Some fear that this is a "power-grab" by a potentially corrupt tribal council that would misuse those tribal funds for personal benefit. Other tribal members fear that approval of such a plan would motivate individuals to "get on the council" so they can invade the proposed endowment fund for their own pet projects.[66] Far from dismaying anyone, such controversy represents a catalytic moment for the Mandan, Hidatsa, and Arikara people as they strive to reclaim responsibility for their economic and social futures. It is a daunting task but only these Indian peoples can successfully reinternalize those values, needs, and circumstances that brought them together originally as the Three Affiliated Tribes. Indeed, the $149.5 million serves as the crude surrogate for these values as the Indian peoples seek to reconstitute their society so as to address their social and economic recovery needs.[67]

Ever since their encounter with Lewis and Clark in 1804, the Mandan, Hidatsa, and Arikara people have been enfolded into a non-Indian historical process that they may now have an opportunity to escape. These people's conscious assumption of their economic and social recovery task will lift them outside of dependency. And because dependency has enveloped them for so long, they will have to expend a great deal of collective social and emotional energy to escape. By penetrating the veil of their burdensome American historical experience, the Mandan, Hidatsa, and Arikara people can restore their distinctive character within a radically resituated Fort Berthold Indian Reservation. Such conscious self-exertion marks the classic strategy of the Indian peoples in carving out a place for themselves within an oftentimes hostile American society. It is the young Black Elk's vision:

And as I looked and wept, I saw that there stood on the north side of the Starving camp a Sacred man who was painted red all over his body, and he held a spear as he walked into the center of his people, and there he laid down and rolled. And when he got up it was a fat bison standing there, and where the bison stood a Sacred herb sprang right up where the tree had been in the center of the nation's hoop. The herb grew and bore four blossoms on a single stem while I was looking—a blue, white, a scarlet and a yellow—and the bright rays of these flashed to the heavens.[68]

As the Mandan, Hidatsa, and Arikara people embark on their path of social and economic recovery, they must confront the high psychic and social costs imposed by the accumulated effects of their historical experience. Cross-cultural psychologists have diagnosed a syndrome called "intergenerational post traumatic stress disorder" that reflects the accumulated adverse effects on Indian peoples of their two-hundred-year experience with United States. It surfaced in a persistent and chronic "spiritual injury" when "the psyche of the community recognized the wounding of the community." A wound to the community was a wound to that community's psyche: harmony had become discord and the community's unconscious perception was that the world was unfriendly and hostile. The problems that were manifested and verbalized were merely symptoms of a deeper wound—the soul wound.[69] To convert $149.5 million into an effective therapy requires the development of strategies that will directly address the assorted maladies that evidence the "soul wound" to the Mandan, Hidatsa, and Arikara peoples. The major task for the Three Affiliated Tribes will be to use these funds in a deliberative, collective effort to "break" the intergenerational transmission of societal trauma.

Repeated and necessary confrontations among powerful tribal constituencies in constructing effective economic and social recovery strategies will eventually result in a new constitution for the Three Affiliated Tribes. In turn the new constitution will reconnect these contesting tribal constituencies and renew their latent and emerging values. At the pragmatic and instrumental level, these confrontations will distill these values and demands into socially accountable political expression, and in turn, effective and responsive institutions of governance. At the societal level, these confrontations will re-embed the tribal government in a renewed tribal identity. Only through such a reconstitutionalizing effort can the tribes reclaim their own institutions from an imposed Americanized identity under John Collier's IRA and federal Indian common law.[70]

I offer only general guidelines for this task; to do more would unduly intrude into the free sovereign choice of these Indian peoples. My recommendations draw upon Amartya Sen's recent constructive approach to social governance as the essential means for realizing human freedom. First, such a tribal constitution would consciously promote the full development of the human capabilities of individual tribal members by according them appropriate opportunities for meaningful social and political participation. Second, such a tribal constitution would explicitly promote the growth of traditional tribal constituencies and encourage the express articulation of their interests and values in a socially comprehensible manner. Third, such a tribal constitution would require the ruling leadership to demonstrate that it "hears" their peoples' demands and needs by responding in a politically and socially accountable manner.[71]

Two additional background requirements provide the context for the "working out" of this new tribal constitution. First, these Indian people must consciously reject what the philosopher Mary Midgley calls the paralyzing "menace of fatalism." This fatalism is embodied in the prevailing American view that innate genetic, cultural, or biological factors have doomed the contemporary Indian societies to decline and eventual disappearance. Many Indian people, including some on the Fort Berthold Indian Reservation, have "bought into" this view. Only by rejecting such fatalism about their future as an Indian people will the Mandan, Hidatsa, and Arikara people avoid such a paralysis of action.[72]

Second, these Indian people must adopt the principle of "enoughness" as expressing their confidence that they can effectively use their existing material and social resources as they define and meet their pressing human needs.[73] Only by agreeing that $149.5 million can be subdivided into enough societal resources—money, food, power, prestige, and authority— to meet peoples' needs in a socially accountable manner, will the constitutionalizing process succeed. This will require future tribal councils to prudently "grow" this $149.5 million in a manner that creates a sustainable "steady-state" economy so as to ensure the fair and equitable distribution of their resources in a socially accountable manner.[74]

The foundational human factors of water, disease, and words have fundamentally conditioned the contemporary "tribal life worlds" of the Three Affiliated Tribes. If Lewis and Clark were to revisit these Indian people today they likely would not fully grasp or appreciate the impact these factors have wrought on the contemporary Mandan, Hidatsa, and Arikara people. But if their return visit occurs two hundred years from today, I believe that they will encounter an Indian people who have reclaimed in large measure their heritage of social and economic vibrancy along the Missouri River. The exact contours of such a re-creation must be left to the working out of their new tribal constitution and their corresponding mode of self-governance. This much is clear: it is up to the Mandan, Hidatsa, and Arikara people to continue their sacred journey upriver as best they can. If history is any guide, great dangers and risks hedge this future journey. But, from 1804 to 2004, the Indian people have encountered and survived many things. This fact alone will likely give them the needed confidence to return to that journey, from which they were only temporarily deflected by an overbearing American historical experience.

NOTES

1. According to Professor Virginia Peters the ancestors of the Mandan Indians settled the upper Missouri River between the mouth of the White River and the Little Missouri around 1100 A.D. to 1400 A.D. See Virginia Bergman Peters, *Women of the Earth Lodges: Tribal Life on the Plains* (North Haven, Conn.: Archon Books, 1995), 19.

2. Ibid., 24–30. This is one of a family of creation myths told by the Mandan, Hidatsa, and Arikara Indians. The Mandan's cultural hero, Lone Man, along with Itsikamahidis, or First Worker, jointly created the ground, grass, trees, animals, birds, and running water over a period of six days. The river that they created to separate their respective works was apparently the Missouri River. The Arikara hold that it was Mother Corn who brought them to the Missouri River region out of the deep darkness of the cave in which they first resided. Skunk, Badger, and Mole helped Mother Corn tunnel out of the cave and into the light of a gracious land.

3. Three Affiliated Tribes Equitable Compensation Act, Reclamation Projects Authorization and Adjustment Act of 1992, Pub L no. 102–575, tit 35, 106 Stat 4731.

4. Raymond Cross, "Sovereign Bargains, Indian Takings and the Preservation of Indian Country in the Twenty-First Century," *Arizona Law Review* 40 (summer 1998): 425–509.

5. Roy W. Meyer, *The Village Indians of the Upper Missouri: The Mandan, Hidatsas and Arikaras* (Lincoln: University of Nebraska Press, 1977), 1–17.

6. Ibid., 2–3.

7. Ibid., 15–16.

8. John Seelye, "Beyond the Shining Mountains: The Lewis and Clark Expedition as an Enlightenment Epic," *The Virginia Quarterly Review* 63 (1987): 40.

9. Ibid., 44–45.

10. Ibid., 45–46.

11. Meyer, *Village Indians*, 42.

12. James P. Ronda, *Lewis and Clark among the Indians* (Lincoln: University of Nebraska Press, 1984), 102–103.

13. Ibid., 92.

14. Ibid., 81–84.

15. Ibid., 2. Also see Elizabeth A. Fenn, "Biological Warfare in Eighteenth Century America: Beyond Jeffery Amherst," *Journal of American History* 86 (March 2000): 1552–1580.

16. The Mandan population's historic high (in the late eighteenth century) was 8,000. After the epidemic had already destroyed many in the closely settled Indian villages, Indian Commissioner Joshua Pilcher proposed that the federal government expend $2,000 on vaccinating all those Indians of the upper Missouri River region who would agree to that procedure. After a long delay in receiving federal approval, Pilcher succeeded in vaccinating about 3,000 members of the nomadic tribes such as the Sioux who, because of their dispersed populations, had not been as adversely affected as the closely settled Mandan, Hidatsa, and Arikara peoples (Meyer, *Village Indians*, 91–96).

17. Ibid., 93, 97.

18. Ibid., 93.

19. Ibid., 94.

20. Ibid., 98–109.

21. Ibid., 109.

22. Ibid., 188.

23. Charles J. Kappler, comp. and ed., *Indian Affairs: Laws and Treaties* (1904–41; reprint, New York: AMS Press, 1971), 1:426.

24. Ibid.

25. The House Subcommittee on Public Lands explained that because of the Garrison Dam the Indians' "homes will be lost, their cattle industry will be ruined, their churches and schools and their social life will be completely disrupted" (H Rep no. 81–544, at 3 [1949]).

26. Roy W. Meyer, "The Fort Berthold Reservation and the Garrison Dam," *North Dakota History* 35 (summer 1968): 215, 233; Cross, "Sovereign Bargains," 499–500.

27. Meyer, *Village Indians*, 186–190.

28. Ibid., 190.

29. Ibid.,190–196. Ironically, many of the Indian dissidents objected to the IRA's effort to "retribalize" the Indians as contrary to the assimilation and acculturation goals of earlier federal Indian policies.

30. Constance E. Hunt, *Down By the River: The Impact of Federal Water Projects and Policies on Biological Diversity* (Washington, D.C.: Island Press, 1988), 116–118.

31. The states in the lower and upper Missouri River basin differed as to why the Missouri River should be controlled by a series of federal dams and reservoirs. The upstream states (North and South Dakota, Montana, and Wyoming) were interested primarily in developing the irrigation potential of the river. The downstream states (Nebraska, Iowa, Kansas, and Missouri) were more interested in flood control. See Flood Control Act of 1944, 16 U.S.C 460d (and various sections of Titles 33 and 43 U.S.C); P.L 78–534, 22 December 1944; 58 Stat 887. Congressman Lemke from North Dakota made it clear that by taking these Indians' lands, Congress was "again violating a treaty solemnly entered into [in 1886] with these tribes—a treaty in which we promised never to disturb them again" (Cross, "Sovereign Bargains," 484).

32. H. D. McCullough, "Social and Economic Report on the Future of the Fort Berthold Reservation, North Dakota," Department of the Interior, Bureau of Indian Affairs, Missouri River Basin Investigations Report no. 46, 24 December 1947 (Billings, Mont.). Also see Michael L. Lawson, *Dammed Indians: The Pick-Sloan Plan and the Missouri River Sioux, 1944–1980* (Norman: University of Oklahoma Press, 1982), 59; and Meyer, *Village Indians*, 213.

33. Meyer, *Village Indians*, 213–214.

34. War Department Civil Appropriations Act, Pub L no. 79–374, section 6, 60 Stat 167 (1946).

35. Lawson, *Dammed Indians*, 62–63

36. Governor Aandahl and Senators Young and Langer of North Dakota agreed that the Garrison Dam must go forward and the Indians must be removed to make way for the dam (Meyer, *Village Indians*, 214–217).

37. War Department Civil Appropriations Act, ch. 411, Pub L no. 80–296, 61 Stat 686, 690 (1947). Roy Meyer comments that Pub L no. 80–296 represented "forced" legislation that ignored the interests and treaty reserved rights of the Mandan, Hidatsa and Arikara Indians (*Village Indians*, 234).

38. Bureau of Indian Affairs, Department of the Interior Report no. 94, "Social & Economic Report of Fort Berthold Indian Reservation" 12, 17 (Supp I, 1949).

39. War Department Civil Appropriation Act, 1948, ch 411, Pub L no. 81–296, 61 Stat 686, 690 (1947) Also see Meyer, "The Fort Berthold Reservation," 257–261.

40. Meyer, "The Fort Berthold Reservation," 261–263. Also see Glynn S. Lunney, Jr., "Compensation for Takings: How Much is Just?" *Catholic University Law Review* 42 (summer 1993): 721–756.

41. Ronald G. Cummings, "Valuing the Resource Base Lost by the Three Affiliated Tribes As a Result of Lands Taken from Them for the Garrison Project" (report prepared for the JTAC, on file with the author).

42. H.R Rep no. 81–544, at 3–4 (1949).

43. 95 Cong Rec 15052, 15051 (1949).

44. H Rep no. 81–544. Also see Cummings, "Valuing the Resource Base."

45. The Senate version of what became House Joint Resolution 33 "struck everything but the legal description of the taking area" (Meyer, "Fort Berthold Reservation," 263). At the conference on the rival bills, "some House members expressed dissatisfaction with the bill in its final form, as they well might, but a sense of urgency and perhaps the futility of further wrangling led them to accept it" (Cummings, "Valuing the Resource Base").

46. Meyer reports that "[t]he approval by the Tribes called for was obtained by a vote in 525 affirmative votes were cast out of 900 eligible voters and on 15 March 1950, council chairman Carl Whitman, Jr., with a seven-man delegation, presented a briefcase containing the ballots to Secretary Chapman" (Meyer, "Fort Berthold Reservation," 264).

47. Quoted in Cummings, "Valuing the Resource Base."

48. Meyer, *Village Indians*, 231.

49. Ibid., 230–231.

50. Ibid., 228.

51. Ibid., 224–228.

52. Ralph Shane quoted in ibid., 228. Also see ibid., 226–231; and Donald L. Fixico, *Termination and Relocation: Federal Indian Policy, 1945–1960* (Albuquerque: University of New Mexico Press, 1986).

53. *Recommendations of the GDUC on H.R 1116, A Bill to Implement Certain Recommendations of the Garrison Diversion Unit Commission Pursuant to Pub L 98–360, Hearings on H.R Before the Subcomm On Water and Power Resources of the House Comm On Interior and Insular Affairs*, 99th Cong 114 (1985).

54. Secretary Donald P. Hodel created the JTAC on 10 May 1985, and that committee submitted its final report to the secretary on 23 May 1986 (see S Rep no. 102–250 [1992]).

55. Ibid.

56. The Supreme Court first enunciated the equivalent value or "make whole" standard for just compensation in *Monongahela Navigation Co v United States*, 148 U.S 312, 326, 341 (1893).

57. Cummings, "Valuing the Resource Base." Cummings notes that Senator Watkins and the rest of the Indian committee were keenly aware that, in light of the MRBI reports, the Fort Berthold Indians would lose the vast majority of their arable and irrigable land base that was the essential means for carrying out the purpose of the 1886 treaty agreement.

58. *Hearings on S 168*, at 16–19; Meyer, "Fort Berthold Reservation," 257–261.

59. S Rep no. 102–250, at 3 (1992). The JTAC's award range reflects the application of these alternative land and resources valuation formulas. In calculating compensation, the JTAC had directed Dr. Ronald G. Cummings to use two alternative formulas.

60. The Senate report notes that the Select Committee on Indian Affairs held three oversight hearings on the JTAC recommendations beginning on 31 March 1987, with a joint oversight hearing with the Senate Energy and Natural Resources Committee and the Water and Power Subcommittee of the House Committee on Interior and Insular Affairs. That hearing examined the need for legislation to implement the recommendations of the JTAC report. The second hearing was held on 19 November 1987, wherein the committee "urged" the tribes to provide "further justification for the level of additional financial compensation to which they felt they were entitled" and "explore a budget neutral to finance the compensation needed to carry out the recommendations." In the third hearing regarding S 168, the tribes "expressed their overall support for the bill" and the GAO "expressed its approval of the compensation figures set forth in [S 168]" (ibid.).

61. Government Accounting Office, *Report to the Chairman, Senate Select Committee on Indian Affairs, Indian Issues: Compensation Claims Analysis Overstates Economic Losses* (May 1991) *Hearings on S 168*, 13–15.

62. *Hearings on S 168*, 31–32.

63. Reclamation Projects Authorization and Adjustment Act of 1992, Pub L no. 102–575, title 25, 106 Stat 4731.

64. Section 3504 of the Authorization and Adjustment Act provides that "[s]uch interest shall be available [to the Three Affiliated Tribes] . . . for use for educational, social welfare, economic development and other programs, subject to the approval of the Secretary." Section 3506 provides that "[n]o part of any in this fund . . . shall be distributed to any member of the Three Affiliated Tribes . . . on a per capita basis."

65. Reclamation Projects Authorization And Adjustment Act of 1992, Pub L no. 102–575, title 25, 106 Stat 4731.

66. An opinion letter by Mr. Jerry Nagel, a tribal member and vice chairman of the Fort Berthold Landowners Association, challenges the proposed tribal investment plan: the "council wants a dowry for themselves not an endowment for you" and describes the proposed tribal referendum on this plan as an option for tribal members to "vote to get 25% of nothing or 50% of nothing and the council gets 100% to spend at will." Likewise, in letters to Senator Byron Dorgan (D., N.D.) Ms. Phyllis Old Dog Cross asks the senator to investigate the proposed "referendum election now being held by the Tribal Council of the Three Affiliated Tribes." She believes the plan is "not a wise move" and asks whether the "funds, principle [*sic*] and interest [are] being protected as well as invested right now?" (copies of both letters in collection of the author).

67. This is my synthesis of governing development theory within Indian country. See Manfred Halpern, "A Theory for Transforming the Self: Moving Beyond the Nation-State," in *Transfomational Politics: Theory, Study and Practice* ed. Stephen Woolpert et al. (Albany: State University of New York Press, 1998), 45–55.

68. Black Elk quoted in Bonnie Duran, Eduardo Duran, and Maria Yellow Horse Brave Heart, "Native Americans and the Trauma of History," in *Studying Native America: Problems and Prospects* ed. Russell Thornton (Madison: University of Wisconsin Press, 1998), 70.

69. Ibid., 64.

_142_ RAYMOND CROSS

70. Amartya Kumar Sen, _Development as Freedom_ (New York: Alfred A. Knopf, 1999), 146–159.

71. Ibid.

72. Mary Midgley, _Wickedness: A Philosophical Essay_ (London: Routledge, 1992), 93–98.

73. Ibid.

74. These issues are explored more fully in Raymond Cross, "Tribes as Rich Nations," _Oregon Law Review_ 79 (winter 2000): 893–980.

Chapter 6

George Shannon and C. S. Rafinesque

Charles Boewe

In the 1820s, when George Shannon was a resident there, Lexington, Kentucky had a population of a little over 5,000.[1] For its size and its geographic location, Lexington was remarkably cosmopolitan, with more than a dozen French names listed in its directory, one of which was that of C. S. Rafinesque.[2] Most of these people knew one another, so it is not remarkable that Rafinesque and Shannon were acquainted—Rafinesque, a professor at Transylvania, the only university west of the Alleghenies, and Shannon, a successful lawyer and a member of the state's General Assembly from 1820 to 1823. In addition to his teaching duties, Rafinesque gave occasional public lectures on various topics; and Shannon, to further his political career, gave speeches before the Lexington Tammany Society. Both were public figures in a small town.

Despite all the attention given in recent years to the lives of members of the Lewis and Clark expedition, the aperçu we have on Shannon through Rafinesque's writings has been overlooked.[3] Rafinesque himself had several reasons to be interested in the expedition and its discoveries. As a naturalist typical of his time, he considered the study of mankind within his purview, especially those little-known Native Americans the Corps of Discovery encountered; and an accomplished linguist himself, he collected vocabularies as avidly as he collected natural history specimens.[4] He was the kind of polymath who appreciated Thomas Jefferson's scientific goals for the expedition. George Shannon, of course, was the expedition's youngest member and helped Nicholas Biddle prepare the first published edition of the expedition journals. By reviewing—and in some cases, retrieving from obscurity—some of the scientific writings of Rafinesque, we find that Shannon's knowledge of Indian languages, acquired during his service in the Corps of Discovery, was considerable. His contributions to Rafinesque's

143

compilations of Indian-language vocabularies came from words he remembered hearing on the journey west. Although the science of linguistics no longer favors the historical approach Jefferson encouraged and Rafinesque embraced—of tracing tribal history through language study—the relationship of Shannon and Rafinesque suggests a new implication of the Lewis and Clark expedition. It probably did encourage the research of better-known linguistic scholars who followed.

It was only reasonable that Rafinesque should seek the acquaintance of Shannon, four years his junior, for he himself had hoped to participate in the expedition sent out in 1804 by his friend Thomas Jefferson.[5] Rafinesque had come to the United States as a young man aged nineteen, but he returned to Europe at the end of 1804, just as the Corps of Discovery was settling into winter quarters in the Dakotas. He stayed in Sicily for a decade, publishing there his first books in natural history, the field for which he is best known, and returned to America in 1815, when naturalists—especially in Philadelphia—were trying to sort out the scientific accomplishments of the expedition.

Though unable to join the Corps of Discovery, Rafinesque was immediately interested in the expedition's scientific findings and written report. At the Academy of Natural Sciences of Philadelphia, of which he was a member, Rafinesque tried to convince George Ord, a distinguished zoologist, that the expedition's *Ovis montana,* as Ord had named a mammal on the basis of its skin and one horn, actually was a goat, not a sheep.[6] Rafinesque's opinion was correct, but such is the confusion between mountain sheep and mountain goats in the Biddle edition of the *Journals* (1814) that Ord stuck to his own belief in the face of the contradictory evidence of the specimen before him.

Rafinesque, too, had ransacked the Biddle edition. Despite its lack of the crucial scientific portion of the journals, Rafinesque got enough information from Biddle to give scientific Latin names to a number of animals he himself had never seen. He gave their specific names, which continue to be used, to the Oregon bobcat, the mountain beaver, the mule deer, and the prairie rattler.[7] The living prairie dog that the expedition had shipped to Peale's Museum in Philadelphia died long before Rafinesque returned from Europe, but he named that animal too, from the description he found in Biddle. So had George Ord, and in this case Rafinesque's generic name, *Cynomys,* has been retained for the prairie dog in preference to Ord's, though Ord gets credit for the specific name, *ludoviciana.*

As a pioneer naturalist, Rafinesque longed all his life to explore the trans-Mississippi West. Unable to obtain either public or private patronage, he never got farther west than Shawneetown, Illinois, the terminal point of his self-financed trip down the Ohio River. Returning overland to Philadelphia in 1818 from this trip, he passed through Lexington, where John D.

Clifford, a merchant friend he first knew in Italy, had now settled and had become a prominent citizen.[8] A trustee of Transylvania University, Clifford got Rafinesque a job at that rapidly developing institution, and there he taught botany and natural history from 1819 to 1826, the only formal professorship he ever held. From Lexington as a base he explored the natural riches of Kentucky, then little known, and published voluminously—mostly on botany—finally achieving the singular record of having devised more new Latin plant names than anyone else who ever lived, before or since. After a dispute with the university's president, Rafinesque returned to Philadelphia in 1826, continued publishing books and articles, and died there in 1840.

In company with Clifford, Rafinesque came upon a new interest in Lexington that led to his brief involvement with the expedition veteran Shannon. It is doubtful that he and Shannon should be called friends, for Shannon's name is not even mentioned in Rafinesque's autobiography. And in the sketch of a utopian society that Rafinesque drew up late in life, he specifically ruled that lawyers would be banned—probably because during a lifetime of many litigious conflicts, most of which he lost, he had had his fill of lawyers.[9]

Clifford, who died in 1820 at age forty-one, had long been interested in geology and paleontology, even though the study of organic fossils had not yet received that name. Before his death Clifford also took up the investigation of prehistoric Indian remains, publishing in Lexington's *Western Review* magazine eight long letters on "Indian Antiquities."[10] All of these were interests shared by Rafinesque, though the last is little known because his biographers have concentrated on Rafinesque's botanical and zoological researches.

In the vicinity of Lexington are a number of prehistoric sites, called, then as now, Indian forts. Whatever their occasional idiosyncrasies in other respects, Clifford and Rafinesque clearly saw that most of these prehistoric sites had nothing to do with fortification. As the few Shawnee Indians remaining in Kentucky had no idea what purpose the earthworks were intended to serve, Rafinesque and Clifford took up the task of trying to understand and explain them. Rafinesque, a cultural nationalist in his adopted land, called these earthworks the "Monuments of America," comparable in a modest way to the monuments of ancient Egypt and Mesopotamia, and believed they were the civil and ecclesiastical ruins of a pacific race of people who had been vanquished by the more warlike ancestors of contemporary Indians. Clifford's conclusion, based on the configuration of the earthworks as well as certain conch shells and ceramic artifacts found in their vicinity, carried the thesis a step further. For him, the earthworks were the ruins of the civilization of an accomplished ancient people who were either identical with or closely related to the ancient Hindus of India. In

Clifford's view, prehistoric life in the Ohio Valley differed little from that on the banks of the Ganges. Little wonder that one of Rafinesque's somber Transylvania colleagues, more familiar with the effort of missionaries to save the souls of the "heathen" Hindus than with the notion that polytheists could be civilized, called Clifford "a vapid, sap-headed booby."[11]

Out of loyalty to Clifford, Rafinesque never wholly dismissed the Hindu thesis, but he had limited enthusiasm for it. Whoever their builders were, earthen mounds and fragments of pottery found near them could tell us little about their long-dead makers. Rather, Rafinesque decided, probably after reading Leibniz in the well-stocked Transylvania library,[12] that the best way to recover something of the unwritten chronicle of the ancient Americans was through a comprehensive study of the history of indigenous languages.

Rafinesque knew that there were similarities among the hundreds of contemporary Indian languages, which he believed he could trace back to about twenty-five ancient "mother languages," and through these could then trace migrations of peoples and lines of linguistic descent back to the dawn of time. Perhaps it is not surprising that Rafinesque theorized as he did about the ethnological value of language, because it was a position many linguists, amateur and scholarly, endorsed at the turn of the century. Thomas Jefferson had suggested in *Notes on the State of Virginia,* for instance, that the noble origins of American Indians would eventually be documented by extended philological analysis. Because Indians left no literary traces, their history would be redeemed, according to Jefferson, by the study of their languages.

Rafinesque's contribution to this school of thought was enhanced by the fact that he was personally well equipped for comparative linguistics; he wrote in English, French, Italian, Latin, claimed a reading knowledge of Spanish and Portuguese, and had a smattering of such exotic languages as Arabic. Later in life he published a book interpreting, to his own satisfaction, the root meanings of words in the Hebrew Scriptures.[13] From travel books in the university and town libraries, he collected vocabularies of languages ranging from Kurdish to Hottentot. He persuaded the federal government to instruct all its Indian agents to collect vocabularies from the oldest people in their charge (a venture that was not very successful), and he personally collected vocabularies from Indians known to him.[14] There was, of course, a fatal flaw in his research program: his concentration on vocabulary alone. Even though there is still some disagreement among linguistic anthropologists over the relative significance of lexicon and grammar, most would concede that indifference to the morphology of languages makes it difficult if not impossible to discover relationships among them. Yet, at the time, few people interested in comparative language study were aware they were taking an inept tack, for Rafinesque was not alone in collecting raw vocabularies. After all, that was one of the missions Jefferson had charged Meriwether Lewis to carry out. And, in any event, some knowledge of the word-stock of a language is a prerequisite to the analysis of its structure.

Through the course of his life, just as he collected plants for his herbarium, Rafinesque collected thousands of pages of vocabularies, most of which were probably carted off to the Philadelphia dump after his death. One document that remained and gives him what little distinction he has among historians is the *Walam Olum*, a long narrative poem in pictographs with a Delaware text that purports—according to some people, including Rafinesque—to describe a prehistoric migration across the Bering Strait. Known today from two bound notebooks (dated 1833) in Rafinesque's hand that are among the treasures of the University of Pennsylvania library, the *Walam Olum* came to Rafinesque in two parts. According to his account, the pictographs alone were given to a "Dr. Ward" by the Indians in 1820 in gratitude for medical treatment; then in 1822 "were obtained from another individual the songs annexed thereto in the original language." He does not further identify Dr. Ward or the other individual, nor does he tell how the two documents reached him. This poem does not, however, account for the so-called Indian mounds near Lexington and elsewhere in the Ohio Valley; they were built by an earlier people only hinted at in the *Walam Olum*. Rafinesque says that he obtained this document while living in Lexington, remarks that only after deep study was he able to read it by 1833; and he did not publish it until 1836, when he was back in Philadelphia.[15]

Partly because of his need to translate and interpret the *Walam Olum* text, Rafinesque was greatly interested in the Delaware-related languages of the West. That surely is the main reason he sought out and interviewed George Shannon, hoping Shannon could recall words from the languages of the various tribes he had visited.

The only reference to this interview in Rafinesque's vast number of publications occurs on two and a half pages of the *Atlantic Journal*, a magazine he published (1832–33) after returning to Philadelphia, and for which he wrote most of the text. The first article, titled "American Languages: Wahtani or Mandan" (132–133), gives words for the cardinal numerals 1 to 10 and lists twenty-three Mandan equivalents for such cardinal nouns as *father, mother, man, woman,* and so on. There Rafinesque says: "I met in Lexington, Ky. Mr. George Shannon, who was one of the companions of Lewis . . . and who furnished me with some words of the Mandans." But it is not clear how many or which, for Rafinesque notes further that he has also "added a few scattered in Lewis' Travels." Hence, it is obvious that, exacting scholar as he was, he was trying to wring all possible evidence for this particular issue from the Lewis and Clark expedition, both from the imperfect Biddle edition of the report and from the only living member available to him. His second article is titled "Languages of Oregon: Chopunish and Chinuc" (133–134), for which Shannon, as informant, was able to supply only twelve words of Chopunish. Although twenty-four words are given for that language, the other half came from "Lewis and [Ross] Cox," and all thirty-three words of "Chinuc" came from "Cox, Lewis, and other sources." However, Rafinesque says, "Mr. Shannon" did confirm "the fact that only 3 languages were met with in the Oregon mts and country"; "but they are spoken in a multitude of dialects." For Rafinesque, the "Oregon country" was the whole expanse of territory from the Rocky Mountains westward, not the present state of Oregon.

It happens that there are, in addition, two extant unpublished manuscripts where Shannon's testimony also appears. The first of these is a four-page essay Rafinesque sent to the American Antiquarian Society in 1824, while he was still in Lexington and probably shortly after his interrogation of Shannon. It is titled "A Short Vocabulary of the Mandan or Wah-tah-neck Language," and it contains twenty-five words that Rafinesque said Judge Shannon "remembered well." This list enables us to see that Shannon contributed all the ten numerals in the *Atlantic Journal* essay as well as twelve other words. It also has three words Rafinesque chose not to include in the *Atlantic Journal* list (equivalents for *Indian, Missouri,* and *Whiskey*), probably because he did not consider these Mandan words indigenous to that language.

Troubled by the variant forms of Indian words when recorded through the filters of English, French, Spanish, and even Swedish used by the Caucasians who had reported them, Rafinesque devised his own phonetic alphabet to render pronunciation more accurately. Essentially, it gave vowels the sounds they have in French and dispensed with silent consonants. Using this "Universal Orthography," as he called it, he recorded the Mandan words recalled by Shannon as follows, pointing out that this language had never been recorded before by philologists:

Man	Nusuakeh	Cold	Shinihush
Woman	Mikeh	Missouri or Water-white	Mini-shoti
Indian	Huatanih	Whiskey or Water of God	Mini-hupanish
Father	Papah	One	Mahanah
Mother	Nayeh	Two	Nupa
God	Hupanish	Three	Namani
Water	Mini	Four	Topa
Corn	Cohanteh	Five	Kehun
White	Shoti	Six	Kima
Knife	Maheh	Seven	Kupa
No	Nicosh	Eight	Tetoki
Meat	Mascopi	Nine	Maapeh
		Ten	Pirokeh

There is another point worth mentioning. William Clark, writing to Albert Gallatin, said he could discover no affinity at all between the language of the Mandans and those of the Sioux, Osage, Minnetarees, or any other tribe known to him.[16] But Rafinesque, on the basis of Shannon's lexical material, concluded that Mandan had "many similarities with the Yancton and Konzas [i.e., Sioux] dialects of the Missouri tribes."[17] In this judgment he appears greatly ahead of his time.

The other unpublished Rafinesque document was unknown until 1982, when it was discovered in Paris in the archives of the Institut de France, where it had lain uncataloged since 1835. For the Volney Prize of that year the institute had announced a competition for the best essay on the grammatical character of the Algonkian languages of North America. Only two essays were received: Rafinesque's and one by his Philadelphia friend Peter S. Du Ponceau, who won the contest. Du Ponceau's essay was eventually published as a book (1838), and Rafinesque's manuscript was filed below Du Ponceau's and forgotten. Rafinesque himself never mentioned in any of his published writing that he had even entered the contest.[18]

Having worked so long already on the language of the Delawares (who called themselves the Leni Lenape), Rafinesque chose their language for his prize essay, a language now usually also called Lenape, as central to all the Algonkian languages, and he tried to trace its analogues all the way from the East Coast to the West, even speculating on its relationship with that of the aboriginal Ainu people in Japan. This led him further to conjecture that the language, with its speakers, must have crossed the Bering Strait, because it was related to the Samoyed languages spoken in eastern Siberia.

This French manuscript of 270 pages, the longest-known linguistic essay by Rafinesque, tells us a great deal about the way he approached the comparative study of languages. Interested primarily in language affinities, since his overriding concern was the prehistoric migrations of peoples—not the science of linguistics for its own sake—he worked out to his own satisfaction a statistical formula for judging the degree of affinity between any two languages. Recent recognition of this accomplishment, crude though it was, has caused him to be called the father of lexicostatistics.[19]

In the prize essay he took up each of the parts of speech in turn and gave a perfunctory description of their grammatical function in Lenape and related languages, as the contest required. Still, Rafinesque's heart really was not in morphological analysis, with the result that the 1835 Prix Volney quite properly went to Du Ponceau. What interested Rafinesque most were the lexical similarities among Indian languages, similarities he fancied sometimes also were found even with Italian and French. Thus, despite the prodding of the Volney contest, he continued to miss the key that might have led to a measure of success in tracing the migrations of peoples through the permutations of their languages. Of course, it should also be noted that a thorough grammatical study of any one Indian language would have required a complete immersion in it through long discourse with one or more native speakers. Neither Rafinesque nor Du Ponceau had this opportunity; both had to depend on material collected by others, and the others were missionaries, trappers, Indian agents, or travelers, who, like Shannon, remembered a few words. In truth, the materials were not yet at hand for anyone to carry out the kind of analysis the French institute wanted to see.[20]

Shannon's appearance, then, comes only in the appendix to Rafinesque's essay (254), where the author attempts to supply a comparative vocabulary of "Chopunish" and "Chinuk," among the twenty-one vocabularies given there. In this list, eight Chopunish words are attributed to Shannon, seven of which Rafinesque had published already in his *Atlantic Journal* essay. The seven are

Sky	Tetoh	Head	Chop
River	Ishkit	Bear	Yahar
Sun	Spokan	Father	Papa
Nose	Nashne		

And in addition, Rafinesque added in the margin of the manuscript:

| Chief | Tayop |

Even if Shannon could recall in total only a dozen words of Chopunish and today we are able to identify only eight of them, this nevertheless tells us something about him and helps confirm Biddle's opinion that he was one of the brightest of the nine young men from Kentucky. It will be remembered that Chopunish, the language of the Nez Perce Indians, baffled the expedition.[21] When Captain Lewis delivered his formal speech to that nation his words had to be translated into French, from that language into Hidatsa, then into Shoshone, and finally into Chopunish. The wonder is that Shannon could pick up any knowledge of the language at all, much less remember, nearly two decades later, words that had reached him through three linguistic filters. (How many people would remember that "boy" is *puer* in Latin if the next speaker intoned *garçon* or perhaps *enfant,* followed by another who said *Junge* or possibly *Knabe* or conceivably *Bube*—while the equivalents of the word jumped about in the sentence according to the syntactical requirements of each language?)

Since the vocabularies collected by Lewis apparently were lost when Jefferson's possessions were rifled on the James River while being shipped to Monticello, even the few words recalled by Shannon now add another heirloom to the memorabilia of the Corps of Discovery. They add nothing, of course, to present-day understanding of Indian languages, and they added little if anything to Rafinesque's reputation as a philologist, since this aspect of his research has itself remained virtually unknown.[22]

It is a pity perhaps that Rafinesque could interview only Shannon. If it is true, as is widely believed, that the best way to learn a foreign language is in bed with a native speaker, then Rafinesque ought to have interviewed York, William Clark's black slave, by all accounts the favorite of the Indian women. York must have been a fountain of linguistic lore.

NOTES

1. See Huntly Dupre, *Rafinesque in Lexington, 1819–1826* (Lexington, Ky.: Bur Press, 1945).

2. A short biography of Rafinesque is in the *Dictionary of American Biography* (1935), a better one in the *Dictionary of Scientific Biography* (1975), and the best in *American National Biography* (1999). An early Filson Club publication, R. E. Call's 1895 biography, though book-length, is little more than a retelling of Rafinesque's own autobiography. T. J. Fitzpatrick also paraphrased the autobiography in his 1911 bibliography, now more accessible in my own *Fitzpatrick's Rafinesque: A Sketch of his Life with Bibliography* (Weston, Mass.: M and S Press, 1982), where the bibliography is revised and enlarged but the biographical sketch left essentially untouched.

3. Gleanings from local archives and extant newspapers were collected and ably assembled by Carolyn S. Denton in *Publication No. 11* (May 1992):15–24, of the Lewis and Clark Trail Heritage Foundation, under the title "George Shannon of the Lewis & Clark Expedition: His Kentucky Years." She mentions the Rafinesque connection in a note.

4. See John C. Greene, *American Science in the Age of Jefferson* (Ames: Iowa State University Press, 1984), esp. ch. 14, "The Sciences of Man: Comparative Linguistics and the Problem of Indian Origins."

5. In his autobiography, *A Life of Travels* (Philadelphia, 1836), Rafinesque says (24), "I was told that I might be admitted as Botanist in the expedition which Lewis & Clark were then preparing." A letter by Jefferson to Rafinesque (15 December 1804) often has been thought to refer to this hope, but it is actually in connection with the ill-fated trip by George Hunter and William Dunbar up the Red River in 1804. At any rate, Rafinesque never received Jefferson's letter because he had already left for Europe. The Jefferson letter was first printed by Edwin M. Betts in the *Proceedings of the American Philosophical Society* 87 (May 1944): 369–370.

6. C. S. Rafinesque to George Ord; New York, 1 October 1817, Academy of Natural Sciences of Philadelphia.

7. According to Raymond Darwin Burroughs, *The Natural History of the Lewis and Clark Expedition* (East Lansing: Michigan State University Press, 1961). A more authoritative reference for currently recognized genera and species is James H. Honacki, et al., eds., *Mammal Species of the World* (Lawrence: University Press of Kansas, 1982), compiled for the American Society of Mammalogists. Through a complicated series of revisions, Ord's generic name for the mountain goat was eventually replaced by Rafinesque's *Oreamnos,* which has current status according to

Honacki. Although Rafinesque proposed names for more than 150 mammalian genera, only 12 of these are recognized at present.

8. There is no biography of Clifford.

9. "To avoid quarrels and trouble, no Drunkards nor Lawyers shall be allowed to join the company," though "pure wines, cider and beer" would be available and "every dispute . . . shall be settled by Arbitrators" according to a pamphlet Rafinesque published in 1837 titled *Plan of the Philadelphia Land Company of Aurora.*

10. Signed only with the initial "C.," these were published during the course of eight months (September 1819–April 1820) under the running title "Indian Antiquities." I have reprinted them, along with related papers and maps by Rafinesque, in *John D. Clifford's Indian Antiquities* (Knoxville: University of Tennessee Press, 2000).

11. Charles Wilkins Short to John Cleves Short; Hopkinsville, Ky., 11 December 1818, Library of Congress.

12. Gottfried Wilhelm von Leibnitz (1646–1716), mostly remembered today as a philosopher and mathematician, was a universal scholar who also had a profound impact on linguistic studies. To him is attributed the idea that "languages are the most ancient monuments of peoples before [the invention of] writing." The books of this German-born author were available to Rafinesque in French. Although Rafinesque's mother was Saxon, German was one language he never learned well enough to use. He also dipped into the writings of Friedrich von Schlegel, seeking lists of Sanskrit words; had he been able to understand German he might have learned Schlegel's opinion that grammar, not vocabulary, is the key to language affinities. He probably was misled by another German scholar, Julius von Klaproth, whom he quoted with approval (in English) as having written that "languages are better guides than physical characters for researches on mankind, and roots more important than grammars" (C. S. Rafinesque, *The American Nations* [Philadelphia, 1836], 1:8–9).

13. C. S. Rafinesque, *Genius and Spirit of the Hebrew Bible* (Philadelphia: Eleutherium of Knowledge, 1838).

14. A letter prepared by Rafinesque was printed and sent out by the War Department's Office of Indian Affairs to 56 recipients, with 10 copies going to General William Clark alone, who was by that time (1825) superintendent of Indian affairs at St. Louis. The letter requested the collection of a vocabulary of 100 words from each of the languages addressed and gave a phonetic guide for their transcription. The Beinecke Library at Yale has one of the letters.

15. How Rafinesque obtained the *Walam Olum* has to be pieced together from enigmatic and ambiguous comments in the 1833 manuscript itself and a few paragraphs in his book *The American Nations* (1:122, 151). The story is so obscure that it gives credence to a recent argument that the whole thing is a hoax; see David M. Oestreicher, "Unraveling the *Walam Olum*," *Natural History* 105 (October 1996): 14–21. The best access to this document is *Walam Olum* (Indianapolis: Indiana Historical Society, 1954), which reproduces Rafinesque's manuscript photographically and contains seven interpretive essays and an elaborate bibliography. The story itself has often been retold, and the pictographs and Lenape text reprinted with new attempts at translation. Most recently (1989) the text was translated into Dutch. Rafinesque published part of the Lenape text and his English translation of the whole of it (but not the pictographs) in *The American Nations,* 1:121–161.

16. Cited by Donald Jackson, ed., *Letters of the Lewis and Clark Expedition with Related Documents, 1783–1854* (Urbana: University of Illinois Press, 1978), 2:644.

17. C. S. Rafinesque, "A Short Vocabulary of the Mandan or Wah-tah-neck Language," *American Antiquarian Society* (1824): 133.

18. Rafinesque's anonymous essay (identified, according to the rules of the contest, by a code) was discovered by Joan Leopold, who is editor of a three-volume book about the significance of the Prix Volney. In volume 2, titled *Early Nineteenth-Century Contributions to General and Amerindian Linguistics* (Dordrecht: Kluwer Academic Publishers, 1999), I have contributed a chapter on the essay, setting it in the context of Rafinesque's life and his other linguistic research. Rafinesque's manuscript (never published) is titled "Examen Analytique des Langues Linniques de l'Amerique Septentrionale, et surtout des Langues Ninniwak, Linap, Mohigan &c avec leurs Dialectes."

19. By Dell H. Hymes, in his "Lexicostatistics and Glottochronology in the Nineteenth Century," in *Essays in the History of Linguistic Anthropology* (Amsterdam: J. Benjamins, 1983), 59–113. Rafinesque first used his statistical formula in another unpublished prize essay, "Mémoires sur l'origine des nations nègres, ou introduction à l'histoire des nègres d'Asie, d'Afrique, Polynésie, Amérique & Europe," of which a file copy exists at the American Philosophical Society. This 105-page essay, written in 1831 for the *concours* of the Société de Géographie of Paris, won for him the consolation prize of a gold medal.

20. In 1826 a better philologist than Rafinesque, Albert Gallatin (Jefferson's secretary of the treasury), tried to encourage the federal government to collect both vocabularies and grammatical analyses through its Indian agents. His effort met with less success than Rafinesque's had the previous year. Few Indian agents had the skills required; almost none had the interest.

21. William Clark wrote that "for want of an Interpreter thro' which we could Speake" with the Nez Perce, it was necessary "to converse altogether by Signs" (Reuben Gold Thwaites, ed., *Original Journals of the Lewis and Clark Expedition, 1804–1806* [New York: Dodd, Mead, 1904–05], 3:85).

22. The best study so far of Rafinesque's linguistic work is a brief essay by the Ukrainian scholar Vilen V. Belyi, "Rafinesque's Linguistic Activity," *Anthropological Linguistics* 39 (spring 1997): 60–73.

PART III

Memories

THE LEWIS AND CLARK TRAIL

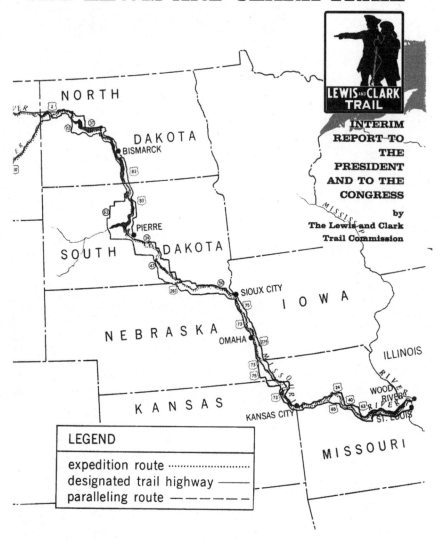

Map 4. The Lewis and Clark trail. From the cover of Lewis and Clark Trail
Commission, *The Lewis and Clark Trail: An Interim Report to the President and to the
Congress* (Washington, D.C.: Government Printing Office, 1966).

   In the post–World War II era, the figure of Sacajawea had fallen out of favor
among expedition enthusiasts and scholars alike. Hence the official logo for the
Lewis and Clark trail eliminates the once familiar silhouette of Sacajawea pointing
the way for the two explorers. The changed depiction of the expedition also
corresponds with new ways to commemorate Lewis and Clark. As the map
indicates, they include a new emphasis on automobile tourism and outdoor
recreation along the "Trail."

Though largely ignored for almost a century, the Lewis and Clark expedition began to take on new meaning and attract new attention in the late 1890s. In the process, this neglected historical subject was transformed into an epic quest that has never since lost its central place in the nation's collective memory. The expedition has become an origin story of the first order that invariably portrays Lewis and Clark as prophets of the future, as if the history of national development were a natural occurrence and the two explorers simply on a journey into the future—with each group of commemorators as their chosen destination.

Lewis and Clark, and Sacagawea even more than the coleaders, were honored in the first decades of the twentieth century with the publication of several books about the expedition, a new edition of the journals, the holding of a successful exposition, and the placement of numerous statues and monuments throughout the country. In every instance, the expedition was celebrated as the foremost symbol of a new century's faith in material progress and overseas empire. By midcentury, the desire to commemorate the expedition with monuments and celebrations was replaced by an increased fascination with the expedition route itself. "The Trail" became a sort of national pilgrimage route, a development that reflected the rise in automobility, along with postwar prosperity and a growing middle-class interest in outdoor recreation. Lewis and Clark's ability to capture the spirit of every age that sought to commemorate them also made the expedition a powerful symbol for critiquing the values it represents. For this reason, the expedition has also served as the subject for potent counternarratives about American progress and development. The three essays in this section speak to these issues in various ways, but all remind us of how memories of Lewis and Clark have often taken on more significance than the expedition itself—and in the process have a great deal to tell us about the way national identity is defined and contested.

Chapter 7

"We are not dealing entirely with the past"

Americans Remember Lewis & Clark

John Spencer

Are we getting too much of Lewis and Clark? The Germans are said to have complained because the Goethe admirers have edited the very shaving-papers of their idol and even the contents of his waste baskets. . . . For our part we are not so minded. In the coming of these heroes the eyes of intelligent men first beheld the nobler features of the beautiful land that is our mother when at last the veil of mystery began to depart from them. From no achievement of our history have flowed consequences more important.
    Book review, *The Nation,* 1904

While we propose that this exposition shall be primarily for the purpose of commemorating the Lewis and Clark exploration expedition, we are not dealing entirely with the past.
    Charles Fulton, U.S. senator from Oregon, 1903

The importance the *Nation's* reviewer attached to Lewis and Clark is striking, considering that books by or about "these heroes" had been hard to come by for most of the nineteenth century. Their route remained obscure to most Americans, and public celebrations of their expedition were apparently unknown. But all of that had changed by the time the reviewer wrote in 1904, a year of centennial celebration of Lewis and Clark. Americans had not completely forgotten the explorers before 1900, but they now remembered them in new ways and new media, including popular literature, reprints of the original expedition journals, and a world's fair. Lewis and Clark have been American icons ever since, with the bicentennial of the expedition providing yet another spike in their visibility. In recent years the historian Stephen Ambrose has written a best-seller about them, the filmmaker Ken Burns has produced a popular documentary film about them, and politicians, historical societies, and history buffs have planned a multitude of public events to celebrate them.[1]

Some of the themes of these commemorations have held constant for more than a century. One is a fascination with the details of the journey itself and with the endurance and heroism of Lewis and Clark—their "undaunted courage," to take the title of Ambrose's book as the most familiar recent example. Another is the didactic importance of the expedition, which enthusiasts have seen as containing larger meanings and a wealth of "lessons," especially for young people.

It is striking, however, amid the ongoing fixation on legacies and lessons in Lewis and Clark, how wildly those meanings have fluctuated over time. At the turn of the twentieth century, publishers, writers, historians, artists, and promoters of world's fairs made Lewis and Clark into standard-bearers for the industrialism, imperialism, and racism that permeated late nineteenth-century society. These centennial images were not entirely new—Thomas Jefferson's expansionism and ethnocentrism were at the heart of the expedition from the first—but they did reflect the special concerns of the moment.[2] A new social order—more hierarchical, more dominated by corporate power, and more focused on the spread of white, Anglo-Saxon supremacy on a world scale—had taken shape after the Civil War, and proponents of that new order invoked Lewis and Clark to justify it. Commemorations of the expedition offered a chance to link the new society to a more fluid, democratic past. In the same way, the social and political upheavals of the 1960s have reverberated into our own time to give us a bicentennial Lewis and Clark who symbolize exactly the opposite of what they stood for a hundred years ago: environmentalism and respect for nature instead of industrial development, multiculturalism instead of racism and imperial conquest. What remains constant is the way in which ideas about the past exploits of Lewis and Clark are shaped by present conflicts over economic growth and inequality, cultural diversity, and the proper role of the United States in the world.

Historians have noted that a golden age of Lewis and Clark scholarship since 1962 has resulted in more varied and thoughtful images of the expedition. These scholars argue that while "popular" or "folk" images of Lewis and Clark were long plagued by distortions and a neglect of such stories as the scientific achievements of the expedition, the gap between those images and a more sober, "literate-elite" tradition is closing.[3] This characterization is certainly accurate to a point, but it must be qualified. Popular and scholarly views of Lewis and Clark were not always so different; both were shaped by the same cultural environment at any given historical moment. What is more, distorted or oversimplified images of Lewis and Clark are not only inescapable; they are revealing. Historical commemorations of Lewis and Clark inevitably say as much about the rememberers as the explorers themselves. They provide a fascinating index of changes in American society and culture over time, reminding us that, as Senator Fulton noted in 1903, "we are not dealing entirely with the past."[4]

Efforts to immortalize Lewis and Clark began as soon as their journey ended in September 1806, but the explorers did not linger in the public mind during the nineteenth century. The leading account of the expedition during that time was Nicholas Biddle's *History of the Expedition Under the Command of Captains Lewis and Clarke* (1814), compiled in consultation with William Clark after Meriwether Lewis died without completing a manuscript of his own. Biddle edited the voluminous field journals into a triumphant tale of national progress, employing what one scholar has called the "language of adventure and empire."[5] But the original print run of 1,417 copies did not sell well. It was poorly timed, appearing nearly a decade after the expedition had ended and competing accounts had begun to circulate, and it did not offer a clear case for the importance and success of the expedition.[6] Jefferson's main goal had been for Lewis and Clark to find a transcontinental waterway—a "passage to India"—that would facilitate the growth and expansion of the United States. Careful Biddle readers discovered no such passage. The president also meant for the expedition to advance science by making detailed observations of the flora, fauna, and native peoples along the way. Biddle edited that material out of his narrative. Meanwhile, as "adventurers" Lewis and Clark did not capture the nineteenth-century imagination the way Kit Carson, Davy Crockett, and a host of other folk heroes did. The Biddle edition soon went out of print.[7]

The work was reprinted several times in the 1840s and 1850s, the first time Americans rediscovered Lewis and Clark for topical reasons.[8] During those decades, proponents of "manifest destiny" saw in Lewis and Clark a compelling justification for their territorial claims in the Far West. In 1845, the year President James Polk sounded the cry of "Fifty-four Forty or fight," one commentator wrote, "from this expedition . . . our claim to Oregon receives not a little accession of strength."[9] Five years later, after the United States had won that claim and the Mexican War as well, another writer celebrated Jefferson and his expedition for "anticipat[ing] the day when the energy and enterprise of American citizens would span the continent, and republican institutions diffuse themselves to the shores of the Pacific."[10]

Such commentary, however, was more the exception than the rule in the nineteenth century. In 1876, as the United States celebrated its centennial, the expedition scarcely appeared in histories of the nation.[11] The Biddle edition of 1814 still stood as the standard account of the expedition, but it was hard to find. The original journal books, today a priceless artifact, languished in obscurity in Philadelphia. In 1893 a natural scientist named Elliot Coues did publish a major revision of the Biddle text, annotating it with copious amounts of scientific material from the journals.[12] He did not alter the basic narrative, though, and the costly, three-volume edition apparently had little impact on public knowledge of Lewis and Clark; among major periodicals, only *The Nation* reviewed it.[13]

As the centennial of the expedition approached, however, Americans began to celebrate Lewis and Clark with something of the fervor Thomas Jefferson had envisioned. Popular accounts of the expedition proliferated as never before. A handful of publishers offered reprints of the 1814 edition. The journals themselves were slated for publication for the first time ever, in an eight-volume edition to be edited by Reuben Gold Thwaites of the Wisconsin Historical Society. Portland, Oregon began planning a federally subsidized world's fair to commemorate the explorers. It was clear, in some of the talk surrounding these developments, that Americans had not completely forgotten Lewis and Clark in the nineteenth century. One booster of the Portland exposition, Senator Charles Fulton of Oregon, called their journey "familiar history to the American public."[14] A publisher of one of the new Biddle reprints wrote that "few names are more familiar upon the tongue than Lewis and Clark." Still, that publisher noted that "a full and adequate account of what they did has long been almost unattainable. The published work of 1814 has quite disappeared from the market."[15] The senator and the publisher, each in his own field of endeavor, were among those who pushed the names and the story of Lewis and Clark into the national spotlight at the turn of the twentieth century.

Why did Lewis and Clark resonate for Americans at the turn of the twentieth century? The fact of the centennial anniversary was part of it, but that alone did not explain why the expedition became one of the most celebrated stories in American history. The country was ripe for Lewis and Clark at the turn of the century. To understand their centennial revival, and the themes that emerged from it, we must examine the social and cultural climate in which it took place.

In the decades prior to the centennial many Americans came to feel that the confident, westward-moving democracy of a former time—Lewis's and Clark's time—was disintegrating. In 1893, at Chicago's Columbian World Exposition, the historian Frederick Jackson Turner crystallized those fears by announcing the "closing" of the nation's frontier, which he defined as the disappearance of "free land" in the West.[16] For Turner and his audience, the news was not just about territory filling up; it was about the future of the United States as a democratic republic. Turner conceived of the frontier in Jeffersonian terms, as a safety valve for Americans who had run out of opportunity in the settled part of the country. It made the United States different from Europe with its multitudes of degraded city dwellers and tenant farmers. It was the basis of America's "manifest destiny." Jefferson had hoped the Louisiana Purchase and the Lewis and Clark expedition would lay the groundwork for a thousand years of agrarian expansion—an "em-

pire of liberty." Less than a century later, Turner lamented the end of the
frontier experience in American history, a turning point that one historian
has described as the "end of American exceptionalism."[17]

Turner's "frontier thesis" was dubious; historians have pointed out that
the West was far less democratic than he believed and that the frontier did
not really "close" in the 1890s.[18] Still, Turner had good reason to feel that
his country was at a crossroads. The Jeffersonian ideal—a nation of self-
sufficient, self-governing farmers—was a distant dream. Capital was concentrated in the hands of a tiny percentage of the population. The gap between rich and poor never had been wider. Nothing symbolized and fueled
these trends more powerfully than the railroad corporations, and nowhere
was their impact felt more powerfully than in the Far West. After the Civil
War the railroads fueled the transformation of a land of homesteaders into
a land of agribusiness and industrial mining. Prices fell and small farmers
suffered as the railroads facilitated large-scale production for national and
international markets.

The class conflicts of the post–Civil War period came to a climax in the
1890s, one of the most turbulent decades in American history. In 1893,
farm debt and a reckless overexpansion of the railroads were among the key
factors that sent the nation spiraling into the worst economic crisis it had
ever known. The panic lasted five years, but the situation hit rock bottom in
1894, when bands of desperate, unemployed men like "Coxey's Army"
crossed the continent on foot and in hijacked trains to demand federal relief in Washington, D.C. A strike wave involving hundreds of thousands of
workers, notably those of the Pullman Palace Car Company, paralyzed the
nation. The administration of Grover Cleveland put down many of the re-
bellions with the help of federal courts and troops, often resulting in violence; one of the worst incidents occurred on the Fourth of July, in Chicago,
when thirteen people died and dozens were wounded in a violent con-
frontation between the U.S. Army and the striking Pullman workers. Meanwhile, the People's Party (also known as the Populists), founded in 1892 by
economically strapped farmers, mounted a serious challenge to the two major parties. In the final decade of a century that began with Jefferson sending his Corps of Discovery into a land of unknown possibility, the nation
faced a crisis over the apparent demise of its democratic promise.

That crisis shaped America's cultural climate in the years leading up to
the Lewis and Clark centennial but so too did the robust recovery and the
return to territorial expansion, this time overseas, that followed the depression and rang in a new century. President William McKinley presided over
an upturn in the business cycle and conquests in Cuba and the Philippines
after his election in 1896, but it was a member of his administration who,
more than anyone else, shaped and symbolized the jingoistic new era. That

man was Theodore Roosevelt, who became McKinley's vice president in 1900 and succeeded him after the president was assassinated the following year.

Roosevelt was the only New Yorker to become president, but his identity was bound up with the West and the meaning of the frontier. Before becoming a politician, he explored those interests as a historian, in his multi-volume study *The Winning of the West.* Roosevelt, like Frederick Jackson Turner, was alarmed at the "closing of the frontier," but for somewhat different reasons. His frontier was not a tide of anonymous farmers steadily converting the wilderness into democratic settlements; it was individual, Anglo-Saxon heroes being put to the test by a violent race war, and winning. Consequently, he was less concerned in the 1890s about the future of democratic opportunity than about the fate of the Anglo-Saxon leadership class of which he was a member. Together with record immigration and declining birthrates among white Protestants (what Roosevelt called "race suicide"), the end of the frontier experience threatened to diminish the potency of the Anglo-Saxon elite just as it faced a new challenge: ruling and bringing order to a modern, industrial society.[19]

Turner was more influential among historians, but Roosevelt made the greater mark on his times by ascending to the presidency and pursuing policies designed to usher in a new era of national greatness. One aspect of his program was progressivism, which to Roosevelt meant a rejection of unchecked corporate power but an acceptance, nonetheless, of the hierarchical society embodied by the modern corporation. Another Roosevelt emphasis had to do with preserving the salutary influence of the frontier, by preserving both its history and select portions of its wilderness, where men might continue to learn the lessons of what Roosevelt called "the strenuous life." And a third, and perhaps most important, element of Roosevelt's pursuit of national greatness was his vigorous extension of McKinley's imperial aggressions in Latin America and Asia—in effect, an extension of the western frontier overseas, under the same banners of white Anglo-Saxon supremacy and market expansion.[20]

The Lewis and Clark centennial thus unfolded in a climate of blustering nationalism layered over depression and doomsaying. Some Americans were dismayed by the transformation of Jefferson's simple republic into a corporatized, imperial nation, while a good many others—notably Theodore Roosevelt and his followers—praised that development as progress. Somewhat ironically, the latter camp would make Lewis and Clark, figures from the bygone era of Jefferson, into icons of its Progressive vision.

The Biddle image of Lewis and Clark held firm at the turn of the twentieth century; centennial celebrants still portrayed the expedition as a heroic "adventure" in the service of national expansion. But, as in Roosevelt's treatment of the "winning of the West," they cast that romantic western tale as a prelude to, and justification for, specific developments of the moment: modernization and the extension of "Anglo-Saxon" power overseas.

In January 1904 the U.S. Senate Committee on Industrial Expositions, calling the Lewis and Clark expedition "one of the most interesting and important events in the history of this country," announced its support for the most visible commemoration of the era: the Lewis and Clark Centennial Exposition and Oriental Fair in Portland, Oregon.[21] Actually, no one in Congress had much interest in Lewis and Clark; the bill might not have passed without the intervention of President Roosevelt, an admirer of Lewis and Clark and, perhaps more important, a friend of the fair organizer and *Oregonian* editor Harvey Scott.[22] Many of the Oregon sponsors of the exposition were not primarily interested in history, either. Like Philadelphia's centennial of the Declaration of Independence in 1876 or Chicago's Columbian exposition of 1893, the Lewis and Clark fair was about the future more than the past, about commerce more than history. What Congress, the president, and the fair organizers did care a great deal about was "mastery of the Pacific," as Scott described the imperatives of Pacific Rim trade, and Lewis and Clark turned out to be convenient symbols for that enterprise.[23]

Congressional debates over appropriations for the fair showed how the present could shape perceptions of the past and how the past could justify policies in the present—especially the pursuit of empire in Asia. Roosevelt, speaking to Congress in support of the fair, praised the Lewis and Clark expedition for "making ready the way for our ascendancy in the commerce of the greatest of oceans."[24] Senator Fulton of Oregon noted that Lewis and Clark had "suffered terribly, yet uncomplainingly, for they realized that they were battling for an empire." And, while the fair was "primarily" for the purpose of commemorating their journey, when Fulton spoke of "empire" he was thinking very much of current foreign policy in Asia. The United States, he said, had assumed "great and grave obligations and responsibilities in the Far East and it now concerns our honor as it concerns our interest that we shall discharge those obligations and meet those responsibilities wisely."[25] One of Fulton's fellow Oregonians in the House, Binger Hermann, was more direct: "The Pacific Ocean," he said, "is the place of battle for the commercial supremacy of the world."[26]

The quest for a commercial empire governed the presentation of the Lewis and Clark story on the fairgrounds, too. The most revealing historical image at the Expo was also the most ubiquitous: Lewis and Clark striding triumphantly into the Pacific Ocean toward the setting sun, accompanied by a flag-draped female figure variously described by contemporaries as "Progress" or "Columbia" (Figure 4). Appearing on posters, maps, tick-

Figure 4. Seal of the Lewis and Clark Centennial and American Pacific Exposition and Oriental Fair. (Oregon Historical Society, OrHi 47301)

ets, and other memorabilia, this image of the next frontier needed little explanation; the fair had an unmistakable "Oriental" theme in its title as well as its exhibits. Most of those exhibits displayed Asian products, but one, the popular Igorrote Village exhibit, displayed people: head-hunting, dog-eating Filipino tribesmen whose "savage" appearance and practices helped legitimize Roosevelt's recent annexation of the Philippines.[27] Special events reinforced the same message; on one occasion, the fair thrilled nighttime visitors with a reenactment of the battle of Manila Bay. For anyone who missed the symbolism of these displays, a large banner greeted fairgoers with the message "Westward the Course of Empire Takes Its Way." The nation that had mourned the closing of its frontier barely a decade before had taken up a new arena of westward expansion. Yet fairgoers learned that the American military and economic advance into the Pacific Rim was not so new after all; it was, according to the banners and iconography, an extension of the hundred-year-old expedition of Lewis and Clark.

Promoters also invoked Lewis and Clark as precursors of industrial progress close to home, in the Pacific Northwest. The *Lewis and Clark Journal*, launched to publicize the fair and the region, trumpeted the Expo as a "timekeeper of development" in northwestern industry since Lewis and Clark and cited railroad expansion as the first step toward an even brighter future.[28] A special "Centennial Number" of *Leslie's Weekly* revealed the poetic flights of fancy taken by some publications in their praise for a century of commercial progress:

> When Clark and Lewis first beheld
> The rippling Willamette,
> The virgin forest round them lay
> with many a snare beset.
> Before them rose Mt. Helen's snows,
> Untrodden, cold, and pale,
> The only path was here and there
> A narrow Indian trail

> Still seaward rolls the Willamette
> With waters bright and clear,
> Still folded in eternal snows
> The mountain peaks appear;
> But now a splendid city rears
> Its roofs to meet the morn,
> And writes its name around the world
> In timber, wheat, and corn.[29]

Promoters even celebrated the Pacific Coast as the latest frontier safety valve for excess population, Turner's 1893 pronouncement notwithstanding. In his opening-day address to dignitaries and fairgoers, the president of the exposition commission, Jefferson Myers, announced that further development of the Northwest's "abundance of industries" would provide "homes of peace and plenty to the people from the over-crowded portions of the country"—a comment that took on pointed significance in light of a concurrent report, in the *Pacific Monthly's* fair coverage, of a Chicago teamsters' strike that had turned into "little less than a social war."[30]

Lewis and Clark to some extent were the vanguard of economic development in the Far West, and that development was in some ways a fulfillment of Jefferson's vision of an "empire of liberty." But the fair's confident proclamations masked underlying conflicts and contradictions. It was a curious distortion to wrap the railroads and other industrial corporations in the mantle of Lewis and Clark; these were the very economic forces that undermined the agrarian ideals of Jefferson's day and that spurred the populist revolt of the late 1800s.

But distortion was exactly the point. Lewis and Clark boosters used the past to serve their needs in the present—in this case to foster national unity at a time of turbulence. Economic boosterism belied class conflicts right on the fairgrounds: several strikes occurred during construction of the temporary buildings. The exposition directors, hoping to dampen labor strife and inspire workers with the magnificence of the grounds and exhibits, declared a Workingmen's Day. Employers throughout the city let their workers take the day off and attend the fair, where they enjoyed reduced admission. As the *Oregon Journal* remarked, no doubt echoing the sentiments of Portland's business elite, "the working people and their families need to see the exposition at considerable length. It will do them good."[31] By the time it closed, the *Oregonian* believed the fair had done a great deal of good, indeed. The paper's editorial page, reflecting on the "lesson" of the exposition, captured the strained exuberance of the time: "America is not an aggregate of little semi-hostile communities antagonistic in feeling and welfare," the paper declared. "We belong to a united and homogeneous Nation, one in aspiration, one in feeling and one in interest. There are no bad Americans. We are all good; and the better we are acquainted the more we like each other.[32]

The Portland extravaganza, despite its heavy commercial emphasis, did fuel a rediscovery of Lewis and Clark history. Having a major exposition named in their honor pushed the explorers into a national spotlight; they became a current event. Writers and editors took the centennial as an occasion to recount the expedition, and when they did, they emphasized the same themes of imperial and industrial progress that were so evident at the fair itself.

Numerous popular accounts of the expedition appeared after 1900, and most praised the expedition as a grand "adventure." Current Lewis and Clark scholars understandably wince at the overblown romanticism of this literature, but it did strike a powerful chord in the cultural context of the early twentieth century, a time that one reviewer of a new Biddle edition referred to as "days of historical romances and adventure stories."[33] America was in the throes of becoming a modern society—urban, bureaucratic, corporate—and writers on Lewis and Clark spoke to a nostalgia for a simpler time.[34] Sounding very much like Theodore Roosevelt and his celebration of "the strenuous life" as an antidote to decadence and overcivilization, they enthused over "hazardous adventures" in "wild nature." "Those were hero days," wrote one, "and they produced hero-types, who flung themselves against the impossible—and conquered it."[35] One Biddle reviewer quietly lamented his own unstrenuous life, writing that "the joy of exploring unknown portions of the earth's surface was a joy of our ancestors, but little for ourselves, and almost none at all for our descendants. . . . Since then," he continued, "there are so few modern explorers telling of new adventures, in new books, we quiet home-stayers must read the old books again." Still, this "home-stayer" held out hope that he might find deliverance from the monotony of modern city life in the "day by day narrative of the explorer, telling of his strife with nature in her most unpleasant hours." Such stories appealed to "that portion of the wild man which, deep down within most of us city-bred men, still calls us to the woods."[36]

Wilderness imagery, as an antidote to effete urban life, went hand in hand with tales of racial violence and conquest. Of the many books that emphasized these themes at the turn of the century, one of the most popular was Eva Emery Dye's *The Conquest*. Dye, a Portland author and suffragette, incorporated the travels of Lewis and Clark into a larger account of the "pressing back of the red race."[37] With its emphasis on racial conquest, her self-proclaimed "Iliad of the West" must have pleased Theodore Roosevelt, who became president the year before it was published.

The Conquest and books like it were not simply backward glances at the favorite themes of Roosevelt the historian (that is, manliness and Anglo-Saxon conquest); they may as well have been polemics for the policies of Roosevelt the president. Dye's account of the past also celebrated imperial ambition in the present. "Five transcontinental lines bear the rushing armies westward, ever westward, into the sea," she wrote. "Bewildered a moment they pause, they turn to the Conquest of the Poles and the Tropics. The Frontiersman? He is building Nome City under the arctic; he is hewing the forests of the Philippines."[38] Dye was not the only author to present Lewis and Clark as act one in a great drama of overseas empire building. Agnes Laut's *Pathfinders of the West* put Lewis and Clark in a pantheon of "heroes who carved empire out of wilderness."[39] A writer for *The Dial* enthused that "all that has come since—the great conquest of 1898, Alaska, Hawaii, Porto Rico *[sic]*, the Philippines, Panama—are but the sequence of that immortal journey in 1804–06."[40]

Asia had been on Jefferson's mind a century before, and Lewis and Clark did launch the United States' expansion across North America. But to describe Lewis and Clark as "conquerors" was a stretch, considering the diplomatic nature of the expedition. What is more, to portray them as imperialists was a politically charged act. Expansion was a matter of intense partisan controversy, as in Jefferson's time, with Democrats in Congress denouncing the overseas ambitions of the Republican presidents McKinley and Roosevelt. It is hard to define a cause and effect relationship between administration policies and the imperialist themes of books like *The Conquest,* but it is safe to say the political climate of 1898 influenced the imperialistic tone of those histories, and vice versa.

The romantic, imperialistic image of Lewis and Clark was not simply a

"popular" view, or a product of crass commercialism; it was standard practice among academic historians, too. James Ronda has noted that Reuben
Gold Thwaites, while predicting that his publication of the complete field
journals would lead to new understandings of Lewis and Clark, offered in
his own writings "nothing more than a vision of the expedition as an agent
of a triumphant Manifest Destiny."[41] To some extent the same was true of
Thwaites's friend Frederic Young, a history professor at the University of
Oregon and a leading booster of Portland's centennial fair. Young exemplified a university-based historical profession that had begun to coalesce
around ideals of objectivity and science, but he and his colleagues could
sound as partisan as any politician or popular novelist. In 1903, Young
pointed to Theodore Roosevelt's assessment of Lewis and Clark in *The Winning of the West*—that they had opened "the door into the heart of the
West"—and suggested that an updated version, based on the recent events
of Roosevelt's own presidency, might say they had "made inevitable the
American mastery of the Pacific and American supremacy among the nations of the world."[42]

The imperial image of Lewis and Clark not only shows how current events
molded the telling of history; it shows how American concepts of empire
and expansionism had turned upside down. For much of the nineteenth
century Americans had conceived of "empire" in Jeffersonian terms, as
the agrarian "empire of liberty." From the Louisiana Purchase in 1803 to
the huge territorial acquisitions of the 1840s, westward expansion was celebrated by Democrats—and disparaged by Federalists and Whigs—as a way
to build and preserve a republic of yeoman farmers. Expansion and empire
took on a more industrial image, however, as railroads transformed the
agricultural economy of the Middle and Far West. Lewis and Clark commemorations revealed this change in the making. Centennial treatments of
the explorers celebrated industrialization at home much as they did imperialism abroad. Indeed, the two themes were closely linked.

Jefferson's idealized yeoman farmer still showed up in turn-of-the-
century writing on Lewis and Clark—many authors saw Roosevelt's "adventurers" and Turner's tide of pioneers as two aspects of the same story—
but he did not necessarily symbolize the agrarian ideal. One writer, for example, praised Lewis and Clark as "world conquerors" who "blazed the
way for thousands of sturdy homeseekers who soon followed in their wake,
building homes, cities, manufacturing plants, railroads, and telegraph lines
where once had roamed the lordly bison."[43] Here, Jefferson's "sturdy homeseekers" had evolved into the builders of the very cities and factories that
Jefferson and many of his Jacksonian heirs had abhorred. The ideolog-
ical shift from agrarian to industrial empire was not entirely new; John
Gast's famous 1873 painting *American Progress*, for example, presented more
or less the same glorification of railroads and telegraph wire. But this writer,

in referring to Lewis and Clark as "world conquerors," linked industrial and imperial progress in a way that was specific to the early twentieth century.

Historically, the relationship between railroads and the "sturdy home-seeker" had been anything but peaceful, and in the 1890s, especially, populists raged at the locomotive and all it symbolized. But this critical perspective did not appear at the Lewis and Clark fair or in the burgeoning literature on the explorers. On the contrary, perhaps the most widely reviewed book on Lewis and Clark at the turn of the century also was the most enthusiastic about the railroads and the industrial development of the West. In *The Trail of Lewis and Clark: 1804–1904,* the amateur historian Olin Wheeler inaugurated a genre and theme that remains popular to this day: retracing the trail and using the Lewis and Clark journals as a benchmark for changes in the landscape. Wheeler brought along several professional photographers—a new approach to illustrating Lewis and Clark—and cited their work as proof of a century of steady American progress.

Wheeler was no stranger to economic boosterism; he also worked for the Northern Pacific Railway, editing the promotional publication *Wonderland.*[44] In fact, *The Trail of Lewis and Clark* originated as one of those shorter books. One of Wheeler's main purposes in writing it, he said, was to "show, without undue prominence, the agency of the locomotive and the steamboat in developing the vast region that Lewis and Clark made known to us."[45] In a 1902 Biddle edition, James Hosmer, a historian and editor, had taken up the same theme, marveling at the tremendous influence of the railroads in Lewis and Clark country; the "New West," he wrote, "may rightly be called the child of the locomotive."[46] Specifically, he might have called it the child of the Great Northern and Northern Pacific Railways; their Northwestern lines, completed in the 1880s, more or less paralleled the explorers' route.

Hosmer hinted at a less approving view among some contemporaries, and he correctly sensed that future generations would grow even more critical of land use practices in the Far West. "It is not strange that some feel we have gone quite too rapidly," he wrote, "and our grandchildren may wish their forbears had been slower in the exploitation of the resources of the fine domain." Likewise, Wheeler anticipated a revisionist stance on Native American history, noting that Lewis's and Clark's "almost uniformly kind reception by and treatment of the Indians, and their absolute and utter dependence upon them, time after time . . . furnishes the most caustic criticism upon the Government's subsequent treatment of the red man."[47]

Still, Hosmer, Wheeler, and the rest of their contemporary commentators on Lewis and Clark were generally uncritical of the racism, imperialism, and industrialism that shaped their culture and, in the process, their ideas about Lewis and Clark. "What Lewis and Clark laid open is a world upon which nature has lavished her bounties," wrote Hosmer. "The present fruition is scarcely calculable: the hope for the future is boundless."[48]

Fast forward several generations and it would be hard to imagine a more different story. In 1975 the *Oregonian*, which in 1905 had gloried in pronouncing the nation "united and homogeneous," expressed a dismal nostalgia for the supposedly golden age of Lewis and Clark. On the eve of the nation's bicentennial, observed one of the paper's reporters, "recalling the epic exploits of this brave little band provides an upbeat in the daily barrage of gloom and doom." He went on to suggest that there was "no better way to spend a holiday, a weekend, or a vacation out of doors than by retracing and perhaps reliving vicariously the way it was in those glorious times."[49] The nation faced serious social and economic problems, as it had at the turn of the century. This time, though, conflicts over economic development, foreign policy, and race relations burst into the open, and it showed in commemorations of Lewis and Clark. The expedition came to stand for exactly the opposite of what it symbolized at the turn of the century.

Public images of the expedition had remained fairly constant for many years after workers dismantled the temporary buildings of the Lewis and Clark exposition. The idea of Lewis and Clark as heroic conquerors and courageous frontiersmen lost none of its appeal. *Life* magazine, in a prominent series entitled "How the West Was Won," devoted a section to Lewis and Clark's "first great adventure."[50] Another article began, "Lewis and Clark didn't know where they were going—but they got there, and clinched our title to a continental empire."[51] Celebrations of industrial development endured, too. Railroad men continued to invoke the land of Lewis and Clark as a symbol of their ongoing story of economic progress. In a booklet published for the sesquicentennial anniversary of the expedition, Robert Macfarlane of the Northern Pacific Railway gushed over the "long way we have traveled as a nation in the past 150 years since Lewis and Clark opened an unexplored wilderness to settlement. With the potential of our natural resources scarcely known and largely undeveloped, a future of great promise still lies ahead of us."[52] In 1950 President Harry Truman sounded a similar note after a nine-day tour of the Pacific Northwest: "Where they found only Indian villages, herds of buffalo, and trackless wilderness and sagebrush," he said, "I saw great cities, immense structures like Grand Coulee Dam, and rich farmland."[53] Alone among Lewis and Clark enthusiasts, the historian and novelist Bernard DeVoto adopted a more critical stance, placing Jefferson's Corps of Discovery within a longer history of grasping American imperialism and considering the impact of that history on Native Americans and western landscapes.[54]

Commemorations of Lewis and Clark changed dramatically after the

1960s, however, as DeVoto's environmental and cross-cultural sensitivities went from being the exception to the rule. By that time, ever-increasing numbers of Americans were getting in their cars to retrace the route of the explorers, and a 1965 travel guide showed that they did so in a very different cultural climate than Olin Wheeler in 1904—or even Harry Truman in 1950. *The Lewis and Clark Trail* was introduced by Secretary of the Interior Stewart Udall, and some of his themes would have been familiar to Americans of previous generations: that the expedition symbolized "the self-reliance with which we probed and later settled the West"; that it showed Americans they possessed the land and water resources to achieve "great national goals"; that it "fired a national spirit of adventure which yet persists." But Udall also sounded a new theme of stewardship. The route of Lewis and Clark offered "an unmatched opportunity to demonstrate a higher concept of conservation," he wrote. "There is even the prospect that we will in time realize the importance of a tie to the out-of-doors with the same intensity we once reserved for the development of material values."[55] In making his call for "resource stewardship," Udall reminded Americans of "the heritage we derive from the expedition"; he believed that Lewis and Clark could and should inspire contemporary environmental awareness. In fact, the opposite process was just as evident, as a cultural shift toward ecological awareness altered the meaning of the expedition.

Udall recognized threats to the nation's natural landscape, but he was optimistic about the government's power to protect it. He believed the Lewis and Clark expedition had left Americans a "land-conscious people." And the secretary of the interior was not alone in stressing what remained of America's scenic heritage. In 1967, for instance, the *New York Times* ran a lengthy feature that promised scenic fulfillment for travelers of the Lewis and Clark trail: "The prairies are tilled now, and much of the swift, 2,135-mile Missouri has been dammed to form placid lakes," the article noted. "However, only a little imagination is needed to recreate much that Lewis and Clark encountered."[56]

Other observers were far less hopeful. Beginning in the 1960s and continuing into the 1970s, some writers and historians embraced the Lewis and Clark journals as a benchmark for measuring a dark side of progress. In 1965, as Udall pointed hopefully to Lewis and Clark as harbingers of the conservation ethic, NBC aired an hour-long news special called "The Journals of Lewis and Clark." The network had commissioned the news producer Ted Yates to recreate the Lewis and Clark expedition "in authentic detail." Yates headed west, expedition journals in hand, looking for scenes the explorers had seen. He was intensely disappointed by what he found—or did not find—and wrote up the experience for the magazine *The American West*. "Their challenge was the wilderness," he wrote. "Our challenge was civilization. In a century and a half of relentless civilizing, the country seen by Lewis and Clark has vanished. It is gone. Their journals seem to be a myth, a romantic fiction, as one compares their observations to the land of today." Yates, like Olin Wheeler sixty-five years before him, ticked off a list of changes in the national landscape. Yet he inverted the symbols of progress that dominated from Wheeler's time through midcentury. Strip mines offended his "eye and intellect," factories "belch[ed] smoke," and dams had turned rivers into "victims of hydroelectric progress"—all in great contrast to the "unwounded" America of Lewis and Clark.[57]

Most striking were Yates's explicit indictments of "civilization" and "progress," the watchwords of American expansionism. "It seems," he said, "that we in our short history have at times confused vandalism with progress, wanton waste with riches. We have not used our resources, we have looted them." Quoting Meriwether Lewis's wish at the Great Falls of the Missouri in Montana—that he "might be able to give to the world some just idea of this truly magnificent and sublimely grand object"—he lamented that the scene had "vanished in a maze of hydroelectric dams, wires, and technology. Progress has concealed it from civilized man." Yates, like Udall, felt the nation's "heritage" was at stake. But if the secretary of the interior defined heritage as an environmental ethic that could be learned from Lewis and Clark, Yates saw it as actual places linked to the expedition, and he condemned their destruction.[58]

Nonetheless, in 1965, millions of television viewers saw an "authentic" reenactment of the Lewis and Clark expedition. Yates, despite mixed feelings, did his best to "crop out the ugliness." "We all felt great sadness," he concluded in his article, "because in a way we had added to a delusion and helped to sustain the myth that America is, from sea to shining sea, a spectacle of beauty, of love and care, instead of a debacle of neglect and abuse."[59]

Yates and Udall were the first of many observers who used Lewis and Clark as the symbol for a critique of progress. The tendency reached a peak in the 1970s, with the rise of the environmental movement. The pages of the *Reader's Digest* reflected the changing times. Prior to the 1960s, the magazine had reprinted articles with titles like "Our Greatest Exploration" and "Heroine in Buckskin" (about Sacagawea). In 1971, by contrast, it featured "The Trampled Trail," a "vivid and troubling journal of nature, a nation, and its people." The author, Jules Loh, captured a sense of environmental concern in the nation and explained the usefulness of retracing the steps of Lewis and Clark, writing: "A twentieth-century American," he wrote, "aroused over the deteriorating quality of a finite environment, can find no better example of man's treatment of nature's resources than to reexamine the route of those two explorers." Like Yates, Loh quoted extensively from the journals of Lewis and Clark as he made his way across the industrialized landscape and chronicled what he called "paradise lost." Like Udall, he pointed to a growing ecological awareness in America, concluding that "people in the final analysis prefer clean Columbias and Missouris and ultimately will insist on them." However mixed the conclusion, though, the meaning of Lewis and Clark was clear: they and their journals had become a symbol of some Americans' disillusionment with the ideology of industrial progress.[60]

This symbolism was evident again in 1976, when the Seattle Art Museum chose Lewis and Clark as the subject of its bicentennial celebration. The exhibit consisted of three parts: a collection of nineteenth-century paintings of western landscapes and Indians (none from the Lewis and Clark expedition, as no painter accompanied them), artifacts from the West Coast Indian cultures they encountered, and a contemporary photographic record of the Lewis and Clark trail. A *New York Times* reviewer emphasized what did not appear in the photographic part of the exhibit:

> There was an opportunity here for a before and after horror show of environmental mutilation, but in the upbeat spirit of the Bicentennial year, Mr. and Mrs. Macapia chose instead to approximate as nearly as possible the record that a photographer would have made if there had been such a thing as a camera to take along in 1803. They were able to find not only secluded woodland spots, but great vistas of mountains, rivers and fields without so much as a distant television aerial to reverse the situation and to reveal the wilderness itself as an anachronism in the 20th century.[61]

The Seattle exhibit, like Ted Yates's NBC news special a decade earlier, had to "crop out the ugliness" at a time when such ugliness was a pressing concern for many Americans. Representations of the Lewis and Clark expedition could inspire with scenes of pristine beauty or shame with "a before and after horror show." Never again, though, would Americans use the expedition to celebrate industrial progress in quite the way Harry Truman had only twenty-five years before.

Environmental destruction was just one of many serious problems that compromised the "upbeat spirit" of the nation's bicentennial. Conflicts over race and foreign policy, largely invisible or marginalized during the turn-of-the-century Lewis and Clark revival, had exploded into view and changed the nation's politics and social relations. The "course of empire" seemed to have run its course in Vietnam. The civil rights and American Indian movements had pressed the nation into painful confrontations over long-suppressed histories of racial oppression. Together with the Watergate scandal, the OPEC oil embargo, and the end of decades of unbroken economic growth, these problems sent the nation spiraling into an unprecedented crisis of confidence. On many of these subjects as on environmental questions, images of Lewis and Clark reflected the larger social situation.

At their annual meeting in 1975, members of the leading group of Lewis and Clark enthusiasts, the Lewis and Clark Trail Heritage Foundation (LCTHF),[62] heard a speech that crystallized the divisiveness and disillusionment of the period and, at the same time, the hope that the legacy of Lewis and Clark held a key to a more harmonious future. Michael P. Gleason, coordinator of the western region of the Virginia bicentennial commission, hinted at the social conflicts of recent years when he spoke of the United States in 1801 and reminded his audience that it was "a divided nation then too." Gleason was optimistic, however, that the study of history could instill a "national spirit" in America's youth. History had "too often been for the elite," he said, and that was wrong; it needed to be "as much for the poor, the working man, the woman, the black, the youth, as anyone else, but only if we can make it exciting!"[63] In that context, Gleason emphasized the value of studying Lewis and Clark, in living history museums and historical reenactments, among other "exciting" formats.

Had it remained the story of two heroic men leading the westward expansion of white, Anglo-Saxon America, the Lewis and Clark expedition would hardly have made a good subject for the more inclusive history proposed by Gleason. But the story had changed a great deal from the day when historians and writers counted racial conquest and imperial expansion as its greatest legacies. The social movements of the 1960s changed the historical profession along with the rest of society, resulting in the development of environmental history, a "new social history," and a "new western history," among other approaches and subdisciplines that emphasized legacies of conflict and diversity in American society. Historians of these fields, in turn, shaped new public understandings of the Lewis and Clark expedition as a symbol of multicultural awareness. The work of James Ronda, to take one of the most important examples of this trend, has influenced scholars and enthusiasts to view the expedition from multiple perspectives—those of its members as well as those of the Native Americans with whom they had contact.[64]

The airing of new perspectives on Lewis and Clark has at times been fraught with tension. In 1993, LCTHF President James Fazio, noting the "frenzy of expose-type articles and protest demonstrations" that marked the five-hundred-year commemorations of Columbus, predicted that Lewis and Clark, too, would be "forced to run the dreaded gauntlet" when "Ph.D. candidates and the mass media" became aware of the expedition's bicentennial commemoration. Indeed, he gave evidence that Lewis and Clark revisionism already was under way, recalling a recent conference in Montana at which critics lambasted Lewis and Clark buffs for their "antiquarian interest" in what the members of the expedition wore, for instance, or what kinds of tools they used. One speaker had charged that such minutiae obscured the real significance of the journey: that it began the invasion of Americans into western Indian country. At least one Lewis and Clark enthusiast left in disgust, reporting a general "berating of all whites for attempted genocide."[65]

Notwithstanding such conflicts, though, Fazio hoped and expected the bicentennial to be less acrimonious than that of Columbus, and with good reason. At the Montana conference, as he noted, the Salish tribe member and historian Betty White had said her purpose was not to vilify Lewis and Clark but simply to offer a native perspective on the "glorification" of the explorers.[66] And by the time enthusiasts began to plan the commemorative activities, simple glorification had been overshadowed by messages of multicultural sensitivity and environmental awareness anyway. Those messages came through clearly in statements made by Henry Hubbard, president of the National Lewis and Clark Bicentennial Council, shortly after the LCTHF created that body in 1993 as a clearinghouse for commemorative activity: "The Council believes that the Bicentennial can be more than the anniversary of a historical event," he said. "Some of the benefits that can accrue from the observance are geographic knowledge, ecological awareness, and the appreciation of cultural diversity." Hubbard went on to acknowledge the explorers' debt to native peoples, noting that they had "skillfully and peacefully negotiated their way through territory dominated by native peoples who, in many instances, aided and supported their efforts."[67]

Six years later, as the bicentennial drew near, the council's executive director, Michelle Bussard, echoed those themes, citing the need for "stewardship of our resources" and "respect for other cultures" as the two most compelling lessons in the Lewis and Clark experience.[68] Those lessons, and with them the changed cultural and political climate since 1905, are dramatically displayed in the bicentennial council's carefully conceived logo (Figure 5). Where Lewis and Clark once strode into the Pacific Ocean, fulfilling the dream of a Northwest Passage to Asia, mountains now stand in the way, symbolizing, according to the council's web site, "the beauty and grandeur of the American landscape as well as the reality that the Northwest Passage existed only in myth." And, exemplifying recent tendencies toward seeing the expedition as a series of encounters with two perspectives rather than one, the council explains that the eight-pointed ring suggests "both a compass and a Native American medicine wheel," that the eagle feathers refer to "peaceful interactions with and contributions by the nearly fifty Native American tribes encountered," and that the tips of the feathers are dipped in blood to signify "the subsequent sacrifices of the native peoples."[69]

Much of the activity that Bussard's organization is coordinating between 2003–06 no doubt will be devoid of history altogether. Commerce, tourism, and regional boosterism will fuel the upcoming bicentennial the same way they did the centennial exposition a century ago. But the bicentennial (again, like the 1905 Expo) also will serve as a showcase for historical inter-

Figure 5. Logo of the National Lewis and Clark Bicentennial
Council. (Reprinted with permission)

pretation, for ideas about the meaning the Lewis and Clark expedition
holds for American society.

Those interpretations of Lewis and Clark are at once timeless and time-
bound. Americans always have been and no doubt always will be fascinated
by what the explorers did and what it must have been like to venture so far
into an uncharted world. At the same time, the historical meaning of the
story has changed dramatically over time, according to changing circumstances. Olin Wheeler, one of the leading commemorators on Lewis and
Clark at the turn of the twentieth century, wrote that it had taken a hundred
years for the United States to "come to something like a real conception
of what Lewis and Clark, the leaders in the exploration of the West, did
for their country." Yet Wheeler's "real conception" of Lewis and Clark—
that they paved the way for the railroads and the industrial development of
America's wilderness—was a product of his time and circumstances. Changing circumstances and political climates—especially the rising influence,
since the 1960s, of critical views on racism, imperialism, and industrialization—have produced different conceptions of Jefferson's Corps of Discovery. In the years ahead thousands will continue to retrace the trail and
reflect with amazement on how the land has changed, but few, if any, will
celebrate those changes as unambiguous progress. Nor will Americans use
the expedition to justify overseas expansion. Those themes have become

historical artifacts, superseded in our own time by the idea that the expedition highlights the importance of ecological awareness and cultural diversity. Wheeler was more nearly correct when he said that the story of Lewis and Clark "gains in interest and value with advancing years, even as wine improves with age."[70] History, unlike wine, does not change, but historians— amateur as well as professional, all with culture-bound perceptions of "interest and value"—do.

NOTES

The author wishes to thank Carl Prince, Ellen Noonan, Stephen Dow Beckham, Kris Fresonke, and Mark Spence for their helpful suggestions and criticisms.

1. Stephen E. Ambrose, *Undaunted Courage: Meriwether Lewis, Thomas Jefferson, and the Opening of the American West* (New York: Simon and Schuster, 1996); Ken Burns, prod. and dir., *Lewis & Clark: The Journey of the Corps of Discovery;* (Burbank, California: PBS Home Video, 1997). The two chapter epigraphs are "Lewis and Clark in Puris Naturalis" (a review of *Original Journals of the Lewis and Clark Expedition, 1804–1806,* ed. Reuben Gold Thwaites), *Nation* 79 (1904): 216–217; and "Speech of Hon. Charles W. Fulton, of Oregon, in the Senate of the United States," on S. 276, Lewis and Clark Exposition, 58th Congress, 18 December 1903 (Washington, D.C: GPO, 1904).

2. James P. Ronda, ed., *Voyages of Discovery: Essays on the Lewis and Clark Expedition* (Helena: Montana Historical Society Press, 1998), 1–14; and James P. Ronda, ed., *Thomas Jefferson and the Changing West: From Conquest to Conservation* (St. Louis: Missouri Historical Society Press, 1997), xi–xv.

3. On the golden age of Lewis and Clark scholarship and Donald Jackson's role in initiating it, see James P. Ronda, "'The Writingest Explorers': The Lewis and Clark Expedition in American Historical Literature," *Pennsylvania Magazine of History and Biography* 112 (October 1988): 621–628; and Gary E. Moulton, "On Reading Lewis and Clark: The Last Twenty Years," in *Voyages of Discovery,* ed. Ronda, 282. On the longstanding split between "folk" and "literate-elite" images of Lewis and Clark, see John L. Allen, "'Of This Enterprize': The American Images of the Lewis and Clark Expedition," in *Voyages of Discovery,* ed. Ronda, 255–277.

4. For recent scholarship on the socially constructed nature of historical memory and the use of distorted memories as a tool of cultural analysis, see David Thelen, ed., *Memory and American History* (Bloomington: Indiana University Press, 1990).

5. Gunther Barth, "Timeless Journals: Reading Lewis and Clark with Nicholas Biddle's Help," *Pacific Historical Review* 63 (1994), 499–519.

6. Biddle was beaten to publication by the ghostwritten journal of the expedition member Patrick Gass, which was followed in turn by several bogus accounts that plagiarized the ethnological observations of other travelers such as Alexander Mackenzie and Jonathan Carver. The Gass book and the "Apocrypha," as the counterfeit journals are generally known, had each gone through six reprintings by the time Biddle's account appeared. For discussions of the various publications, see Paul Russell Cutright, *A History of the Lewis and Clark Journals* (Norman: University of Oklahoma Press, 1976).

7. See Allen, "Of This Enterprize," 265–269; and Ronda, "Writingest Explorers," 611–612, on the limitations and lack of commercial success of the Biddle edition.

8. For an inventory of nineteenth-century Biddle editions, see Victor Hugo Paltsits, "Bibliographical Data," in *Original Journals of the Lewis and Clark Expedition, 1804–1806*, ed. Reuben Gold Thwaites (1904–05; reprint, New York: Arno Press, 1969), 1:lxi–xciii.

9. "The Northern Pacific: California, Oregon, and the Oregon Question," *Southern Quarterly Review* 8 (1845): 231.

10. "Lewis and Clarke's Expedition to and from the Pacific," *Western Journal and Civilian* 3 (1850): 363.

11. See, for example, *The First Century of the Republic: A Review of American Progress* (New York: Harper and Brothers, 1876), which devotes one page to "the Pacific Coast Settlements" and does not mention Lewis and Clark anywhere in its seventeen chapters.

12. Elliot Coues, ed., *History of the Expedition Under the Command of Lewis and Clark,* 3 vols. (New York: F. P. Harper, 1893).

13. "The New Lewis and Clark," pts. 1–2, *Nation* 57 (1893): 312–313; 331–333.

14. "Speech of Charles W. Fulton."

15. Publisher's note, *History of the Expedition of Captains Lewis and Clark*, ed. Nicholas Biddle (1814; reprint, Chicago: A. C. McClurg, 1902).

16. Frederick Jackson Turner, *The Frontier in American History* (New York: Holt Rinehart and Winston, 1920). Turner followed the lead of the U.S. Census Bureau, which defined the frontier as those places where population density was less than ten persons per square mile. In 1890, the bureau announced that no such areas remained.

17. David Wrobel, *The End of American Exceptionalism: Frontier Anxiety from the Old West to the New Deal* (Lawrence: University Press of Kansas, 1993).

18. See, for example, Donald Worster, "Beyond the Agrarian Myth," in *Trails: Toward a New Western History*, ed. Patricia Nelson Limerick, Clyde A. Milner II, and Charles E. Rankin (Lawrence: University Press of Kansas, 1991), 3–25; and Richard Slotkin, *Gunfighter Nation: The Myth of the Frontier in Twentieth-Century America* (New York: Atheneum, 1992), 30.

19. Slotkin, *Gunfighter Nation*, 22–62; and Gail Bederman, *Manliness and Civilization: A Cultural History of Gender and Race in the United States, 1880–1917* (Chicago: University of Chicago Press, 1995).

20. For a useful discussion of Roosevelt's progressivism, including his emphasis on nationalist and imperialist themes, see Slotkin, *Gunfighter Nation*, 51–62.

21. "Fair Is Indorsed," *The Oregonian*, 12 January, 1904.

22. Carl Abbott, *The Great Extravaganza: Portland and the Lewis and Clark Exposition* (1981; reprint, Portland: Oregon Historical Society Press, 1996), 16–17.

23. H. W. Scott, "The Momentous Struggle for Mastery of the Pacific," *Pacific Monthly* 14, no. 1 (July 1905).

24. "President Roosevelt's Recommendation to Congress in Behalf of the Lewis and Clark Fair," *Lewis and Clark Journal* 1, no. 1 (January 1904): 5.

25. "Speech of Charles W. Fulton."

26. "Speech of Hon. Binger Hermann, of Oregon, in the House of Representa-

tives of the United States," Lewis and Clark Exposition, 58th Congress, 4 March 1904 (Washington, D.C.: GPO, 1904).

27. "Five Filipino Villages to be on Grounds," *Lewis and Clark Journal* 3, no. 1 (January 1905): 6; "The Igorrote Tribe From the Philippines," *Lewis and Clark Journal* 4, no. 4 (October 1905): 4; Robert Rydell, *All the World's a Fair: Visions of Empire at American International Expositions* (Chicago: University of Chicago Press, 1984), 193–197.

28. "The Exposition, a Timekeeper of Development," *Lewis and Clark Journal* 3, no. 4 (April 1905); "Era of Railroad Building," *Lewis and Clark Journal* 4, no. 5 (November 1905): 7.

29. "The Lewis and Clark Exposition," *Leslie's Weekly*, 22 June 1905, 580.

30. "Address of Jefferson Myers," in *Report of the Lewis and Clark Centennial Exposition Commission for the State of Oregon* (Salem, Oreg.: J. R. Whitney, State Printer, 1906), 16; "Social War in Chicago," *Pacific Monthly* 14, no. 1 (July 1905): 98.

31. Quoted in Rydell, *All the World's a Fair*, 192.

32. "The Lesson of the Fair," *The Oregonian*, 15 October 1905, 6.

33. "Lewis and Clark," review of Biddle's *History*, *New York Times Book Review*, 1 November 1902.

34. On the rise of the new order, see Olivier Zunz, *Making America Corporate, 1870–1920* (Chicago: University of Chicago Press, 1990); Alan Trachtenberg, *The Incorporation of America: Culture and Society in the Gilded Age* (New York: Hill and Wang, 1982); Robert H. Wiebe, *The Search for Order, 1877–1920* (New York: Hill and Wang, 1967).

35. Charles H. L. Johnston, *Famous Scouts: Including Trappers, Pioneers, and Soldiers of the Frontier* (1910; reprint, Freeport, N.Y.: Books for Libraries Press, 1972). Agnes Christina Laut, *Pathfinders of the West* (1904; reprint, Freeport, N.Y.: Books for Libraries Press, 1969), 332–333.

36. "Four Books of the Month: The Lewis and Clark Expedition," *The Bookman* 23 (1906): 428.

37. Eva Emery Dye, *The Conquest*, 10th ed. (New York: Wilson-Erickson, 1936). Quotation from review of *The Conquest*, *Oregon Historical Quarterly* 3 (1902): 427.

38. Dye, *The Conquest*.

39. Laut, *Pathfinders*, 332.

40. John J. Halsey, "The Beginnings of Expansion in Retrospect," *The Dial* 37 (1904): 113.

41. Ronda, "Writingest Explorers," 306–307.

42. Frederic G. Young, "The Lewis and Clark Centennial: The Occasion and its Observance," *Oregon Historical Quarterly* 4 (1903): 3, 5. Young's exuberant expansionism, including his characterization of the native Indians as a "race destined to melt away before the onslaughts of the sturdier European," was influenced by a far more prominent exemplar of the new academic history, Frederick Jackson Turner. Turner may have been less fixated than Roosevelt on the violence and romance of racial conquest, but he did write, with two coauthors, that American history was "inferior to that of no other country in the romance of discovery, border warfare, and frontier life. . . . The three centuries of strife between these native races and the white invaders—what Parkman calls 'the history of the forest'—is one of the world's treasure houses of romantic episodes, comparable with the history of chivalry" (Ed-

ward Channing, Albert Bushnell Hart, and Frederick Jackson Turner, *Guide to the Study and Reading of American History*, 2d ed. [Boston: Ginn, 1912], 5).

43. Johnston, *Famous Scouts*, 138.

44. For a sample, see Olin D. Wheeler, *Indianland and Wonderland: Once Roamed by the Savage Indian and the Shaggy Buffalo, Now Dotted by Ranches, Towns, and Cities* (St. Paul: Northern Pacific Railway, 1894).

45. Olin D. Wheeler, *The Trail of Lewis and Clark, 1804–1904*, 2d ed. (New York: G. P. Putnam's Sons, 1926), xiii.

46. James K. Hosmer, introduction to Biddle's *History*, xxxv.

47. Olin D. Wheeler, "Lewis and Clark Expedition," *Lewis and Clark Journal* 2, no. 3 (September 1904): 7.

48. Hosmer, introduction, xxxv.

49. Don Holm, *The Oregonian*, 24 March 1975, G10.

50. A. B. Guthrie, Jr., "How the West Was Won," pt. 1, *Life*, 6 April 1959.

51. Richard L. Neuberger, "Our Greatest Exploration," *Reader's Digest*, March 1941, 67.

52. Robert Macfarlane, "The Lewis and Clark Country a Century-and-a-Half Later," in *Lewis and Clark: Our National Epic of Exploration, 1804–1806* (St. Paul: Northern Pacific Railway, 1954).

53. "Text of Truman's Address on the Jefferson Papers," *New York Times*, 18 May 1950, 26:1.

54. Bernard DeVoto, *The Course of Empire* (Boston: Houghton Mifflin, 1952). See Ronda, "Writingest Explorers," 617–621, for an appraisal of *Course of Empire* as a ground-breaking book that "fell into a vacuum."

55. Stewart L. Udall, introduction to *The Lewis and Clark Trail*, by Calvin Tomkins (New York: Harper and Row, 1965).

56. Donald Janson, "Retracing the Lewis and Clark Trail," *New York Times*, 26 February 1967, 10:1.

57. Ted Yates, "Since Lewis and Clark," *The American West* 2, no. 4 (1965): 23–30.

58. Ibid.

59. Ibid.

60. Jules Loh, "The Trampled Trail," *Reader's Digest*, February 1972, 217–240.

61. John Canaday, "Glimpses of Lewis and Clark's Expedition," *New York Times*, 1 August 1976, 2–24.

62. Founded in 1969, the foundation succeeded the Lewis and Clark Trail Commission, which Congress established in 1964 to promote tourism and recreation along the expedition route. The purpose of the foundation, according to its mission statement, is to stimulate public interest in the Lewis and Clark expedition on a national scale and to publicize the contributions made to Ameri-can history by expedition members. Today the group consists of about three thousand Lewis and Clark enthusiasts and publishes the monthly newsletter *We Proceeded On*.

63. Michael P. Gleason, "Wants Living History," *We Proceeded On* (July 1975): 3.

64. James P. Ronda, *Lewis and Clark among the Indians* (Lincoln: University of Nebraska Press, 1984).

65. "Message from President Fazio," *We Proceeded On* (February 1993): 2.

66. Ibid.

67. Harry Hubbard, "The Lewis and Clark Bicentennial," *Oregon History* 38, no. 3 (1994): 28–29.

68. Michelle Bussard, telephone conversation with author, Portland, Oregon, 29 August 2000.

69. Other symbolic elements include seventeen stars, for the states at the time of the journey, and thirteen wavy stripes, for the original colonies and the "nautical nature of much of the group's travel" as well as its original purpose of finding a water route to the Pacific Coast (http://www.lewisandclark200.org/logo.html/).

70. Olin D. Wheeler, *The Lewis and Clark Exposition* (St. Paul: Northern Pacific Railway, 1905), 11, 15.

Chapter 8

Sacajawea, Meet *Cogewea*
A Red Progressive Revision of Frontier Romance

Joanna Brooks

The *Journals* of Meriwether Lewis and William Clark offer incidental, idio-syncratic glimpses of Sacajawea: her pregnancy and delivery (January–February 1805); her skill as a gatherer of wild artichokes, apples, and "Lickerish" (April and May 1805); her extended illness (June 1805); her relationship with the sometimes abusive French trapper Toussaint Charbonneau (August 1805); her return to the site of her childhood abduction and her reunion with family (July–August 1805); her vote to establish winter quarters at a site plentiful with "potas" (November 1805); and her insistence on seeing the Pacific Ocean (January 1806). Clark additionally acknowledges her work as a "pilot," negotiator, and "interpretess."[1] Two hundred years of Lewis and Clark studies have confirmed little more about the factitious Sacajawea. Some local historians still like to debate her name, her tribal origins, her role in the Lewis and Clark expedition, and the circumstances of her death.

Her postfactual afterlife has meant fuller celebrity and broader circulation for Sacajawea. In her most recent incarnation, she has joined a select group of American Indians—real and imagined—to be featured on the currency of the United States. Now, as a replacement for the ill-fated Susan B. Anthony, she appears on a golden dollar, smiling, an infant strapped to her back. Ironically, this image of Sacajawea was invented and popularized by Anthony and other suffragettes a century ago. In 1902, the Oregon suffragette Eva Emery Dye published *The Conquest: The True Story of Lewis and Clark.* Dye's novelistic treatment of the expedition recuperated Sacajawea as a heroine of western women's history, amplifying her role as an expeditionary guide and emphasizing her travails as a new mother in the wilderness. Dye also presented Sacajawea as a pioneering liaison between white and Indian worlds—in sum, as the "Madonna of her race."[2] Dye set out to materially incorporate her vision of Sacajawea with the organization of the Saca-jawea Statue Association in 1903. The association raised more than $7,000 to commission from the sculptor Alice Cooper a seven-foot bronze of the Shoshone woman as Dye had imagined her: a pioneer-Madonna, facing westward, carrying a cradle-boarded infant. The statue was unveiled and dedicated on 30 June 1905, "Women's Day" at the Lewis and Clark Centennial Exposition. Officials of the National Woman Suffrage Association, which had been invited to hold its annual convention concurrently with the exposition, spoke at the dedication ceremony. In her opening address, Susan B. Anthony hailed Sacajawea as an unsung heroine of western history:

> This recognition of the assistance rendered by a woman in the discovery of this great section of the country is but the beginning of what is due. Next year the men of this proud State, made possible by a woman, will decide whether women shall at last have the rights in it which have been denied them so many years. Let men remember the part that women have played in its settlement and progress and vote to give them these rights which belong to every citizen.[3]

Following Anthony at the podium, Anna Shaw, the association's president, lauded Sacajawea in the popular, pathetic rhetoric of the "Vanishing Indian":

> Sacajawea. . . . Your tribe is fast disappearing from the land of your fathers. May we, the daughters of an alien race who slew your people and usurped your country, learn the lessons of calm endurance, of patient persistence and unfaltering courage exemplified in your life, in our efforts to lead men through the pass of justice, which leads over the mountains of prejudice and conservatism, to the broad land of the perfect freedom of a true republic.[4]

Shaw and Anthony poetically transferred the westward movement of the Lewis and Clark expedition onto the movement for women's suffrage. They claimed for Sacajawea historical value as the woman who "made Oregon possible" and symbolic value as an icon of woman-piloted progress (Figure 6). But Sacajawea's career as a suffragette was short-lived: after Oregon voters defeated women's suffrage in a 1906 state referendum, her statue was rededicated to "the pioneer mothers of old Oregon" and permanently installed at Portland's Washington Park.[5]

Following the Lewis and Clark exposition, more conservative clubwomen redefined Sacajawea as a mascot of true western womanhood and regional pride. Monument campaigns and historical pageants in North Dakota, Washington, and Montana honored her as both an instrument of Manifest Destiny and a model of its civilizing successes. Typical of these projects was the North Dakota Women's Club's effort to install a statue of Sacajawea on the state capitol grounds in Bismarck. Promotional pamphlets published by

Figure 6. Statue of Sacajawea in Washington Park, Portland, Oregon. (Photo by Andrew Gulliford, Center of Southwest Studies, Fort Lewis College)

the club erroneously celebrated the Shoshone woman as the "first Indian west of the Missouri River to convert to Christianity." In 1912, when the *Bird Woman* statue was dedicated, the secretary of the North Dakota State Historical Society claimed that Sacajawea made it possible for "our good friends" the Indians to be educated in government schools. His eulogy of Sacajawea as an emblem of Indian education was met with an ironic response from Native Americans in the audience. A group of young Shoshone, Hidatsa, Mandan, Arikara, and Sioux government-school graduates, featured as honored guests, told reporters from the *Bismarck Tribune* that they had never heard of Sacajawea before the statue campaign.[6] Her incorporation into colonialist historical romance did not secure Sacajawea's legacy among American Indians.

American Indian intellectuals were solicited to settle emerging disputes over the Shoshone woman's biography. Conventional historians held that Sacajawea died in Missouri in 1812, but the University of Wyoming professor Grace Raymond Hebard asserted that Sacajawea died in Wyoming in 1884. Controversy flared in 1924 when Hebard lobbied for a federal Sacajawea memorial in Wyoming. The Bureau of Indian Affairs commissioned Charles Eastman (Santee Sioux), a Dartmouth- and Boston University–educated medical doctor then serving as general inspector for the agency, to establish an authoritative account of Sacajawea's final years. After collecting testimony from tribes in Wyoming, North Dakota, and Oklahoma, Eastman concluded in support of Hebard: Sacajawea had outlived Charbonneau, wandered south, married a Comanche man, and died in Wyoming in 1884. Eastman also offered an explanation for the shadowy, contested character of Sacajawea's history:

> At the time history was unknown to even some of the Rocky Mountain white men, much more so with the Indians. One of the striking characteristics and habits of the Bird Woman is that she is very modest in claiming any honors of being guide to that party; one reason for this is the Indian woman will put her husband as the head in any matter of that kind. She never considered herself as a guide or interpreter. She evidently assumed that the great duties performed by her were the natural consequences of the expedition. . . . It was not her choice but fate seemed to have compelled her to live the life that she did.[7]

In his books *Indian Boyhood* (1902) and *The Soul of the Indian* (1908), Eastman had promoted Indian culture as an innately, if primitively, virtuous alternative to anxious, ills-ridden modernity. The same aims shaped his public presentation of Sacajawea as a model of traditional Indian modesty. Privately, Eastman maintained a more radical view of Sacajawea, describing her in his personal correspondence as the "Ben Hur" of Native America.[8] What began as a project of historical reconnaissance, for Eastman, ultimately produced another species of Sacajawea romance.

Sacajawea's transformation from historical personage into cultural icon ensured her survival in popular memory, but it sacrificed important dimensions of her story. As Philip Deloria demonstrates in *Playing Indian,* the long American tradition of turning Indians into symbols—a tradition reaching from Pocahontas, Chief Logan, and King Tammany to Chief Seattle—both perpetuates and masks the darker aspects of colonialist cultural politics. The celebration of Sacajawea as protosuffragette ignored, if not obscured, the federal disenfranchisement of Native Americans: most Indians, male and female, did not enjoy the right to vote until granted citizenship by an act of Congress in 1924. More egregious was conservative clubwomen's use of Sacajawea to affirm their assimilationist programs and policies. Charles Eastman's presentation of Sacajawea as a model of traditional gender values may have appealed to the nostalgia of white audiences, but it did little to advance respect for Native women as modern beings. Indeed, little about Sacajawea's story was traditional: her career as interpreter and borderlands guide significantly extended and complicated white-Indian relations. Romantic representations of Sacajawea transmitted little of this complexity.

We find a very different view of Sacajawea in one of the first novels published by a Native American woman. Christine Quintasket (1885?–1936) grew up a Salish-speaking Okanogan, indigenous to northeastern Washington. Like many Native people of her generation, she was educated in convent and government schools with intensely assimilationist agendas. In 1912, while living in Portland, Oregon, Quintasket chose a pen name—Mourning Dove—and penciled a first draft of a novel. There, in the birthplace of the iconic Sacajawea, Mourning Dove developed her own story about a young northwestern Native woman negotiating the dislocations of colonialism. The protagonist was an interpreter and mediator between white and Indian worlds; she eventually rejected romance with an exploitive white fortune seeker for a more satisfying partnership with an Indian man. Down to the detail of its protagonist's nearly homophonous name, Mourning Dove's *Cogewea, the Half-Blood: A Depiction of the Great Montana Cattle Range* suggests a critique of popular Sacajawea romance. Mourning Dove used the novel to record, preserve, and perpetuate tribal perspectives—once passed down as oral narrative—on the coming of the Lewis and Clark expedition. Her story also offers distinctive insights into the complexities of contact between white men and Indian women in the aftermath of the expedition. According to the novel, what Cogewea experiences as a conflicted, race-conscious, thoroughly modern "half-blood" is a predicament shared by northwestern Native women since the time of Sacajawea. Cogewea's survival and happiness depend on her ability to hear, understand, and interpret that legacy.

Cogewea is a revisionist Western, a love story that rejects the premises and reworks the novelistic conventions of frontier romance. Mourning Dove knew these conventions well: she first learned the English alphabet by reading dime novels, introduced to the Quintasket household by an adopted white orphan named Jimmy. She also learned from her Okanogan elders an indigenous perspective on the story of Lewis and Clark. She explains in her *Autobiography*,

> When Lewis and Clark made their famous exploration, they did not reach Okanogan territory, but my people heard many stories of white-skinned

strangers who wintered at the mouth of the Columbia. The stories came from the south—from Yakima who told Wenatchi, who told Okanogan. . . . The first white explorer to enter our country was David Thompson of the Northwest Company of Montreal, a rival in the fur trade with the great Hudson's Bay Company.[9]

The conventional American view of Lewis and Clark did not hold for her people: among them, "the first white explorer" was a Canadian fur trader. Lewis and Clark entered Okanogan territory as a story, a story transmitted from tribe to tribe. Mourning Dove's account deauthorizes Lewis and Clark as producers of their own history, and it decenters their party as one among several to "explore" the region. Additionally, it emphasizes that the land was already inhabited by distinct Native populations—Yakima, Wenatchi, Okanogan, and others—who were known to one another before their "discovery." To Mourning Dove, the story of Lewis and Clark was not an unprecedented epic, a narrative progressing from east to west. Rather, it was another installment of the stranger-comes-to-town genre, a story set entirely in the Pacific Northwest.

Mourning Dove brought this perspective to bear on the composition of *Cogewea*. Its frontier setting is not the boundary between civilization and wilderness, nor between white and red. Rather, it is a simultaneously wild and settled space, where cattle ranches abut open rangeland; it is a social borderlands, home to a range of highly differentiated and dynamic identities. Its protagonist, Cogewea McDonald, is a half-blood, the daughter of an Okanogan mother and an errant white father, and a recent graduate of Carlisle Indian School in Pennsylvania. Both her situation as a half-blood and her education place her in the borderlands of racial identity and cultural belonging. She has returned home to the Horseshoe Bend—or "H-B," for "half-blood"—Ranch, which is owned by her sister Julia and her white brother-in-law, John Carter. The ranch hands are a comic crew of mixed-bloods and migrants: "Rodeo Jack," a "quarter-blood Texan of uncertain qualities"; "Celluloid Bill," a trickster "half-blood Cheyenne"; "Silent Bob," a displaced, drawling West Virginian; and James LaGrinder, the half-blood Flathead foreman.

The plot of *Cogewea* feminizes frontier-adventure by mixing in key elements of the captivity narrative and the novel of seduction. As the novel opens, Cogewea stands on a bluff overlooking the Pend Oreille River, facing west, surveying the landscape, and musing aloud over her future. "What had the future in store for her? What would it bring? Would it, through her, illuminate the pathway of others?"[10] Mourning Dove positions her protagonist to pilot readers through the social complexities of Indianness in the twentieth century. The plot thickens with the arrival of Alfred Densmore, a dastardly, duplicitous city dweller "with a cold, calculating grey eye" (43).

Cogewea finds herself strangely attracted to the Eastern fortune seeker, and she volunteers herself as Densmore's guide to life on the range. Densmore erroneously believes that Cogewea owns large land holdings; he plots to seduce, marry, and abandon her. Densmore's seduction strategy is a calculated appeal to Cogewea's liminality: he feigns interest in Indian customs and sympathy for Cogewea's situation as a half-blood. This indulges her tendency to lapse into impassioned soliloquy, to play the native informant, to reveal and explain her vulnerabilities. At times, Cogewea becomes so absorbed in her own internal debates that she fails to read and interpret Densmore's motivations. Here Mourning Dove remakes the novel of seduction in modern Indian terms, and she turns the captivity narrative formula into an indictment of white men who entrap Indian women.

The voice of Native tradition in the novel belongs to Cogewea's grandmother Stemteema, a full-blooded Okanogan who has been entrusted with the stories of the tribe. Stemteema staunchly opposes her granddaughter's deepening fascination with Densmore, whom she sees as the latest in a series of opportunistic "Sho-yah-pee," or white men, who have come west to take advantage of the women of the tribe. Stemteema recounts their fates to Cogewea: an ancestor given as a wife to a member of the Lewis and Clark expedition; a childhood friend seduced and abandoned by a white American soldier; and Cogewea's own mother, left alone by her gold miner husband with three girls to raise. She warns,

> My grandchild! You talk too much to that pale face. He does not mean right by you! He is having sport with you. He wants to make a fool of you, that all the young people may laugh. You think he has love because he follow you. Not so! He is blind you with false words. He is here to cheat you; all that any white man wants of the Indian girl. It is only to put her to shame, then cast her aside for his own kind, the pale faced squaw. (103)

In an attempt to derail the romance, Stemteema insists that Densmore and Cogewea meet with her to hear the customs and histories of the tribe. "I will tell this Sho-yah-pee a tale of the long ago. I will tell him of the coming of the pale face; when the tribes were many and strong. . . . Yes! I will tell him of the invasion by the despoiler, and of the wasting of my people. . . . I will speak and you shall interpret my words" (105). In commanding Cogewea to interpret these difficult stories, Stemteema forces her to disengage from her solipsistic, romantic reverie and to recognize the historical context of her relationship with Densmore. Stemteema's story contests the privileged discourse—the romance of discovery—which assures Densmore that the West and its indigenous people exist to be explored and exploited.

The meeting between Densmore, Cogewea, and Stemteema takes place in Stemteema's tepee, located at some distance from the H-B ranch houses. Similarly, Stemteema locates her story and her authority in the context of tribal tradition: "This story I am telling you is true. It was given me by my father who favored me among his many children. . . . He told me the tales that were sacred to his tribe; honored me with them, trusted me. Treasured by my forefathers, I value them" (122). She describes Okanogan life as it existed before contact, then recounts the portents, history, and impact of colonial incursion. According to Stemteema, "Black Robes," or priests, preceded Lewis and Clark among the Okanogan. She continues, "Then they saw the pale face again, two of them. They had no black robes, but the people tried to pray to them, as they remembered the words of the Black Robe. The pale faces only laughed at them. But this is another story which I may tell you some time" (128). As they leave the tepee, Densmore interrogates Cogewea about the accuracy of Stemteema's narrative. His motive is "more to court favor" with Cogewea than to advance his understanding of Native history, "a subject in which he felt no particular interest": "Cogewea! are all those supposed facts as narrated by your grandmother concerning the first coming of the white man, or only legend? They seem to be no part of the chronicles. . . . Lewis and Clark were the first Caucasians to reach and explore the great Northwest. That is recognized history" (129).

Cogewea defends Stemteema's story: "They were the first white *explorers* of the Northwest, but *not* the first to penetrate its sylvan wilds. It is my belief that the last two 'pale faces' Stemteema mentioned were the famous pathfinders sent out by the Government, and I am sure that when you hear her story of these men, you will agree with me on that score. Stemteema was a small child at the time of this second coming, and she has certainly seen more than a hundred snows" (129–130). Cogewea continues, goaded by Densmore's resistance into a critique of Christianity, white supremacy, and the Bureau of Indian Affairs. Densmore does not find these subjects "altogether engaging" but nonetheless assumes a look of "studied intent" (133). Ultimately, he begs to learn more about "tribal marriage ceremonies," as a way of distracting and entrapping her (136). When she tells him she must marry a half-blood, he appeals to her sense of modernity: "Why erect an imaginary barrier about your life? A true mate is one who has sympathy for your ideals; who understands and is willing to adapt himself to your ways. Don't you think I would make a good half-breed?" (150). Densmore successfully captivates Cogewea with the absurdity of his question, and the significance of Stemteema's story is lost. Cogewea and Densmore never return to hear the complete history of Lewis and Clark, and the seduction scheme advances.

Stemteema finds a more reliable audience in the ranch's half-blood foreman, Jim LaGrinder. LaGrinder shares her suspicions about Densmore, and he watches over Cogewea with protective affection. "You are an Indian," she pleads, "you will understand me, what I am to tell you I am distressed and need your help" (216). To enlist his help in preventing Cogewea's impending elopement, Stemteema relates the story of "the second coming of the Shoyahpee." She herself witnessed the arrival of Lewis and Clark as a child "more than a hundred snows" ago: "The men with hair on their pale faces impressed me. . . . I remember well both Shoyahpees. I was afraid! I clung to my mother for protection. With pleading and coaxing, she made me to understand that I was not to be afraid of them; that they were not common mortals as we were the warriors and medicine men, but were gods—a higher people than the Indians—which all my tribe believed to be true" (218).

Stemteema relates how her father established contact with Lewis and Clark, seeking them out at their camp. "The pale faces were both holding weapons against us. Even the strange Indian woman who was with them, held a gun in aim. She was a brave squaw! We found afterwards that she came to show them the trail to the big water, towards the sunset" (220). She continues, recounting a prophecy made by one of her ancestors:

> Evil and death will come to my people in the wake of these two pale faces. . . .
> I saw on this great new trail a might nation sweeping over our hunting grounds,
> armed with dread weapons of war. I saw our villages made desolate with fire
> and the graves of our fathers profaned. I saw the death-trail worm smooth by
> the moccasined feet of the dead and the death wail grew loud on the storm-
> rack of night. (224)

Stemteema concludes by connecting the story of Lewis and Clark directly to Cogewea's predicament. "You now know why I do not want Cogewea to marry this Shoyahpee. They are all false to our race" (226). As a half-blood, Jim hears the story of Lewis and Clark as a commentary on his white ancestors. His responds feelingly, "I have heard Stemteema and I am not proud of my white blood" (226–227). Jim tells Stemteema that "the white man's law" trumps "tribal rules" and allows Cogewea to choose her husband. However, he promises to take revenge if Densmore proves false. With Jim as her audience, Stemteema successfully rehistoricizes the mythology of frontier romance. Her testimony confirms the agency of Indian women—Sacajawea *and* Cogewea—as accomplices to white explorers' schemes. Jim also recognizes Cogewea's autonomy in negotiating the terms of white-Indian contact, and for this reason he refuses to interfere as she chooses her own path.

As Mourning Dove reconnects the predicament of Sacajawea to the situation of modern half-breeds, she comments on the strategies used by her Indian contemporaries to address the white world. Her generation of Indian intellectuals, like Cogewea, had been educated in both white schools and tribal customs. They cultivated a ground-breaking awareness of their shared status as Indians and founded intertribal organizations such as the Society of American Indians to advance their common cause. The so-called "Red Progressives"—including Charles Eastman; Henry Roe Cloud (Winnebago), the first Native graduate from Yale University; the noted authors Gertrude Bonnin / Zitkala Sa (Sioux) and Francis LaFlesche (Omaha); the anthropologists Arthur Parker (Seneca) and Ella Deloria (Yankton Sioux), and others—were deeply divided over how Indians should advance into modernity. Some were strong advocates of complete assimilation; others were firebrand opponents of the Bureau of Indian Affairs. All seemed to share a consciousness of the opportunities for cultural and political power their precarious position as Indian intellectuals afforded them. Philip Deloria explains that the Red Progressives "wanted to become bridge figures, using antimodern primitivism to defend native cultures against the negative stereotypes left over from colonial conquest."[11] Like the Sacajawea of popular imagination—if not the Sacajawea of history—the authority and power of the Red Progressives derived from their liminality and their skills as interpreters and mediators.

Mourning Dove experienced the limits of this power and authority in the process of composing and publishing her novel. *Cogewea* was the product of editorial collaboration between Mourning Dove and Lucullus V. McWhorter, a West Virginia–born archeologist and Indian affairs activist. Mourning Dove first met McWhorter in 1914 at the Walla Walla Washington Frontier Days celebration; he encouraged her literary ambitions and offered his assistance in securing publication for her drafted manuscript. During the winter of 1915–16, Mourning Dove lived in the McWhorter home and dedicated herself to manuscript revisions.[12] Consequently, the published novel is marked by McWhorter's editorial interventions: poetic epigraphs, anthropological annotation, and extended political invective.[13] While awaiting the long-delayed publication of *Cogewea*, Mourning Dove began work on a collection of Okanogan folklore. There too she found her efforts hampered by the intervention of white "professionals." She wrote to McWhorter:

> There are some that are getting suspicious of my wanting folklores and if the Indians find out that their stories will reach print I am sure it will be hard for me to get any more legends without paying the hard cash for them. A whiteman has spoiled my field of work. . . . This Mr. James Teit has collected folklores among the Indians and has been paying five dollars a piece for good Indian legends. (viii)

Teit, an assistant of Franz Boas, compiled wordlists and folklores still considered authoritative. Still, Mourning Dove did manage to compile her Okanogan folklore, which was published as *Coyote Stories* in 1933.

In Cogewea, Mourning Dove created a protagonist who shared her Red Progressive authorial ambitions and who encountered many of the same limitations.[14] Cogewea states early in the novel that her ambitions are to be an "authoress." One motive for this ambition is to correct inaccurate and demeaning literary representations of Indians. Cogewea reacts violently to *The Brand,* a dime novel romance in which a self-hating half-breed hero offers himself in a self-abasing marriage to a white girl of the Flathead range. Pitching the book into the kitchen stove, she criticizes the colonialist misconception of Indianness: "Cogewea reflected bitterly how her race had had the worst of every deal since the landing of the lordly European on their shores; how they had suffered as much from the pen as from the bayonet of conquest; wherein the annals had always been chronicled by their most deadly foes and partisan writers" (91–92).[15] Cogewea considers it her responsibility to use her education to advance public awareness of and respect for Indian culture. She also envisions print as a venue for the preservation of Indian traditions. Cogewea fears that "the new order of things" threatens the survival of tradition and believes that "her people's philosophy must be irretrievably lost unless speedily placed on record" (33). Her duality, her liminality positions her uniquely between white and Indian, oral tradition and print literacy. As the novel explains,

> Most of the old people do not make use of English, although the majority of them understand many words and can speak them but will not do so unless absolutely necessary. If alone with the whites, they will talk if occasion demands; but if in the presence of the younger Indians, they can hardly be induced to do so. . . . Recognizing the linguistic ability of the educated youth, it is expected to them to assume the role of interpreter. (118)

Only an English-literate Indian like Cogewea could translate traditional Indian lore into the modern medium of print. Cogewea's liminality between white and Indian worlds also situates her in a unique position to mediate Indian culture for a broader reading public.

Yet the offices of translation, mediation, and interpretation place Cogewea and her contemporaries in a difficult position. Education in government schools could teach them English literacy, but it could also inculcate a deep resentment of white incursions into Indian territories, cultural and geographic. Thus, while younger Indians knew how to communicate with outsiders, they were more distanced from Indian traditions and more resentful of the beneficiaries of their translation. The complexities of this situation are demonstrated in an anecdote from the novel, an anecdote—according to McWhorter's annotations—drawn from Mourning Dove's life. One winter when Stemteema, Cogewea, and her sisters were living on the banks of the Columbia River, two young white men came to ice-fish. The fishermen inquired at the tepee about the condition of the ice; Cogewea and her sisters pretended not to understand English. Chastised by Stemteema for failing to warn the fishermen about the thin ice, "What did you learn the language and books of the pale face for? They do no good unless you make use of them when needed!" Stemteema cried out in "a jargon of English," successfully warning the boys off (119). The McDonald sisters' mischievous refusal to interpret for and to guide the two young white explorers reveals the potential for resistance. This strategy is corroborated also by the half-breed ranch foreman, Jim LaGrinder, who admits that he and the boys of the HB ranch have fed would-be white authorities tall tales and half-truths about range life and Indian lore. When Alfred Densmore suggests that "confidence" might improve Indian relations with whites, "facilitating both social and business interests," Jim replies, "That there 'confidence' card has been our undoin" (94). The indictment of Densmore as confidence man becomes more provocative when considered in connection with his last name; Frances Densmore was the early twentieth century's leading scholar of American Indian music. Perhaps Alfred Densmore is a stand-in for all the opportunistic "friends of the Indian," from Lewis and Clark to the romancers, land speculators, and anthropologists of the modern age. Jim's comment reveals a little recognized aspect of the Sacajawea predicament: in a colonialist context, the relationship between Indian and white, "interpreter" and explorer, is never in good faith.

Indeed, Cogewea herself will discover the bad-faith basis of Densmore's marriage plot. After the pair elopes, Densmore learns that his intended bride has no large land claims. He robs her of a small cash fortune, ties her to a tree, and abandons her on the range. But Mourning Dove does not leave Cogewea to die in the wilderness. Resisting the conventions of the seduction novel, she allows Cogewea to recover and learn from her mistakes. In a chapter entitled "The Cost of Knowing," the heroine is rescued by Jim LaGrinder, to whom she reveals, with some humiliation, the extent of Densmore's duplicity. At novel's end, after a lapse of some years, an older, wiser Cogewea and LaGrinder resolve to marry in a happy joining of half-blood equals. The conclusion of *Cogewea* marks a way to survive the Sacajawea predicament: it is "knowledge," self-knowledge, rather than service as someone else's tutor or guide. Playing Sacajawea subscribes Indians to the schemes of whites rather than advancing their own independent interests. Acting as an interpreter recycles and reinscribes the colonialist mythology of the frontier.

Here, then, is a powerful Red Progressive response to popular representations of Sacajawea. In historical novels, on statehouse lawns, in public parks, and at roadside historic sites, the name and the image of Sacajawea indexed a broadly accepted romance of how the West was won with the help of a Indian woman, a story white people told themselves about their relationships with Indians. For many Indian intellectuals of the Progressive era, playing the Sacajawea role—patient guide and interpreter—seemed one of most effective avenues to broadening Indian cultural and political power.

But Mourning Dove's novel reveals a darker aspect of the Sacajawea predicament. It challenges Native women to resist the bad-faith lure of colonialist romance and to pilot their own meaningful path through the chaos of modernity.

Cogewea also challenges contemporary readers to imagine the Corps of Discovery from the perspective of the "discovered." From this perspective, Meriwether Lewis, William Clark, and Sacajawea are not singular characters. Rather, they belong to a broader genre of strangers-come-west stories, a genre that the expedition neither pioneered nor exhausted. *Cogewea* restores this sense of multiplicity to the record. It decenters the legacy of Lewis and Clark. It reminds us that there were multiple Indian witnesses to the expedition, that Sacajawea was not the only Native woman with a Lewis and Clark tale to tell, and that our singular fascination with her proceeds from a paucity of knowledge about American Indian women. Similarly, the novel resists our ambitions to "discover" and establish new knowledge about Lewis and Clark; it will not use Native oral tradition to authenticate or legitimate our historical fascinations. Rather, it counters the heroic formulas of historical narrative with a more profound, primeval, place-based, and cyclical sense of story. As Louise Erdrich asks in the conclusion to her novel *The Antelope Wife,* "Did these occurrences have a paradigm in the settlement of the old scores and pains and betrayals that went back in time? Or are we working out the minor details of a strictly random pattern? Who is beading us? Who are you and who am I, the beader or the bit of colored glass sewn onto the fabric of this earth?"[16] Mourning Dove's novel *Cogewea* suggests that Lewis, Clark, and Sacajawea were but beads in a more extensive pattern. They were the elements but not the authors of randomness and chaos. *Cogewea*—like the best Native American literature—asks us to confront the idea of sovereignty: to recognize that "discovery" does not confer authority, mastery, or ownership. Two hundred years after Lewis and Clark, we have yet to learn this lesson.

NOTES

1. In an 1805 register of corps members, Clark explains that "Shabonah and his Indian Squar," "Sah-kah-gar-wea," were to "act as an Interpreter and interpretess for the snake Indians" (Gary E. Moulton, ed., *The Journals of the Lewis & Clark Expedition* [Lincoln: University of Nebraska Press, 1988], 4:11); he emphasized these responsibilities during her June 1805 illness, "her being our only dependence for a friendly negociation with the Snake Indians" (4:299). Later, Clark credited Sacajawea's mere presence in the corps with "reconsil[ing] all the Indians, as to our friendly intentions" because "a woman with a party of men is a token of peace" (5:268). Finally, on 13 July 1806 Clark records with appreciation Sacajawea's "great service to me as a pilot" (8:180). James Ronda offers a terse review of Sacajawea history and

scholarship in an appendix to *Lewis and Clark among the Indians* (Lincoln: University of Nebraska Press, 1984).

2. Quoted in Jan C. Dawson, "Sacagawea: Pilot or Pioneer Mother?," *Pacific Northwest Quarterly* 83, no.1 (1992): 25.

3. Ida Husted Harper, *The Life and Work of Susan B. Anthony* (Indianapolis: Hollenbeck Press, 1908), 3:1365.

4. G. Thomas Edwards, *Sowing Good Seeds: The Northwest Suffrage Campaigns of Susan B. Anthony* (Portland: Oregon Historical Society Press, 1990), 229.

5. Grace Raymond Hebard, "Memorials to Sacajawea," *Annals of Wyoming* 13, no. 3 (July 1941): 184.

6. Donna J. Kessler, *The Making of Sacagawea: A Euro-American Legend* (Tuscaloosa: University of Alabama Press, 1996), 91–93.

7. Charles Eastman, "Report," *Annals of Wyoming* 13, no. 3 (July 1941): 192.

8. Raymond Wilson, *Ohiyesa: Charles Eastman, Santee Sioux* (Urbana: University of Illinois Press, 1983), 179.

9. Mourning Dove / Christine Quintasket, *Mourning Dove: A Salishan Autobiography*, ed. Jay Miller (Lincoln: University of Nebraska Press, 1990), 149.

10. Mourning Dove / Christine Quintasket, *Cogewea, the Half-Blood: A Depiction of the Great Montana Cattle Range*, ed. Dexter Fisher (1927; Lincoln: University of Nebraska Press, 1981), 17. Any parenthetical page citations in chapter 8 text are to this work.

11. Philip Deloria, *Playing Indian* (New Haven: Yale University Press, 1998), 122.

12. Steven Ross Evans, *Voice of the Old Wolf: Lucullus Virgil McWhorter and the Nez Perce Indians* (Pullman: Washington State University Press, 1996), 56.

13. On Mourning Dove's relationship with McWhorter, see Susan K. Bernardin, "Mixed Messages: Authority and Authorship in Mourning Dove's *Cogewea, the Half-Blood: A Depiction of the Great Montana Cattle Range*," *American Literature* 67, no. 3 (1992): 487–509; Alanna K. Brown, "Mourning Dove's Voice in *Cogewea*," *Wicazo Sa Review* 4, no. 2 (1988): 2–15; Alanna K. Brown, "Looking through the Glass Darkly: The Editorialized Mourning Dove," in *New Voices in Native American Literary Criticism*, ed. Arnold Krupat (Washington, D.C.: Smithsonian Institution Press, 1993); and Linda K. Karrell, "'This Story I am Telling You Is True': Collaboration and Literary Authority in Mourning Dove's *Cogewea*," *American Indian Quarterly* 19, no. 4 (1995): 451–465. See also Evans, *Voice of the Old Wolf*.

14. Arnold Krupat connects *Cogewea* to its Red Progressive context in "From 'Half-Blood' to 'Mixedblood': Cogewea and the 'Discourse of Indian Blood,'" *Modern Fiction Studies* 45 (spring 1999): 120–145.

15. See Peter G. Beidler, "Literary Criticism in *Cogewea*: Mourning Dove's Protagonist Reads *The Brand*," *American Indian Culture and Research Journal* 19 (1995): 45–65.

16. Louise Erdrich, *The Antelope Wife* (New York: Harper Collins, 1998), 240.

Chapter 9

On the Trail

*Commemorating the Lewis & Clark Expedition
in the Twentieth Century*

Wallace Lewis

Concerned over the nation's inadequate commemoration of the explorers' 1804–06 journey to the Pacific Ocean and back, delegates from more than twenty communities in the Pacific Northwest and Montana gathered at Lewiston, Idaho in 1929 to form the Lewis and Clark Memorial Association (LCMA). "It seems almost incredible," the group's initial report states, "that through all those years there has been no national monument erected in their honor. Perpetuated only in a few place names, they claim but scant present attention, except from close students of western history." The association may have overstated the case, ignoring the two world's fairs that commemorated the centennial of the expedition in 1904 and 1905, as well as the many statues, monuments, and books those two events inspired in the ensuing decades. Nevertheless, popular interest in Lewis and Clark had diminished considerably since the early twentieth century, as had the number of people who even knew where or when the expedition occurred. Though disheartening, it was probably not surprising to the members of the LCMA when their efforts failed to stir much interest in the approaching 125th anniversary of the trek across the continent.[1]

While they failed in their initial goals, the members of the association realized that part of the problem lay in the ways that Lewis and Clark had been memorialized in the past. Their first goal was to inculcate a "better understanding" among the American public, which would in turn "inspire a higher conception of what is suitable to commemorate them." That "higher conception" apparently involved road building along the expedition route, since promotion of a multistate Lewis and Clark highway underlay the association's agenda. Making the route of the expedition serve as the nation's memorial to the expedition represented a radical new way of commemorating the past, and no one at the 1929 meeting of the LCMA seemed to recognize what their goals implied or how to enact them. This partly reflected the new but half-understood excitement about automobile tourism that appealed to every kind of western booster. This new leisure industry briefly flourished in the late 1920s with the availability of inexpensive vehicles and the construction of continuous paved highways across the Great Plains and the mountain west, then faded altogether in the midst of the Great Depression and wartime rationing. It required the economic expansion of the post–World War II era to make automobile tourism a persistent and widespread feature of American culture, which in turn provided the context in which the expedition route developed into the principal monument for commemorating the Lewis and Clark expedition. "The Trail"— as the route became known—was not the result of "better understanding," as the LCMA once predicted. Rather, it became the means through which many Americans came to understand the Lewis and Clark expedition. In the process, touring the Trail provided an important benchmark for assessing the magnitude of change in the American landscape over the short course of two centuries.[2]

Commemorating the past has commonly been a way for Americans to validate the present and create a sense of common identity. This usually occurs in one of two ways: traditionally through plaques, statues, and other monuments, the most visible and fundamental means of memorializing; or through "public historical imagery" like rituals, reenactments, and pageants. While both types of commemoration marked public awareness of the significance of the Lewis and Clark expedition after the turn of the century, new ways of identifying historic sites have proliferated in the past forty years or so and become meaningful to the public in ways that traditional commemorative types do not. These include simple markers to elaborate replicas of structures and multimedia interpretive centers that interpret historical events at a particular site. The popularity of these new forms of commemoration probably derives from their convenience to vacationers and purported educational value, but they also appeal to the imagination in ways that commemorative statues and monuments simply cannot. Place becomes the hero: *this* is where something significant occurred.[3]

While all of this has been fairly recent, it clearly distinguishes past commemorations of Lewis and Clark from more recent efforts to memorialize their expedition. Lewis and Clark received relatively little attention in the nineteenth century. The national government seems to have permitted the fiftieth anniversary of the expedition to pass unrecognized. Local communities, which normally would have celebrated the passage of the expedition through their vicinity, were few and far between. For Captain John Mullan, builder of the Mullan trail across the Bitterroot and Rocky mountains, the explorers' fame as forerunners of civilization seems to have been adequately memorialized by progress and settlement. "Here with you," he told the Historical Society of the Rocky Mountains in 1861, "their [Lewis and Clark's] monument is to be found, industrious people, who have built towns & cities where there was the wilderness, & their epitaphs are found engraved upon the hearts & affections of an appreciating people, who are ever willing to pay homage & respect to the very mention of the names of Lewis & Clark." But Mullan castigated the national government for its failures to "maintain the claim . . . established by the explorations" and to fully publish the journals produced by the explorers.[4]

The unavailability of the original journals partially explains early failure to commemorate the expedition. After the 1814 Biddle edition, which sold relatively few copies, no legitimate narrative of the journey again appeared until Elliott Coues's in 1893. Moreover, no original edition of the journals was published until Reuben Gold Thwaites's in 1904 and, according to Paul Russell Cutright, no "book of consequence *written about* the Expedition" until Olin D. Wheeler's two-volume *Trail of Lewis and Clark,* also in 1904. As the historian Donald Jackson observed, the two explorers do not occupy the same sort of mythical frontier space as figures like Davy Crockett, Daniel Boone, or even Zebulon Pike; consequently, books must be "the real source of public knowledge about the expedition." Publications of the original journals in the twentieth century by such editors as Thwaites, Milo Milton Quaife, Ernest S. Osgood, Jackson, and Gary Moulton, as well as Bernard DeVoto's popular condensation, largely account for expanding interest in the expedition. During the nineteenth century, in contrast, disillusionment and lack of interest obscured its history. The Corps of Discovery's accomplishments had already begun to be overshadowed by events when Biddle's history of them finally appeared, the scientific observations remained all but unknown for eighty years, and the path they blazed fell quickly out of favor. Soon after the explorers' views of the Pacific Northwest had been distorted to promote settlement in the Oregon country during the 1830s, Lewis and Clark "receded into the American memory" until the Thwaites edition of the journals and the centennial celebration brought them to the fore.[5]

A "merging and melding" of what John L. Allen calls "literate elite" and "folk" images of Lewis and Clark in the twentieth century helps explain shifts in the way the expedition has been commemorated. The "folk image," on the one hand, has tended to focus on "the explicit purpose of exploring and evaluating the newly acquired lands," essentially the viewpoint expressed by Captain Mullan. The "literate elite" image, on the other hand, focuses on the scientific purposes of the expedition and, as Donald Jackson noted, the "personalities involved." For the elite image, the journals became central, and they made the specific path taken by the expedition central as well. The geographic regions through which that path runs, however, were not settled until the last three decades of the nineteenth century, and long stretches of the expedition route remained largely inaccessible through the first half of the twentieth century. Though these conditions certainly help explain a previous lack of local interest in the history of the expedition, they also forced the elite image of the expedition to remain book-bound until the 1950s.[6]

The folk image of the expedition flowered during the 1904 Louisiana Purchase Centennial Exposition in St. Louis and the 1905 Lewis and Clark Centennial and American Exposition and Oriental Fair in Portland, Oregon. The two centennials came at a time when American imperialistic ambitions were in full flood and providing an anodyne to anxiety about the recent closing of the frontier. The image of Lewis and Clark carrying an American flag to the edge of the Pacific fit very well into a vision of the nation expanding its trade and influence across the ocean to Asia, while anxiety over the loss of the frontier inspired a growing interest in the history of the American West. As Warren I. Susman notes, Americans sought in the frontier past "a native epic, an epic that extolled the virtues of extreme individualism, courage, recklessness, aloofness from social ties and obligations." The story told in the journals provided an ideal candidate and has in fact been called "our national epic" on the basis of those qualities and virtues with which it represents the nation's ideals.[7]

The world fairs held in St. Louis and Portland stimulated public interest in "our national epic," but they largely presented the Lewis and Clark expedition as an emblem of progress and national expansion. At the Louisiana Purchase exposition in St. Louis, the Oregon exhibit included a rather grandiose and nonhistorical representation of Fort Clatsop surrounded by a log stockade and "gardens of rose-flushed Clarkia," and other plants discovered by the explorers. Organizers also claimed to fly the same "flag carried by" Lewis and Clark over the structure. Still, history was overshadowed by boosterism and commercialism, much as had been the case at the great centennial celebration in Philadelphia (1876) and the Columbian World Exposition in Chicago (1893). To borrow from Karal Ann Marling, the exposition was " a vast entertainment to which a dollop of history lent some semblance of high-minded dignity." At Portland's Lewis and Clark exposition in 1905, ceremonies honored Lewis and Clark and speakers like Exposition President Harvey W. Scott expounded upon the magnitude of their achievement: "through as humble an undertaking as the settlement at Plymouth or Jamestown, [the expedition] was the prologue to the theme of our later national expansion." Yet, despite these ostensible signs of commemoration, the Portland exposition was overshadowed by the promotion of municipal and regional economic investments and claims that "the twentieth century was to be America's Pacific century." Carl Abbott points out that such commercial concerns reflected more national interests, which became evident when exposition organizers approached the federal government for assistance in planning their "Great Extravaganza." "No one in Congress," he writes, " had much interest in the historical heroes and their . . . trek." What they were interested in was the "vision of Pacific trade that had motivated the exploration and settlement of the Oregon Country." In order to garner support, "Oregonians learned quickly in the winter of 1903–04 to cut the references to Lewis and Clark and to hammer home the idea that a Portland fair was 'an undertaking of national interest and importance.'"[8]

Their being identified with America's commercial destiny probably worked against popular appreciation for the explorers and their party. Abetting national expansion and stimulating economic development, no matter how much reverent praise it may earn in 1905, is decidedly less exciting or dramatic in the public mind than conquering by force of arms or heroically and tragically failing. But the figure of Sacagawea invited celebration of a more human and personal type of heroism. This would become manifest in the dozens of statues, monuments, and markers that have been erected in her honor, as well as the countless stories, place-names, musical compositions, paintings, pageants, and other forms of representation that have been commissioned over the years. Indeed, Sacagawea often seems to occupy a plane apart from the rest of the expedition, and her story, historical or legendary, has been put to various uses over the past century. The beginnings of Sacagawea's transformation in the popular imagination can be traced back to Elliott Coues, who emphasized her heroic contribution to the expedition, and to Eva Emery Dye's book *The Conquest: The True Story of Lewis and Clark,* which described Sacagawea as an Indian princess of equal or greater significance to the expedition than either Lewis or Clark.[9]

Sacagawea assumed the leading historical role at the Lewis and Clark Centennial Exposition when the National American Woman Suffrage Association accepted an invitation to hold its 1905 national convention in Portland. In the convention's presidential address, Anna Howard Shaw called voting rights for women "the logical conclusion of Sacagawea's heroic efforts." The Woman's Club of Portland had already established a "Sacajawea Statue Association," with Eva Emery Dye as president, and raised money for a statue by selling souvenir "'Sacajawea spoons' and 'Sacajawea buttons.'" The finished bronze statue, designed by Alice Cooper of Denver, which portrayed Sacagawea pointing the way for the explorers, was unveiled on 6 July 1905 at a ceremony in which both Susan B. Anthony and the Portland suffragist Abigail Scott Duniway were on hand to praise her in speeches. Anthony noted that it was "the first time in history that a statue has been erected in memory of a woman who accomplished patriotic deeds."[10] Cooper's statue was only the beginning. Also in 1905 the General Federation of Women's Clubs in North Dakota raised money and commissioned a twelve-foot-high bronze statue entitled *Bird Woman,* which was completed by the Chicago sculptor Leonard Crunelle in 1910 and dedicated in 1912 on the

North Dakota state capitol grounds in Bismarck before an estimated 5,000 spectators. More typical monuments to Sacagawea included a bronze plaque on granite that was placed at the site of Camp Fortunate near Armstead, Montana by the Daughters of the American Revolution in 1915. The Camp Fortunate monument came a year after Laura Tolman Scott of Armstead spoke at a meeting of the Montana Federation of Women's Clubs, and called Sacagawea the "unsung heroine of Montana." While these monuments certainly reflected the interests of western suffragists, Sacagawea symbolized more than the progress toward women's rights in the early part of the century. As Donna Kessler points out, Sacagawea came to embody many of the characteristics that had long been attributed to Pocohantas; at least as often as she represented political equality between men and women, Sacagawea also became an "Indian princess" who served as handmaiden to the noble cause of manifest destiny.[11]

Public monuments to Meriwether Lewis and William Clark appeared less frequently in the early twentieth century, and sometimes with considerable difficulty. In 1843 the state of Tennessee had erected a marble monument and column more than twenty feet high to mark Meriwether Lewis's grave, and in 1904 Congress authorized the War Department to place a second monument at Hohenwald, Tennessee. The gravesite of Sergeant Charles Floyd on Floyd's Bluff near Sioux City, Iowa had also drawn attention, particularly in 1857 when local residents, noticing that the remains of the Corps of Discovery's only fatality were in danger of crumbling into the Missouri River, reinterred them in a safer spot. Then in 1895 a national Floyd Memorial Association was formed, which placed a stone slab on the grave site and set out to raise money for a more imposing monument. That memorial, a one-hundred-foot sandstone obelisk dedicated in 1901, is said to be the first registered National Historic Landmark in the United States. One of the monument's plaques commemorates not only the "heroic members" of the Lewis and Clark expedition, but also the Louisiana Purchase, the "valor of the American soldier," and the "courage and fortitude of the American Pioneer." Perhaps the earliest heroic-scale statue (life-size or larger) that includes both Meriwether Lewis and William Clark, was created in 1919 by the New York sculptor Charles Keck and placed in Charlottesville, Virginia's Midway Park. Set atop a fourteen-foot pedestal surrounded in bas-relief depicting scenes from the expedition, the bronze statue rises another eight feet, four inches and portrays the two explorers standing beside a sitting Sacagawea.[12]

While the state of Montana commissioned a number of large murals for the new west wing of the state capitol building in Helena, including Charles M. Russell's *Lewis and Clark Meeting Indians at Ross' Hole* (1912) and Edgar Paxson's *Lewis and Clark at Three Forks* (1912), state and community leaders failed to establish any other monuments to the explorers for several decades. The first of many unsuccessful efforts apparently began with a proposal around the time of the Portland exposition to place a statue on the site of Camp Fortunate, where the expedition met the Shoshone and bargained for horses, but nothing came of this original proposal. In 1917 a bill introduced in the Montana Legislature called for heroic bronze statues of Meriwether Lewis and William Clark at Great Falls and at the three forks of the Missouri River. The measure passed in both houses but for some reason was never acted upon. A Montana governor's commission appointed in 1926 to propose means of honoring the explorers also called for a substantial monument and considered several cities for the site, including Great Falls, Three Forks, Helena, Butte, Bozeman, and Livingston. The commission ultimately recommended monuments in both Great Falls and Three Forks, but if only one were approved, it should be at Great Falls. Once again, nothing came of this proposal—possibly because of the intense municipal rivalry and the commission's apparent inability to decide whether to have monuments in different places or just one. Yet the competition among towns continued. A committee of the Three Forks Chamber of Commerce published an elaborate pamphlet in 1928 arguing that community's claim for a national monument on the basis of it being practically on the site of the expedition's "first and most important goal" (the headwaters of the Missouri River) as well as the point where the "great Yellowstone Trail, the National Parks Highway and the Geysers to Glacier Trail" all came together. Montana Senator Burton K. Wheeler even introduced, fruitlessly as it turned out, a bill in Congress that would have appropriated $50,000 to erect a memorial at Three Forks. In 1929, the same year the regional Lewis and Clark Memorial Association was formed to address the problem of public neglect, the Montana Legislature passed a resolution designating Fort Benton as the single site for a Lewis and Clark monument, using an earlier design for Great Falls done by the artist Charles M. Russell. Still, nothing came of the design or the resolution, and interest in constructing monuments to Lewis and Clark seems to have dissipated altogether.[13]

The sesquicentennial of the expedition brought a sharp increase in national interest in the Lewis and Clark expedition. *The Far Horizon*, a romantic depiction of the expedition starring Fred MacMurray (Meriwether Lewis), Charlton Heston (William Clark), and Donna Reed (Sacajawea), was released by Paramount Studios in 1955. The Pulitzer prize-winning author Bernard DeVoto also published books related to Lewis and Clark, *The Course of Empire* (1952), which won the National Book Award, and the still widely read *Journals of Lewis and Clark* (1953). Such popularity did not translate into a national memorial, but the sesquicentennial did inspire a great deal of local and regional interest in commemorating Lewis and Clark. For the most part, these commemorative efforts steered clear of monument building and focused instead on community celebrations that would foster local pride and attract tourists to sites along the expedition route.[14]

In the midst of this growing national interest in the Lewis and Clark expedition, the governors of Washington, Oregon, Idaho, and Montana proclaimed 1955 as "Lewis and Clark Year." They subsequently appointed a joint committee of representatives from the sesquicentennial committees in those states, who met in Spokane, Washington in December 1954 to plan commemorative celebrations. Events were scheduled to take place between May and October and spaced so that none would conflict. In some cities a Lewis and Clark theme was added to regular annual events, while other communities staged elaborate celebrations dedicated to the sesquicentennial. In Astoria, Oregon a full week of activities accompanied the dedication of a newly completed replica of Fort Clatsop, the 1805–6 winter quarters of the expedition. In Salmon, Idaho a large cast performed the *Salmon River Saga,* which combined drama, music, poetry, and narration to tell the story of Lewis and Clark and Sacagawea in eight episodes that began with Sacagawea's abduction by the Minatarees and concluded with Old Toby leading the expedition over the Bitterroots. At the Missouri River headwaters near Three Forks, Montana, Professor Bert Hansen of the University of Montana directed a pageant that had been performed each of the previous four summers. Episodes depicting the expedition's outward bound and homeward bound journeys were each performed twice on alternate evenings. In conjunction with the Three Forks celebration, the American Pioneer Trails Association, which served as the national sponsor of the sesquicentennial, held its twenty-sixth annual "Rendezvous" at the Sacajawea Hotel in Three Forks—and event that included an appearance by the grandson of the expedition member Patrick Gass. Just five days after the pageant at Three Forks, an estimated five thousand spectators crowded a "natural amphitheater near the site of Camp Fortunate on the Beaverhead River as Dillon offered its commemoration, a two-hour dramatization directed by Professor Joe Ryburn of Western Montana College of Education that featured a cast of "more than 100."[15]

A new emphasis on the expedition's route appeared during the sesquicentennial, and many commemorative events were not specifically tied to towns or cities in the region. Approximately one thousand Boy Scouts gathered in Great Falls, Montana to begin retracing the expedition's route from the great portage to Astoria, using dugout canoes and packhorses. The Greater Clarkston (Washington) Association sponsored an "automobile caravan" that would travel over the Lewis and Clark route for nine days between Bismarck, North Dakota and the Oregon coast. The caravan planned to camp along the way and to stop at "all Lewis and Clark museums and roadside markers." Celebrants even took to the air, as one hundred pilots made an air tour over the trail from St. Louis to Astoria with stops in Missoula, Montana and Walla Walla, Washington. In a public relations coup that trumped all other efforts to retrace the explorers' route, the Montana state committee announced that it would help pay expenses for seventeen-year-old Meriwether Lewis of Tacoma, Washington, "a seventh direct descendant of an uncle" of the famous explorer, to travel the length of the trail from St. Louis to the Pacific.[16]

Besides these various retracings of the Trail, other commemorative efforts were targeted more broadly to the various communities in the vicinity of the expedition route. The Washington state committee prepared outlines for talks on Lewis and Clark as well as lists of available speakers and offered suggestions for program topics and activities, including art displays, pageants, and radio or television programs. The Northern Pacific Railway Company agreed to finance a special sesquicentennial book with maps to familiarize readers with events in the journals and the nature of the country the explorers traversed. Oregon Senator Richard Neuberger introduced bills in July 1955, cosponsored by Senators Wayne Morse of Oregon and Henry Dworshak of Idaho, to establish national monuments at what was believed to be the original site of Fort Clatsop near Astoria and the rock cairns at Indian Post Office on the Lolo trail in Idaho. But many residents of Idaho and Montana would have preferred that Congress provide the means for completing the Lewis-Clark Highway between Lewiston, Idaho and Lolo Pass on the Idaho-Montana state line. The highway (now U.S. 12), which follows the route Lewis and Clark took down the Clearwater River and roughly parallels the Lolo trail for about a hundred miles, still had not been completed some forty years after construction first began. The completion of the highway had been a special concern of the now defunct Lewis and Clark Memorial Association, and now fewer than thirty miles remained to be constructed along the Lochsa River as the region prepared to celebrate the Corps of Discovery's 150th anniversary.[17]

Following the sesquicentennial, the Lewis and Clark trail—the combination of routes from Wood River to the Pacific Ocean and back to St. Louis, as described in the journals kept by several of the company—became the true memorial to the expedition. For many enthusiasts in the second half of the twentieth century, the most inspiring and appropriate way to commemorate Lewis and Clark has been to follow in their footsteps, to retrace as much of the route as possible. The tradition of following in the footsteps of Lewis and Clark goes back to the turn of the twentieth century and Wheeler's two volume *Trail of Lewis and Clark*. In order to prepare a separate chapter on Lewis and Clark for the 1900 issue of the Northern Pacific's annual publication, *Wonderland,* Wheeler set out to "visit many places that were important and critical points in their exploration." Closely relating sites and landmarks visited to passages in the journals, Wheeler attempted to match them with the geographic features he encountered in order to connect "the exploration with the present time."[18] Of particular significance are the hundreds of photographs Wheeler took of the entire journey from Missouri to Oregon and back, providing the first complete visual record of the places visited by the expedition.

Retracing the expedition route became easier in the 1920s, when a rudimentary system of national highways permitted auto tourists to drive along the Missouri, the Yellowstone, the Jefferson, and the Columbia Rivers and gain access to at least some of the significant campsites and other landmarks. Few people ever made this pilgrimage in the decades before World War II, however, and none wrote books about their journeys in the same way as Wheeler. All this would change in the postwar era, when a number of latter-day explorers "rediscovered" Lewis and Clark and published illustrated accounts of their journeys. Albert and Jane Salisbury, Calvin Tomkins, and Ingvard Eide all effectively depicted the ground covered by Lewis and Clark and stimulated strong public interest in seeing and marking the trail. Wheeler's effort to trace the exact route of the expedition, even over the tortuous Lolo trail, would also find new expression in the efforts of Ralph Space, John J. Peebles, and others to plot the exact routes and pin down the precise locations of campsites in some of the most remote parts of northern and central Idaho.[19]

Whereas following the expedition by water and foot might represent the "Holy Grail" of Lewis and Clark aficionados, experiencing the route by highway and road has become the goal of many enthusiasts and engendered a body of related writings. For example, Dayton Duncan's engaging and personal observations based on his own retracings of the Lewis and Clark trail juxtapose present-day people and places to those described in the journals. Books by Roy E. Appleman for the National Park Service and by Archie Satterfield have contributed detailed maps indicating how to drive to Lewis and Clark sites, and several tourist guides now exist that offer practical advice for following all or part of the route.[20]

One of the most challenging sections of the expedition route to retrace by foot or car has always been the stretch through Idaho's Bitterroot Range. In his 1955 speech to the Senate memorializing Lewis and Clark, Senator Neuberger said he thought that he and his wife were "among the comparative handful of people who have traveled the whole Lolo Trail." That was true, but by the 1950s it was probably a fairly large "handful." The Lolo Motorway, a nearly one-hundred mile forest road completed in 1932 that approximates the route taken by Lewis and Clark over the Lolo trail, had become surprisingly popular with motor tourists. In 1953 the writer Ralph Gray and his family took on the rough, narrow road in their station wagon rather than detour north or south as they traced the Lewis and Clark trail across the country from east to west. Rather than turn back when a tire blew after only five miles, the Grays persevered without a spare for the remaining ninety-five miles to Pierce, Idaho, averaging about ten miles an hour up and down, skirting "the brink of yawning chasms" without encountering "any vestige of civilization" other than the road itself. Two years later Space led an automobile caravan over the same road, an excursion from Pasco, Washington to Fort Benton, Montana to promote completion of the Lewis-Clark Highway's missing link along the Lochsa River. But only a handful of other intrepid motorists had tried that road by the early 1960s when the Lewis-Clark Highway finally opened, making it possible to approximate the route on pavement at much lower elevation.[21]

When the summer of sesquicentennial celebrations in the Pacific Northwest came to a close with a two-day gala in Lewiston, Idaho, interest in somehow preserving and interpreting the trail of Lewis and Clark as a national memorial began to gain momentum. In 1956 Senator Warren G. Magnuson of Washington headed a campaign for a Lewis and Clark "national tourway," that would include State Highway 14 along the Washington side of the Columbia River. It was a more ambitious version of a proposal made in 1948 by the National Park Service, a designated "Lewis and Clark tourway" along the Missouri River between St. Louis and Three Forks, Montana. One critic of Senator Magnuson's proposal questioned its appropriateness. The secretary of the South Dakota Historical Society sniffed that "while the idea of [a] Lewis & Clark Highway is picturesque they were only one [sic] of hundreds of pioneers . . . who used the Missouri as a path to the development of the Northwest." The remark suggests that Lewis and Clark represented something different in the Pacific Northwest than they did in the Northern Plains states. In fact, the sesquicentennial celebration had been a Montana, Idaho, Washington, and Oregon thing, while the Dakotas and states further downstream had scarcely participated, but that would all change once the idea of commemorating the entire route from the mouth of the Missouri River to the Pacific Ocean gained currency. While the issue of appropriately selecting and labeling highways remained, emphasis in the 1960s shifted to the actual path of exploration and the campaign to establish a national historic trail.[22]

While anxiety over the closing of the frontier may have stimulated interest in Lewis and Clark at the turn of the twentieth century, anxiety in the 1960s over the loss of parts of the historical landscape almost certainly did the same for creating a nationally designated Lewis and Clark trail, as did the relative isolation of the route by the new interstate freeway system. Donald B. Alexander, executive director of the National Conference on State Parks, complained in 1966 that the expedition had disappeared into the history books and that, except for "a few memorial stones and restored camp sites," most of which could not be seen from the new interstate freeways, almost nothing of historical interest remained. In the same year, Roy E.

Appleman pointed out that "only in the high Bitterroot Range of Idaho and in the badlands of the White Rocks section of the Missouri in Montana can one today see this western wilderness for any considerable extent essentially as Lewis and Clark saw it." Hydroelectric power dams had shorn the Great Falls of the Missouri and its companion waterfalls of much, or in some cases, all, of their spectacular beauty. Camp Fortunate, where Lewis and Clark had conferred with the Shoshone and bargained for horses to cross the mountains and where Sacagawea had immeasurably improved their chances by recognizing her brother Cameahwait, had been covered over by the reservoir waters behind Clark Canyon Dam in 1963. At Kamiah, Idaho on the Clearwater River, a sawmill had obliterated the site of Long Camp where the expedition prepared to recross the Bitterroots in the spring of 1806. Ted Yates, who made a film based on the journals for NBC in the early 1960s, bemoaned the "relentless civilizing" that had made the "country seen by Lewis and Clark" vanish, through cultivation, dam building, and other forms of development. Clear-cut logging marred the Lolo trail, even at that time. "Our film remained unexposed until we reached North Dakota," Yates noted bitterly, because reservoir impoundments on the Missouri River had obliterated so many of the sites mentioned in the journals, and there still remained another hundred miles in Montana covered by the waters of Fort Peck Reservoir. As for the Columbia River, Yates found it "impossible to photograph most of the way. Its technology, its wires and signs and roads and motels and picnic sites and highways and barges and locks and docks, defied our best efforts to film the wild and awesome river that the explorers wrote about." Even without "road signs and high-tension wires," the Lolo trail was difficult to photograph, he said, because of the pervasive evidence of clear-cut logging. Yates concluded that he and his crew had with great difficulty "reconstructed America to look the way many of us dream it looks," yet they had also managed to add to a "delusion" and "sustain" a myth of American scenic beauty.[23]

Awareness, at least among many affluent members of the middle class, that a significant part of the country's historical heritage was slipping away combined in the 1960s with heightened concern for the environment to generate public and governmental support for a national Lewis and Clark trail. In 1961 the Iowa conservation writer and newspaper cartoonist J. N. "Ding" Darling proposed creating "a scenic avenue" and "recreation ribbon" along the entire length of the expedition's route. A foundation in Darling's name created after his death pushed the concept, while the Department of Interior's newly created Bureau of Outdoor Recreation studied the feasibility of a national historic trail through ten states. In October 1964 Congress established a national Lewis and Clark Trail Commission to identify and seek means for making the route "available" for the American people and to "advance public awareness and knowledge of [its] far-reaching and historic influence." Perhaps the most grandiose and interesting proposal for a monument heard by the commission came in 1968 from the sculptor Archie M. Graber, who had designed a "landsculpture . . . for the space age" that would alter the natural topography at the confluence of the Missouri and Yellowstone rivers with earthmoving equipment to "create cameo-like statues of the explorers" visible from the air, with one head facing east and the other west. This superheroic commemoration never became reality, of course, but it demonstrates the degree of imaginative vision inspired by the commission's mandate. And its outright rejection also underscores the new emphasis away from monument building and the strong interest in maintaining or recreating the physical conditions of the expedition route as experienced by Lewis and Clark. The original intent of the original Lewis and Clark trail proposal was best captured in the Bureau of Outdoor Recreation's final report in 1975, which recommended that the entire 3,700 mile route be designated as the Lewis and Clark national historic trail and that recreational development be planned for twenty-one selected segments. On 10 November 1978 it officially became part of the National Scenic and National Historic Trails system.[24]

As the Lewis and Clark bicentennial begins, the array of "suitable" means for commemorating this national epic and the list of individuals who participated in it have both widened considerably over the past century. The emergence of a national network of paved highways and mass automobile tourism had incalculable effects on public attitudes toward the Corps of Discovery, as did intense concern for historical heritage in a landscape altered and threatened by economic development. There will be many more monuments, pageants, and other traditional means of expressing the expedition's significance, but the Trail itself, as it exists both within the journals as a literary representation and as a physical entity marked by signs and interpretive features, will certainly assume the central role.

NOTES

1. RS 164, folder 4, Montana Historical Society Archives (hereafter cited as MHS).

2. Ibid. On western automobile tourism in the 1920s, see Paul Sutter, *Driven Wild: How the Fight Against Automobiles Launched the Modern Wilderness Movement* (Seattle: University of Washington Press, 2002), 19–53.

3. David Glassberg, *American Historical Pageantry: The Uses of Tradition in the Early Twentieth Century* (Chapel Hill: University of North Carolina Press, 1990), 3–4, 269.

4. John Mullan, handwritten original of speech delivered before the Historical Society of the Rocky Mountains at Fort Owen, Montana, 24 December 1861, pp. 31 and 38, SC 547, MHS.

5. Paul Russell Cutright, *A History of the Lewis and Clark Journals* (Norman: University of Oklahoma Press, 1976), 227; Donald Jackson, "The Public Image of Lewis

and Clark," *Pacific Northwest Quarterly* 57 (January 1966): 1–2; John L. Allen, "'Of This Enterprize': The American Images of the Lewis and Clark Expedition," in *Voyages of Discovery: Essays on the Lewis and Clark Expedition*, ed. James P. Ronda (Helena: Montana Historical Society Press, 1998), 266–271.

6. Allen, "Of This Enterprize," 260, 274–276; Jackson, "Public Image," 4.

7. Warren I. Susman, *Culture as History: The Transformation of American Society in the Twentieth Century* (New York: Pantheon Books, 1984), 30; Helen B. West, "Lewis and Clark Expedition: Our National Epic," *Montana, the Magazine of Western History* 16 (July 1966): 4–5.

8. For descriptions of the Oregon exhibit at the Louisiana Purchase Exposition, see *Lewis and Clark Journal* 1 (February 1904): 4; Karal Ann Marling, *George Washington Slept Here: Colonial Revivals and American Culture, 1876–1986* (Cambridge, Mass.: Harvard University Press, 1988), 156; Harvey W. Scott, "Historical Significance of the Lewis and Clark Expedition," *Lewis and Clark Journal* 1, no. 1 (January 1904): 6; Carl Abbott, *The Great Extravaganza: Portland and the Lewis and Clark Exposition*, rev. ed. (Portland: Oregon Historical Society, 1996), 3, 16.

9. Ella E. Clark and Margot Edmonds, *Sacagawea of the Lewis and Clark Expedition* (Berkeley: University of California Press, 1979), app. D: Sacagawea Memorials; Donna J. Kessler, *The Making of Sacagawea: A Euro-American Legend* (Tuscaloosa: University of Alabama Press, 1996), 66–67. Also see Joanna Brooks's chapter 8 in this collection.

10. For the Portland statue and Anthony's speech, see Ronald W. Taber, "Sacagawea and the Suffragettes: An Interpretation of a Myth," *Pacific Northwest Quarterly* 58 (January 1967): 7–11.

11. Laura Tolman Scott, paper read before the Montana Federation of Women's Clubs at Lewistown, Montana (June 1914), VF 2606, Washington State University Special Collections; "Historical Sites Preserved and Markers Erected by the Montana Society, Daughters of the American Revolution and Its' *[sic]* Chapters, 1899–1917," VF Lewis and Clark Expedition—Statuary, Markers, Monuments, etc., MHS; Kessler, *Making of Sacagawea*, 90–92.

12. Olin D. Wheeler, *The Trail of Lewis and Clark, 1804–1904*, 2d ed. (New York: G. P. Putnam's Sons, 1926), 68–69, 74, 87–90, 171 (photo); 58th Congress, 2d sess. (1903–04), H. R. 6483; *Lewis and Clark Trail Newsletter* (Missouri committee) 4 (April 1977); *The Unveiling of the Lewis-Clark Statue at Midway Park in the City of Charlottesville, Virginia* (Charlottesville, Va., 1919), frontispiece.

13. Dr. H. J. Wunderlich (Lewis and Clark Bicentennial Celebration Committee) to Montana Governor Stan Stephens, 9 February 1991, VF Lewis and Clark, MHS; Lewis and Clark Memorial Committee, "The Three Forks of the Missouri River: Logical Site of a National Memorial to Captains Lewis and Clark" (Three Forks, Montana: Chamber of Commerce, 1928) 3, 13, 16, Leggat-Donahoe Collection, Montana State University (Bozeman) Special Collections; Montana Legislative Assembly, 15th sess. (1917), House Bill 167; *House Journal*, 167, 305, 637, in papers of the (1929) Lewis and Clark Memorial Commission: minutes of 1 May, 26 May, and 10 September meetings, and undated copy of the final report to the Montana Legislature, RS-164, folders 1–4, MHS. Not until the national bicentennial in 1976 would a heroic-size bronze statue commemorate the explorers in Montana, a composite statue of Clark, Lewis, and Sacagawea created by the Browning sculptor Bob

Scriver and placed at Fort Benton. Scriver's ambitious project to carve a limestone monolith on "Clark's Lookout," the point near Dillon where Clark climbed to view the valley, did not come to fruition, but he did complete the fourteen-foot-high bronze group at Great Falls, entitled "Lewis and Clark at the Portage," which was unveiled at ceremonies for Montana's state centennial in 1989. The monument portrays Lewis, Clark, York, and the dog Seaman (Bob Saindon, "'Lewis and Clark at the Portage' Unveiled," *We Proceeded On*, no. 15 [August 1989]: 23).

14. Rudolph Maté, dir., *The Far Horizon*, produced by William H. Pine and William C. Thomas, written by Della Gould Emmons, Winston Miller, and Edmund H. North (Hollywood, Calif.: Paramount Studios, 1955), based on Emmons, *Sacajawea of the Shoshones* (Portland, Or.: Binfords and Mort, 1943); Bernard DeVoto, *The Course of Empire* (Boston: Houghton Mifflin, 1952); Bernard DeVoto, ed., *The Journals of Lewis and Clark* (Boston: Houghton Mifflin, 1953).

15. *New York Times*, 8 May 1955; Northwest Lewis and Clark Sesquicentennial Committee Minutes for 18 December 1954, and undated committee report, pp. 5–6 in Lewis and Clark Trail Papers, box 3, South Dakota State Historical Society archives; program for "The Salmon River Saga" by Vio Mae Powell, VF 2609, Washington State University Special Collections; *Montana Standard* (Butte-Anaconda), 24 July 1955; *Dillon* (Montana) *Daily Tribune*, 28 July and 1 August 1955. The American Trails Association had also sponsored Montana's celebration of the expedition in 1945, which sought to make the expedition route "a special highlight of the American Pioneer Trails Association's 1945 project—Explorers of America." Meetings and programs were scheduled in communities from Missoula to the North Dakota line, and on parts of both the Missouri and Yellowstone rivers (*Great Falls* [Montana] *Tribune*, 18 February 1945).

16. "Northwest Lewis and Clark Sesquicentennial Committee Report," *New York Times*, 8 May 1955, 4–5.

17. "Washington State Committee's Speech Outline for the Sesquicentennial" and "Suggested Programs for Clubs and Organizations" (prep. Ruth M. Babcock) in VF 906, Washington State University Special Collections; James Stevens, Robert MacFarlane, and Kenn E. Johnston, *Lewis and Clark: Our National Epic of Exploration* (Tacoma: Northern Pacific Railway and Washington State Historical Society, 1955); Senator Richard L. Neuberger, "150th Anniversary of the Great Expedition of Lewis and Clark," speech in the U.S. Senate, 12 July 1955 (Washington, D.C.: GPO, 1955), 3. The history of the Lewis-Clark highway is detailed in Wallace G. Lewis, "Building the Lewis-Clark Highway," *Idaho Yesterdays* 43 (fall 1999): 21–22.

18. Wheeler, *Trail of Lewis and Clark*, xi–xiii.

19. Albert and Jane Salisbury, *Two Captains West: An Historical Tour of the Lewis and Clark Trail* (Seattle: Superior Publishing, 1950); Calvin Tomkins, *The Lewis and Clark Trail*, with an introduction by Stewart L. Udall (New York: Harper and Row, 1965); Ingvard Eide, *American Odyssey: The Journey of Lewis and Clark* (New York: Rand McNally, 1969); Ralph Space, *The Lolo Trail: A History of Events Connected With the Lolo Trail Since Lewis and Clark* (Lewiston, Id.: Printcraft Printing, 1970); John J. Peebles, "Rugged Waters: Trails and Campsites of Lewis and Clark in the Salmon River Country," *Idaho Yesterdays* 8, no. 2 (summer 1964): 2–17; and his "On the Lolo Trail: Route and Campsites of Lewis and Clark," *Idaho Yesterdays* 9, no. 4 (winter 1965–66): 2–15.

20. Dayton Duncan, *Out West: A Journey Through Lewis & Clark's America* (New York: Viking, 1987); Roy E. Appleman, *Lewis and Clark: Historic Places Associated with Their Transcontinental Exploration (1804–06)* (Washington, D.C.: Department of the Interior, National Park Service, 1975); Archie Satterfield, *The Lewis & Clark Trail* (Harrisburg, Pa.: Stackpole Books, 1978). Recent guidebooks include Julie Fanselow, *Travelling the Lewis & Clark Trail* (Helena: Falcon Press, 1994); Barbara Fifer and Vicky Soderberg, *Along the Trail with Lewis and Clark,* with maps by Joseph Mussulman ([Helena]: Montana Magazine, 1998); and Thomas Schmidt, *National Geographic's Guide to the Lewis and Clark Trail* (Washington, D.C.: National Geographic Society, 1998).

21. Neuberger, "150th Anniversary," 2; Ralph Gray, "Following the Trail of Lewis and Clark," *National Geographic Magazine,* June 1953, 748; Eastern Washington Chapter of the Northwest Conservation League, *Conservation Newsletter* 1 (17 August 1955): 2.

22. 85th Congress, 1st sess. (8 May 1957), S. R. 88; Department of Interior, Bureau of Outdoor Recreation, *The Lewis and Clark Trail: A Proposed National Historic Trail* (1975), 6; Will Robinson to Chapin D. Foster, 24 July 1957, in Lewis and Clark Trail Commission Papers, box 3, South Dakota State Historical Society archives.

23. Donald B. Alexander, "Tracking Down a Heritage," *Parks and Recreation* 1 (March 1966): 224; Roy E. Appleman, "Lewis and Clark: The Route 160 Years After," *Pacific Northwest Quarterly* 57 (January 1966): 12, 10–11; Ted Yates, "Since Lewis and Clark," *American West* 2 (fall 1965): 24–25, 30. Also see John Spencer's chapter 7 in this collection.

24. Alexander, "Tracking Down a Heritage," 225; *U.S. Statutes at Large* 88 (1964): 630 and 89 (1966): 475; Archie Satterfield, "Park with Land Sculptures Proposed," *Seattle Times,* 28 January 1968; *U.S. Statutes at Large* 95 (1978): 625; Department of Interior, Bureau of Outdoor Recreation, *The Lewis and Clark Trail Study Report* (Denver, 1975), 2–3, 6. In its final report in 1969, the Lewis and Clark Trail Commission recommended that its mission be carried on by various state Lewis and Clark trail committees. However, its mandate was assumed by the national Lewis and Clark Trail Heritage Foundation in 1970.

PART IV

New Perspectives

Map 5. Lewis and Clark National Historic Trail. National Park Service, Department of the Interior. This is the map currently used in the National Park Service brochure for the Lewis and Clark National Historic Trail. Along with noting brief sections of "Water Trail," "Motor Trail," and "Land Trail," the map also shows the locations of 83 national, state, local, and private historic sites and recreation areas along the expedition route.

With the bicentennial of the expedition approaching, interest in Lewis and Clark has grown exponentially. From St. Louis, Missouri to Seaside, Oregon, various states, counties, and cities are planning to cash in on the millions of latter-day explorers who will cruise the expedition route in the next few years. In the words of David Borlaug, president of the National Lewis and Clark Bicentennial Council, the bicentennial "is shaping up to be the tourist event of the 21st century." All of this reflects an increased focus on the Trail as the appropriate site for commemorating the expedition, but a four-thousand-mile, two-and-a-half-year "event" raises new questions and problems about how to understand and incorporate the lessons of the past.

The three essays in this section present very different assessments of the promises and prospects of the Lewis and Clark bicentennial. In many regards, there is much to celebrate—not about Lewis and Clark, but in the opportunities that such a unique commemorative event presents. Fascination in the expedition has led countless individuals and families to "rediscover" largely unvisited portions of the United States, from the Dakotas to the Columbia Plateau, and in the process learn a great deal about the peoples and histories of these places. Likewise, the bicentennial represents a powerful opportunity for Native peoples to tell their stories and in the process shape the nature and significance of this massive commemorative event. Because two hundred years have profoundly altered the lands traversed by Lewis and Clark, the bicentennial also gives pause for reflection on the expedition's destructive legacies. Yet it remains to be seen whether such reflection will lead to constructive understanding, or if it will become little more than a brief and unproductive lament.

Chapter 10

Let's Play Lewis & Clark!

Strange Visions of Nature and History at the Bicentennial

Mark Spence

The middle weeks of October can be a cruel time of year in the Dakotas. It is not uncommon to experience four seasons in a day, when a mild afternoon can give way to cold rain and a bone-chilling night. Travelers in the open must contend with the blasting winds of the Great Plains, which swing wildly about the compass as continental weather patterns shift between the Gulf of Mexico and the Arctic. Gray skies from the north become more prevalent with each passing day, however, and early morning frosts settle into the dry grasses and put an urgency to the winter preparations of all living things. For the Sahnish (Arikara), Mandan, and Hidatsa villagers who lived along the upper Missouri River in the early nineteenth century, the short autumn season was a time for brief hunts, final harvests, and preparations for the move to more sheltered dwelling sites. This time also marked the end of the business season for nonresident traders from St. Louis, who left in early fall before the river level dropped to its lowest ebb and the water turned frigid. How strange it must have seemed, then, for a group of nearly forty men and three watercraft to arrive from the south in the fall of 1804.[1]

For the members of the Lewis and Clark expedition, "strange" was probably too mild a word. Something with more sinister connotations might have better described their predicament, as weather and the Missouri River seemed to conspire against their efforts at every turn. On the morning of 5 October, just a day after passing into the territory of the Sahnish, they were surprised to awake beneath a white frost. The following day, shallow water and a cold north wind forced expedition members to drop sail and drag their fifty-five-foot single masted keelboat across sandbars and gravel shoals. William Clark described these efforts in brief but telling fashion: "we have been obgd [obliged] to hunt a Chanl. for Some time past the river being devided in many places in a great number of Chanels" (3:147).[2] Their struggles soon brought them to a principal village of the Sahnish, the southernmost of the three horticultural groups that lived and farmed along the upper Missouri River, and "Great numbers of Spectators" gathered along the river to watch and comment on the expedition (3:151). The diplomatic goals of Lewis and Clark and the ritual hospitality of the Sahnish allowed for a brief respite from the challenges of river travel, but the winds of the Northern Plains still found a way to stymie the expedition: the first official meeting with village leaders was postponed because, in Clark's words, it was too "windey rainey . . . and Cold" (3:155).[3]

A few consecutive days of fair weather seemed to bode well for the expedition, and after several meetings with different village leaders the self-described Corps of Discovery renewed its daily struggle against shallow currents and variable winds. Its number was increased by the addition of a Sahnish leader named Piahito (Eagle Feather) and his retinue, who agreed to accompany the captains upriver for a series of meetings with the Mandan and Hidatsa. For several days they passed smaller Sahnish settlements and encountered returning parties of hunters. According to the observations of a French trader who lived among the Sahnish and served the expedition as a translator, all marveled at the keelboat and the strange instruments it carried as "supernatural and powerful."[4] For Piahito at least, the most peculiar aspect of the expedition and its members was manifest not so much in their tools as their behavior. A day after the Sahnish leader was brought on board, the captains initiated a court-martial of Private John Newman. Charged with "having uttered repeated expressions of a highly criminal and mutinous nature," Newman was sentenced to seventy-five lashes on his bare back (3:170). As the punishment was being delivered, Piahito cried out in alarm and apparently tried to halt the whipping. Corporal punishment in public was completely foreign to the peoples of the upper Missouri, and he protested that no one ever whipped another person for any reason. Clark "explained the Cause of the punishment and the necessity," which he believed was sufficiently convincing to his guest, but it is impossible to assess how much was understood between these two men. Nevertheless, the event was certainly discussed at length by Piahito and the Sahnish who visited the boat later that day.

Nothing quite so dramatic or unsettling would occur again during the one-hundred-mile journey to the Mandan and Hidatsa villages, but upriver travel grew increasingly difficult. On 17 October, Clark reported that a wind from the northwest blew so hard that the expedition was forced to halt after just a few hours, making no more than six miles the entire day. Strong headwinds and cold squalls of rain not only made it impossible to use the sail but also caused the keelboat to swing about as it was poled through the shallows or hauled with towlines from the shore. The expedition also included two smaller pirogues—open vessels with low-slung gunwales—but these were perhaps even more difficult to operate; their smaller sails were also useless and, when the oarsmen were not fighting their way into a constant spray of cold spindrift, they too were forced to clamber along the frozen clay banks of the river and pull their vessels against the current (3: 179–181, 222).

As they made their way toward the great bend of the Missouri, where the eastward-flowing river makes a broad sweeping turn toward the south, it was clear that five months of river travel were rapidly coming to an end.[5] The expedition members had experienced the first snow of the season and already suffered through several "verry Cold" nights. On the day before their first official meeting with Mandan leaders, and under the curious gaze of numerous onlookers from shore, they suffered through one of their most difficult days yet. Clark gave a brief summary: "this evening passed a rapid and sholde [shoaled] place in the river were obliged to get out and drag the boat—all the leaves of the trees have now fallen—the snows did not lye" (3:222). The cold and strain proved especially hard on Clark and at least two or three others, who complained of a severe, debilitating rheumatism once they finally stumbled into the Mandan villages.[6]

For the Sahnish and Mandan who watched this little flotilla move slowly upriver, covering in two weeks what a heavily laden and equally large group might travel by foot or horseback in just a few days, the Corps of Discovery presented a bizarre sight indeed. Made up of an odd assortment of young American backwoodsmen, a black slave, several French Canadian engagés, a number of men of mixed Indian and European or American parentage, and two military officers, the expedition defied easy interpretation. At times it must have been a quite humorous spectacle as the members of the expedition slipped in the freezing mud, cursed in various languages, and struggled to pull "towlines that remained slick and stiff with ice until mid-morning."[7] Far stranger was the captains' boast that they planned to travel in this fashion all the way to the headwaters of the Missouri River, where they would cross the Rocky Mountains and head downriver a short ways to the Pacific Ocean. What made these plans so audacious was not the vast distances they entailed, but the manner in which they would be covered. The Sahnish knew that peoples they traded with, including the Comanche and Kiowa, made journeys between the upper Missouri River and what is now the American Southwest in a matter of weeks. Likewise, the Hidatsa, who lived just upriver from the Mandan, were familiar with the headwaters of the Missouri and frequently raided the peoples who lived on the western slope of the Rockies; yet they also made the journey in a fairly short time.[8]

Though it must have seemed a form of collective madness, the Sahnish no doubt judged the behavior of the Corps of Discovery with a generous eye.[9] Based on close observation and intimate contact, they may well have concluded that the Lewis and Clark expedition was a sort of mass vision quest. In many respects this was brilliant deduction. No other reasoning could so completely explain the unnecessary hardships that expedition members endured, the physical abuse they inflicted on one another, or their pathological devotion to river travel. The two captains were obviously not traders, given the time of year they arrived and the stingy manner in which they hoarded a relatively large amount of valuable goods. Their declared intention to move on to the Rocky Mountains and the Pacific Ocean also distinguished Lewis and Clark from other traders, as did their relatively potent collection of firearms, but the expedition did not seem to have any immediate military objectives. Instead, the expedition's behavior mirrored a common form of vision questing among the Sahnish and other groups along the upper Missouri. Though usually done by individuals within a particular community context, this powerful and deeply personal ritual often involved self-torture, arduous travel, and the hauling of terrible burdens to the point of absolute physical and mental exhaustion. A state of self-induced delirium, achieved through personal deprivation and sacrifice, opened one up to visitation by a spiritual helper or reciprocated for a previous divine intervention.[10]

Lewis or Clark would have dismissed such an interpretation as ridiculous and "not worth while mentioning," but it serves as a good indication of just how absurd the idea of *exploration* must have seemed to peoples already familiar with the places to be *discovered*.[11] More significantly, the Sahnish interpretation should also draw our attention to a simple yet frequently overlooked fact: no one would travel with so much pain, hardship, and deliberate slowness, except on purpose. The expedition members did not throw themselves against the "challenge of the continent" and "triumph over an unforgiving wilderness," as so many Lewis and Clark aficionados proclaim. Such romantic hyperbole disguises what the Sahnish and others saw so clearly: the Corps of Discovery brought its own obstacles and proved the source of nearly all the physical adversities it encountered.

Understanding the significance and purposes of the expedition must begin with a clear sense of how and why Lewis and Clark dragged so many burdens across the continent. This should in no way undermine our appreciation for the arduous nature of their task, but it can provide a meaningful alternative to the simple recipe of "heroism" and wilderness adventure espoused by Steven Ambrose and others.[12] Focusing less on the physicality of the expedition's task and more on the reasons why Lewis and Clark would have viewed their actions as appropriate and worthwhile (as opposed to unnecessarily difficult) can also provide a new basis for interpreting the expedition's significance at the bicentennial. In the process we might begin to recognize how current efforts to commemorate Lewis and Clark draw on popular ideas about history and nature that cloud our understanding of the expedition, ignore its historical legacies, and perpetuate a set of social and ecological burdens that are becoming increasingly intolerable.

FOR THE PURPOSES OF COMMERCE

Over nearly half of the territory they crossed, Lewis and Clark were not the first "civilized men" to experience the lands and peoples of the Missouri and Columbia watersheds.[13] And of course, their claims of "discovery" in the areas where they knew that no European or American had ever visited were still anywhere from twelve to twenty thousand years late. Nevertheless, they were the first to experience these places within the context of Thomas Jefferson's vision of an expanding agrarian empire. As Jefferson's "eyes," Lewis and Clark saw the West in terms of the president's ideas on Indian relations, foreign policy, and the role of the federal government in shaping future national economic development.[14]

The objectives and route of the expedition, as well as the time and tools required to make it possible, reflect two fundamental aspects of Jefferson's goals for Lewis and Clark. According to the president's instructions, the expedition's entire energies were devoted to a careful survey of two major river systems "for the purposes of commerce," and an effort to convince Native leaders of the "peaceful and commercial dispositions of the United States." These concerns were manifest in the vast array of equipment and trade goods carried by the expedition, which constituted the bulk of the cargo it so laboriously hauled up the Missouri River. Jefferson also made explicit his desire that Lewis and other members of the expedition keep journals. While paper and ink did not represent a weighty physical burden, their use required a great deal of time and care. According to Jefferson's instructions, most of this was devoted to descriptions of "the soil and face of the country, it's growth and vegetable productions," "the animals of the country generally," "the mineral productions of every kind; but more particularly metals, limestone, pit coal, & saltpetre; salines & mineral waters," "volcanic appearances," and climate. In other words, the journal writers were to methodically observe and report on the potential of these lands for future commercial development and agricultural settlement.[15]

The combined writings of Lewis, Clark, and other expedition members have often been called a "national epic," but the journals do not fit this genre at all. Daily records of temperature, longitude, soils, Native markets, river courses, plants, minerals, and animals are not the stuff of epic poetry. Rather, they more closely resemble the crude field notes of a land assessor or early-nineteenth-century surveyor, and in that respect they are absolutely true to the original purpose of the expedition.

While the expedition was primarily an extended venture in land assessment, it was predicated on the desire to initiate a strong American presence in the western fur trade. Toward these ends, Jefferson directed Lewis and Clark to seek a river route across the continent, announce to Native leaders that the United States was now their primary commercial partner, and appraise the trade possibilities of the West Coast. The immediate interest in a transcontinental water route reflected the desire to make St. Louis the center of a global fur trade that extended to the Pacific and the markets of the Far East. Establishing diplomatic and commercial relations with Native leaders would also undermine the position of imperial rivals in North America's lucrative fur trade, thus confirming the authority of the United States in the newly acquired Louisiana Territory and bringing much needed revenue into the fledgling nation.

As important as these concerns were both financially and diplomatically, they were only the necessary preliminaries to Jefferson's vision of a vast expanse of American farms stretching out to the Pacific. Once the West had been skinned of its peltry, commercial ties with Native leaders would become irrelevant. As Jefferson wrote Benjamin Hawkins in 1803, the period of the fur trade should be a time to "familiarize [Indians] to the idea that it is for their interest to cede lands at times to the United States, and for us thus to procure gratifications to our citizens, from time to time, by new acquisitions of land."[16] "The obtaining [of] lands from the Indians . . . as fast as the expansion of our settlements," as Jefferson put it in a letter to Andrew Jackson that same year, "was the ultimate goal of the Louisiana Purchase and the Lewis and Clark expedition.[17] The establishment of commercial and diplomatic relations with Native leaders was thus a necessary first step in Jefferson's aggressive efforts to convert tribal lands into American farms.

"TWO HUNDRED YEARS TO THE FUTURE"

Two hundred years after Thomas Jefferson formulated his disturbing vision of Native dispossession and national expansion, the Lewis and Clark expedition has acquired a new set of meanings that reflect the concerns of the twenty-first century. Zealous desire to "develop" the West has been tempered by fears of global ecological crisis, and the cultural certitudes that explained the motives of an early-nineteenth-century imperial enterprise have been eclipsed by more relativistic thinking. These changes are not unrelated, and both are found in recent films and books in which Lewis and Clark are presented as protoecologists and culturally sensitive diplomats of the frontier.

The contrasts between the Jeffersonian vision that produced the expedition and the concerns that are shaping current bicentennial understandings of Lewis and Clark are both subtle and dramatic. They are also bizarre. One need only wonder at how William Clark, suffering from a severe rheumatism brought on by physical strain and intense cold, might have responded to the following description of the Missouri River in the recent Ken Burns documentary of the expedition: "[The Missouri] is a river that immediately presents to the traveler, 'I am a grandfather spirit. I have a source; I have a life.' . . . [T]hat grandfather spirit . . . of the Missouri River helped draw them on. . . . [It is a] river which seems to say to the traveler, 'Come up me.'"[18] Clark would certainly have found the "grandfather spirit" description of the Missouri River somewhat daft, but he would no doubt be even more perplexed by a new twist on the old Sahnish interpretation of their expedition. As we learn in the companion volume to the Burns documentary, "Lewis and Clark, on behalf of America, set off up the great Missouri on a kind of national, if unrecognized, vision quest."[19]

The bicentennial version of the vision-quest theory comes with some important new elements while it omits other key aspects of the old Sahnish interpretation. It does not emphasize the peculiar behavior of the expedition members or the difficulties they created but instead presents the expedition in mythic yet elemental terms. As we learn from recent depictions of Lewis and Clark, their purpose was simply to proceed on with undaunted courage and face whatever challenges wild nature threw their way. According to the precepts of dramatic storytelling, the expedition members were transformed by the experience and, through a strange kind of alchemy, both they and the territories they encountered became more fully American.[20] To paraphrase from Robert Frost's poem "The Gift Outright," Lewis and Clark opened up a "still unstoried, artless, unenhanced" country and gave of themselves "outright" so that Americans could realize that "the land was ours . . . [and] we her people."[21] In short, the expedition was nothing less than a holy act of national transubstantiation.

The expedition across the continent has also come to represent a journey *through* time as well. It might seem unfair to single out Ken Burns and company, but their *Lewis & Clark: The Journey of the Corps of Discovery* is certainly the most potent example of contemporary understandings of the expedition, and we hear in the conclusion of that documentary one of the clearest statements on the timeless qualities of Lewis and Clark: "It matters less what they went to find as what it is that they did find. . . . They discovered the American future. They went, literally, from east to the west coast, and that is what America did in their footsteps. It was . . . a physical journey of the nation to go to the Pacific Ocean to discover its own future."[22]

Jefferson may not have included time travel in his instructions to Meriwether Lewis, but these concerns obviously speak more to the current fascination with Lewis and Clark than the original purposes of the expedition. Using the past to satisfy the desires of the present is hardly a new development, nor is it especially unique to commemorations of the expedition. Like all origin stories, whether religious or secular in nature, the expedition retains a peculiar ability to conflate the past with the present with each retelling. When the National Park Service proclaims "two hundred years to the future" as the motto for its Corps of Discovery II bicentennial program, the agency is participating in a long tradition of using Lewis and Clark to celebrate the values and conditions of the present. Yet there is a quality about the bicentennial version of this story that sets it apart. Past commemorations have invariably placed Lewis and Clark at the beginning of a celebratory narrative about unrelenting national progress. At the 1905 Lewis and Clark Centennial Exposition in Portland, Oregon, for instance, technological and commercial developments subsequent to the expedition were highlighted to connect the past to the present, explain the expedition's original purposes, and illustrate its ongoing inspirational significance for future national growth.[23] The bicentennial version of the expedition continues to see in Lewis and Clark the embodiment of current needs and concerns yet rejects the old narrative of national progress through conquest and industrial development. Instead, the bicentennial is seen as an elusive chance to incorporate the virtues of the distant past, erase the mistakes of the past two hundred years, and set the American future back on the course it should have followed at the beginning of the nineteenth century.

MILLENNIAL HISTORY

A recent membership solicitation from the Lewis and Clark Trail Heritage Foundation begins with a simple but telling statement: "As we start the third millennium, we approach the third century since the Corps of Discovery made its epic journey across the young American continent."[24] To understand the ideas and concerns that are shaping the bicentennial observance of the Lewis and Clark expedition, we must first begin with an appreciation for its millennial context. More than a simple accident of calendars and centuries, the bicentennial is rooted in the classical sense of the millennium as a time of apocalypse and regeneration. Indeed, the Lewis and Clark bicentennial reflects the abiding sensibility of a nation that continues to present itself in millennial terms—as "the last best hope of earth," to use Abraham Lincoln's powerful phrase. True to these deeper sentiments, the bicentennial of the expedition is increasingly described as nothing less than a unique and profound opportunity for national redemption. With almost religious zeal, fans of Lewis and Clark see the bicentennial as an opportunity to incorporate the virtues of a mythic past (when the continent was "young"), leave behind the mistakes of more recent history, and press ahead with a new sensitivity. Commemorating the expedition is "a chance to finally get things right, to start over," a member of the National Lewis and Clark Bicentennial Council recently told me. "We need to get back to the original spirit of Lewis and Clark. They cooperated with Indians and appreciated Nature; they didn't try to dominate."[25]

It is nice to see that multicultural concerns and a certain environmental-ist sensibility have begun to take the place of older mythologies about con-quest and national progress. Replacing one misguided understanding of the past with another historical fiction is not a satisfying alternative, how-ever. Native peoples certainly assisted the expedition on repeated occasions, but it is wrong to assume that Lewis and Clark represent a tragic lost opportunity in the history of Indian-white relations. "The sorrow behind the Corps of Discovery," according to the writer William Least-Heat-Moon (a.k.a. William Trogdon), "is that what they did so well, later people were not able to do half so well, and that is in, in dealing with the native peoples who were there."[26] Such an interpretation overlooks an essential feature of the expedition: a transient group of people in unfamiliar country was almost entirely dependent on the hospitality and support of resident com-munities. Aggressive or belligerent behavior would have undermined the objectives of the expedition and could well have proved suicidal. The fact that Lewis and Clark did not maniacally blast their way across the West is hardly the result of a special cultural sensitivity that future generations of Americans failed to emulate.

No one was more conscious than Meriwether Lewis of the need to main-tain what Jefferson called a "most friendly & conciliatory manner" toward Native peoples. Lewis's journal entries are full of references to his frequent struggles to keep his fears and prejudices in check when dealing with people he regarded as capricious "savages who are ever as fickle as the wind" (5:106). The young captain was not always successful in these matters, how-ever. On the occasions when his deeper sentiments did determine his ac-tions, especially during the expedition's encounters with the Lakota, the winter at Fort Clatsop, the eastward and westward journeys along the Co-lumbia River, and among the Blackfeet, Lewis was not above theft, threats of violence, or killing.[27] Such behavior may have been rare by necessity, but it hardly contradicted the ultimate purpose of the expedition. The conver-sion of Native lands into American farms was always the central tenet of Jefferson's Indian policy, and thus a guiding force behind the expedition. The president did warn Lewis to prepare for "hostility" during the expedi-tion but also forbade him to engage "superior force[s]" since "we value too much the lives of citizens to offer them to probable destruction." Yet Jeffer-son did not shy from advocating extreme violence to achieve his larger ob-jectives. "[I]f ever we are constrained to lift the hatchet against any tribe," he wrote William Henry Harrison in 1807, "we will never lay it down till that tribe is exterminated." "[I]f they wish to remain on the land which covers the bones of their fathers," he continued, "[they must] keep the peace with [us] who ask their friendship without needing it." "In war," Jefferson added ominously, "they will kill some of us; we shall destroy all of them."[28]

It would be wrong to attribute an entire century of conquest to the attitudes and behaviors of Lewis and Clark or the bellicosity of Thomas Jefferson. And yet it does no good to view the expedition as some kind of innocent encounter, a fleeting moment in the wilderness when Native peoples and Americans managed to briefly escape the violent course of history. Native leaders certainly did not receive Lewis and Clark as the harbingers of a bright future of cooperation and harmonious cultural exchange. Most viewed the expedition with apprehension or, like the Sahnish, outright confusion. At best, "even those Indians whom [Lewis and Clark] came to know best regarded the explorers as the advance party of a great trading company, 'the United States.'"[29] At worst, the expedition represented a dangerous new rival in the contest to shape the scope and terms of wide-ranging trade networks. This was certainly the case for the Lakota and Blackfeet, as well as the peoples of the lower Columbia River. With key political and commercial interests at stake on all sides, violence or the threat of violence was often a central feature of the expedition's encounters with these and other groups.[30]

At times a bitter and abiding prejudice developed on both sides of the diplomatic and commercial divide. Within a few years of their return to St. Louis, at least three members of the expedition were killed by Blackfeet while trapping beaver near the Rocky Mountains, and another lost a leg as a result of a violent incident among the Sahnish.[31] William Clark, in particular, harbored a deep hatred for the Lakota through his more than twenty years as a superintendent of Indian affairs. His views of the Lakota grew out of the expedition's tense encounters with several bands along the Missouri River but also reflected that powerful nation's ability to challenge and thwart the objectives of the federal government. Clark's ideas about a people he described as "fierce deceitfull unprencipaled robers" (3:483) were also conditioned by his previous experience in the brutal wars of the 1790s that ravaged the Native communities of the Ohio country—an arena of conflict that had earlier made his brother, George Rogers Clark, a national icon.[32]

MILLENNIAL NATURE

The temper of the expedition's relations with the various groups they encountered was intimately connected to the manner in which they perceived and described the lands they coveted. That is, both were described in accordance with the purposes of commerce. In a strange parallel, current efforts to celebrate Lewis and Clark have linked the expedition's supposed good intentions toward Native peoples with a special ability to appreciate nature. Not surprisingly, modern readers and editors of the journals often pause at the two captains' frequent use of the word "beautiful" when describing the lands they traversed along the Missouri River. While this conjures up images of an unspoiled landscape for present-day readers and implies a stark contrast with the "ugly" developments that have since altered an earlier vista, this was certainly not the intent of the original journal writers. In American dictionaries of the early nineteenth century, the primary definition for "beautiful" was: "fair arrangement" or "pleasing quality."[33] This carries into our own usage in a phrase like "Everything comes together beautifully; the villain loses and the heroes live happily ever after." It is less a reference to scenic qualities than a description of how well various features of a place match a particular end or purpose. On a very few occasions the journals do make explicit reference to the purely aesthetic, as when Lewis described the white cliffs of the Missouri: "As we passed on it seemed as if those scenes of visionary enchantment would never have an end" (4:226). On the countless other occasions when Lewis, Clark, or some other member of the expedition described an area as "beautiful," the meaning was something that modern tourists would find infinitely less exciting— as in William Clark's description of modern-day Kansas City as "a butifull place for a fort, good landing place," or his use of "butifull Plain" to describe the agricultural potential of an area in what is now southeastern Nebraska (2:113, 157).

This is hardly the kind of stuff that would inspire a national celebration. A book titled *Lewis and Clark: First Assessors of Western Agricultural Potential* might be good history, but it hardly stands a chance against something along the lines of *Saga of Lewis and Clark: Into the Unknown West*, or *Those Tremendous Mountains: The Story of the Lewis and Clark Expedition*.[34] What excites people today is to imagine being in the shoes of Lewis and Clark. No one, it seems, tries to get inside their heads. Though it is an interpretation that would have made no sense to the members of the expedition, Lewis and Clark have become symbols of environmental appreciation and preservation. At a recent demonstration in Washington, D.C., two men dressed as Lewis and Clark to advocate for the restoration of salmon populations in the Pacific Northwest by removing dams from the Columbia and Snake Rivers. Dam removal may be sound policy, but using Lewis and Clark to symbolize the virtues of salmon and wild rivers is deeply ironic. The expedition generally avoided salmon as a food source (preferring dogs instead), struggled often with the fierce and turbulent nature of the Columbia, and held a pronounced disdain for the Native peoples who lived along the river. If anything, they would have supported the construction of dams that decimated salmon, eased river navigation, and undermined Native communities.[35]

Using the expedition as a symbol for environmentalist causes is part of a deep-seated American fascination with wilderness and national origins. In the case of Lewis and Clark the symbolic order is especially wilderness-driven since they are situated within the very heart of a simple but profound maxim: American History Begins When Americans Encounter Nature. Of course, the uninhabited places that outdoor enthusiasts seek out today are devoid of the peoples who actively shaped and maintained the cultural landscapes they called "home" when Americans first "encountered Nature." Consequently, the idea that history begins at the point of contact with this modern recreational wilderness erases thousands of years of human history and equates national origins with the commercial and aesthetic experience of the modern tourist. This presents a dual tragedy: on the one hand it ignores the dispossession of Native peoples that makes current "wilderness experiences" possible; on the other it promotes an idealized sense of nature in which a human is never more than "a visitor who does not remain."[36]

These are central problems with the upcoming bicentennial, which advertises outdoor recreation as the best way to imbibe the special environmental sensitivities of Lewis and Clark. At scenic locales along the trail, tourists are encouraged to "relive the adventure" at places that still "look much the same *as* they did when Lewis and Clark explored."[37] Of course it depends on what your definition of "as" is, but this generally means seeing "what" the expedition members saw as opposed to how they saw it. In either case, little is gained and much is lost when Lewis and Clark are fashioned as the first ecotourists.

Two centuries of history have transformed the cultural landscapes that Lewis and Clark experienced (what they saw), as well as the ideas they carried in their heads (how they saw them). Of course there is a direct if problematic correlation between these transformed places and ideas, and any effort to understand the changes in one must also look to changes in the other. However, using Lewis and Clark to celebrate today's conception of wilderness or to criticize two centuries of exploitation, environmental degradation, and Native dispossession creates a false distinction between the past and the present, between nature and history. The tools and time required for outdoor leisure pursuits are available only because of the hyperdevelopment and mass consumption that define our society. The wilderness ideal we associate with Lewis and Clark is actually a product of the comforts and desires that characterize early-twenty-first-century America. Using a contemporary idea of wilderness to find the virtues of the distant past and escape the mistakes of the last two centuries is a perversion of historical understanding that builds dreams on false premises.

RE-CREATION AND RECREATION

Much as wilderness is largely understood in recreational terms, ideas about history have also recently become influenced by the ethic of re-creation. Placing a premium on reenactments or *living* history, historical re-creation first became a popular form of recreation in the early 1970s. This is a phenomenon that only continues to grow, particularly in regards to subjects like the Civil War, overland migrations, and the fur trade. In the story of Lewis and Clark, of course, reenactment is most closely linked with popular ideas about wilderness. And in the upcoming Lewis and Clark bicentennial, outdoor recreation certainly provides the means for developing "a true sense of exploration." According to an outfit called Lewis and Clark Trail Adventures, all one needs to understand history and appreciate the environments that Lewis and Clark experienced is "a sense of adventure and a desire to discover the *Trail* as Lewis and Clark did nearly two hundred years ago!" Even purchasing merchandise from "the Lewis & Clark Collection provides an ideal way for today's outdoor oriented person to capture The Adventure In Their Life!"[38]

Playing Lewis and Clark can offer an exciting, personalized sense of history, but there is something insidious about the way recreational concerns are shaping our conceptions of history and nature. Among other things, they allow us to assume that a beckoning "river spirit" has relevance across all time, and not just within the context of a pleasant excursion on the Missouri River. To persist in such a claim, as if this "spirit" represented an essential truth about "discover[ing] the *Trail* as Lewis and Clark did," is to commit a series of profound historical errors. For starters, it implies that all peoples on the Missouri somehow longed for the Corps of Discovery to *come up* to them. The fact that most Indian communities encountered by the expedition did not themselves migrate up the Missouri also suggests a certain deficiency in Native abilities to hear or answer the river's calling. This conception of the river also perverts the objectives of the expedition into a mystical quest across space and time: they did not set out with Jefferson's instructions so much as they were beckoned onward by a vast continent patiently awaiting their arrival; or, as First Lady Laura Bush noted at a recent White House ceremony for the bicentennial, "the new frontier begged for exploration."[39] Gone are the encounters with Native peoples, gone are the two hundred years of environmental and cultural change that succeeded the expedition; in their stead is a long-silent spirit that once again calls the Lewis and Clark enthusiast.

As absurd as this sounds, what compounds it further is a penchant to view the expedition as a kind of ecotourist fantasy. Hardly the difficult and mundane imperial venture described in the expedition journals, the Corps of Discovery has instead become an ideal model for a "true wilderness experience."[40] When the Lewis and Clark expedition becomes "the greatest camping trip of all time," to quote Stephen Ambrose, we can be certain that the musings of a comfortable excursionist at the beginning of the twenty-first century have completely redefined a continent and its history.[41] The two hundred years that separate the tourist in 2004 from the historical Lewis and Clark all but disappear, and the many thousands of years that preceded the expedition become irrelevant.

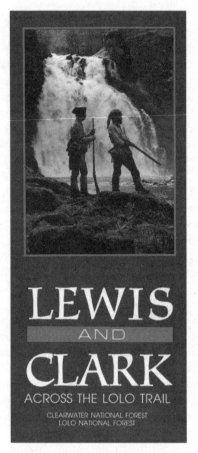

Figure 7. Lewis and Clark across
the Lolo trail, United States Forest
Service Brochure.

Much as current efforts conjoin Lewis and Clark to problematic ideas
about Nature as recreational space, attempts to reenact the expedition are
fraught with peculiar understandings of the past that entertain without
teaching. They are not unique to the bicentennial or the subject of the expedition, but their source is the same emphasis on leisure that shapes the
"outdoor oriented" person's desire "to capture The Adventure In Their
Life." Nothing better illustrates the problems endemic to this kind of approach to history as re-creation, or recreation, than the current passion
for Civil War reenactments. The real war was certainly about slavery, race,
and fear. But Civil War reenactors convert this into a story about heritage,

courage, and valor. With its intense focus on the historical accuracy of costumes, weaponry, and troop movements, this recreational form of history gives its participants and audiences a powerful sense of authenticity. The result is a pleasant, even exciting excursion to "the past, a more authentic time," to quote a Union soldier I recently met.[42] But this only ignores the unseemly legacies of slavery, race, and fear and, by actively ignoring them, only encourages their perpetuation into the future. In short, "living history" does not lead to deeper understandings of the past, nor does it let us see how the past shapes our world—it too often leads to shallow escapes from the deep historical problems of the present. In regards to the Lewis and Clark bicentennial (Figure 7), one need only reflect on the absence of Native participants from living history portrayals of an expedition that was shaped by "[n]nearly two and a half years of almost constant contact between explorers and Indians."[43]

PROBLEMS AND PROMISES

When nature is regarded as a place "out there," and history is "back then," they are not processes with which we live. At best, nature and history become abstracted into commodities for tourism. In this context, "experiencing" nature or history through recreation becomes an escape from both. How history shapes our world, and how the environment connects where we work and where we play, become invisible. In terms of Lewis and Clark, the world they helped create becomes divorced from the purposes of the expedition, and the world we inhabit loses its historical grounding. The personalized sense of history that comes from visiting expedition sites or reconstructing early-nineteenth-century experiences can hardly be considered a bad thing. However, the tendency to conflate the distant past with the immediate, individuated present tends to make the historical roots of ecological and cultural issues disappear—the very issues that shape current understandings of Lewis and Clark. Through a sort of mental sleight of hand, the comforts of tourism both escape and satisfy multicultural and environmental concerns. Perhaps therein lies the real appeal of these newly constituted heroes for the new millennium, and there also can be found reasons for deep concern about our abilities to meet the challenges of the new century.

The problems and promises of the bicentennial surfaced at a recent planning meeting between the Army Corps of Engineers and members of the Columbia River Treaty Tribes. The corps announced it had $200 million to help Native communities present their side of the Lewis and Clark story. The money could largely be used to construct signboards, parking lots, and bathrooms at interpretive waysides. The corps also hoped to use this money for a new pet project: a bike path from the Rocky Mountains to the Pacific. It assumed everyone would favor a plan that equated playing on the Lewis and Clark trail with the best way to commemorate the expedition.

Presented with a huge sum of money, and the tangled strings that came attached, Native participants balked. They certainly welcomed support for their efforts to engage and inform tourists, but the emphasis seemed too focused on the visitor experience and not tribal concerns. One woman captured the mood perfectly: "What good will parking lots, bathrooms, and bike paths be in a few years? We are thinking about where we will be in 200 years. What about funding to support language instruction, or restore some important cultural sites and animal habitats, or tearing down some of your dams?"[44] Her point was sharp but simple. Honoring the past obliges us to make history part of our present and relevant to our future. For her and many others, *living history* is not a game of dress up or a chance for touristic rediscovery. It means commemorating the past by confronting persistent problems and actively incorporating their solutions into the places where we live.

Coming to terms with the legacy of Lewis and Clark must begin with an honest assessment of the expedition as a long, difficult, imperial venture with tragic consequences for the peoples and places they encountered. But that is only a beginning. Understanding the world that Lewis and Clark encountered is important, but that means commemorating the expedition in a way that ensures that world's continuing relevance. Nothing could be more relevant than strengthening the vitality of the languages that first described the expedition, and no obligation to the future could be more pressing than working to ensure the economic and political autonomy of the people who first described Lewis and Clark. Making the bicentennial into a grand extravaganza for recreational tourism and automobile pilgrims only ensures that those priorities will be ignored and old problems will persist.

If the bicentennial is a chance to "get things right," then residents of the areas crossed by the expedition should demand that the attention and fantastic amounts of money it attracts must first—and perhaps only—go toward building connections between the world Lewis and Clark experienced and the places millions of people now call home. Imagine the lasting impact of a bicentennial project that helped people build parks and plant gardens to attract healthy and sustainable populations of currently threatened species—and bring them back in to the places where people live and work. Compare that with current plans to accommodate a fleeting parade of tourists by constructing directional signposts, parking lots, interpretive waysides, campgrounds, marinas, forest roads, and visitors centers with no more than a three-year life span.

Commemorating Lewis and Clark is frequently presented as an opportunity to "relive history" and recapture "a spirit of adventure." Yet this tends to reject the mundane or unsettling aspects of history by simply ignoring them. The bicentennial offers a real chance to address historical problems and start the process of actively recovering what has been lost, damaged, or threatened. Spending enormous sums of money to play at Lewis and Clark or rediscover past values that never existed is something the future cannot afford.

NOTES

This essay was composed with the generous support of a fellowship from the Humanities Center at Oregon State University. I also gratefully acknowledge research funding and assistance from Knox College. Portions of this essay appeared in different form in "Harmless Fun or Reckless Abandon? Re-Creation and Recreation as History at the Lewis & Clark Bicentennial," *History News* 56 (spring 2001): 17–21.

1. W. Raymond Wood and Thomas D. Thiessen, *Early Fur Trade on the Northern Plains: Canadian Traders Among the Mandan And Hidatsa Indians, 1738–1818* (Norman: University of Oklahoma Press, 1985); Frank H. Stewart, "Mandan and Hidatsa Villages in the in the Eighteenth and Nineteenth Centuries, *Plains Anthropologist* 19 (November 1974), 287–302; Roy W. Meyer, *The Village Indians of the Upper Missouri: The Mandan, Hidatsas and Arikaras* (Lincoln: University of Nebraska Press, 1977), 36–58.

2. This and all subsequent references to journal entries in text and notes come from Gary E. Moulton, ed., *The Journals of the Lewis & Clark Expedition*, 13 vols. (Lincoln: University of Nebraska Press, 1983–97).

3. Because theatrical aspects of Lewis and Clark's diplomacy needed fair weather to best show off flag raising, discharge of firearms, marching, and distribution of gifts, the two captains conferred with Sahnish leaders to put off the first of their formal meetings to the next day (James P. Ronda, *Lewis and Clark among the Indians* [Lincoln: University of Nebraska Press, 1984], 56). Clark's commission did not bestow on him the official rank of captain, but for the duration of the expedition he was regarded as a co-equal with Captain Lewis.

4. Pierre-Antoine Tabeau, *Tabeau's Narrative of Loisel's Expedition to the Upper Missouri*, ed. Annie Heloise Abel, trans. Rose Abel Wright (Norman: University of Oklahoma Press, 1939), 201. As a leader in one of the Sahnish towns, Piahito was also known as Arketarnashar (chief of the village).

5. While making preparations for the expedition, Clark estimated that it would take from 190 to 240 days to reach the Rocky Mountains. This was based on a total estimated distance of 2,400 miles at 10 to 12 miles per day. Clark was off by only 100 miles in his estimate of the distance to the Mandan villages, but the expedition arrived four to six weeks later than originally planned. The mileage estimate to the Continental Divide was off by more than 600 miles (John L. Allen, *Passage through the Garden: Lewis and Clark and the Image of the American Northwest* [Urbana: University of Illinois Press, 1975], 160–167).

6. In the early morning of 22 October, "at 1 oClock [Clark] was violently and Suddinly attacked with the Rhumetism in neck which was So violent [he] could not move." This was the night of the first snow. The ailment eased up the following day

but soon returned and proved so debilitating that Clark was unable to attend the first official meeting with Mandan leaders. The other members of the expedition who complained of similar ailments were Pierre Cruzatte, Reuben Fields, and perhaps another unnamed man (see entries for 22–26 October, 3:191–202).

7. Quote is from Allen, *Passage through the Garden*, 205.

8. A Hidatsa raid of a Lemhi Shoshone band near the headwaters of the Missouri River probably explained the presence of Sacagawea among those people (the Hidatsa knew her as Sakakawea).

9. Because the Sahnish had a long history of contact and cohabitation with Europeans, they were accustomed to the strange behavior from outsiders. Not surprisingly, Lewis and Clark do not figure prominently in Sahnish oral history and the expedition's brief passage through their villages left no measureable impact. But the Sahnish keenly remember Piahito, who traveled to Washington, D.C. in 1805 at Lewis and Clark's request. His unexplained death in Washington on 7 April 1806 caused a bitter sadness among the Sahnish. There is currently an outstanding request to Senator Brian Dorgan (North Dakota) that Piahito's remains be located and returned to his people (Rhoda Star, telephone interview by author, 9 July 2002). Piahito's death is noted by Thomas Jefferson in Donald Jackson, ed., *Letters of the Lewis and Clark Expedition with Related Documents, 1783–1854*, 2d ed. (Urbana: University of Illinois Press, 1978), 1:306.

10. This interpretation is based on speculation. For contemporary descriptions of what might generally be called "vision questing" among the Sahnish, and their views of Lewis and Clark, see Tabeau, *Tabeau's Narrative*, 191–193, 200; Henry M. Brackenridge, *Journal of a Voyage up the Missouri River Performed in Eighteen Hundred and Eleven* (1816), reprinted in Reuben Gold Thwaites, ed., *Early Western Travels, 1748–1846* (Cleveland: A. H. Clark, 1904–07), 6:126; and Ronda, *Among the Indians*, 64. Lewis and Clark did not observe this widespread element of upper Missouri Native cultures, but see Edwin Thompson Denig in *Five Indian Tribes of the Upper Missouri: Sioux, Arickaras, Assiniboines, Crees, Crows*, with an introduction by John C. Ewers (Norman: University of Oklahoma Press, 1961), passim.

11. This was William Clark's response to Piahito's explanations about a "number of their Treditions" (3:180).

12. Stephen E. Ambrose, *Lewis & Clark: Voyage of Discovery* (Washington, D.C.: National Geographic Society, 1998), 22.

13. A. P. Nasatir, *Before Lewis and Clark: Documents Illustrating the History of the Missouri, 1785–1804*, 2 vols. (1952; reprint, Lincoln: Bison Books, 1990); Barry M Gough, *The Northwest Coast: British Navigation, Trade, and Discoveries to 1812* (Vancouver: University of British Columbia Press, 1992), 155–156, 182.

14. Albert Furtwangler makes a similar observation in his *Acts of Discovery: Visions of America in the Lewis and Clark Journals* (Urbana: University of Illinois Press, 1993), 201–202.

15. For Jefferson's instructions to Lewis, see Jackson, *Letters*, 1:61–66.

16. Jefferson to Benjamin Hawkins, 18 February 1803, in Andrew A. Lipscomb and Albert Ellery Bergh, eds., *The Writings of Thomas Jefferson* (Washington, D.C.: Thomas Jefferson Memorial Association of the United States, 1903–04), 9:363–364, quoted in Anthony F. C. Wallace, *Jefferson and the Indians: The Tragic Fate of the First Americans* (Cambridge, Mass.: Harvard University Press, 1999), 223.

17. Jefferson to Andrew Jackson, 16 February 1803, in Lipscomb and Bergh, *Writings*, 10:357, quoted in Anthony F. C. Wallace, "'The Obtaining Lands': Thomas Jefferson and the Native Americans," in *Thomas Jefferson and the Changing West*, ed. James P. Ronda (Albuquerque: University of New Mexico Press in Association with the Missouri Historical Society Press, 1997), 25, 30.

18. This description of the Missouri River comes from the transcript of an interview with William Least Heat-Moon for the Ken Burns documentary on the expedition, first presented by PBS in November 1997 (http://www.pbs.org/lewisandclark/archive/moon.html [18 March 2000]). These comments are also synopsized in the documentary's companion volume by Ken Burns's preface, "Come Up Me," in Dayton Duncan and Ken Burns, *Lewis & Clark: The Journey of the Corps of Discovery, an Illustrated History* (New York: Alfred A. Knopf, 1999), ix–xvii.

19. William Least Heat-Moon, "Vision Quest," in Duncan et al., *Lewis & Clark*, 62–67.

20. The clearest representation of these sentiments can be found in Stephen E. Ambrose, *Undaunted Courage: Meriwether Lewis, Thomas Jefferson, and the Opening of the American West* (New York: Simon and Schuster, 1996).

21. Robert Frost, "The Gift Outright," in *A Witness Tree* (New York: Henry Holt, 1942), 43.

22. These words are Dayton Duncan's (http://www.pbs.org/lewisandclark/archive/moon.html [12 January 2000]).

23. Also see the essays by John Spencer and Wallace Lewis in this collection.

24. Quotation is from a brochure entitled "Live the Spirit," received by the author in a membership application mailing dated 11 August 2000.

25. Anonymous, interview with the author, 12 December 1999, Toppenish, Washington.

26. As in http://www.pbs.org/lewisandclark/archive/moon.html (18 March 2000).

27. Many scholars have described Lewis's fears and actions as slight blemishes on an otherwise perfect record of peaceful coexistence with Native peoples. The several dozen violent encounters mentioned in the journals suggest a different conclusion but were never severe enough to end the expedition.

28. Jefferson's instructions to Lewis in Jackson, *Letters*, 1:64; Jefferson to William Henry Harrison in Lipscomb and Bergh, *Writings*, 2:344–345, quoted in Wallace, *Jefferson and the Indians*, 313.

29. Quotation is from John C. Ewers, "Plains Indian Reactions to the Lewis and Clark Expedition," *Montana, the Magazine of Western History* 16 (1966): 12.

30. For an overview of encounters that involved violence or the threat of violence, see Ronda, *Among the Indians*, 31–40, 171–176, 203, 219–221, 238–243, 250. When contrasted with other nineteenth-century government-sponsored explorations, the Lewis and Clark expedition stands out as particularly violent and deadly.

31. Roy E. Appleman, *Lewis and Clark: Historic Places Associated with Their Transcontinental Exploration (1804–06)* (Washington, D.C.: Department of the Interior, National Park Service, 1975), 249–252.

32. For a brief but excellent treatment of George Rogers Clark's military actions in the old Northwest, see Richard White, *The Middle Ground: Indians, Empires, and Re-*

publics in the Great Lakes Region, 1650–1815 (Cambridge: Cambridge University Press, 1991), 368–378. On William Clark's military activities, see Jerome O. Steffen, *William Clark: Jeffersonian Man on the Frontier* (Norman: University of Oklahoma Press, 1977), 19–25. White also helps to place the younger Clark's career in a broader context (*Middle Ground,* 454–468).

33. Thomas Sheridan, *A Complete Dictionary of the English Language* (Philadelphia: Printed for W. Young, Mills and Son, 1796), 28; John Entick, *Entick's New Spelling Dictionary* ([Wilmington, Del.]: Printed and sold by Peter Brynberg., 1800), 24.

34. Thomas Schmidt and Jeremy Schmidt, *Saga of Lewis and Clark: Into the Unknown West* (New York: Dorling Kindersley Press, 1999); David Freeman Hawke, *Those Tremendous Mountains: The Story of the Lewis and Clark Expedition* (New York: W. W. Norton, 1998).

35. John Hughes, "Snake Again Called 'Most Endangered' River in America," Associated Press State and Local Wire Services, 9 March 2000.

36. Quote is from the Wilderness Act; Public Law 88–577 (16 U.S. C. 1131–1136), 88th Congress, 2d sess. (3 September 1964). I detail the connections between wilderness preservation and Native dispossession in *Dispossessing the Wilderness: Indian Removal and the Making of the National Parks* (New York: Oxford University Press, 1999).

37. "Relive the Adventure" is the theme for LewisAndClarkTrail.com. Though a widely expressed sentiment, the second quote comes from Barbara Gibbs Ostmann, "Big Sky Country," *Travel America,* May–June 2000, 56. In its brochure for the Lewis and Clark National Historic Trail, the National Park Service positively gushes: "Today you can follow in the footsteps of Lewis and Clark, exploring the route they traveled and reliving the adventure of the Corps of Discovery."

38. *Lewis and Clark Trail Adventures,* http://www.trailadventures.com/ (4 May 2000). "The Lewis and Clark Collection" is advertised by *The Catalog of the Great American West,* http://www.webwest.com/lewis-clark/ (4 May 2000).

39. Quote is from C-SPAN, "President Bush participates in Bicentennial of Lewis & Clark's 'Voyage of Discovery' Summit," 3 July 2002.

40. Quote comes from *Lewis and Clark: Resources About the Trail,* http://www.lcsc.edu/lewis.clark/resources/trail.html (9 May 2000)

41. Ambrose, *Lewis & Clark,* 21.

42. Anonymous, interview with the author, 26 August 2000, Galesburg, Illinois. This reenactor apparently preferred the virtues of early industrial-scale warfare to the morally suspect postmodern variety.

43. Quote is from Ronda, *Among the Indians,* xi. The person of Sacagawea is occasionally played by individuals of Native descent, but there are no living history portrayals of the expedition that involve full-scale "encounters" between historically garbed Indians and explorers. For most Native peoples, the aversion to these kinds of scenarios is visceral.

44. Comments from a Lewis and Clark bicentennial planning meeting between the Army Corps of Engineers and representatives of the Columbia River Treaty Tribes, 12 December 1999, Yakama Indian Reservation, Toppenish, Washington.

Chapter 11

On the Tourist Trail with Lewis & Clark

Issues of Interpretation and Preservation

Andrew Gulliford

Western states are bracing for a huge influx of Lewis and Clark tourists who will follow the explorers' routes before, during, and after the 2004–06 Lewis and Clark bicentennial. Tourists will travel along a 4,000-mile route from St. Louis, Missouri to Astoria, Oregon, even though some scholars argue that the Lewis and Clark trail begins not in St. Louis, but in Pittsburgh or in Washington, D.C. These matters are of little or no concern to those who readily identify the two explorers with the lands they encountered. Some especially dedicated enthusiasts will follow the entire Trail, embarking from St. Louis then paddling and walking in the footsteps of their heroes. Most will travel in a more comfortable manner, with some opting for luxurious accommodations aboard vintage trains like the *American Orient Express* or modern cruise ships on the Columbia and Snake Rivers like the *Columbia Queen*, the *Spirit of the West*, and the *Spirit of Discovery*. Besides first-class meals and sumptuous accommodations, these rail and ship tours have established guided excursions where historians and naturalists lecture on everything from the location of Lewis and Clark campsites to Sacagawea's love for wapato roots. Just how many will don backpacks, board cruise ships or set out in the family car is anyone's guess, but certainly thousands, possibly hundreds of thousands, and maybe millions will follow some portion of the expedition route in the next few years. Regardless of how Americans will get up the Missouri River, across the Dakotas and Montana, through the Bitterroot Range of Idaho, and down the canyons of the Snake River into the magnificent Columbia River Gorge, they will come.[1]

Unlike other commemorations or celebrations of historical events, the Lewis and Clark bicentennial is unique in that visitors want to cover the route, see the terrain, smell the prairie after a thunderstorm, and hike steep mountain slopes in Montana and Idaho.[2] Revisiting the route of the Corps of Discovery is an unprecedented commemoration in terms of geography, length of the trip, and potential lessons. Though tourists seek deep, personal experiences with the landscape, the flood of banal curios is anything but unique and is an unavoidable corollary of the explorers' newfound popularity.[3] The bicentennial is drawing Americans out of the suburbs and on to the Great Plains. It is without precedent as a commemorative event. Citizens visit Civil War battlefields, and the Oregon trail's 150th anniversary generated much travel along that migration route, but this is a different sort of patriotic pilgrimage, and one that may have lasting impacts. In the process, this bicentennial event is focusing unprecedented attention upon a vast, linear western corridor, and this essay reflects what tourists expect, what they will experience, and what they may learn.

PERSONAL DISCOVERIES

Most Americans have seen the central regions of their country only from 30,000 feet out the window of commercial jets, or through the car window as they sped along interstate highways. The Lewis and Clark route, however, like the old Indian trails, follows the contours of the land. Tourists have rarely been drawn up the Missouri River to North and South Dakota, but that is changing. Today, people want to come into the country the way the captains did: slowly, upriver, moving out of the humid east and across the vast western landscape of open sky and few fences.[4] The prairie states are delighted with this newfound tourist desire, and momentum for the bicentennial is resulting in everything from new visitor centers to extra motel rooms along the route. On the western edge of the continent, traveling on the Columbia River is more developed and luxurious than in the Dakotas. Yet in both parts of the continent, river travel is a new medium for most Americans and is growing in popularity thanks to the newfound excitement about Lewis and Clark.

Travelers following the Corps of Discovery are not arriving at a single tourist destination; instead they are encountering an entirely new landscape not visible from jets or four-lane highways. The entire route has its appeal and no one particular historic campsite, mountain ridge, or museum visitor center can claim to be the tourist nexus. Just as the explorers had not completed their journey until they had arrived back home, this commemoration is about crossing America—by river, trail, and back roads—and returning with new understanding. Following the captains' route is a personal voyage of discovery, a tourist odyssey linking landscape and history as described by the Lewis and Clark journals.

Walking down the main street of Three Forks, Montana, after rocking on the porch of the Sacagawea Inn, provides a special delight for suburban tourists who may never have experienced a western barbecue cooked in an old oil drum behind a restored railroad hotel. Few Americans have visited small Montana towns with only two stoplights but at least six bars. The open prairies of the Dakotas have been habitually shunned by traveling tourists, but now as they follow Lewis and Clark, they are stopping to see the wild-flowers, staring at the buffalo, and marveling at the prairie dogs. The Lewis and Clark lens focuses on a large landscape, and Americans in search of Lewis and Clark are encountering one another in small towns, quiet valleys, forested hills, and shallow unpolluted rivers they never knew existed.

Four things the captains had in abundance that we have lost in the twenty-first century are silence, solitude, darkness, and proximity to mammals like wolves and grizzlies. These qualities of the wilderness landscape are unknown in subdivisions and on city streets. Nevertheless, the words of T. K. Whipple from *Study Out the Land* still apply to the Corps of Discovery as well as to the legions of tourists traveling the Lewis and Clark trail: "All America lies at the end of the wilderness road, and our past is not a dead past, but still lives in us. Our forefathers had civilization inside themselves, the wild outside. We live in the civilization they created, but within us the wilderness still lingers. What they dreamed, we live, and what they lived, we dream."[5]

Lewis and Clark tourists reawaken their senses on the plains of eastern Montana, on the Weippe Prairie of Idaho, and on open riverboats at the Missouri River's Gates of the Mountains near Helena, Montana. There travelers can visit Meriwether Campground and view the Joe and Reuben Fields Gulch where the expedition stayed on 19 July 1805.[6] For many suburban visitors to the West, just seeing an uncluttered starry sky makes the trip worthwhile. For others, following the Lewis and Clark trail is both a historical pilgrimage and a personal spiritual quest.[7]

Lewis and Clark in their buckskin shirts and with their hunting rifles symbolize a freedom and independence unknown in modern America. They represent an irresistible draw for the young who want to follow in Lewis and Clark's footsteps and learn about the landscape as they learn about themselves. For senior citizens it is also a journey about youth and self-discovery. Sitting around a campfire at the Triple O Hunting Camp deep in Idaho's Bitterroot Range, a woman from Rhode Island more accustomed to cocktails and card parties explains after a week of rafting, hiking, and horseback riding along the trail, "I never knew I could do these things. My friends told me I was a fool to come. Now I know that they are the fools. Why have I limited my life? I was ready to lie down and retire and snooze away my afternoons. Not now. Not ever. I hurt. I'm sore, but I'm stronger than I've ever been."[8]

A widow from Baton Rouge, Louisiana stares into the fire and says, "I've never been so free. The kids are grown. I'm on my own. All my life I've wanted to follow Lewis and Clark and see these woods. This journey has changed me." For Harlan and Barb Opdahl of Triple O Outfitters, such campfire revelations are nothing new. Get the right people sleeping in those canvas tents, drinking that deep black Idaho camp coffee, and eating ham for breakfast and steak for dinner, and they'll forget all about that dark, chilly trip to the outhouse behind the corrals. Slowly, tourists realize that they do not need all those creature comforts and all that internet access. What endures is the landscape and the stories of those who came before.[9] The appeal is more than nostalgia, more than a longing for a return to some frontier golden age. Instead, it is about movement, about distance; it is about personal exploration along a shared historic route. Tourists find a piece of themselves they did not know they had lost.

PATRIOTISM AND SUSTAINABLE HEROES

Both the young and the old are rediscovering America in a patriotic impulse not seen since the nation's bicentennial in 1976. Patriotism is back in style, and the Lewis and Clark expedition is being recognized as the precursor to Manifest Destiny and the settlement of the West as well as a symbol of America's national virtues. Thomas Jefferson may have bought Louisiana, but Lewis and Clark gave us the continent. By embracing them, we embrace ourselves and our yearning for a simpler time. Imagine the members of the Corps of Discovery struggling along rocky shoals near the three forks of the Missouri as they tried to find a nonexistent water route across the continent.[10] In many ways, their epic journey represents one of the nation's primal origin myths just as the Pilgrims who shivered through their first winter near Plymouth Rock gave us the first Thanksgiving. But this story is different, and Americans are fascinated by the distances covered and the immense difficulties the corps faced.

Lewis and Clark tourists are also captivated by the leaders' bonds of friendship, and they retrace the journey as an antidote to much of the negative history taught since the 1960s. A quarter century after the Vietnam War, Americans want to be proud of themselves and their accomplishments. Captains Lewis and Clark have earned their place as heroes, and tourists want to visit the exact spots where heroic deeds took place.[11]

Lewis and Clark are sustainable heroes and role models who reflect human weakness and prejudice. Their ultimate success is therefore all the more remarkable. Clark's anger at the Sioux who blocked their river route as the corps ascended the Missouri River, and Lewis's fatal use of weapons against young Blackfeet can be understood as errors in judgment. Despite the mistakes, including almost losing one of the young Kentucky hunters who had been missing for three days, deep friendships and human bonds forged by both the prairie heat and the frigid Great Plains winters kept them all together.

Near present-day Great Falls, Montana, cactus thorns reduced the soles of William Clark's feet to a pulpy mass, and his good friend Meriwether Lewis had to remove those thorns by firelight. Later on the homeward journey, when all the men wore elkskin, Pierre Cruzatte mistakenly shot Lewis in the buttocks with his .54 rifle. The bullet went through both cheeks, and Captain Clark cleaned the wounds to stave off infection.

The captains' respect for each other represents one of the great friendships in American history. As Stephen Ambrose has pointed out, theirs was a shared command, unheard of in military annals, and yet it succeeded. American veterans who are tourists, and who remember when they were young and seemingly invincible, recall in the captains' friendship their own deep bonds with soldiers and comrades now at rest.

The Lewis and Clark journey was as complicated and as full of danger as going to the moon and back, but more so because the Apollo astronauts had maps and photographs of the moon. Lewis and Clark had their Indian guides, but no reliable maps, and certainly no photographs. Beyond Fort Mandan in North Dakota, they were on their own.[12] The appeal of Lewis and Clark to many Americans is that the captains did not know where they were most of the time, and yet they persevered. Today's tourists may panic driving across the plains with a quarter tank of gasoline and no small towns in sight. The openness of the prairies can be unnerving, but Lewis and Clark never panicked. Perhaps they faced a longer interval between meals, but they had the inner resources we seem to have misplaced. We depend upon technology instead of on ourselves. That, too, is part of the captains' appeal—their resourcefulness across so many different landscapes.

Tourists who are business professionals and chief executive officers ponder the logistical aspects of outfitting the expedition, worrying about the subcontractors, and finding all the supplies. Executives contemplate Lewis and Clark's management style and the captains' ability to hone forty-five disparate young men into efficient soldiers, explorers, and the vanguard of what became mountain men. Not surprisingly, Lewis and Clark's leadership style has become a model for corporate management seminars. The expedition's accomplishments are all the more remarkable when compared to the next exploring party to head from St. Louis to the Pacific Coast. Financed by the millionaire John Jacob Astor in 1811, this group had the benefit of Lewis and Clark's information and took comfort in the fact that supplies would come by water to the mouth of the Columbia River. Many of these Astorians died en route, others starved, and at least two men went mad. Why did the captains succeed while other later and better-equipped companies fell apart? Tourists are justifiably impressed by the group cohesion exemplified by the Corps of Discovery, and they marvel at the captains' ability to lead their men through such diverse and difficult terrain, under trying circumstances and with an unswerving common purpose. Retired business leaders and executives are awed at the consummate skills of the captains to organize, motivate, inspire, and even heal their men.[13]

The appeal of Lewis and Clark stems, in part, from the American fascination with wilderness. As the historian James Ronda makes clear, however, the American West of the early nineteenth century was "a crowded wilderness."[14] The expedition would have failed miserably without the constant support and guidance of Native Americans. Contemporary Native Americans can tell us about the captains' dependence upon their ancestors. The captains may have been self-sufficient woodsmen blazing trails through the wilderness, but they also depended upon Indian women, wapato roots, and the kindness of strangers.

SACAGAWEA'S LEGACY AND WOMEN'S HISTORY

By far the most important Native individual to assist the expedition was Sacagawea, the Shoshone (some say Hidatsa) woman who joined the expedition in the spring of 1805. Not surprisingly, Sacagawea elicits a great deal of conversation on the Lewis and Clark tourist trail. Some of this reflects the influence of romantic novels like Anna Lee Waldo's *Sacajawea* (1984), some pulls from debates among historians, and some comes from unclear or inconclusive passages in the expedition journals. Invariably, questions arise about the pronunciation and spelling of her name—is it Sacajawea, Sacagawea, or Sakakawea? The answer is never definitive, but it is usually "Sacagawea," with a hard "g."[15] The question, or the answer, matters less than the continuing fascination that surrounds the historical figure. Although each generation wants to see a different symbol in Sacagawea, she remains central to how people understand the expedition and its significance. Of course, there is always deep fascination about her personal and psychic survival as the only female among two dozen men. In the early twentieth century, this made her a key symbol for the women's suffrage movement.[16] At other times, her position within the expedition has led to more personal reflection—for artists, writers, and tourists alike.

The expedition journals provide some dramatic scenes that have piqued the imaginations of many. In the freezing Bitterroots, facing starvation, Sacagawea offered to share with Captain Clark a crust of bread that she had kept hidden on her person to feed her baby, Jean Baptiste. And during that cold, wet Christmas at Fort Clatsop she presented Captain Clark with a stunning gift of two dozen white weasel tails—the most valued fur from the Rocky Mountains.[17] Did she admire Clark, because he was such a contrast to her lout of a husband, Charbonneau, or was there more to their relationship? Historians and Lewis and Clark aficionados lightly pass over such questions, but tourists on the Trail still wonder. After all, for months Lewis,

Clark, Charbonneau, Sacagawea, and the baby stayed together in the same quarters whether it was a tepee or wooden hut.[18]

Until very recently no one has dealt with the complex issues of female representation surrounding Sacagawea. This is surprising, since she has more statues erected to her honor than any other American woman. The height of Sacagawea representation came at the turn of the twentieth century as the Daughters of the American Revolution and other women's groups sought to create a female heroine to take her rightful place in American history. Sacagawea succeeded as a female symbol of bravery and personal independence, yet she also represented stoicism, loyalty, motherhood, and Native participation in the expedition. What does that say about us as Americans, and what does that say about her?[19]

Besides frequent debates on the correct form of her name, tourists on the Lewis and Clark trail frequently discuss Sacagawea's tribal origins, her life after the expedition, and her final resting place. Today, she is claimed by the Northern Shoshone at Fort Hall, Idaho, the Eastern Shoshone at Fort Washakie, Wyoming, and the Hidatsa in North Dakota. The National Park Service and the historian James Ronda are convinced that Sacagawea died of a "putrid fever" on 20 December 1812 and was buried at Fort Manuel, on the Missouri River near the present-day border between North and South Dakota. According to John C. Luttig, the clerk at Fort Manuel, "she was a good and the best woman in the fort, aged abt 25 years."[20] The Eastern Shoshone Indians have a different story and believe she lived to be an old woman and is buried in the Wind River Mountains to the west of the Sacagawea Cemetery near Fort Washakie. When asked to explain the contradiction between the Park Service's version of her death and their own, Eastern Shoshone elders smile and state that when Charbonneau took Sacagawea for a wife, he had a second young wife who did not make the trip, and she is the one who died in the Dakotas. In other words, Luttig erred.[21]

Sacagawea's story thus becomes a prism, which reflects not only the history of the Lewis and Clark expedition, but also the significance of the bicentennial to Native peoples. She is enormously important to western tribes who regard her with compassion and treat her as a valued ancestor. The old woman who came to live on the Shoshone reservation knew many strange things, told interesting stories, sang beautiful songs, and remembered visiting the great water and seeing the great fish, that is, the beached whale at the Pacific Ocean near Cannon Beach. What is the truth? When will we let Indian tribes interpret their own story of contact with the Corps of Discovery? Encouraging American Indians to tell their stories may become a significant achievement of the bicentennial.[22]

From the Native American perspective, a band of white men wandered through their territory begged for food, made many promises they never kept, and then in a different season came blundering back on their return route. For Columbia Plateau tribes who have fished and prayed and hunted in the same valleys and creek bottoms for eleven thousand years, the expedition's brief visits in 1805 and 1806 are but moments in time.

The Nez Perce tell the story of an old woman who had been taken captive as a child, much like Sacagawea. The woman regained her freedom when a Canadian trapper helped return her to her people. She was there when Lewis and Clark stumbled starving out of the Bitterroots, bloated themselves with salmon and camas roots, and suffered miserably from intense stomach pains. The Nez Perce seriously considered killing the explorers for their valuable rifles and ammunition, but the old woman said, "Do them no harm." A white man had once befriended her so she felt they should be spared. The Nez Perce had never seen whites before and distrusted them, but she argued that the debilitated explorers should be nursed back to health and not killed for their guns.

For Native American tribes two elements of this story are important. The first element is that in the history of the expedition two different Indian women saved the corps—Sacagawea, as a translator whose brother Cameahwait sold them horses, and a Nez Perce female elder who spared their lives. Second, though white women had little social standing in the Virginia of the captains' birth and were rarely consulted on important decisions, among Indian communities, then and now, women's opinions are highly respected. Few interpreters get that story straight or understand the nuances of Native American history. Clearly, Indian interpretation needs to be central to the bicentennial.[23]

Tourists need to know that Lewis and Clark moved, not through an unknown wilderness world, but rather through an Indian landscape where even the rocks and trees had names. The Corps of Discovery were strangers at the mercy of powerful tribes who let them pass in peace. To see Lewis and Clark as explorers of a vast wilderness is to miss the context of the expedition and the reasons for its successful completion.[24] Lewis and Clark ran out of trade goods on their way home and even had to barter their buttons.

Tourists should learn about the corps's desperation, but Americans also need to understand the irreversible changes the captains wrought including the spread of diseases, the availability of guns, and the disappearance of certain Indian bands who befriended them. Tourists have always seen Lewis and Clark as the epitome of "Great White Men" who led America westward, but in 2004–06 tourists must rethink their stereotypes and learn that American history is not the seamless, unchangeable past they once believed. Such an awakening will be jarring, but inevitable. Whether or not tourists set out to find cultural diversity along the Lewis and Clark trail, they will find it anyway, and the full richness and complexity of American history will resonate deeply. Understanding the cultural complexity of the expedition, in terms of its survival and success, may be one of the real achievements of the bicentennial. The National Park Service and the National Lewis and Clark Bicentennial Council are committed to this crucial reappraisal.

CLEAN CAMPSITES AND THE ABSENCE OF ARCHAEOLOGY

Given the vast expanse of land covered by the Lewis and Clark expedition, and the changes wrought by two hundred years, tourists are understandably curious about what sites can still be visited. If commemorating the expedition means following its trail, then how can visitors still walk in the actual footsteps of the Corps of Discovery? Their concern gives special importance to archaeology, because this science can significantly aid interpretation at wayside exhibits, visitor centers, and local, state, and regional museums. Emphasis on the archaeology of Lewis and Clark sites is a recent phenomenon, but it illustrates well some of the special challenges of commemorating the expedition. Unlike a Civil War battlefield or a visit to a historic antebellum house, the expedition's route yields very little physical evidence. Lewis and Clark campsites have been difficult to validate, because the explorers left few traces. After years of searching, Ken Karsmizki, the curator of history at the Columbia Gorge Discovery Center, has found only a rifle flint, a wooden stake, and butchered buffalo bones at Lower Portage Camp, where the corps spent weeks near Great Falls, Montana (Figure 8). The results have been equally dismal along the entire eight thousand mile round-trip route.[25]

One interesting new lead in the hunt for traces of Lewis and Clark has to do with sex, venereal disease, and three pewter penis syringes, which Lewis bought in Philadelphia and took along the trip. He used them to inject mercury compounds up the urethra of the enlisted men who found too much delight with Indian women. Mercury is a deadly heavy metal and some of the corps probably went to early graves because of their promiscuity. Archaeologically, heavy metals remain deep in stratified soil, so a search has been undertaken to find the latrine at Fort Clatsop and to use that location to identify the fort's actual site. This archaeological strategy assumes the captains followed strict military procedure in building the latrine at a specified distance from the fort. Archaeology may prove the exact location of the 1805–6 winter quarters along the cold and wet Oregon coast.[26]

INTERPRETIVE CENTERS

Lewis and Clark tourism is an economic reality among western states and a potent force reshaping small towns along the expedition's route. Tourists will traverse the Lewis and Clark trail, which is now clearly marked and identified, thanks in large part to the efforts of the Lewis and Clark Trail

Figure 8. Excavation of Lower Portage Camp. (Photo by Andrew Gulliford, Center of Southwest Studies, Fort Lewis College)

Heritage Foundation from Great Falls, Montana. Begun only thirty years ago, the heritage foundation has gone from 1,200 members to 2,500 members in the last few years. It has also succeeded in building a multiagency, $7 million-dollar Lewis and Clark National Historic Trail Interpretive Center at Great Falls, Montana, which features dramatic exhibits on the 18-mile portage around the falls.[27] Other public and private agencies are building or upgrading interpretive centers in the Columbia River Gorge and along the trail in North Dakota. The Columbia River Gorge National Scenic area may get a $7 million gateway center near Washougal, Washington to interpret the 292,615-acre scenic area traversed by Lewis and Clark two centuries ago.[28] Camp Wood, Illinois will see its own 15,000-square-foot, $7 million interpretive center to commemorate the site where the Corps of Discovery spent the first winter of 1804 near the junction of the Mississippi and Missouri Rivers. Likewise, Sioux Falls, Iowa gets a new $2.5 million visitor center to honor the corps's only fatality, Sergeant Floyd, who probably died of appendicitis.

The size and scope of the upcoming bicentennial is perhaps best indicated by the attentions of the federal government. Congress has designated a special caucus just to oversee the bicentennial and to appropriate additional commemorative funds, which are being hotly contested by states along the route. Eleven federal agencies, including the National Park Service, the Bureau of Land Management, the U.S. Forest Service and others have signed a memorandum of agreement and appointed full-time staff members to handle logistics and interpretive issues. The National Park Service has its own full-time superintendent for the Lewis and Clark National Historic Trail. Out of his Omaha, Nebraska office, Gerard Baker keeps track of a mailing list with 1,200 names and his staff continually updates the Park Service web site.[29]

Park Service plans also include driving three diesel tractor-trailers on the route and stopping at selected sites during the same time of year as the corps's visits. One truck would hold artifacts, another would contain satellite dishes and e-mail links to school children across the nation, and the third truck would be staffed with scientists and biologists who would study plants and animals at each stop and compare them with historic descriptions from the journals.[30] As its name—The Corps of Discovery II—suggests, the concept is a "multi-agency project designed to augment and enhance, but not duplicate or replace, local bicentennial events already in the planning stages. Hundreds of communities and Indian nations throughout the United States will be visited by this traveling education center."[31] The Park Service also plans to join forces with Amtrak to place interpretive guides aboard trains between Grand Forks, North Dakota and Portland, Oregon.

NEW INTERPRETATION ON THE WASHINGTON COAST

Along with these novel interpretive efforts, the bicentennial may also lead to significant, and permanent, changes in how visitors access Lewis and Clark sites. In southwestern Washington state, Rex Ziak has urged the removal of portions of U.S. Highway 101 along the coast because he believes it runs too close to campsites where Lewis and Clark suffered miserably from cold November winds, pelting rain, surging tides, and high waves. A close reading of the journals, expertly combined with a local's knowledge of the raw fall weather and with tidal charts from the U.S. Navy, have helped Ziak to understand that those November days on the Washington coast represented epic endurance in the face of miserable weather, rotting elk-skin clothing, and starvation so severe that Clark named one site "Camp Despair."

The state of Washington has funded a feasibility study to move U.S. Highway 101 away from the coast to provide more walking access to these valuable sites. Ziak's personal vision for commemoration includes creation of a large rotunda near the beach to be shaped like the Jefferson Memorial in Washington, D.C. Inside the rotunda, a bronze plaque would repeat Jefferson's instructions to the captains. Ziak believes the true success of the expedition was achieved when the corps finally made it to the ocean some days after Clark exulted in his journal: "Ocian in view! O! The joy."[32]

Ziak's efforts have even begun to alter accepted approaches to Lewis and Clark interpretation in the Pacific Northwest. For decades Oregon has claimed the significant West Coast site for the end of the Lewis and Clark trail at the Fort Clatsop National Memorial near Astoria. Now historians and experts are scrutinizing campsites on the Washington side. The state of Washington may implement a new state park at Station Camp near Long Beach where the explorers stayed between 16–25 November 1805.[33] The competition between Washington and Oregon over what is more historically important to Lewis and Clark—the Washington side or the Oregon side of the Columbia River, is creating interesting new scholarship and will inevitably result in increased interpretation.[34]

SUPPORTING ROLES

One of the marvels of the Lewis and Clark saga is that American tourists are attracted to more than just the captains, and this affection is leading to bicentennial commemorations of Sacagawea's offspring and even the corps's faithful canine companion. There are new children's books about Seaman, Lewis's loyal Newfoundland dog who guarded the camp at night, woofed and barked at grizzlies, and was so powerful he could kill fleeing deer and drag them out of rushing rivers. Sculptors have even completed statues of the dog![35]

Dozens of men in western states have joined Lewis and Clark reenactor groups, which are thriving in the Northwest and in Montana. Reenactors study the journals and become first-person interpreters of the voyageurs, privates, sergeants, and captains of the Corps of Discovery. Men grow beards, hand-sew leather clothing, hack out wooden dugout canoes, practice their black powder shooting, and try to entice their wives with blue beads.[36]

Irish Americans now claim an affinity for Sergeant Patrick Gass and his carpentry expertise. Never mind that Captain Lewis loathed the fact that Gass got his book published first, Irish Americans are proud to claim him. Likewise, African Americans want to learn more about York, who accompanied Captain Clark the entire route, and French Canadians want to know more about Drouillard, or "Drewyer" as the captains called him.[37] A Drouillard descendant explained that family members know what Drewyer knew— how to cook muskrat in a savory fashion. The recipe has been handed down for generations.[38] Fiddlers, of course, choose to reenact the nearsighted French-Canadian Pierre Cruzatte.

Just as Lewis and Clark campsites have been discovered on the Washington coast, also coming out of historical obscurity is the grave of Jean Baptiste in the high deserts of eastern Oregon. Born in a frigid North Dakota winter after his mother, Sacagawea, swallowed a potent folk remedy of warm water and crushed rattlesnake rattles to help her through a difficult childbirth, Jean Baptiste earned the adoration of Captain Clark, who nicknamed him "Pomp" and named Pompeys Pillar along the Yellowstone River after him.[39] Following Sacagawea's death, Clark paid for her son to have formal parochial schooling in St. Louis; then Jean Baptiste went to Europe to learn new languages. Pomp eventually returned to the West to guide for European royalty on hunting expeditions, worked with Kit Carson, and helped lead John C. Fremont to California. Jean Baptiste died from an unknown illness in 1866 while crossing eastern Oregon on his way to the gold strikes in Montana. Now his grave has been relocated, authenticated, and spruced up for the truly dedicated tourist for whom no Lewis and Clark related historic site is too remote. Pompeys Pillar along the Yellowstone River has been designated a new national monument to be administered by the Bureau of Land Management.[40]

INDIAN VOICES

Rarely do historic site staff discuss Lewis and Clark as the vanguard of expanding American capitalism, as a moving front of the lucrative fur trade, and as the progenitors of enormous social and economic transformations. Those perspectives need to be raised along with the historical impact of forcing tribal peoples into the orbit of American diplomacy.[41] Tourists know about Sacagawea, but they need to learn about the other western tribes who befriended the Corps of Discovery and their descendants' perspectives on the bicentennial. Moreover, contemporary issues including sacred site protection and the return of human remains and burial goods should be more central to how the legacies of the expedition are understood.[42]

Because of the bicentennial, at least one sacred site on the Great Plains may now become protected. The National Park Service is working to acquire Spirit Mound in South Dakota. Native beliefs about this lone hill in the midst of a vast expanse of flat prairie greatly intrigued the two explorers. On 25 August 1804, accompanied by nine expedition members and Lewis's dog Seaman, the captains crossed the Missouri River from their camp and hiked for nine miles in hot, humid weather to climb the mound and determine the reasons for its sacred attributes. The captains noted an abundance of insects, and hence bird life, but they sensed no spirits, despite the Indian name. Native Americans will be glad to have that site in public ownership as a vindication of their oral traditions. Besides Spirit Mound, other sacred sites along the expedition route that need protection include the Smoking Place in the Bitterroots (Figure 9) and, along the Columbia River, the rock

Figure 9. The Smoking Place, Bitterroot Range, Idaho. (Photo by Andrew Gulliford, Center of Southwest Studies, Fort Lewis College)

outcroppings called the Twin Sisters, sacred to the Cayuse and Umatilla tribes and now marred by roadside graffiti.[43]

The bicentennial will also shed new light on relations between the Corps of Discovery and Native peoples that may help confirm a number of Indian stories about the expedition. The Nez Perce claimed that when the corps delayed their departure because of deep snow in the spring of 1806 and had to stay on the Weippe Prairie an extra two weeks, William Clark fathered a son. This may be an Indian legend that is provable. Recent DNA evidence verified that Thomas Jefferson and Sally Hemmings had a romantic liaison. As part of the forthcoming Lewis and Clark Bicentennial Exhibition sponsored by the Missouri Historical Society, a telescope from the Clark family went to Colonial Williamsburg for cleaning. Conservators found a red hair between two glass lenses. DNA testing may be possible, and if Nez Perce genealogy is accurate, and if a descendant of the supposed offspring of Captain Clark still lives, another story from the expedition could be proven. The journals frequently mentioned dalliances of other men, but perhaps the captains also enjoyed the attentions of Native American women.

At Fort Clatsop, so much fraternizing went on between the enlisted men and the local Indians that the captains felt obligated to close the doors to the fort after dark and require all Indians to leave. Far too often the men came down with venereal diseases, which weakened their ability to work. Despite the fort's closed door policy, Natives remained friendly, and the corps could not have survived the winter without help from the Clatsop and Chinook Indians. Now two centuries later those Native peoples are almost invisible on the Pacific Coast after being decimated by disease and forced into assimilation with white coastal communities. In the Northwest, the Clatsops no longer exist, yet in Pacific County, Washington about 1,800 Chinooks remain. For decades they had to go underground, hide their culture, tolerate local racism, and disguise their Indian identity. Beginning in the 1950s, and with increasing fervor over the last two decades, the Chinooks applied for federal recognition, but to no avail. Finally, in December 2000 the Bureau of Indian Affairs officially recognized the Chinooks on the Washington coast as an American Indian tribe. Kevin Grover, assistant secretary of Indian affairs, stated, "Today we have the opportunity to address directly a historical injustice lasting many years. What more fitting memorial for the bicentennial than to honor those coastal tribes who helped the Corps of Discovery survive that dreary, wet winter." Given this explicit reference to the upcoming bicentennial of the Lewis and Clark expedition, it is especially unfortunate that President George W. Bush decided to perpetuate the old historical injustices when he reversed the earlier ruling and unilaterally stripped the Chinook Indian tribe of its government-to-government relationship with the United States. Consequently, the Chinooks will no longer receive federal funds to help restore their language, improve economic development, housing, and health care, and acquire their own land base where their ancestors once lived along the Columbia River and Willapa Bay. Regardless of the Bush administration's actions, Lewis and Clark tourists should meet the last descendants of those coastal tribes who befriended the corps and provided a variety of foodstuffs to supplement their meager rations of "pore elk."[44]

CONTROVERSY AND THE DEATH OF CAPTAIN LEWIS

William Clark's grave can be found in the prestigious Belle Fountain Cemetery of St. Louis where the gravestone reads, "His life is written in the history of his country." Well known in his own lifetime, and a significant figure in the history of the American West, Clark administered Indian affairs for all of the Upper Louisiana Territory from 1813 until his death in 1838. In the process he earned the respect of tribes who nicknamed him "the Red-headed Chief," and referred to St. Louis as "Red Hair's Town." Such respect, and the tremendous service he provided his country through most of his life, never brought William Clark a captaincy in the U.S. Army. While Thomas Jefferson's best efforts to confer an equal rank to Lewis and Clark never succeeded, another outcome of the bicentennial has been Congress's posthumous awarding to Clark of the rank of captain. Such a fitting tribute for his military service matches the prestige of his massive tombstone in the heavily populated Belle Fountain Cemetery.[45]

In contrast, Captain Lewis's remains lie in a remote area of rural Tennessee far from the Lewis and Clark trail, yet at a site integral to understanding the Lewis and Clark legacy in the nineteenth century. The site is important as a link to other Lewis and Clark sites in the east, specifically Monticello, Virginia, the home of Thomas Jefferson. The bicentennial will make the Lewis gravesite better known and incorporate it into the tourist pilgrimage, because understanding Lewis's death makes the contributions of his short, vital life more meaningful. Lewis's prolonged downfall into alcohol and drug addiction, his several suicidal attempts, and finally his violent death along the Natchez Trace in Tennessee, lend tragedy to the expedition's heroism.

The story of Lewis's death resonates deeply; as Stephen Ambrose has written, it "is the great mystery of Lewis's life." Ambrose rightly argues that Lewis's suicide served to obscure the success of the expedition. Nineteenth-century scholars could not come to terms with Lewis's death, and so the value of the corps's contribution to American exploration diminished. According to Ambrose, "Lewis's suicide hurt his reputation. Had Cruzatte's bullet killed him, he would be honored today far more than he is. . . . [T]hrough most of the nineteenth century he was relatively ignored and in some danger of being forgotten."[46]

Lewis's stone grave marker in Lewis County, Tennessee has recently been repointed and structurally assessed by the National Park Service whose experts pronounced the 1848 Tennessee monument to be sound. Designed to "express the difficulties, successes and violent termination of a life which was marked by bold enterprise, by manly courage and devoted patriotism," the monument's broken shaft represents Lewis's premature death.[47]

Amateur historians claim Lewis was murdered by members of the Grinder clan, who owned the run-down cabin where he stayed that fateful night, but he died by his own hand. Besides the wide acceptance among Lewis's contemporaries that he died by his own hand, scholars are convinced that Lewis was clearly inclined toward suicide.[48] A forthcoming book by the Lewis interpreter Clay Jenkinson discusses Meriwether Lewis and the "Other," an anthropological term often used to consider explorers and their ambiguous relationships with Native peoples. Jenkinson believes that after his return to St. Louis, Lewis failed to adjust back to "civilization"; indeed, he claimed never to have slept on a bed after returning from the journey but instead slept on wooden floors wrapped in his robes. Scholars also question Lewis's sanity and his relationship to other men. In one of Lewis's last letters, posted from New Orleans, he confessed that there was always an emptiness in him that he could not fill, except in the bracing presence of other men—with Captain Clark and Thomas Jefferson, for example, or in the U.S. Army. The psychiatrist Alfred J. R. Koumans writes about Lewis's "unusual actions . . . not to mention his awkward approaches to marriageable women, even with his good looks, and his intense attachment to his mother." Dr. Koumans muses about Lewis: "Was he the kind of man who excels only when closely linked to another man?" Because William Clark married, did that leave Lewis with a "painful inner emptiness and unable to live up to the expectations the successful expedition brought him?"[49]

Meriwether Lewis's botched management of the Louisiana Territory, his alcoholism and painful bouts of depression, his egregious failure to publish the journals, his difficult social adjustments after the expedition, and his poignant inability to impress marriageable women all point to a complex, tortured personality that tourists still debate but cannot fathom two centuries later. One explanation for his death has been described by the noted epidemiologist Reimert Thorolf Ravenholt, who believes Lewis contracted syphilis in Chief Cameahwait's camp the same evening he struck the bargain to procure horses. Ravenholt argues that the onslaught of neurosyphilis resulted in skin eruptions, weeks of convalescence, erratic behavior, poor financial decisions, febrile attacks with extreme disorientation, and at least two suicide attempts en route to Memphis.[50]

Few people visit Meriwether's grave on the historic Natchez Trace just south of Nashville, but at least the National Park Service, which manages the Lewis Monument, has resisted all efforts by self-seeking archaeologists to exhume Lewis to prove or disprove his suicide. Along the Natchez Trace, current National Park Service interpretation leaves open the matter of Captain Lewis's death but honors his life and his outstanding accomplishments. As befitting the bicentennial, visitors need to pay homage to his grave but let Lewis's remains stay buried in Tennessee soil. Let him receive in death the peace he could not find in life.[51]

ENVIRONMENTAL IMPACTS

An understanding of the corps and its significance at the bicentennial requires an understanding of landscape change. Twenty-first-century tourists must recognize what has been forever altered in the American West since 1806, and tourists must appreciate the captains not only as frontier patriots, but also as naturalists in elkskin who provided us with scientifically valid observations on a once diverse and healthy environment. The bicentennial commemoration must also be aware of its own environmental "footprint," as tens of thousands of people follow in the footsteps of Lewis and Clark and seek out the same remote locales.

Positive and negative environmental impacts of the 2004–06 Lewis and

Clark bicentennial are numerous and will vary from too many tourists visiting fragile riparian ecosystems to tourist-driven recreational vehicles getting stuck in Montana mud or snowed in on remote Idaho mountain passes. Yes, there will be too many visitors to a few very special places, but in the end if our appreciation for natural ecosystems in the West is heightened, and if some of those ecosystems are restored, then the short-term bicentennial impacts may result in long-term ecological gains. Environmental understanding must come with historical appreciation. One of the great opportunities for the Lewis and Clark bicentennial is to blend visitation along the historical landscape with environmental restoration.

The conservation biologist Daniel Botkin's *Passage of Discovery: The American Rivers Guide to the Missouri River of Lewis and Clark* (1999) may well become the cornerstone for a major movement during the bicentennial to restore the Missouri River, one of the most dammed rivers in the West, and make portions of it free flowing. The U.S. Army Corps of Engineers dammed the Missouri at great cost, but with few benefits. The Missouri was made safe for heavy barge traffic that never materialized. The dams generated hydroelectric power for markets that did not need it, and reservoirs stored irrigation water for crops that do not need to be grown. Now, however, the Corps of Engineers may turn over a green leaf and undo some of the needless damage. In both *Passage of Discovery* and *Our Natural History: The Lessons of Lewis and Clark* (1995), Botkin wrote superbly about the mighty force of the Missouri in spring flood and the roils of muddy water that forced the men of the Corps of Discovery to tug and pull on tow lines as they dragged their keelboat upriver in the spring of 1804. Their accounts of fish, animal, and bird life stand as vivid biological markers of all that has been lost, and as a challenge in the twenty-first century to restore natural wetlands cleared for agriculture. This may be a lasting legacy of the Lewis and Clark bicentennial—returning the Missouri River watershed into bird sanctuaries, rich river meanders, and Great Plains habitat for small mammals and white-tailed deer.[52]

Equally pressing are environmental issues related to survival of endangered stocks of salmon. In the Shoshone camp of Chief Cameahwait, Lewis tasted his first piece of broiled salmon and realized he was about to cross into the Columbia River system. For millennia salmon have been a sacrament for Native peoples of the Pacific Northwest. In little more than a century, however, logging, agriculture, urbanization, bad fishery science, and dams along the Columbia and Snake Rivers have diminished the salmon runs to tiny fractions of what they once were. When Lewis and Clark passed the great fishery at Celilo Falls, they marveled at its seemingly infinite supply of huge fish. The fishery was drowned in 1957, behind the waters of The Dalles Dam.[53]

It would be appropriate to combine the commemorative tourist bicen-

Figure 10. Grandfather Tree at Lemhi Pass. (Photo by
Andrew Gulliford, Center of Southwest Studies, Fort
Lewis College)

tennial brouhaha with serious science and environmental restoration. Biological audits should be conducted, and baseline studies should compare
plant and animal species in specific locations with those described two centuries ago in the journals. Protecting and designating historic vegetation
will also enhance the tourist experience. A few trees that are two hundred
years old remain along the expedition route. At the top of Lemhi Pass, just
on the east side of the Continental Divide, there are two grandfather trees
that were young when Jean Baptiste was a baby and Sacagawea a new mother
(Figure 10). These are sacred trees for northwestern tribes, and biological
commemorations are in order, too.

The bicentennial has already resulted in special issues in *Sierra,* the magazine of the Sierra Club, about wild and scenic places and the need to save special areas along the four-thousand-mile route.[54] The best places to visit are the upper Missouri wild and scenic river section in eastern Montana, which Lewis wrote about in grand detail; Lemhi Pass on the Montana and Idaho border along the Continental Divide; select sites like the Sinque Hole and Smoking Place deep in the Bitterroot Range of Idaho; steep trails on the Oregon side of the Columbia River Gorge; and the last twenty miles of the wild, western Washington coast. Here tourists confront the dynamic wilderness landscape of Lewis and Clark where ecological integrity of place still exists. To stand on the top of Lemhi Pass at dawn, to be caught in a freezing late November rain in the Columbia Gorge, and to walk among the wild, windswept bracken on the Washington coast is to experience a new sense of awe for the captains and their tenacity. Here is an opportunity to come face to face with both ecological wonder and ecosystem loss.

For the bicentennial, dedicated Lewis and Clark enthusiasts will canoe the Clearwater River and paddle down the Snake to the Columbia. They will traverse the many locks and dams of the U.S. Army Corps of Engineers. Sea kayakers will travel the Washington side of the Columbia passing sloughs, islands, and sheltered stretches of backwater. There is a proposal for a Lewis and Clark Columbia River water trail from Portland to Astoria for tourists who favor canoes, kayaks, and small shallow-draft boats. Thus, for seasoned paddlers, Lewis and Clark's journey will become a personal voyage of discovery.[55]

Using waterways to experience history is one more special aspect of the bicentennial, and these forms of ecotourism represent a whole new form of historical commemoration. A century ago local business leaders, Daughters of the American Revolution, and small-town promoters erected statues, parks, immense log buildings, and other edifices including the Astoria Column at Astoria, Oregon, which features scenes from the expedition. A century ago the heroes were commemorated for bringing the seeds of civilization, which they helped to sow; now they are being commemorated for the wild spaces they traversed, the rapids they shot, and their hardy endurance in crossing barren landscapes.[56]

In 1904 Americans revered the expedition for what changes the captains wrought. Hitting the tourist trail with Lewis and Clark a hundred years later is a different experience. In the twenty-first century Americans seek the solitude, the silence, and the darkness that come only from wild landscapes and undeveloped stretches of the American West. Tourists want to experience the Lewis and Clark landscape as the explorers saw and traversed it, and this longing suggests that we may have come of age as a nation. Perhaps at last we are willing to consider Manifest Destiny and western conquest not

ON THE TOURIST TRAIL   259

just for what was gained, but also for what was lost and what should be restored.

NOTES

The author would like to thank Mark Spence for his editorial encouragement, and David and Linda Tozer for locating Oregon newspaper sources. Betty Bauer and Alfred J. R. Koumans read early drafts. Rex Ziak gets a thank-you for his enthusiasm and wisdom when it comes to Lewis and Clark in Washington state. Thanks also to Gary Ripley of Portland, Oregon, for designing a Smithsonian Associates study tour of Lewis and Clark sites in Montana and Idaho and for helping me lead the Smithsonian tours by horseback and canoe.

1. For an analysis of the 2004–06 Lewis and Clark bicentennial see the essays in "Lewis and Clark: 200 Years Later," a feature edition of *History News* 56 (Spring 2001). A great deal of the interest in Lewis and Clark has been inspired by Stephen E. Ambrose's best-selling *Undaunted Courage: Meriwether Lewis, Thomas Jefferson, and the Opening of the American West* (New York: Simon and Schuster, 1996); no doubt, large numbers of tourists will have copies by their side as they travel the expedition route. Other major texts include David Lavender, *The Way to the Western Sea: Lewis and Clark Across the Continent* (New York: Doubleday, 1988); and James P. Ronda, ed., *Voyages of Discovery: Essays on the Lewis and Clark Expedition* (Helena: Montana Historical Society Press, 1998).

2. One of the author's favorite access points for the Lewis and Clark National Historic Trail is at Howard Creek Picnic area in Montana along Lolo Pass. See Thomas Schmidt, *The Lewis and Clark Trail* (Washington, D.C.: National Geographic Society, 1998). For a better understanding of Lewis and Clark's actual route with up-to-date maps, see Cathy Riggs Salter, "Lewis and Clark's Lost Missouri: A Mapmaker Re-Creates the River of 1804 and Changes the Course of History," *National Geographic Magazine*, April 2002, 90–97.

3. The upcoming commemoration is generating an avalanche of kitsch including Lewis and Clark shot glasses, replica telescopes, blue bead necklaces, baseball caps, refrigerator magnets, and the ubiquitous T-shirt. See Mark Spence, "Selling Out Lewis and Clark," *The Oregonian*, 14 May 2000, B1; and, for a dissenting opinion, Chet Orloff, "Lewis and Clark bicentennial More Than a Party," *The Oregonian*, 20 May 2000, B9.

4. Two personal artistic voyages of discovery include paintings of the trail by Kenneth Holder, and a photo series by Mike Venso. See Jennifer Hattam, "An Artistic Adventure: Following the trail of Lewis and Clark with Paintbrush in Hand and History in Mind," *Sierra* 85 (July–August 2000): 73–74; and Joan Abrams, "A Journey Recreated," *Lewiston Tribune*, 6 August 1999, 1C.

5. T. K. Whipple, *Study Out the Land* (Berkeley: University of California Press, 1943), 65. Whipple's lines serve as the epigraph for Larry McMurtry's Pulitzer-prize-winning novel *Lonesome Dove* (New York: Simon and Schuster, 1985).

6. Most of the Lewis and Clark landscapes are on public land, but Gates of the Mountains is also protected by private easements. The establishment of the Gates of

the Mountains Foundation in 1973 eventually resulted in the Hilger family's donating of a conservation easement to the Montana Land Alliance in 1984 to protect the southern side of the historical and scenic canyon.

7. There are numerous Lewis and Clark Historic Trail guidebooks and well illustrated reference books. Schmidt's *Lewis and Clark Trail* is the best small guidebook, but also see the excellent maps in Barbara Fifer and Vicky Soderberg, *Along the Trail with Lewis and Clark* ([Helena]: Montana Magazine, 1998). For excellent photos see Dayton Duncan and Ken Burns, *Lewis & Clark: The Journey of the Corps of Discovery* (New York: Alfred A. Knopf, 1998); Stephen E. Ambrose, *Lewis & Clark: Voyage of Discovery* (Washington, D.C.: National Geographic Society, 1998), photographs by Sam Abell; and Thomas and Jeremy Schmidt, *Saga of Lewis and Clark: Into the Unknown West* (New York: Dorling Kindersley Press, 1999).

8. Campfire conversation on a Smithsonian Associates' study tour at the Triple O Outfitters Bitterroot Camp, July 2000.

9. Marjorie Belk on the Smithsonian tour, Bitterroot, July 2000.

10. Donald F. Nell and John E. Taylor, eds., *Lewis and Clark in the Three River Valleys, Montana, 1805–1806* (Tucson: Patrice Press and Lewis and Clark Trail Heritage Foundation, Headwaters chapter, 1996).

11. Patricia Limerick has coined the phrase "sustainable heroes" in speeches where she has discussed the need not only to tell the truth about history but also to find suitable role models who are not just Great White Men who own slaves or possess robber baron tendencies.

12. For an intellectual history of the journey and attitudes toward geography and landscapes see Albert Furtwangler, *Acts of Discovery: Visions of America in the Lewis and Clark Journals* (Urbana: University of Illinois Press, 1993).

13. On the trials and tribulations of the Astorians, see James P. Ronda, *Astoria & Empire* (Lincoln: University of Nebraska Press, 1990), 165–195. For an excellent discussion on discipline and morale within the corps, see Gunther Barth, ed., *The Lewis and Clark Expedition: Selections from the Journals Arranged by Topic* (Boston: Bedford/St. Martin's, 1998), 45–80.

14. James P. Ronda, *Lewis and Clark among the Indians* (Lincoln: University of Nebraska Press, 1984), 2.

15. Irving W. Anderson, "Sacajawea, Sacagawea, Sakakawea?" *South Dakota History* 8 (fall 1978): 305–311.

16. Donna J. Kessler, *The Making of Sacagawea: A Euro-American Legend* (Tuscaloosa: University of Alabama Press, 1996), 65–98.

17. Bernard DeVoto, ed., *The Journals of Lewis and Clark* (Boston: Houghton Mifflin, 1953), 294.

18. For background information on the Charbonneau family, see Irving W. Anderson, "A Charbonneau Family Portrait: Profiles of the American West," *American West* 17 (March–April 1980): 4–13, 58–64. This article was republished in 1992 by the Fort Clatsop Historical Association for sale to tourists.

19. Jeannine Aversa, "The Search for Sacagawea," *The Oregonian*, 28 December 2000, B1–2.

20. I worked with the Eastern Shoshone Cultural Center and the Skaggs Foundation of Oakland, California to erect an interpretive plaque at the Sacagawea Cemetery near Fort Washakie, Wyoming. The plaque was dedicated on Memorial Day

1998. The Daughters of the American Revolution erected a large granite monument at the site in the 1930s.

21. Ronda, *Among the Indians*, 256–259.

22. See Roberta Conner's chapter 12 in this collection. In October 2000, eighteen tribes with their own histories of Lewis and Clark met at Lewiston, Idaho to discuss the upcoming celebration and to make recommendations to numerous federal agencies.

23. Ibid.

24. No author makes this clearer than Ronda in *Among the Indians*. Though there are three different major Lewis and Clark exhibitions scheduled for the bicentennial, only the National Lewis and Clark Bicentennial Exhibition being produced by the Missouri Historical Society in St. Louis will focus on the corps from an Indian perspective. For historical context see Anthony Wallace, *Jefferson and the Indians: The Tragic Fate of the First Americans* (Cambridge, Mass.: Harvard University Press, Belknap Press, 1999). To understand Indian concepts of landscape and the naming of rocks, trees, and fishing places see Carolyn M. Baun and Richard Lewis, eds., *The First Oregonians* (Portland: Oregon Council for the Humanities, 1991); and Richard White, *The Organic Machine: The Remaking of the Columbia River* (New York: Hill and Wang, 1995), 18–23.

25. Archaeological survey work includes verifying the corps' route on the Lolo trail by Historical Research Associates of Missoula, Montana. The National Trust for Historic Preservation purchased in 1999 a site near Helena, Montana that may be the original September 1805 campsite known as "Travelers Rest." The corps returned there in 1806 on its speedy route home.

26. Richard Hill, "Hunting for the Explorers' Fort," *The Oregonian*, 14 November 2001, B1.

27. Dustin Solberg, "A Lewis and Clark Revival Hits the Northwest," *High Country News*, 27 September 1999, http://www.hcn.org/servlets/hcn.Article?article_id = 5275 (25 June 2002).

28. Rick Bella, "Gorge May Finally Get a Front Entrance," *The Oregonian*, 26 December 2000, B1.

29. See Lewis and Clark National Historic Trail—National Park Service Administrative Update, no. 13 (October 1999) and no. 14 (March 2000). One of many lasting contributions of the commemoration could be respect for Native peoples and preservation of tribal historic and sacred sites they deem significant. Dollars spent for new tourist visitor centers should be matched for tribal preservation issues and respect for Indian sacred places.

30. Though there are some errors in the text, the standard book on Lewis and Clark's biological achievements is Paul Russell Cutright, *Lewis and Clark, Pioneering Naturalists* (Urbana: University of Illinois Press, 1969). Also see Ron Fisher, "Lewis and Clark: Naturalist-Explorers," *National Geographic Magazine*, October 1998, 76–93. Plants plucked by Lewis and Clark and held by the Academy of National Sciences Museum in Philadelphia will be displayed in Idaho in 2005–06. Also see the special Homes and Gardens of the Northwest edition of *The Oregonian* titled "Lewis and Clark: The Legacy Grows," 24 May 2001 (http://www.nwrac.org/lewis-clark/oregonian [25 June 2002]).

31. Midori Raymore, technical editor, "Corps of Discovery II Update," *The Corps*

Explorer 17 (January 2001): 1 (published by the Park Service's Omaha Support Office). Federal dollars for the project may not be forthcoming; see Peter Sleeth, "Funding May Trip Lewis and Clark Plan," *The Oregonian*, 17 February 2002, A23.

32. Gary E. Moulton, ed., *The Journals of the Lewis & Clark Expedition* (Lincoln: University of Nebraska Press, 1983–99), 6:33. Ziak has other grand plans as well. Along with the author Dayton Duncan, he believes that democracy in America begins not with the framing of the U.S. Constitution, but with the first vote in American history in which a black (Clark's slave, York) and a woman (Sacagawea) voted as equalswith white men to determine where to spend the winter. At the spot near where the corps voted and where its members carved their names in trees now long gone, Ziak would place stone tree trunks etched with the names and dates of birth and death for each member of the corps. On quiet Baker Bay where the Field brothers shot a huge California condor with an eleven-foot wingspan, Ziak would like to see a life-size sculpture of the men holding up the almost mythical bird.

33. Erin Middlewood, "Washington Seeks Lewis-Clark Park," *The Oregonian*, 24 December 2000, A1, 12.

34. Jonathan Nelson, "Lewis and Clark Feud Resolved," *The Oregonian*, 19 May 2000, D11; and Karen Mockler, "Lewis and Clark Effort Takes Unified Stance," *The Daily Astorian*, 19 May 2000, 1. Ziak is working on his own book, which will cover the expedition's movements from 7 November to 7 December 1805.

35. For the definitive canine history see Ernest S. Osgood and Donald Jackson, "The Lewis and Clark Expedition's Newfoundland Dog: Two Monographs," supplement to [Lewis and Clark Trail Heritage Foundation's official publication] *We Proceeded On*, no. 10 (September 1990). Of the many children's books and magazines about Lewis and Clark see "Lewis and Clark: Buffalo tongue for lunch . . . mmmmm good?" *Kids Discover* (New York, 1998).

36. Reenactor friends greeted me at the Nez Perce National Historic Park in Spalding, Idaho with a present of a replica Lewis and Clark Corps of Discovery lead powder canister. Lewis ingeniously devised the lead container to carry gunpowder and when it was empty the container could be melted down into bullets. I truly appreciate the gift, but getting it home through the Portland International Airport was not easy. It looks and feels almost exactly like a bomb!

37. Robert B. Betts, *In Search Of York: The Slave Who Went to the Pacific with Lewis and Clark*, rev. ed. (Boulder: University Press of Colorado, 2000).

38. While giving a Lewis and Clark lecture at New Harmony, Indiana in February 2000 for Harmonifest, I met a Droulliard descendant with plenty to say about family history and muskrat recipes. He offered to cook up a batch for me, but I told him I was holding out for more beaver tail. A group is working to publish a genealogy of the trek's descendants (see Peter Sleeth, "Mapping Descendants of Lewis and Clark," *The Oregonian*, 10 December 2001, 1).

39. The Bureau of Land Management manages a visitor center and 473 acres near Pompeys Pillar, a site visited and named by William Clark on 25 July 1806.

40. Peter Sleeth, "Overgrown Grave Site Breathes Life into State's Expedition History," *The Oregonian*, 3 May 2000; and "Paying Tribute to Expedition's 'Pomp,'" *The Oregonian*, 25 June 2000. Also see Donald Olson, "On the Trail of Sacagawea's son," *Sunset*, June 2001, 48–49. President William Clinton declared Pompeys Pillar a national monument, but an agricultural company wants to erect four 150-foot-

high grain towers within a mile of the new monument, seriously damaging the view-
shed (Sleeth, "A Monumental Debate," *The Oregonian,* 21 January 2001, A17).

41. Only Idaho has so far taken Indian interpretation seriously. The Idaho Department of Commerce has produced a handsome color pamphlet titled "Lewis and
Clark and the Native Peoples."

42. Another fitting bicentennial tribute in 2004 would be to return Native
American bones to the volcanic soils of the Columbia Plateau. Archaeologists disin-
terred tribal dead during the hasty salvage archaeology that preceded dam construction on the Columbia River. Those remains should respectfully go back to the
earth. Grave goods now on display should also be reburied, including original
Thomas Jefferson peace medals dug up from burials along the Columbia.

43. See Andrew Gulliford, *Sacred Objects and Sacred Places: Preserving Tribal Traditions* (Boulder: University Press of Colorado, 2000); see 74–75 for photos of the
Smoking Place and how Clark described it.

44. Erin Middlewood, "80 Chinook Gather at Park in Rally for Recognition from
Government," *The Oregonian,* 17 June 2000, D4; and Angie Chuang, "Native American, Mayor in Dispute on Lewis and Clark Commemoration," *The Oregonian,* 8 November 2000, C11. Karen Mockler, "Chinook Tribe Recognized," *High Country News,*
12 February 2001, 5; also see Courtenay Thompson, " Chinook Quest Opens New
Era," and "Chinook Tribe wins Struggle for Federal Recognition," *The Oregonian,*
7 January 2001, A9, 17. On the Bush administration's actions, see Office of the Assistant Secretary for Indian Affairs, "Final Determination Declines Chinook Recognition," Bureau of Indian Affairs press release, 5 July 2002, http://www.doi.gov/
news/chinook.htm (15 July 2002); and Bryan Denson, "Chinook Stripped of Tribal
Recognition," *The Oregonian,* 6 July 2002, A8.

45. Rick Bella, "Explorer William Clark will be promoted to rank of captain
posthumously," *The Oregonian,* 16 January 2001, B1, 8. Additional honors for Clark
may include naming the summit of Tillamook Head in Oregon after him. See Peter
Sleeth, "Making a Mountain Out of a Headland," *The Oregonian,* 18 June 2001, 1.

46. Ambrose, *Undaunted Courage,* 468, 474.

47. Midori Raymore, technical editor, "Restoration of the Meriwether Lewis
Monument Completed," *The Corps Explorer* 17 (January 2001): 9–10.

48. See recently published letters included in James J. Holmberg, *Dear Brother:
Letters of William Clark to Jonathan Clark* (New Haven: Yale University Press, 2002).

49. Dr. Alfred J. R. Koumans, personal letter to author, 3 November 2000. Other
evidence for suicide includes the obituary of the slave who gave Meriwether Lewis
his last cup of water; see Jill K. Garrett, "Historical Sketches of Hickman County,
Tennessee," *Hickman Pioneer,* 5 April 1878, 6. The excerpt reads, "Peter Grinder, a
colored man, was the property of Robert Grinder, Sen., and was at an early day our
village blacksmith. He came from what is now Lewis County and with his master then
lived at the Grinder stand, on the Natchez Trace, where the monument is erected
over the grave of Gov. Lewis, and was the boy of all work at the hotel; was with Gov'r
Lewis during his stay at the hotel, and the first one that saw him after he had committed the rash act of self-destruction. He was, like most of his race, superstitious,
and did not like to talk of the event." Also see Elliott Coues, ed. *History of the Expedition Under the Command of Lewis and Clark* (1893; reprint, New York: Dover, 1965),
1:xv–xxii.

50. Reimert Thorolf Ravenholt, "Triumph then Despair: The Tragic Death of Meriwether Lewis," *Epidemiology* (1994); and "Trail's End for Meriwether Lewis: The Role of Syphilis," *Cosmos* (1997). Also see discussion on the History News Network for 8 April 2002; and Ravenholt's essay "Did Stephen Ambrose Sanitize Meriwether Lewis's Death?"

51. Judge Thomas A. Higgens of Nashville, Tennessee has ruled that the remains of Meriwether Lewis are not to be disturbed despite an exhumation request by Dr. James E. Starrs and a proposal supposedly supported by 160 Lewis family members.

52. Daniel B. Botkin, *Our Natural History: The Lessons of Lewis and Clark* (New York: Perigree Books, 1995), and *Passage of Discovery: The American Rivers Guide to the Missouri River of Lewis and Clark* (New York: Perigree Books, 1999). For another perspective on environmental change along the trail, see Benjamin Long, *Backtracking: By Foot, Canoe and Subaru along the Lewis and Clark Trail* (Portland: Sasquatch Books, 2000). Also see Traci Watson, "Missouri River Levels May Change," *USA Today,* 30 November 2000, 11A.

53. See Tim Palmer, *The Snake River: Window to the West* (Washington, D.C.: Island Press, 1991); Daniel L. Boxberger, *To Fish in Common* (Seattle: University of Washington Press, 2000); Lisa Mighetto and Wesley Ebel, *Saving the Salmon: A History of the U.S. Army Corps of Engineers' Efforts to Protect Anadramous Fish on the Columbia and Snake Rivers* (Seattle: Historical Research Associates, 1994); and Charles Wilkinson, *Messages from Frank's Landing: A Story of Salmon, Treaties, and the Indian Way* (Seattle: University of Washington Press, 2000).

54. Page Stegner, "Beyond the Sunset: Two Centuries after Lewis and Clark, A Chance to Rediscover the American West," *Sierra* 85 (May–June 2000): 44–59. The Plum Creek timber company, which is cutting timber too close to a trail easement, has endangered the trail in Montana.

55. Terry Richard, "Pioneer Trail: Lower Columbia Offers a Historic Ride," *The Oregonian,* 17 October 1996, D2. To understand today's dedicated canoeists see Robin Cody, *Voyage of a Summer Sun: Canoeing the Columbia River* (Seattle: Sasquatch Books, 1995). In addition to canoeists following Lewis and Clark, bicyclists will travel from Fort Clatsop to Hartford, Ill. (Katy Muldoon, "Cyclist Ready to Peddle in Pioneers' Path," *The Oregonian,* 14 October 2001, E8).

56. For discussions of the centennial celebrations of Lewis and Clark, see the essays by Mark Spence and Jonathan Spencer in this collection. New books about Lewis and Clark and the trail will chronicle landscape change along with the authors' and photographers' perspectives. The University of North Texas photography professor Brent Phelps is retracing the trail (Joseph B. Frazier, "On the Trail of Lewis and Clark," *The Oregonian,* 20 January 2002, A21). Also see James R. Fazio, *Across the Snowy Ranges: The Lewis and Clark Expedition in Idaho and Western Montana* (Moscow: University of Idaho Press, 2001); and Long, *Backtracking.*

Chapter 12

The Lewis & Clark Bicentennial
Putting Tribes Back on the Map

Roberta Conner

*passed above our camp a small river called Youmalalam riv. . . . we continued our
march accompanied by Yellept and his party to the village. . . . This chief is a man
of much influence not only in his own nation but also among the neighbouring tribes
and nations. This village consists of 15 large mat lodges. . . . Yellept haranged his
village in our favour intreated them to furnish us with fuel and provision and set
the example himself by bringing us an armful of wood and a platter of 3 roasted mul-
lets. The others soon followed his example with rispect to fuel and we soon found ourselves in possession of an ample stock. . . . the Indians informed us that there was a
good road which passed from the Columbia opposite to this village to the entrance of
the Kooskooske on the S. side of Lewis's river; they also informed us, that there were
a plenty of deer and Antelopes on the road, with good water and grass. We knew that
a road in that direction if the country would permit would shorten our rout at least
80 miles. The Indians also informed us that the country was level and the road
good, under these circumstances we did not hesitate in pursuing the rout recommended by our guide whos information was corrobertated by Yellept & others.*
Captain M. Lewis, 27 April 1806

*some time after we had encamped three young men arived from the Wallahwollah vil-
lage bringing with them a steel trap belonging to one of our party which had been
neglegently left behind; this is an act of integrity rarely witnessed among indians.
during our stay with them they several times found knives of the men which had been
carelessly lossed by them and returned them. I think we can justly affirm to the honor
of these people that they are the most hospitable, honest, and sincere people that we
have met with in our voyage.*
Captain Lewis, 1 May 1806

The descendants of the people described in these journal entries still live in
much the same area as when the expedition traversed their homeland in
1805 and again in 1806.[1] The Walla Walla, Umatilla, and Cayuse tribes, as
they are now known, make up the Confederated Tribes of the Umatilla
Indian Reservation just east of Pendleton, Oregon. The population of the
confederacy is about 2,200 enrolled members. About two-thirds of the

tribal membership plus about 1,000 Indians from other tribes and 1,700 non-Indians reside within the present-day reservation. Relative tribes include, among others, the Warm Springs, Wanapum, Palouse, Yakama, and Nez Perce.

The Umatilla and Walla Walla dialects of the Sahaptin language were very different from the Cayuse language isolate. Now that the Cayuse language is extinct, save about 350 documented words, most Cayuse descendents who speak a native language speak lower or upper Nez Perce. The few persons who speak Walla Walla as a first language are all elders. Those who speak Umatilla as a first language are a handful of adults and the rest elders. Like the cultures, the landscape and all the species that inhabit the Blue Mountains and Columbia River Plateau have undergone many dramatic changes in the past two hundred years.

More than fifty modern tribal governments representing over a hundred tribes will decide in the next eighteen months whether they will observe and participate in the National Lewis and Clark Bicentennial. Some tribal leaders met with delegates of federal agencies to begin discussing their plans in the spring of 1999. Then, and in every subsequent meeting, the following themes emerge consistently. For us, this is not a celebration. It is an observance or commemoration. We want both sides of the story told—the army expedition's and our own—and we want to tell our own story. We want to protect resources on the Lewis and Clark National Historic Trail, including burial sites. We want to help create economic opportunities for our people. We want the nation to realize and recognize tribal contributions to this great country including aid given the Corps of Discovery. We want the U.S. government to do what it has promised. And, above all, we want to protect the gifts the Creator gave us.

Why should I want to know Native peoples' perspectives on the Lewis and Clark bicentennial? There are some easy, glib answers. Because people like colorful, intimate stories. Oral histories from Native communities are often likened to quaint and entertaining folklore. Because we say we want the truth, the unvarnished, unadulterated truth until it spills over us with overwhelming force, or volume and repetition, as in the Clinton impeachment hearings of 1999. Because people are curious about what happened to the Indians that met the expedition, now almost two hundred years later. Because it is very unlikely that you have heard our story. It is not typically represented in history books or classroom lessons or contemporary politics.

Another obvious reason is that we rarely see ourselves the way others see us and vice versa. The journal entries by Meriwether Lewis and William Clark, as well as those by the other writers of the expedition, tell us what they observed, what they perceived, and what they believed. They cannot reflect the impressions of the only other participants in this significant time in history—the indigenous peoples. The travelers were clearly at a disadvantage in language and knowledge of the terrain. As deft as Clark was at measuring and as astute as Lewis was in observation and dialects, they were still left to conjecture frequently. As remarkably thorough as their diplomacy and records are, they are not always aware of how they have insulted Natives or crossed a cultural taboo, nor do they tell of their own liaisons with Indian women. There is no need to demonize these American heroes; the Native observers' perspective humanizes them and brings history to life.

Another reason to consider our perspective is that President Jefferson considered Indians important, as evidenced in his second inaugural address and first, third, and sixth annual messages to the Senate and House of Representatives as well as his directive to Captain Lewis. This great man—who was a student of science, culture, and linguistics and authored the Declaration of Independence, declaring to the world the thirteen colonies' independence from all nations—wrote about Indians.

In his 20 June 1803 missive to Captain Lewis, along with all other studies, reports, and transactions Jefferson instructs Lewis:

> The commerce which may be carried on with the people inhabiting the line you will pursue, renders a knolege of these people important. You will therefore endeavor to make yourself acquainted, as far as diligent pursuit of your journey shall admit, with the names of the nations & their numbers; the extent & limits of their possessions; their relations with other tribes or nations; their language, traditions, monuments; their ordinary occupations in agriculture, fishing, hunting, war arts, & the implements for these; their food, clothing, & domestic accommodations; the diseases prevalent among them, & the remedies they use; moral and physical circumstance which distinguish them from the tribes they know; peculiarities in their laws, customs & dispositions; and articles of commerce they may need or furnish & to what extent . . . it will be useful to acquire what knolege you can of the state of morality, religion & information among them, as it may better enable those who endeavor to civilize & instruct them, to adapt their measures to the existing notions & practises of those on whom they are to operate. . . . In all your intercourse with the natives treat them in the most friendly & conciliatory manner which their own conduct will admit; allay all jealousies as to the object of your journey, satisfy them of it's innocence, make them acquainted with the position, extent, character, peaceable & commercial dispositions of the U.S., of our wish to be neighborly, friendly & useful to them, & of our dispositions to a commercial intercourse with them. . . . Carry with you some matter of the kine-pox, inform those of them with whom you may be of it's efficacy as a preservative from the small pox; and instruct them & encourage them in the use of it. This may be especially done wherever you may winter.[2]

In his second inaugural address on 4 March 1805, President Jefferson reports,

The aboriginal inhabitants of these countries I have regarded with the com-
miseration their history inspires. Endowed with the faculties and the rights of
men, breathing ardent love of liberty and independence, and occupying
a country which left them no desire but to be undisturbed, the stream of
overflowing population from other regions directed itself on these shores;
without power to divert, or habits to contend against, they have been overwhelmed by the current, or driven before it. . . . These persons inculcate a
sanctimonious reverence for the customs of their ancestors; that whatsoever
they did, must be done through all time; that reason is a false guide, and advance under its counsel, in their physical, moral, or political condition, is perilous innovation; that their duty is to remain as their Creator made them, ignorance being safety, and knowledge full of danger.[3]

One obvious reason for wanting to know our perspective is that we are
still here to offer it. Against pretty overwhelming odds, many indigenous
groups have survived the past two hundred years. Many also perished. Languages of our ancestors are no longer spoken in many Native communities.
Despite efforts to document and preserve dialects, languages, and songs,
many are dangerously close to language loss. Contemporary life makes traditional tribal activities compete with every new entertainment device or
program targeted at American youth. Two hundred years from now, distinct
cultural practices and oral histories may not exist in living cultures if we are
passive now. By trying to learn more about our historical accounts, visitors
reinforce the notion that our knowledge has value and help inspire our
young people to pursue learning more.

How about an even more urgent reason? The United States of America
is a great nation as well as a large one, and it is located on lands obtained
from Native people through conquest, purchase, treaty, and governmental
protections that didn't work. Less than a half century after Lewis and Clark's
troupe went right through the middle of the homelands of the Walla Walla,
Umatilla, and Cayuse, we ceded in peace treaty proceedings over six million
acres of land to the United States. In the Walla Walla Treaty Council of 1855,
we reserved for ourselves a half million acres so that we might continue to
live according to the natural laws given to us by the Creator. The half million acres became a quarter million acres when the Umatilla Reservation
was surveyed in 1871. It became 158,000 acres after the Slater Act of 1885
allotted lands to individual Indians and the U.S. government declared
the balance to be surplus and open for settlement. And we are among the
"lucky" ones. Some tribes have no lands. Some no longer live anywhere near
their home on the Lewis and Clark trail. The federal government does not
recognize some tribes. Some agreed to treaties that were never ratified by
Congress. And still other tribes were "terminated" by federal policy.

Interestingly enough, loss of ownership rights did not extinguish our
personal or tribal responsibility for the more than six-million-acre aborigi-

nal homeland or the rivers or the creatures that rely on our covenant with them and the Creator. We pursue clean water, clean air, restored habitats, and watershed protection and hope to prevent species extinction in our homeland—regardless of who else lives here and who claims title—because we promised to do so in exchange for the sustenance the Creator provides. Great nations should honor their treaties and promises.

Tribes were regarded as nations when President Jefferson dispatched the expedition to conduct their exploration, and they are nations today. The lessons we have learned along the way in assimilation, subjugation, termination, and litigation, as well as mitigation, cooperation, and collaboration, should be worth something to the planners of tomorrow. We should not have to ask to have our voices heard. Unfortunately, we have contemporary national elected officials who still think the government gave Indians land. These leaders think that tribes should not be allowed to exercise their sovereignty through fishing and hunting rights or gaming enterprises. In some states citizens have voted to disestablish reservations.

The journals of the expedition comprehensively document our fishing practices, our numerous tule mat lodge villages, our vast horse herds, and our games of chance and skill. We have used games and gambling to redistribute wealth for centuries if not millennia; get used to it. There is an uninterrupted continuum present in the mid-Columbia region in our culture and people. Sadly, our once great horse culture is now a remnant of what it once was, and the richest salmon fishery in the West is no longer visible. And tribes like ours that have successfully reintroduced spring Chinook salmon to the Umatilla River after an absence of seventy years must endure the genetic purist arguments about hatchery fish. As nations, we should join forces to solve our problems.

As communities, towns, counties, states, and an assortment of organizations including federal agencies make plans for commemorating the national bicentennial, tribes are getting invitations to participate. That's not surprising considering that tribes were the only chambers of commerce for the first visitors. These recent invites run the gamut. The more predictable ones are requests to provide Indians in regalia for drumming and dancing at a local festival. The more extraordinary invitations are inquiries about whether we all might have mutual goals or how we might create substantive partnerships on lasting projects.

Many groups are creating maps for itineraries and tours. The National Park Service is working on a new Lewis and Clark trail map. The map project coordinator states that the new one will include the names of tribes, unlike the last one, which showed state boundaries that didn't exist during the expedition but did not reflect the presence of tribes who had dealings with the expedition. Communities and trail states that are creating plans that will "put them on the map" should consider putting tribes on their maps. Without tribal homelands, Indian reservations, or Indian attractions, the maps tell domestic and international travelers that we are no longer here. And, after all, we helped Lewis and Clark with content for their maps.

Historians, interpreters, teachers, tour guides, and heritage travelers all make decisions about which events, people, and places are sufficiently significant to warrant their attention. Each determines what is interesting as well as believable or valid and authentic. During the bicentennial and at any other time, visitors will vote with their feet, or tires, or itineraries. Those who choose to travel the expedition route should come prepared for a variety of experiences, just as the first group did.

In Indian country, tribes may choose to boycott the bicentennial, bear silent witness to another migration of non-Indians through their lands, develop visitors' facilities and interpretive activities, publish accounts of contact with the expedition, or create reenactments or documentaries. In our region, we have been welcoming travelers for a couple of centuries. We are hospitable and friendly, but please be mindful this is the place the Creator gave us. It is our only home. We may reside elsewhere temporarily but this is the only place we'll ever be from. It is part of us, and we are part of it. And just as the first travelers did, bring gifts.

THE INFAMOUS BUSINESS TRIP
A Umatilla Story on the Lewis and Clark Bicentennial

Wish-low-too-la-tin (Raymond Burke), Umatilla Tribal Chairman

The Umatilla Indian tribe's story of the Lewis and Clark journey is at best a story about a couple of guys out west on a "not so well Intended" business trip. In 1803 the president of the United States, Thomas Jefferson, ordered Lewis and Clark to head up a trip into unknown territory to develop trading partners with the local residents and open trade routes for U.S. business interests before the Russians, British, or Spaniards got a foothold in the marketplace.

Indian tribal leaders have recently been looking at this upcoming bicentennial as the last chance for our generation, and further removed generations, to give an accurate account of "our side of the Lewis and Clark story." I think I can speak for the Umatilla tribes in saying we have been looking with too much emphasis at interpreting this historic moment in the past when our story is in the present and the future.

In 1805, when Lewis and Clark passed through our homeland, we were (relatively speaking) a wealthy nation. Our successful business interests were built on trading with our Indian partners near and far. Our business interests consisted of our salmon fishery, our extensive herds of cattle and horses, and the natural returns from the assets of our land base. The extent of our market distribution areas reached into Mexico. We traded willingly and shrewdly with these potentially new business partners from the United States in expectation of a mutually beneficial business relationship as outlined by their leader, President Jefferson.

Through the moccasin telegraph, Indians out west had already been warned by eastern tribes of the potential dangers of this so-called business partnership. "It's your land they want to take and sell, and you will have to fight to keep it." Over the next 50 years United States government sanctioned business interests were, indeed, not just interested in opening trade to new market but planned to exploit the vast land-based assets that were the foundation of our Indian people's business livelihood. The U.S. government's business plan was based on a much farther reaching concept, that of Manifest Destiny. A doctrine of the time that said, "Anglos, as the chosen people, will dominate the Western Hemisphere."

For the last 150 years, the Umatilla tribe's businesses have been in a state of recession and oppression that would have bankrupted and dissolved most any other national corporation. Only because we have a homeland, a cultural and spiritual identity, and blood ties to hold us together, has our nation's corporation survived. Like most U.S. businesses, we have had our share of help from government subsidies, tax breaks and concessions, deregulations and bailouts. In our case, they did not come from political power, special interest groups, paid lobbyists, or public opinion. Fortunately our survival has been based on a much stronger legal commitment than a quick fix from Congress. It is the right to do business as a sovereign nation by contract; that is, the treaty negotiated by our visionary leaders at the Walla Walla Treaty Council in 1855.

After 150 years of government control that diminished our asset base, blocked our trade routes, suppressed our trading partners, and systematically broke down the self-respect and productivity of our nation's people, we have staged an unprecedented business recovery.

Today, the Umatilla Indian nation is in the process of building a diverse multimillion-dollar corporation that not only is gaining wealth and improving the well-being of its member stockholders but contributing significantly to the regional economy by increasing employment opportunities, payroll, and support of local businesses, as well as human and community development.

Our story is about taking control of our destiny. Our original 1855 Treaty Lands comprised 512,000 acres. However, the federal government surveyed out 245,000 acres. The 1885 Allotment Act again reduced our lands to 158,000 acres and allowed white people to buy land on the reservation. Consequently, the reservation is a checkerboard of Indian and non-Indian lands. The tide of land loss and fragmentation is ending, and today we have increased the agriculture, timber, and grazing land holdings on our reservation so that now more than 50 percent of the land base is in Indian ownership.

For the first time since the federal government began "surplusing" our homeland to nonmember stockholders, more than half the people who live on the Umatilla Reservation are Indians. After 75 years of depletion of our salmon fishery, tens of thousand of salmon are returning to our homeland waters.

We have been successful politically by uniting with other tribes in the Northwest to remove from office one of the strongest opponents in the U.S. Congress to Indian sovereignty and a successful Indian business climate, Slade Gorton.

We have planned, financed, built, and are now operating a successful resort complex employing over 500 people (Indian and non-Indian) providing quality customer service to the public.

We are now in the process of partnering with other local governments and businesses to build an environmentally and technically correct power plant to contribute to the diversification of our economy and do our part to reduce the energy shortages in the region without damaging vital northwestern resources.

We are, for the first time, operating our own agriculture, timber, and grazing enterprises to assure more sustainable and resource sensitive management yields from our natural assets.

We have cooperated successfully with our neighbors in the agriculture and business community and continue to work toward achieving a balance of competing objectives for the region's interest as a whole on the use of limited water supplies. For example, in northeastern Oregon the Umatilla River and Walla Walla River Basin Projects, respectively, are designed to restore salmon and water, and at the same time protect the local economies that are dependent upon irrigation. Although these projects repair damages to treaty rights, support from all stakeholders and beneficiaries is needed to make them successful. We are also working with the larger Columbia River Basin Forum, the Wheat Growers Columbia River Forum, and Save Hanford Reach to ensure that there is enough water for salmon.

We have employed and retained the skills and experience of competent professionals and managers in the fields of finance, law, community and economic development, human resources, public safety, health, education, government affairs, investment, and business operations to build a strong corporate nation and Indian community.

The Lewis and Clark bicentennial provides a benchmark for measuring the business recovery of the Umatilla nation's history. We have just begun to rebuild the weal and cultural pride that 200 years ago belonged to our people. But rebuilding our business and economy is just the start. We now must look to the future, and that future is to rebuild the self-respect, well-being, and health of our people, the respect of our neighbors, the citizens of this country, and the businesses that have prospered for the last 200 years on the Umatilla Indian nation's assets. We now and over the next 50 years will continue to work with our neighbors to restore the natural resource base and environmental qualities that once were the basis of our strong economy.

As Umatilla national sovereignty and self-government grow stronger, we are better able to temper the exploitive excesses of the Manifest Destiny doctrine. For example, hydroelectric power does not have to decimate the Pacific Northwest's salmon runs. People built the dams, and people can save the salmon. Because the Umatilla nation and other Northwest tribes have treaty fishing rights, our interests are essential to the design of effective and lasting good salmon policies. Salmon and hydroelectricity do not have to be incompatible, any more than economic strength and cultural vitality have to cancel each other out. Of course, economic empowerment does not solve all our problems, but you have a better chance to keep your culture, and your salmon, if you build and own the system yourself.

This legacy of struggle, survival, and recovery of the Umatilla nation's business corporation and people is our most important bicentennial story.

NOTES

1. Gary E. Moulton, ed., *The Journals of the Lewis & Clark Expedition* (Lincoln: University of Nebraska Press, 1983–99), 7:173–174, 196–197.

2. Donald Jackson, ed., *Letters of the Lewis and Clark Expedition with Related Documents, 1783–1854,* 2d ed. (Urbana: University of Illinois Press, 1978), 1:62–64.

3. Noble E. Cunningham, Jr., ed., *The Inaugural Addresses of President Thomas Jefferson, 1801 and 1804* (Columbia: University of Missouri Press, 2001), 77–78.

Epilogue

"We proceeded on"

Dayton Duncan

One January afternoon years ago, I found myself huddling next to a fire inside an earth lodge near Stanton, North Dakota. The temperature outside had managed a high of only 3 degrees below zero. A north wind howled across the prairies. The sun was slipping below the horizon, to be followed by nearly sixteen hours of darkness. The word *cold* does not begin to express where the night was clearly headed.

Across from me, patiently feeding the fire with cottonwood logs, sat Gerard Baker, a Mandan-Hidatsa and park ranger for the National Park Service. He had built the earth lodge as a "living history" demonstration for the Knife River Indian Villages National Historic Site, where three Hidatsa villages once stood when Lewis and Clark wintered in the area. I was retracing the explorers' route, trying to connect their experience with my own over a gap of nearly two centuries and had asked if I could spend a night in the earth lodge, which with a dusting of snow looked something like a sod igloo. Gerard had seemed bemused by my request, but he agreed to accompany me, even provided our supplies.

First he smudged the interior in all four directions with the smoke from a bundle of sweetgrass. "For the spirits," he explained. Then, in an iron pot, he boiled potatoes, onions, red peppers, and buffalo tripe, the spongy membranes of a buffalo stomach—a rubbery meal that we ate with our hands. I told him tales about my trip upriver from St. Louis, about all the changes I had seen compared to what the captains had described in their journals. He shared stories of his ancestors and sang some Hidatsa chants. Outside, the northern lights began to dance while the temperature kept sinking. It was time to go to bed.

Gerard had brought along five large buffalo robes, and he advised me to

275

place one of them, fur up, on the dirt floor as my mattress. The other four, he said, would provide more warmth stacked on top of me, fur down.

"But what about you?" I asked, thinking that he was taking Indian hospitality to a foolish extreme. In the back of my mind, I recalled Clark's journal entry about the two Indians who had stayed out all night on the frozen prairie and survived—proof, he wrote, that the "customs and habits of those people have inured them to bear more cold than I thought possible for a man to endure." The smudge ceremony, the meal of buffalo, the stories around the campfire, *and now this,* I thought. History was repeating itself.

"Are you sure you'll be okay?" I insisted.

Gerard smiled at me, his eyes twinkling in the firelight. "I'll be all right," he answered, and he unrolled a fancy down-filled sleeping bag next to my buffalo robes. "This one's guaranteed to twenty below."

I have been out and back across the entire Lewis and Clark trail two complete times since that evening in the earth lodge with Gerard. And more times than I can count, I have visited individual sites along their route. Yet every time my path has crossed theirs, I have wondered what the two captains would think if somehow they were magically transported back to life in the modern world and sent out as, say, a Corps of Rediscovery. What would they recognize? What would confound them? What would they regret? What would they appreciate?

Certainly, a frigid night on the Northern Plains would be almost painfully familiar to them. These were two Virginia-born gentlemen, accustomed to the mildest of winters; I doubt that they could ever forget their experience at Fort Mandan, where they were exposed to one of the harshest weather extremes this continent has to offer.

I, too, have stood on the banks of the Missouri and been awestruck by its raw power as huge chunks of ice floated relentlessly downstream, only to be even more stupefied the next morning on finding the mighty river frozen solid, conquered by the coldness. It's something you remember. (In my case, the memory is aided by a minor case of frostbite in my nasal passages: it still acts up whenever the mercury drops below zero.) In the column titled, "unchanged," place a big checkmark for the ferocity of winters on the upper Missouri.

Nor would the captains find anything new in a meal of buffalo, or in a Mandan's willingness to share it with a stranger. But Lewis, I imagine, would be fascinated by Gerard's sleeping bag—so lightweight, yet so warm; just the kind of scientifically advanced equipment he had scoured Philadelphia to find for outfitting his expedition. Whether the captain would appreciate the irony that in this case it was an Indian showing off the latest in technology to a white man—and poking a little good-natured fun in the bargain—depends on your own assessment of Lewis's psyche. Personally, I doubt it. In my mind's eye, I see him bristling silently as he tucked himself in between the buffalo robes. Clark's the one who might have enjoyed the joke, even if it was on him. But he would also have been the one more troubled by a story Gerard had told as the embers turned crimson.

In 1836, while an aging Clark was still Indian agent for the territory, the government sent two doctors up the Missouri with instructions to vaccinate all the tribes along the river against smallpox. They inoculated most of the tribes until winter turned them back, before they had reached the Mandan, Arikara, and Hidatsa. For some reason, the secretary of war did not dispatch them to finish the job the next spring (and even misled Congress into believing the project was completed). That summer, catastrophe struck.

When a fur trading boat filled with supplies paid its annual visit, it unintentionally also brought the smallpox virus, which quickly spread among the unprotected Indians. Gerard has read all the eyewitness accounts, as well as listened to oral history passed down through the tribes' generations. Smallpox, he says, causes a "very, very ugly death"—sores that ooze and burst on the victim's skin, swelling, aching, vomiting, delirium, and finally loss of life. In the villages, people began dying at a rate of eight to ten a day. Corpses piled up; the stench of rotting bodies could be smelled for miles.

Fearing their protective spirits had abandoned them, some Mandan sought escape through suicide. After debating the bravest way to die, one warrior cut his own throat while another forced an arrow into his own lungs. Some drowned themselves in the Missouri.

Among those struck by the sickness was Four Bears, a Mandan chief of some note. As a warrior, he had killed five chiefs of other nations in hand-to-hand combat, wrested a knife from a Cheyenne warrior and used it to kill its owner, taken many prisoners, survived an enemy arrow and six gunshot wounds. But, like the rest of his people, he had always felt nothing but friendship for the white man. When the fever first hit him, he put on his ceremonial garments, mounted his horse, and rode through his village singing his sacred songs. And then, as he, too, began to succumb to the dread disease, he gave a final speech to his people. A fur trader transcribed it, and it's preserved in a book of tribal history that Gerard loaned me:

> Ever since I can remember, I have loved the whites. . . . To the best of knowledge, I have never wronged a white man. On the contrary, I have always protected them from the insults of others, which they cannot deny. The Four Bears never saw a white man hungry, but what he gave them to eat, drink and a buffalo skin to sleep on in time of need. . . . And how they have repaid it! With ingratitude! I have never called a white man a dog, but today I do pronounce them to be a set of black-hearted dogs. They have deceived me. Them that I have always considered as brothers have turned out to be my worst enemies.

I have been in many battles, and often wounded, but the wounds of my enemies I exalt in. But today I am wounded, and by whom? By those same white dogs that I have always considered and treated as brothers.

I do not fear death, my friends. You know it. But to die with my face rotten, that even the wolves will shrink with horror at seeing me, and say to themselves, "That is the Four Bears, the friend of the whites."

Along with Four Bears, 90 percent of the tribe perished in the epidemic. The once-prosperous nation, whose villages had constituted the biggest city on the plains during Lewis and Clark's time, was reduced to barely a hundred individuals, huddled together with remnants of the Arikara and Hidatsa.

Word of the devastation would have reached Clark in St. Louis shortly before he died. He was experienced in the loss of friends, but it must have greatly saddened him, "the Red-Headed Chief," to ponder the fate of the people who had so warmly welcomed the expedition thirty years earlier. Showing up in Gerard's earth lodge nearly two centuries later would undoubtedly flood him with even stronger emotions. Outside, the three villages once teemed with life and noise, and the smoke of cook fires once curled from the tops of hundreds of earth lodges, and neighbors and explorers alike shared food, music, and laughter to ward off winter's chill. Now there are only large, circular depressions in the ground marking where each lodge stood, like so many supplicating palms oustretched on the barren plain.

My guess is that Clark would have had the same trouble sleeping that I did that night, hearing echoes of Four Bears's words whenever the night wind hissed or a cottonwood groaned as it shook in the gale. And I imagine that he, too, would have uttered a silent prayer that Gerard had adequately appeased the spirits of friendship with the smudge of his sweetgrass.

"We proceeded on" is the most recurrent phrase in the journals of the Lewis and Clark expedition. Charles Floyd wrote it several times in the brief diary he kept before he died far from home—the first United States soldier to die west of the Mississippi, but certainly not the last. His comrades Patrick Gass, Joseph Whitehouse, and John Ordway used it all the time as well. So did the captains.

With three matter-of-fact words they could describe the act of getting up each morning, facing an unknown horizon whose only certainty was another day of hard work, and pushing forward with, if not confidence, then at least dogged determination to move at least a little farther toward that horizon before the sun went down.

"We proceeded on." It became, in effect, the Corps of Discovery's unofficial motto, a mantra that kept them going in the face of every obstacle.

When I travel in their footsteps, I usually adopt it as my own. It reminds me that they didn't have the luxury to look backward, to pause and contemplate the past. And it helps me conjure up their spirits to join me on my modern journey.

The captains in particular were Jeffersonian men, imbued with the Enlightenment notion of steady progress. "We proceeded on" could summarize their view of how the universe works. It would also influence their reaction to many of the starkest changes to be found along their route across the continent.

Lewis, who devoted so much time to scientific descriptions, would no doubt be enthusiastic about the agricultural transformation of the Louisiana Territory. The Missouri, he had written his mother from Fort Mandan, "waters one of the fairest portions of the globe, nor do I believe that there is in the universe a similar extent of country equally fertile." He would probably nod his head, as if to say "I told you so," when he learned that the area is now the food basket for the nation and much of the world.

Clark, with his keen eye for terrain, had marked locations on his map as likely places for future forts and settlements. The mouth of the Kansas River, where the Missouri bends sharply toward the east, was such a spot. He would enjoy, I think, the vista from his old campsite. Where once two rivers met in the wilderness, now rises the skyline of Kansas City, the largest city along the Lewis and Clark route west of St. Louis. Later I would show him Omaha and Bismarck and Portland, other cities that grew up at strategic places that he had identified. "We proceeded on," he might say.

More changes. A series of dams, built to prevent flooding and to provide irrigation and hydroelectricity, has turned much of the Missouri into more lake than river. The "sublimely grand spectacle" of the Great Falls, which Lewis described so ecstatically, is now dominated by a concrete barrier that holds back the Missouri; except in times of unusually high water, the falls themselves are dry rocks. The same goes for the Columbia. Celilo Falls, the Long and Short Narrows, the Cascades—places that Clark noted for their "horrid appearance of this agitated gut swelling, boiling & whorling in every direction"—are now entombed under reservoirs.

What would the explorers think of the two mighty rivers now? To them, the raging cataracts were uncommonly magnificent, but they were also impediments. I can imagine Lewis noting ruefully at the Great Falls that their majesty had once reduced him to wishing for better words to adequately describe their beauty—and then walking excitedly into the powerhouse to see how the turbines work. On the Columbia (and its tributary, the Snake), Clark would be wide-eyed at the sight of deep-draft vessels blithely carrying cargo toward the twin cities of Clarkston and Lewiston, now officially designated as *sea*ports though they are four hundred miles inland from the Pacific.

It would not escape their notice that the same dams that tamed the Columbia for boat traffic, and that generate electricity used as far away as California, have also virtually eliminated the salmon. The number of salmon, Clark wrote in 1805, was "incrediable to say." Even attempting to estimate their numbers seemed preposterous. I think he would be equally speechless today if he went with me into one of the deeper recesses of the Bonneville Dam, where one employee literally—and rather easily—counts each adult salmon that manages to swim past a window looking out on the dam's fish ladder.

Lewis and Clark would have other questions about wildlife. They would remember beaching their canoes for hours as a buffalo herd forded the river; going for several months in which encountering a grizzly bear was almost a daily event; seeing enormous elk herds and packs of wolves; being kept awake at night by the slapping of beaver tails; witnessing a midday sky darkened by huge flocks of wild geese; filling their journals with description after description of animals they had never seen before, in numbers beyond imagination; passing through a landscape in which, as they wrote, "the game is getting so plenty and tame in this country that some of the party clubbed them out of their way."

As we retrace their steps, I can almost see the captains craning their necks at every turn, looking expectantly for an abundance of animals and then turning to me for answers of what happened. I would have to tell them that some of the species they recorded have vanished entirely; others are struggling back from the brink of extinction. "Most of your animals can still be found," I would assure them, "but in smaller numbers and more secluded locations. We probably won't be seeing many on this trip." Another side of the same coin upon which the nation emblazoned, "We proceeded on."

Likewise, we would encounter fewer Indians. Lewis and Clark had been the first to tell them they had a new "great father." In their speeches, the captains promised that he "has offered you the hand of unalterable friendship, which will never be withdrawn from your nation." Moving from reservation to reservation along the modern trail, they would hear instead tales of lands lost and promises broken. For the Lakota, the Nez Perce, the Shoshone, the Blackfeet, and the tribes along the Columbia, the offered hand had turned into a fist. And even for those tribes that never experienced war with the United States—like the Salish and Hidatsa and Mandan—the handshake of friendship proved a bad bargain.

"Follow these councils," Lewis had concluded his first speech to western Indians, "and you will have nothing to fear, because the great Spirit will smile upon your nation, and in future ages will make you to outnumber the trees of the forest." Even by the standards of the Virginia gentry, Lewis was acutely sensitive about matters of honor; seeing how his word was so cavalierly disregarded would start him sputtering, and then, perhaps, send him into dark despair. Clark's face, I think, would turn as crimson as his hair, out of both anger and shame.

To cheer them, I'd take the captains through the White Cliffs of the Missouri in north central Montana, protected by Congress from damming and development. This is another place where Lewis waxed rhapsodic, writing for pages about "scenes of visionary enchantment." I'd invite him to do what friends and I have done on several occasions: read passages from his journal and then look up from our campsite or canoe to see precisely what he had struggled so hard to describe. With luck, we might even see a bighorn on the cliffs.

On our journey together, the captains would learn that the western sky is still as big as it was for the Corps of Discovery, the horizons still as simultaneously intimidating and exhilarating. Nothing has changed the broiling summer heat on the plains or the startling fury of a prairie hailstorm—not to mention the maddening persistence of mosquitoes up and down the Missouri. And the mountains? To Clark they were the "Shineing Mountains." Lewis called them "tremendious . . . covered with eternal snows." Snow still covers their peaks in midsummer; from a distance they still shine. Farther west, winters on the Pacific coast are still sodden with rain.

It was on the coast where the Corps of Discovery got into the habit of carving their names into tree trunks. From the journal accounts, it seems, few trees near the sea escaped their knife blades. Reading between the lines, I get the impression they emblazoned the date and their names and initials with particular gusto, relief, and pride, as the most tangible evidence they could think of to prove they had actually crossed the continent. But mixed in with those emotions was also a tinge of fear—fear that they might not make it back to their homes, that they would never be heard from again, that they and their remarkable achievements would be lost to history. Marking a tree was both a boast and a plea to be remembered.

The tree markings have long since disappeared. But other things now bear their names. On our hurried return toward St. Louis, I would point some of them out: towns, counties, and national forests, rivers and mountain passes, high schools and colleges, campsites and cafes, the Lewis and Clark Search and Rescue Association and the Lewis and Clark 24-Hour Wrecking Service. Where they ran out of whiskey, there is a Lewis and Clark Distillery. And where they switched from eating horses to eating dogs, there is the Lewis and Clark Animal Shelter.

We could follow federal highway signs marked "Lewis and Clark Trail" all the way from the Pacific to the east bank of the Mississippi, where they had embarked on their epic journey. Near St. Louis I would drive them over the Lewis Bridge and then the Clark Bridge before I dropped them off on the

Illinois side, at the Lewis and Clark Motel. "We proceeded on," I would tell them on behalf of their nation, "but you weren't forgotten."

There would be much for them to report on to Mr. Jefferson, some of it with great pride, some of it with profound sorrow. Before we parted, I would add one more bit of information, telling the captains about what happened back in North Dakota on the morning after the cold night in the earth lodge with Gerard Baker.

Thanks to his sleeping bag, Gerard woke up warmer than I did. My feet felt like blocks of ice, and it took some time near the fire to restore them. Gerard teased me, saying that in honor of my experience he might give me an Indian name; what did I think of "Man Who Sleeps in Buffalo Robes" or "Smells Like Tripe"? Once more we shared stories over the fire. He invited me back for the summer, promising that we could visit a traditional sweat lodge he had built along the banks of the Missouri. A friendship was forming that has now lasted for a decade and a half—despite the distances between our homes and the differences of race and culture.

We have learned that we have many things in common. Among them is a passion for history, not just out of intellectual curiosity but based on a more practical belief: that the journey to a better future must include discovering the past and learning from it. And while our approach is to explore history by being clear-eyed about its darker moments, we both try to pay attention and respect to the spirits of those who came before us.

Gerard's desire to honor his ancestors and keep alive the traditions of his people had led him to the journals of Lewis and Clark, one of the best written records about the Mandan and Hidatsa before the cataclysmic epidemic that nearly ended the tribes' very existence. My search to understand my nation, by retracing its pursuit of the next horizon, had led me to the same source. Along the trail of the Corps of Discovery, our paths had crossed, and if I could meet their spirits I would thank the two captains for bringing us together.

That morning was as cold as the morning before. The sun was rising, but the temperature was not going to reach zero. The north wind still howled. We had planned on hiking to the site of Fort Mandan, a walk guaranteed to be both bone-chilling and fatiguing. For a moment we considered staying put, near the warm comfort of our fire. But, like Lewis and Clark, we were moved by the spirit of discovery. We packed up our gear, ready to face the new day. And then we proceeded on.

CONTRIBUTORS

PETER APPEL is an assistant professor at the University of Georgia School of Law, where he specializes in environmental and natural resources law. After completing his undergraduate and legal education at Yale University, Peter clerked for Chief Judge Gilbert S. Merritt of the United States Court of Appeals for the Sixth Circuit. Peter then practiced environmental and natural resources law for the United States Department of Justice, where he argued over fifty cases at the appellate level.

FRANK BERGON is a novelist and professor of English at Vassar College. He is the author of *Stephen Crane's Artistry* and the editor of the Penguin Nature Classics edition and the London folio edition of *The Journals of Lewis and Clark* (Viking, 1989). He is also the editor of *The Wilderness Reader* and *A Sharp Lookout: Selected Nature Essays of John Burroughs* and the coeditor with Zeese Papanikolas of *Looking Far West: The Search for the American West in History, Myth, and Literature*. His novels include *Wild Game, The Temptations of St. Ed & Brother S,* and *Shoshone Mike.*

With a doctorate in American Studies from the University of Wisconsin, CHARLES BOEWE taught in several American universities and lectured in Europe before spending sixteen years in south Asia, where he was director of the Fulbright foundations in Iran, Pakistan, and India. Editor of the papers of C. S. Rafinesque and Rafinesque's bibliographer, he now lives in North Carolina. His most recent book is *John D. Clifford's Indian Antiquities; Related Material by C. S. Rafinesque* (Tennessee, 2000).

JOANNA BROOKS is an assistant professor of English at the University of Texas at Austin, where she teaches early American, African American, and Native American literatures. She is the author of *American Lazarus: Religion and the Rise of African-American and Native American Literatures* (Oxford, 2003). Her poetry, fiction, and scholarship have appeared in *African American Review, Zyzzyva, South Dakota Review, Blue Mesa Review,* and edited collections.

EDWARD C. CARTER II (1928–2002) was librarian of the American Philosophical Society, adjunct professor of history at the University of Pennsylvania, editor-in-chief of the ten-volume edition of *The Papers of Benjamin Henry Latrobe* completed in 1995, and the author or editor of seven other books, and numerous articles and book reviews. His most recent publications are *Surveying the Record: North American Scientific Exploration to 1930* (APS, 1999) and *Three Journals of the Lewis and Clark Expedition 1804–1806,* a facsimile edition (APS, 2000).

ROBERTA CONNER is the recipient of several achievement awards and serves as director of Tamastslikt Cultural Institute. A member of the Confederated Tribes of the Umatilla Indian Reservation, she holds a master's of art from Willamette University's Atkinson Graduate School of Management.

RAYMOND CROSS is a professor of law at the University of Montana School of Law in Missoula, Montana. Prior to joining the law faculty in 1993 he served as tribal attorney for the Three Affiliated Tribes (Mandan, Hidatsa and Arikara nations) of the Fort Berthold Reservation. He also served as staff attorney and director of the Indian Law Support Center for Native American Rights Fund in Boulder, Colorado. He has published several major law review articles on Indian law and public natural resources law. He is an enrolled member of the Three Affiliated Tribes and lives now with his wife, Kathy, and his two children, Cade and Helena, in Montana.

A native Iowan who now lives in Walpole, New Hampshire, DAYTON DUNCAN is an award-winning author and filmmaker. His books include *Out West: A Journey Through Lewis & Clark's America* (Viking, 1987), and *Lewis & Clark: The Journey of the Corps of Discovery* (Knopf, 1998), the companion book to the PBS documentary of the same name, which he wrote and coproduced with Ken Burns. He and Burns have collaborated for many years; they are currently at work on *Horatio's Drive,* a documentary film about the first transcontinental automobile trip, which occurred in 1903, exactly 100 years after Meriwether Lewis began his own historic trip.

KRIS FRESONKE is an assistant professor of English at Adelphi University, where she specializes in nineteenth-century American literature. She is the author of *West of Emerson: The Design of Manifest Destiny* (California, 2002) and numerous articles on the literature of the American West. A native westerner, she lived for some years with her husband in Florence.

ANDREW GULLIFORD is professor of Southwest studies and history and director of the Center of Southwest Studies at Fort Lewis College in Durango,

Colorado. He is the author of *America's Country Schools, Boomtown Blues: Colorado Oil Shale,* and *Sacred Objects and Sacred Places: Preserving Tribal Traditions* (Colorado, 2000). For the Smithsonian Associates program he has led tours by cruise ship on the Columbia and Snake Rivers in Washington and Oregon and on the Lewis and Clark trail by canoe and horseback in Montana and Idaho.

WALLACE LEWIS is an associate professor at Western State College in Gunnison, Colorado, where he has taught U.S. history since 1991. A native of Idaho, he has lived in several western states and researched and written about early highway development.

RONALD LOGE is in the private practice of medicine at the Southwestern Montana Medical Clinic in Dillon, Montana. He is also a clinical associate professor at the University of Washington School of Medicine.

MARK SPENCE is an assistant professor of history at Knox College. He is the author of *Dispossessing the Wilderness: Indian Removal and the Making of the National Parks* (Oxford, 1999); *Lewis and Clark and the Nature of Nation, 1804–2006* (W. W. Norton, forthcoming); and *The American West: Peoples, Frontiers, and Regions* (Oxford, forthcoming). His favorite way to play on the Lewis and Clark expedition route is surfing at Tillamook Head, near Seaside, Oregon.

JOHN SPENCER is the associate education director of the American Social History Project/Center for Media and Learning, based at the City University of New York. He holds a Ph.D. in U.S. history from New York University. A native Oregonian, he is also the editor of *A Sight So Nobly Grand: Joel Palmer on Mount Hood in 1845* (Oregon Historical Society, 1994).

INDEX

Ackerman, Bruce, 86–87, 101–102, 108, 109
Adams, Henry, 85
Ambrose, Stephen, 1, 33, 159–160, 222, 231, 243, 254
American Philosophical Society (APS): archivists of *Journals*, 2, 24; as Lewis and Clark expedition sponsors, 9, 19, 21–36; and Thomas Jefferson, 21–24; training Meriwether Lewis, 25, 71–72
Ames, Fisher, 42
Anthony, Susan B., 11, 14, 187–188, 202
APS. *See* American Philosophical Society
Arikara (Sahnish), 10, 85, 219, 220, 221, 278; before Lewis and Clark expedition, 119–120; and European diseases, 121–122; Garrison Dam compensation, 135–137; on Lewis and Clark expedition, 220–222; Piahito, 220; since Lewis and Clark expedition, 117–142
Articles of Confederation, 90–91
Audubon, John James, 41

Baker, Gerard, 275–278, 282
Barton, Benjamin Smith, 25, 39, 62
Bartram, William, 39–40, 42, 60, 62
Biddle, Nicholas, 164; APS membership, 28; defacing *Journals*, 30; *Eulogium* for Jefferson, 28; hiring of, 26, 42; *History* of, 3, 5, 24, 26–30, 43, 143, 144, 161, 171, 200; prose style of, 2–3, 168–169
Black Elk, 125

Blackfeet, 80, 227, 228, 280
Bodmer, Karl, 64
Bolton, Herbert, 8
Bonaparte, Napoleon, 92–95, 98
Botkin, Daniel, 256
Brautigan, Richard, 7
Brown, Everett Sommerville, 85
Brown, Mary, 14, 15
Brown, William Wells, 103
Buell, Lawrence, 7
Buffalo tripe, 275
Buffon, Comte Georges-Louis Leclerc, 52
Bunyan, John, 4
Burroughs, John, 41, 67

Calhoun, John (Sen. South Carolina), 103
Candle fish *(Thaleicthys pacificus)*, 61
Catlin, George, 64
Cavell, Stanley, 6
Cayuse, 265–266
Charbonneau, Toussaint, 187
Chardon, Francis A., 122
Chopunish, 148, 150. *See also* Nez Perce
Clark, William, 26; ailments of, 77; animal drawings, 2; brother, 228; diary lawsuit, 85; first glimpse of Pacific, 3; grave of, 253; Indian territory governor, 102, 253; laconic prose style of, 57–58; and Lakota, 228; and Mandan, 277–278; maps by, 26, 27, 48–50; as physician, 77–81; publication efforts, 26, 42; weather observations, 219–221

Compositor: G & S Typesetters, Inc.
Text: 10/12 Baskerville
Display: Baskerville
Printer and binder: Sheridan Books, Inc.